Developmental Continuums:

A Framework for

Literacy Instruction

and Assessment K–8

Developmental Continuums: A Framework for Literacy Instruction and Assessment K–8

Bonnie Campbell Hill

Christopher-Gordon Publishers, Inc.
Norwood, Massachusetts

Credits

The *Fountas and Pinnell Guided Reading Leveling System*™ is used by permission of Heinemann, a division of Reed Elsevier, Inc. Portsmouth, NH. All rights reserved.

Excerpts from *Matching Books to Readers: Leveled Books in Guided Reading,K-3* by Irene C. Fountas and Gay Su Pinnell. Copyright © 1999 by Irene C.Fountas and Gay Su Pinnell. Published by Heinemann, a division of Reed Elsevier, Inc., Portsmouth, NH. Reprinted by permission.

Excerpts from *Guiding Readers and Writers Grades 3-6: Teaching Comprehension, Genre, and Content Literacy* by Irene C. Fountas and Gay Su Pinnell. Copyright © 2001 by Irene C. Fountas and Gay Su Pinnell. Published by Heinemann, a division of Reed Elsevier, Inc., Portsmouth, NH. Reprinted by permission.

all student work and profiles used with permission.

Every effort has been made to contact copyright holders for permission to reproduce borrowed material where necessary. We apologize for any oversights and would be happy to rectify them in future prints.

Christopher-Gordon Publishers, Inc.
1502 Providence Highway, Suite 12
Norwood, MA 02062
1-800-934-8322
781-762-5577

Printed in the United States of America

10 9 8 7 6 5 4 3 2   06 05 04 03 02

Library of Congress Catalog Card Number: 2001088608

ISBN: 1-929024-30-4

Contents

Acknowledgments

This book would not have been possible without the hundreds of hours my husband, Steve Hill, spent creating the database, editing chapters, and formatting forms for the CD-ROM. I would also like to thank my three children (Keith, Laura, and Bruce) for their support and patience as I traveled and typed my way through this year. I particularly appreciated Laura's help editing chapters and writing book annotations. The four of you made this book possible.

I would like to thank Sue Canavan at Christopher-Gordon for her unflagging support and willingness to tackle daunting projects. I also appreciated the feedback from the reviewers, particularly from Carol Wilcox and Katherine L. Schlick Noe, whose thoughtful suggestions meant many more days of work on my part, but resulted in a much stronger book.

Many teachers contributed their time and ideas to various chapters in this book. Throughout the book I refer to teachers at Brighton School, in Lynnwood Washington. These teachers generously allowed me to interview them about continuums. They helped me level books and provided feedback on forms, drafts of chapters, and continuum descriptors. Special thanks to Linda Johnson (K), Sue Elvrum (K), Diana Kasner (1st), Donna Kerns (2nd), Sandy Figel (2nd), Linda Horn (3rd), Cindy Flegenheimer (3rd/4th), Gabrielle Catton (4th), Julie Ledford (4th/5th), and Judy Cromwell (6th/7th/8th) at Brighton School. Chapter 10 could not have been written without the ideas and suggestions from Janine King, one of the innovative middle school teachers at Brighton. I also want to thank the principal, Cliff Nelson, for his support for the ongoing continuum revisions and staff development at Brighton School.

Many of the most practical and useful ideas and student samples in this book came from Lisa Norwick and Anne Klein. A seasoned teacher, Lisa Norwick is currently home with two young children in Michigan and Anne teaches fourth and fifth grade in Edmonds, Washington. My co-author for two assessment books, Cynthia Ruptic, was part of the team of teachers who developed the continuum ten years ago on Bainbridge Island. Now teaching in Osaka, Japan, Cynthia emailed helpful suggestions for this book I would also like to thank Megan Sloan (a primary teacher in Snohomish, Washington) and Christy Clausen (a former primary teacher and Reading Recovery teacher who is currently in a staff development role in Everett, Washington). Both teachers provided practical ideas for assessing primary students. Ingrid Stipes and Marilyn O'Neill from Mercer Island, Washington made assessment and continuums an exciting part of their classrooms and contributed ideas and examples to this book.

Chapter 4 could not have been written without the help of Carrie Ekey, the Lead Literacy Resource Teacher for Jefferson County School District, near Denver, Colorado. Carrie knows the early stages of the continuums better than anyone I know and I relied heavily on her expertise as I fine-tuned the continuum descriptors and leveled books. Conversations with Laura Benson from Denver also helped clarify issues about early reading and books. Many other people provided suggestions on book leveling. Thanks to Roz Duthie and Nancy J. Johnson who edited chapters on plane trips and to Dan and Colleen Kryszak who emailed feedback from Moscow, Russia.

I am especially grateful to my colleagues and friends, Nancy J. Johnson (Western Washington University) and Katherine L. Schlick Noe (Seattle University). They graciously allowed me to build upon the database we created for *The Literature Circles Resource Guide* (Hill, Schlick Noe, and Johnson, 2001). The database in this book would not have been possible without their generosity. Thanks to Irene Fountas, Gay Su Pinnell, and Heinemann Publishers for allowing me to use the *Fountas and Pinnell Guided Reading Leveling System*™ in the database, charts, and book lists.

Anna Marie Amudi, Kathryn Blatch, and Cecilia Vanderhye created the English as an Additional Language (EAL) continuum and support materials in Chapter 9. Teaching now respectively in Saudi Arabia, Thailand, and Belgium, their multiple perspectives made this chapter a rich addition to the book. Special thanks to Cecilia Vanderhye and Enrique Mejía who translated the parent surveys and reading and writing continuums into Spanish. Olivia Ruiz, Claudia Miller, and Sally Nathenson-Mejía also helped with the EAL chapter and continuum translations.

A final thanks to the teachers in the international schools in Saudi Arabia, Bahrain, the United Arab Emirates, Sri Lanka, Bangladesh, Mexico, and Belgium. Their work with continuums in the international schools confirms my beliefs in the universal nature of literacy acquisition and the realization that educational challenges and hopes are the same around the world.

Reading and Writing Continuums

A continuum is like a map showing where students have gone and where they're going. The stages are like signposts along the way.

—*Anne Klein, Intermediate Teacher, Edmonds, Washington*

When you are planning a trip, it is helpful to look at a map in order to know where you are going. In the same way, the reading and writing continuums in this book provide a map for literacy growth. This book provides practical examples of how teachers use developmental continuums to guide their teaching, assess students, and communicate with families. It is important, however, to recognize that continuums are only one piece of the assessment puzzle.

Finding the Corner Pieces

The *Corner Pieces Series* is structured around four key aspects of assessment: classroom-based assessment, developmental continuums, student portfolios, and reporting student growth (Figure 1.1).

What if you have collected a great deal of information about one of your students named Malika? Even by January, her portfolio and your assessment tools show that she has made great gains as a reader and writer since the beginning of the year. When Malika moves to another school, however, her family is dismayed to learn that her literacy skills are far below those of her peers. You have been able to document growth, but have not been able to measure progress toward widely-held expectations for students Malika's age. Without benchmarks or standards, you only have part of the puzzle. Developmental continuums, linked to standards, provide the missing piece.

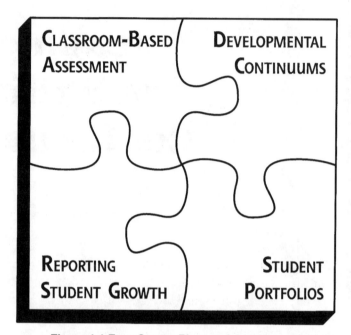

Figure 1.1 Four Corner Pieces of Assessment

The heart of assessment should be the information you collect on an ongoing basis in your classroom. The first book in the series, *Classroom Based Assessment* (Hill, Ruptic, and Norwick, 1998), explores ways in which you can collect and organize assessment information about your students. In this second book, *Developmental Continuums: A Framework for Literacy Instruction and Development K–8*, I will show how continuums and standards can provide a developmental anchor for your assessment information. I also provide examples of how students can use the continuums for self-evaluation and portfolio selections. Additional information about portfolios will be included in the next book in the series, *Student Portfolios*. Finally, incorporating the continuums into your report card provides a shared language for teachers, students, and their families. The fourth book in the assessment series, *Reporting Student Growth*, will address the challenges of using continuums as part of the reporting process.

Connecting the Pieces

Developmental continuums connect the nine key components of education (Figure 1.2).

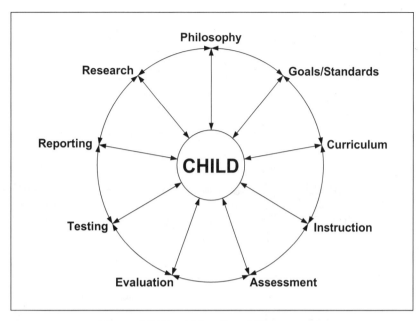

Figure 1.2 Nine Educational Components

The continuums are based on current research about literacy acquisition and reflect a child-centered, constructivist, developmental philosophy of teaching and learning. The continuums can also be aligned with national, state, and district standards. The learner is at the center of the figure, since your instructional decisions will be influenced by the needs of your particular group of students. The arrows extend in both directions because student learning should also impact your decisions about curriculum, instruction, assessment, and evaluation. Rather than lofty goals and five-inch curriculum binders, the continuums provide a practical and manageable way to see the connection between standards and curriculum and your daily focus lessons. Student learning, rather than curriculum or lessons plans, should be at the heart of education. Ideally, your curriculum and daily instructional practices should match the new standards and tests and the reading/writing continuums. Further alignment occurs when criterion-referenced state tests are based on standards and tested by teams of teachers. The final puzzle piece falls into place when continuums are used by students for self-evaluation and shared with families during student-led conferences as part of the reporting process.

Defining Continuums

A continuum is a visual representation of literacy development using descriptors to depict the developmental stages of learning. Fifth graders on Bainbridge Island, Washington, provided their own definitions of a continuum (Hill and Ruptic, 1994, p. 235):

A continuum is a way to tell where you are in a process.

A continuum is a factual time line of your learning and knowledge. It helps you keep track of your abilities.

A continuum is like your family; it goes on and on.

I like using a continuum because I like to know where I am, instead of +, ✓, – or 4, 3, 2, 1.

A continuum is a timeline to show where you are in reading and writing. There is no good or bad place. Everyone is different and more successful in different subjects.

A continuum is an everlasting list of where you are.

The continuums in this book describe the typical path that readers and writers follow from kindergarten through the end of middle school. Figure 1.3 shows an example of the reading continuum. The 11 x 17 inch reading and writing continuums and student versions of the continuums are included at the end of this book and on the CD-ROM. Several other versions of the continuums are also included on the CD-ROM.

READING CONTINUUM

Preconventional Ages 3–5	Emerging Ages 4–6	Developing Ages 5–7	Beginning Ages 6–8	Expanding Ages 7–9
Begins to choose reading materials (e.g., books, magazines, and charts) and has favorites. Shows interest in reading signs, labels, and logos (environmental print). Recognizes own name in print. Holds book and turns pages correctly. Shows beginning/end of book or story. Knows some letter names. Listens and responds to literature. Comments on illustrations in books. Participates in group reading (books, rhymes, poems, and songs).	Memorizes pattern books, poems, and familiar books. Begins to read signs, labels, and logos (environmental print). Demonstrates eagerness to read. Pretends to read. Uses illustrations to tell stories. Reads top to bottom, left to right, and front to back with guidance. Knows most letter names and some letter sounds. Recognizes some names and words in context. Makes meaningful predictions with guidance. Rhymes and plays with words. Participates in reading of familiar books and poems. Connects books read aloud to own experiences with guidance.	Reads books with simple patterns. Begins to read own writing. Begins to read independently for short periods (5-10 minutes). Discusses favorite reading material with others. Relies on illustrations and print. Uses finger-print-voice matching. Knows most letter sounds and letter clusters. Recognizes simple words. Uses growing awareness of sound segments (e.g., phonemes, syllables, rhymes) to read words. Begins to make meaningful predictions. Identifies titles and authors in literature (text features). Retells main event or idea in literature. Participates in guided literature discussions. Sees self as reader. Explains why literature is liked/disliked during class discussions with guidance.	Reads simple early-reader books. Reads harder early-reader books. Reads and follows simple written directions with guidance. Identifies basic genres (e.g., fiction, nonfiction, and poetry). Uses basic punctuation when reading orally. Reads independently (10-15 minutes). Chooses reading materials independently. Learns and shares information from reading. Uses meaning cues (context). Uses sentence cues (grammar). Uses letter/sound cues and patterns (phonics). Recognizes word endings, common contractions, and many high frequency words. Begins to self-correct. Retells beginning, middle, and end with guidance. Discusses characters and story events with guidance. Identifies own reading behaviors with guidance.	Reads easy chapter books. Chooses, reads, and finishes a variety of materials at appropriate level with guidance. Begins to read aloud with fluency. Reads silently for increasingly longer periods (15-30 minutes). Uses reading strategies appropriately, depending on the text and purpose. Uses word structure cues (e.g., root words, prefixes, suffixes, word chunks) when encountering unknown words. Increases vocabulary by using meaning cues (context). Self-corrects for meaning. Follows written directions. Identifies chapter titles and table of contents (text organizers). Summarizes and retells story events in sequential order. Responds to and makes personal connections with facts, characters, and situations in literature. Compares and contrasts characters and story events. Reads between the lines with guidance. Identifies own reading strategies and sets goals with guidance.

Bridging Ages 8–10	Fluent Ages 9–11	Proficient Ages 10–13	Connecting Ages 11–14	Independent
Reads medium level chapter books. Chooses reading materials at appropriate level. Expands knowledge of different genres (e.g., realistic fiction, historical fiction, and fantasy). Reads aloud with expression. Uses resources (e.g., encyclopedias, CD-ROMs, and nonfiction texts) to locate and sort information with guidance. Gathers information by using the table of contents, captions, glossary, and index (text organizers) with guidance. Gathers and uses information from graphs, charts, tables, and maps with guidance. Increases vocabulary by using context cues, other reading strategies, and resources (e.g., dictionary and thesaurus) with guidance. Demonstrates understanding of the difference between fact and opinion. Follows multi-step written directions independently. Discusses setting, plot, characters, and point of view (literary elements) with guidance. Responds to issues and ideas in literature as well as facts or story events. Makes connections to other authors, books, and perspectives. Participates in small group literature discussions with guidance. Uses reasons and examples to support ideas and opinions with guidance.	Reads challenging children's literature. Selects, reads, and finishes a wide variety of genres with guidance. Begins to develop strategies and criteria for selecting reading materials. Reads aloud with fluency, expression, and confidence. Reads silently for extended periods (30-40 min.). Begins to use resources (e.g., encyclopedias, articles, Internet, and nonfiction texts) to locate information. Gathers information using the table of contents, captions, glossary, and index (text organizers) independently. Begins to use resources (e.g., dictionary and thesaurus) to increase vocabulary in different subject areas. Begins to discuss literature with reference to setting, plot, characters, and theme (literary elements), and author's craft. Generates thoughtful oral and written responses in small group literature discussions with guidance. Begins to use new vocabulary in different subjects and in oral and written response to literature. Begins to gain deeper meaning by "reading between the lines." Begins to set goals and identifies strategies to improve reading.	Reads complex children's literature. Reads and understands informational texts (e.g., want ads, brochures, schedules, catalogs, manuals) with guidance. Develops strategies and criteria for selecting reading materials independently. Uses resources (e.g., encyclopedias, articles, Internet, and nonfiction texts) to locate information independently. Gathers and analyzes information from graphs, charts, tables, and maps with guidance. Integrates information from multiple nonfiction sources to deepen understanding of a topic with guidance. Uses resources (e.g., dictionary and thesaurus) to increase vocabulary independently. Identifies literary devices (e.g., similes, metaphors, personification, and foreshadowing). Discusses literature with reference to theme, author's purpose, and style (literary elements), and author's craft. Begins to generate in-depth responses in small group literature discussions. Begins to generate in-depth written responses to literature. Uses increasingly complex vocabulary in different subjects and in oral and written response to literature. Uses reasons and examples to support ideas and conclusions. Probes for deeper meaning by "reading between the lines" in response to literature.	Reads complex children's literature and young adult literature. Selects, reads, and finishes a wide variety of genres independently. Begins to choose challenging reading materials and projects. Integrates nonfiction information to develop deeper understanding of a topic independently. Begins to gather, analyze, and use information from graphs, charts, tables, and maps. Generates in-depth responses and sustains small group literature discussions. Generates in-depth written responses to literature. Begins to evaluate, interpret, and analyze reading content critically. Begins to develop criteria for evaluating literature. Seeks recommendations and opinions about literature from others. Sets reading challenges and goals independently.	Reads young adult and adult literature. Chooses and comprehends a wide variety of sophisticated materials with ease (e.g., newspapers, magazines, manuals, novels, and poetry). Reads and understands informational texts (e.g., manuals, consumer reports, applications, and forms) Reads challenging material for pleasure independently. Reads challenging material for information and to solve problems independently. Perseveres through complex reading tasks. Gathers, analyzes, and uses information from graphs, charts, tables, and maps independently. Analyzes literary devices (e.g., metaphors, imagery, irony, and satire). Contributes unique insights and supports opinions in complex literature discussions. Adds depth to responses to literature by making insightful connections to other reading and experiences. Evaluates, interprets, and analyzes reading content critically. Develops and articulates criteria for evaluating literature. Pursues a widening community of readers independently.

Types of Texts and Oral Reading · Attitude · Reading Strategies · Comprehension and Response · Self-Evaluation

Figure 1.3 Sample Reading Continuum

The continuums are based on four basic concepts. First, they focus on what students *can do* by stating the descriptors in a positive way. For example, rather than stating that a student's writing is disorganized, you can provide focus lessons on paragraphing, then note when a child "Begins to use paragraphs to organize ideas." Second, the emphasis is on what students learn, rather than on what is taught. The strength of this approach is that the focus is on the learner. The continuums are not based on any particular teaching methodology, but reflect both the cumulative knowledge of classroom teachers and current research about literacy development. Third, the stages are only approximations. Children's behaviors may fit primarily into one stage, but they are probably still consolidating one or two strategies from the previous stage and showing evidence of a few new skills at the next stage. Progress is also uneven as students take developmental leaps, then spend time solidifying new strategies. Finally, the continuums clearly show that reading and writing are complex processes. Literacy skills evolve over time and build upon each other in a developmental progression. Rather than viewing reading and writing as something to be "taught" in first grade, we now know that children acquire many concepts about print at an early age. Many two-year-olds can spot favorite restaurants and preschoolers often act as though they are "reading" the books they have memorized. Literacy learning, and indeed, all learning, occurs on a continuum. The purpose of using a continuum is to monitor progress and growth in order to support further learning.

Describing the Continuums

Stages

There are ten developmental stages on the reading and writing continuums included in this book.

CONTINUUM STAGES

Preconventional (Ages 3–5)
Emerging (Ages 4–6)
Developing (Ages 5–7)
Beginning (Ages 6–8)
Expanding (Ages 7–9)
Bridging (Ages 8–10)
Fluent (Ages 9–11)
Proficient (Ages 10–13)
Connecting (Ages 11–14)
Independent

The names of the stages were a source of great debate over the years. Names were used, rather than numbers, to highlight growth, rather than competition and to avoid the tendency to equate stages with grade levels or scores. The names reflect an aspect of a particular stage. For example, although we want children at all ages to work toward independence, the hallmark of the Independent stage is that students are able to select, read, write, analyze, and evaluate a wide range of sophisticated texts independently. The overlapping ages also emphasize a developmental perspective.

Age Ranges

All teachers know that there's no such thing as a "third-grade reader" or "fifth-grade writer." A wide range of reading and writing levels exists in every classroom. For example, in second grade, there will be a few students still reading Dr. Seuss books and many others enjoying early readers, like the *Frog and Toad* books by Arnold Lobel. Some students will be reading easy chapter books, like the *Cam Jansen* books by David Adler. This is the normal developmental range for seven-

and eight-year-olds, as indicated by the age-level span in the Beginning and Expanding stages on the reading continuum.

Just as babies learn to walk and talk at different rates, the same is true for readers and writers. Parents learn the normal developmental benchmarks for children through experience, talking with friends and family, and reading books about child-rearing. The reading and writing continuums provide a similar set of benchmarks for children's literacy development. As children begin to read and write, parents want to know if their child is learning at the appropriate rate. They want to know if their child's behaviors fall inside the normal developmental range. Focused assessment, based on the continuum descriptors and backed by examples of student work, can help students, parents, and teachers measure growth against the path of typical literacy development.

The continuum stages are defined by chronological age, rather than by grade level. The ages of the continuum stages overlap, so that a student at a particular age could be in several stages, yet still fall within the acceptable developmental range. The continuums are particularly useful in multiage classrooms where the concept of grade level blurs and the age range is even greater than in other classrooms. It's important to note that no student's behaviors will fall neatly into one stage or another and that children grow at different rates. The continuums paint a picture of the general sequence and patterns of literacy acquisition from kindergarten through the end of middle school.

Should chronological age ranges be included on the continuums? On one hand, if you truly believe that learning is a developmental process, the continuums could be used without ages. As educators, you might hope this would de-emphasize the competitive nature of our society and allow students and families to focus on learning rather than comparisons. The continuum could be used to highlight growth and to identify each child's next steps. At University Child Development School in Seattle, Washington, for instance, teachers felt that by the very name and nature of their school, a continuum without ages would best reflect their beliefs about learning. Many parents, however, held a different perspective. Parents at this school and at many others schools feel that the ages are important, not for comparisons in a negative sense, but as benchmarks. They want the ages on the continuum as one way to know if their children are within the normal developmental range for literacy acquisition. Some teachers also feel that the age ranges provide a "red flag" to identify students whose behaviors fall outside the typical developmental progression. Whether it's a language challenge, a learning disability, issues at home, or other factors, using the continuums can help describe specifically what the child already *can* do in order to develop a plan for supporting the student's next steps.

In most schools, teachers have decided to keep the ages on the continuums for assessment and reporting purposes. In order to de-emphasize competition and to focus students on the descriptors, the ages have been omitted on the student self-evaluation continuums and checklists. If you decide to use the continuums for reporting, do you plan to use the adult version with ages or the student version without ages? Your decision should be based on the educational philosophy of your school, your purpose for using continuums, and input from families.

Young children move rather quickly through the first part of the continuum. This progression is reflected in the three-year age spans in the first seven stages on the reading and writing continuum. We find that students take more time to consolidate and internalize skills in the upper intermediate grades and in middle school. The ages ranges are in four-year increments in the Fluent, Proficient, and Connecting stages, since this is a time of consolidation. Roz Duthie, a former primary teacher on Bainbridge Island, Washington, observed: "As the complexity of the stages grows, the child's rate of progress slows." Moving from performing a skill with guidance to applying that skill independently requires a great deal of adult modeling and student practice. There are no ages for the Independent stage, since these are skills that many students are still fine-tuning in high school or even as adults.

When primary children are given plenty of opportunities to write, their placement on the writing continuum is often ahead of their placement on the reading continuum. This phenomenon supports the notion that for many children, writing can provide an avenue into literacy. As children move into the Beginning stages on the continuums, their reading and writing skills become more even. In later stages, writing growth seems to lag behind reading growth. It's difficult to ascertain whether this is due to development, the emphasis placed on reading, the general skill level and expectations for writing in our society, or the quality of writing instruction. Growth in reading and writing will certainly be affected by the opportunities provided inside and outside of school, the curriculum, and the quality of instruction. It would be interesting to explore the relationship between reading and writing growth in districts where data could be collected and analyzed on a large scale.

Grade Levels

No matter what grade you teach, you probably have students with a wide range of skills and abilities. What would be the typical range of continuum stages you would expect to see at your grade level? The general age ranges and grade levels for each of the continuum stages are presented in the following chart.

Continuum Ages and Grade Levels		
Continuum Stage	**Ages**	**Grade Level**
Preconventional	3–5	PreK/K
Emerging	4–6	**K** 1
Developing (Early)	5–7	K 1
Developing (Later)	5–7	K 1 **2**
Beginning (Early)	6–8	K 1 **2**
Beginning (Later)	6–8	1 2 3
Expanding (Early)	7–9	1 2 3
Expanding (Later)	7–9	2 3 4
Bridging (Early)	8–10	2 3 4
Bridging (Later)	8–10	3 4 5
Fluent	9–11	4 **5** 6
Proficient	10–13	**5** 6 7
Connecting	11–14	6 **7** 8
Independent		**7** 8+

For instance, at the Expanding stage, students will generally be ages seven, eight, or nine. This means that these students will most likely be in second or third grade. By the end of first grade, you may have a few seven-year-olds who demonstrate some of the behaviors at the Early Expanding level. In some schools, you may also have some nine-year-olds in fourth grade at the beginning of the year who are still working on some of the literacy behaviors described in the Later Expanding descriptors. The age spans reflect a wider and more developmental range for each stage.

Teachers in Jefferson County School District near Denver, Colorado, have felt increasing pressure for accountability and testing at the state level. In response, they have had to draw arbitrary lines between stages in order to set benchmarks and standards. For instance, the expectation in Jefferson County, is that all students will reach the end of the Bridging stage by the end of fourth grade. An Individual Learning Plan (ILP) is developed for any students who do not meet the established goals in kindergarten through third grade (the Emerging through Bridging continuum stages). A Literacy Support Plan (LSP) is developed for any students who do not meet the established goals in grades four through six (the Bridging through Proficient stages). In the Jefferson County School District, the Bridging stage would include third- and fourth-grade students and the Fluent stage would include only fifth-grade students. The bold type in the chart above indicates the narrower range reflected in many districts based on state standards. If you are not facing these political pressures, you may not have to draw such definitive lines between stages.

Rationale for Continuums

Some of the benefits and challenges of using developmental continuums are listed in the following chart. As you can see, the greatest challenge is finding time to talk, to plan, and to assess. Teachers who use the continuums, however, say it's worth the time because they know their students better and their teaching is stronger than before. Improving instruction and assessment are certainly two worthwhile reasons for using continuums.

Benefits of Using Continuums
- Create a common language for teachers, parents, and students
- Reflect progress and growth
- Provide a roadmap for instruction
- Create a structure for classroom-based assessment
- Provide clear targets and benchmarks
- Provide specific information about each student
- Involve students in the assessment process and facilitate goal setting
- Communicate clear information to families
- Encourage professional conversations

---

cont.

Challenges of Using Continuums
- Require time to talk and share ideas and student work
- Require time to match the continuums to curriculum and standards
- Require time to develop consistency within and between schools
- Require time to develop and refine assessment tools
- Require time to observe and assess students
- Require time to help students learn to self-evaluate and set goals
- Require organization and demand a high level of accountability
- Require parent education and support
- Require administrative support and ongoing professional development

Benefits of Using Continuums

Create a Common Language for Teachers, Students, and Families

A wide range of teaching styles exists in any school. One teacher's classroom may be filled with literature as he centers his curriculum around several broad themes for the year. Another teacher at the same grade level may use a basal to structure her reading groups. Both are excellent teachers, but their teaching beliefs and styles can become a source of conflict or division within a school. One of the greatest strengths of the continuums is that they can provide a common framework for both teachers so that they can work toward similar goals.

The continuums are manageable. Instead of a three-inch curriculum document, reading and writing development K–8 are each presented on one piece of paper. Rather than vague terms like "writes clearly" or "reads at grade level," the continuums contain specific and concise terminology. In some districts, teachers have re-designed their curriculum guides to match the language from the continuums and their state standards. The continuums provide teachers with a common language for describing literacy development.

The continuums also provide a shared language for students and families. You can use the continuums and your focus lessons to develop charts about the characteristics of good readers and writers. Students can then use charts to develop rubrics and evaluate their own work. They can also fill out the student versions of the continuums and select quality work for their portfolios as evidence. The continuums, rubrics, self-evaluation forms, and portfolio samples can provide the focus and structure for student-led conferences. By using the continuums, students and their families can discuss reading and writing growth with great specificity.

Reflect Progress and Growth

When they discuss student learning, teachers often prefer small brush strokes that portray each child's development. Administrators and legislators require broader brush strokes that capture the expectations for all students as readers and writers. How can we reconcile these differences? The most helpful explanation has been the distinction by Grant Wiggins (1994) between "progress" and "growth." Progress is measured against a definable goal, such as the distance between Seattle and Denver. In education, student progress toward standards can be measured by using criterion-referenced, standardized tests.

Growth, on the other hand, is unique to each individual. Using the travel analogy, the time it takes to get from my house in Seattle to the hotel in Denver varies widely, depending on freeway traffic, overbooking, delayed flights, snow on the runway, and lost baggage. These are individual variables that affect my travels in much the same way that students' attitudes, learning styles, educational opportunities, family support, interests, and other factors impact learning. As teachers, you naturally highlight growth. You may hang fall and spring self-portraits side by side in the hall. You probably marvel at how a student's writing has improved since September and how many books a youngster has read. Students may collect and select representative samples of their work in portfolios to show how much they have learned. Work samples from the end of the year inevitably show changes since the beginning of the year. "Developmental assessment shifts the focus in assessment from notions of 'passing' and 'failing' to the concept of growth: from an emphasis on comparing one individual with another, to an emphasis on students' developing skills, knowledge and understanding." (Masters and Forster, 1996, p. 8)

In our society, however, growth is not enough. Parents want assurance that their children are developing at an appropriate rate and keeping step with other children their age. Developmental continuums provide a way to measure both progress and growth. If standards are embedded into the continuums, you can ascertain how far students have to go in order to meet the benchmarks or standards (progress). By using color highlighters for each grading period on the continuums, supported by student work, you can show individual change over time (growth).

For students with special needs, standardized test results may show that they are miles from their destination as they struggle year after year to meet the high expectations that have been set for all children. By using the continuum, you can show that although they may not have "met the standard," they are making significant growth each year. Rather than closing doors with low grades or test scores, you can provide honest feedback, yet still celebrate growth and set realistic goals for learners' next steps.

Provide a Roadmap for Instruction

How do you know what to teach? What types of revision can you expect from your students? How do you plan your lessons for next week? You most likely rely on a combination of intuition and experience, grounded in knowledge of your particular age group. You probably also refer to curricular material, professional books and resources, and talk with your colleagues. As you teach, you probably collect information, make observations, jot down notes, and examine work samples. But what do you do with all the information you collect? How much of that wealth of information do you share with families or pass on to next year's teachers? How do you know your students are growing at the appropriate rate? How can you be sure that your students will perform well on high-stakes tests? Many of these questions can be answered by using reading and writing continuums. The continuums provide a developmental picture of student learning K–8. You can create focus lessons based on the descriptors, then use your classroom-based assessment tools to monitor progress and set individual goals for students. Rather than passing along your anecdotal notes, running records, and other assessment data, you can use that information to fill out the one-page reading and writing continuums. The continuums are then shared at parent conferences and passed along to the child's next teacher.

The continuums provide a framework for planning instruction since every descriptor on the continuums for your particular age group should be taught and modeled. Some of your instruction can occur with your whole class, providing a common frame of reference for your students. For instance, Megan Sloan, a primary teacher in Snohomish, Washington, has developed a whole series of focus lessons on revising for specific writing traits (Culham, 1998; Fletcher and Portalupi, 1999; Spandel, 1997). At other times, instruction is more effective in small groups, such as when Megan models and discusses reading strategies during guided reading groups. Megan then uses a variety of assessment tools to collect information about her young readers and writers, consciously linking both her whole-group and small-group instruction and assessment. For example, she uses her anecdotal notes to record specific reading strategies (DC Form 6.9) and a Six-Trait Guide (CBA Form 7.11) to assess her students' writing skills.

Do you remember feeling overwhelmed and unsure of what you were supposed to teach your first year? Were you filled with anxiety the first time that you changed grade levels? Like new parents, many beginning teachers don't have the big picture. If you were new to a grade level or you were a first-year teacher, well-meaning colleagues probably handed you stacks of curriculum guides, worksheets, and manuals. How can you possibly wade through all that material? What new teachers first need is a broad picture of reading and writing development. Many teachers have told us that the continuums were particularly beneficial their first year in a new job or grade level (see Chapter 11).

After teaching intermediate grades for several years in Seattle, Washington, Lisa Norwick moved to Michigan where she taught second grade. The continuums helped Lisa individualize her instruction to meet each student's needs. Sandra, one of Lisa's students, was struggling with reading and writing. Lisa sat down in early November with all of her classroom-based assessment tools and anecdotal notes. As she filled out the reading and writing continuums, her hunch that Sandra was significantly below the range of normal development in both areas was confirmed. This information prompted Lisa to have an early conference with Sandra's parents and to recommend that a team of specialists do further assessments and take a closer look at Sandra's specific learning needs. The continuums provided clear information as well as a starting point for planning how to meet this student's needs.

Teachers are also sometimes equally at a loss about how to meet the needs of students who are clearly farther ahead than other students. That same year, Lisa discovered that Tom was far above the normal range of developmental growth in reading and writing as she collected assessment information and filled out his continuums. The continuums helped Lisa design specific activities that would challenge him and encourage his growth as a reader and writer. Even as a second grader, Tom consistently added description and detail to his writing. His stories had a clear beginning, middle, and end and he used paragraphs to organize his ideas. Lisa looked at the next stage on the writing continuum as a guide for developing appropriate lessons for Tom. For example, during an individual conference, Lisa showed him how he might experiment with leads. The continuums provided a structure for Lisa to meet the needs of both Sandra and Tom.

Phyllis Keiley-Tyler, an educational consultant in Seattle, Washington, found that middle school teachers often complain that their students "can't read." When she shows teachers the reading continuum and asks for specific examples, they can see that their students actually do demonstrate many reading strategies listed on the continuum. Since middle school teachers rarely have training in the developmental nature of early reading, the continuum can provide a new lens for assessing struggling students and planning instruction.

Create a Structure for Classroom-Based Assessment

The school parking lot is usually full the nights before parent conferences as teachers gather their anecdotal comments and stacks of student work, then finish filling out report cards. Most conferences are a pleasure, and it's exciting to be able to show progress and growth to families; however, there are two types of conferences that most teachers dread. One is with the family of the child about whom you are most concerned. These conversations can be emotional and draining. The other type is with the "high maintenance parents" who want assurance that their child's needs are being met and that he or she is being adequately challenged. When you meet with both types of parents, you may feel as if you need to come "armed" with answers. Sometimes, you may end up feeling inadequate or defensive.

The best response to both of these challenges is better assessment. Teachers say that the classroom based assessment tools, especially their Teacher Notebook, their anecdotal notes, and the continuums increase their confidence as professional. Teachers say, "I know my children better than I've ever known them before." Chapter 5 and Chapter 6 include specific examples of how teachers at various grade levels have linked their assessment to the continuums.

Provide Clear Targets and Benchmarks

Most parents know the developmental milestones for their children's physical development. They know approximately when babies learn to roll over or when toddlers start to walk. When children enter school, parents want to know the educational benchmarks. When do students usually learn to read? When do they learn cursive? At what age should students spell most words correctly? In the past, educational benchmarks have not been clearly communicated to parents. All too often, students "slip between the cracks" or families do not discover a problem until it is too late for effective intervention and support. Particularly if their child is struggling, most parents want to know what support you will provide at school and specific information about how they can help their child at home. The continuums provide specifics about what young readers and writers can do, as well as outlining their next steps. The Family Support documents in Chapter 8 provide suggestions for what families can do at home to support reading and writing at each continuum stage.

Continuums also provide a broader perspective on learning than is captured in one classroom or one year. "A progress map [continuum] draws on experience and evidence from a wide range of classrooms. It also sets student growth in the context of progress made in earlier years of school and progress that can be reasonably expected in the future. In other words, a progress map provides a 'whole-school' view of learning" (Masters and Forster, 1996a, p. 8).

Standards also describe what we expect students to be able to do at various ages. In 1993, the Washington State Legislature created a Commission on Student

Learning, whose task was to develop new academic standards. The standards were developed with teacher input and feedback from the community. As the standards and tests were developed, conversations in schools, in the community, and in the media began to focus more on what we want students to learn, rather than on the curriculum. The Washington State standards include the following general guidelines for reading and writing:

**WASHINGTON STATE ESSENTIAL
ACADEMIC LEARNING REQUIREMENTS**

Writing
The student writes clearly and effectively.
The student writes in a variety of forms for different audiences and purposes.
The student understands and uses the steps of the writing process.
The student analyzes and evaluates the effectiveness of written work.

Reading
The student understands and uses different skills and strategies to read.
The student understands the meaning of what is read.
The student reads different materials for a variety of purposes.
The student sets goals and evaluates progress to improve reading.

These guidelines were spelled out more specifically at fourth, seventh and tenth grades. When the continuums were revised in 1996, the Washington State standards were woven into the reading and writing continuums. Eighty percent of the fourth- and seventh-grade Washington state benchmarks for reading and writing have been incorporated into the continuums. Of course, not every state has connected high-stakes state tests with developmentally appropriate standards. You'll need to look at your own standards and state tests to decide where they match the continuums and where there are gaps. We have included the reading and writing continuums on the CD-ROM so that you can make changes in order to match your own curriculum and standards.

Provide Specific Assessment Information about Each Student
Continuums serve as an observation guide for teachers. What strategies and behaviors should you be looking for and assessing? After you introduce a particular strategy, such as using "energetic verbs," you can use anecdotal notes to record when your students actually apply the strategy in their work. By connecting your anecdotal notes to the continuums, you will have precise information about each student. Your anecdotal notes also give specificity and voice to your narrative comments on report cards and at parent conferences. More information about manageable ways to take anecdotal notes can be found in Chapter 6.

Involve Students in the Assessment Process and Facilitate Goal Setting
Students need clear educational targets. How can students meet high expecta-

tions when they don't know what they are? How clear are the criteria for evaluation? How can you help students learn to evaluate their own progress and set goals independently? Surely all of you with children have been plagued on road trips by the incessant question, "Are we there yet?" This question is not unreasonable from a child who can barely see out the window and who has no perspective on how far your family has driven or the distance to your destination. At the beginning of a trip, it helps to show your child the map and explain where you are going and how long the trip will take. The educational route to literacy has been no less mysterious for students. Developmental continuums provide the roadmap that shows students where they are and how far they have to go. By using the student version of the continuums, written in "kid-language," students can begin to internalize the language of self-reflection. The specificity of the descriptors also makes goal setting much easier for students.

Communicate Clear Information to Families

There is a tendency for teachers and parents to blame each other for gaps in a child's learning. I believe that this adversarial relationship has arisen because of a lack of trust in schools, which is exacerbated by current legislative and media attacks on public education. The only possible way to combat the highly-charged accusations is to become more knowledgeable about current research, more politically proactive, and more articulate about what you do and why. In *Literacy at the Crossroads* (1996), Regie Routman claims that one of the best responses to the emotionally-charged plea for better education is meaningful assessment:

> If you want to make "back to basics" a nonissue with parents, move to more meaningful assessment practices. When parents "see" what students are learning, producing, thinking, and evaluating – as well as what the expectations are – in spelling, math, phonics, science, all areas, they stop asking for "the basics" because they know first-hand it underpins all that is happening in the teaching-learning process (pp. 157–158).

Parents become more respectful of teachers as professionals when they can see first-hand evidence of quality assessment. Your Teacher Notebook (Chapter 5), anecdotal notes (Chapter 6), and the developmental continuums show families that you have clear expectations and that you know precisely what their child can do and needs to learn next.

Traditionally, we report to parents at parent conferences and by sending home report cards. If a child is receiving acceptable grades, most parents assume their child is making adequate progress. However, letter grades are not the straightforward answer they appear at first glance. Does the "C" reflect average work compared to other students in the class or district? Is the grade based on test scores, attitude and participation, progress, or growth? If traditional report cards and letter grades do not provide families with meaningful information, how can we report student progress and identify areas for growth? The specificity of the descriptors and the differentiation of the strands on the continuums provide significantly more information to teachers, parents, and students than letter grades.

Even after sharing student portfolios and listening to your assessment information at conferences, some parents inevitably ask, "But how is my child doing?"

Student work samples may have deomonstrated growth, but they still want to know about progress. How does their child compare to others in the class? Parents want to know the "ballpark" or "widely-held expectations" for students of a particular age. Especially if this is their first child, they may not have a frame of reference for what students at different ages can do as readers and writers.

In response to these questions, some teachers have created a graph of the range of literacy behaviors in their classroom. For instance, when she taught a multiage primary classroom on Bainbridge Island, Washington, Cynthia Ruptic talked to parents at Curriculum Night about children's physical and oral language development. She explained that just as children learn to walk and talk at different ages, not every child will learn to read at the same time or in the same way. She then showed a graph from the previous year, covering up the students' names, with the first five stages of the continuum for both reading and writing (see Figure 11.1 in Chapter 11). She used a dot in the fall to indicate the general stage where each child's general behaviors fell. At the end of the year, she marked where students were on the continuum by using a second dot. By drawing a line between the two dots, it was clear how much progress her students had made in one year. Cynthia used the graph (again, without names) during individual conferences if parents voiced concerns about their child. The continuums and the graph helped parents understand the developmental aspect of reading and writing and the age spans on the continuums showed the normal range of literacy behaviors. "By mapping the achievements of a number of students it is possible to show parents how an individual is achieving in relation to other students of the same age or grade" (Masters and Forster, 1996, p. 60). More information about collecting data is included in Chapter 11.

We can also change the relationship between school and the community by creating avenues for families to become involved as partners in children's learning. In many schools and districts in the United States and Canada, the reading and writing continuums have become part of the reporting process. Teachers who are just starting to use the continuums often share them informally at conferences, without sending them home as part of the official report card. In some schools or districts, the continuums become the reading and writing sections of the report card. Each grading period, teachers mark the descriptors with different colored highlighters. The continuums enable you to share very specific information with families about what their child can do as a reader and writer. Chapter 8 includes a list of activities families can do at home to support reading and writing at each of the continuum stages. This information can be distributed at conferences, at a Curriculum Night, or included in a Parent Handbook, along with copies of the continuums.

Encourage Professional Conversations

I believe that the most effective path to staff development and change is through the door of assessment. The process of aligning and revising the continuums provides an opportunity to articulate and re-examine our beliefs and teaching practices. In *Conversations* (2000), Regie Routman states that "It is the conversations around curriculum that push us to change, not the documents themselves." (p. xxxviii). In the same way, the continuums themselves are not as valuable as the professional dialogue that is fostered by talking together about students and their work. Chapter 11 includes a description of the typical questions and issues that arise over a five-year period as schools and districts implement the continuums.

Challenges of Using Continuums

The greatest obstacle to change is time. In order for new ideas to take root, teachers desperately need time to talk, to share ideas, and to work together. You start teaching early in the morning and run full-tilt until students leave at the end of the day. Many of you stay for hours after students have left. Many evenings and vacations are spent doing schoolwork, attending workshops, and reading professionally. How can you add one more thing to your already-full plate? If you are going to use continuums successfully in your classroom, school, or district, you have to build in time during the school day to talk about the descriptors using samples of student work. You need time for professional conversations in order to build consistency within and between grade levels. You need time to align the continuums with your teaching and assessment. It also takes time to introduce your students to the continuums and to teach them the language of self-evaluation. Students will need time to fill out the continuums and set goals. If continuums are to be used by an entire school or district, administrators need to build in release time for teams of teachers to align the continuums with standards and curriculum. Time is also needed in order to develop continuum support materials to share with families.

The schools and districts where the continuums have been implemented most successfully are ones in which there is administrative leadership and support, as well as opportunities for ongoing professional development linked to continuums. Suggestions for staff development are included at the end of every chapter and in Chapter 11.

Developing the Continuums

Getting Started

The reading and writing continuums in this book began over ten years ago. Bainbridge Island is a small district a 20-minute ferry ride west of Seattle, Washington with three elementary schools. Teachers were frustrated with the fact that their traditional report card with columns of checkboxes did not reflect the kind of instruction and learning that were occurring in their classrooms. In 1990, teachers on Bainbridge Island met with me to create a report card that actually matched what they taught. In an educational system that has focused for the last 50 years on what and how to teach, rather than on what students are learning, this required a major shift in stance. Teachers began meeting in grade levels to articulate what they expected from incoming students in September and what they thought that most students could do by the end of the year.

What can most second graders do as readers by the end of the year? What kinds of writing skills do most students demonstrate by the end of fourth grade? Despite a wide range of experience and philosophy, the teachers were able to pinpoint common patterns. As the grade-level lists were compiled, teachers began to notice overlapping skills. Third-grade teachers were observing some of the same characteristics in their students as the fifth-grade teachers. The second-grade list and fourth-grade lists looked remarkably similar. Rather than listing skills by grade levels, we decided to place the skills and strategies in a developmental progression. A core group of teachers transformed these grade-level lists into developmental continuums. The Bainbridge Island teachers developed continuums for reading, writing, and spelling. After lengthy discussions, they decided that spelling is not a subject area, but a tool for writing, so the spelling descriptors were embedded in the writing continuum.

This "top-down" method of constructing a continuum is described by Geoff Masters and Margaret Forster (1996a):

> A progress map (or continuum) usually begins with teachers' understandings. Through their day-to-day experiences, teachers gain an understanding of how student development usually occurs in an area of learning. They come to recognize indicators of progress. An initial sketch of a progress map is made by putting on paper the understandings that teachers already have. (p. 1)

The continuums were developed as teachers articulated their knowledge of how readers and writers develop, based on their expertise and experience. The conversations were both exciting and enlightening and often led to further professional reading about literacy acquisition. Beginning with teachers' own experience fostered an important sense of ownership.

After early drafts evolved into an organized continuum, the committee next began to explore literacy continuums from other states and countries. At that time, very little information about continuums was available from mainstream publishers. We examined several continuums from other districts and provinces, such as the ones from the Juneau School District in Alaska (1993) which were also created through a "top-down" process, beginning with teachers' experience.

Other continuums have been developed as "bottom-up" documents, based on an analysis of student performances on assigned task. The continuums are then tested in classrooms and revised. "A progress map (or continuum) must be constantly checked, updated and enriched. Careful observations and records of actual student performances provide valuable information for revising and enriching a progress map" (Masters and Forster, 1996, p. 7). The Resource Documents from the Ministry of Education in British Columbia (1994) included "reference sets" which were also useful as we revised our own continuums. In Australia, the continuums are called "progress maps" or "profiles." The Curriculum Profiles from Australia (Curriculum Corporation, 1991, 1994) were modified for an American audience and published by Heinemann as the *American Literacy Profiles Scales* (Griffin, Smith, and Burrill, 1995). The First Steps (Heinemann, 1996) materials were also originally developed by the Education Department of Western Australia, then modified for use by teachers in the United States. First Steps includes continuums for oral language, spelling, writing, and reading. Looking at these materials from around the world side by side, the similarities are apparent. Indeed, this is not surprising, since all of the continuums describe how readers and writers develop. The most informative published materials about using continuums are *Developmental Assessment* (1996a) and *Progress Maps* (1996b), both written by Geoff Masters and Margaret Forster from Australia. These two magazines present information about developing and using continuums (progress maps) in various countries around the world.

There are, however, differences between the continuum described above and the continuums and support materials in this book. The first difference is that the continuums in this book are not linked to a district, province, country, or program. This book was developed with the recognition that no continuum or package of materials will exactly meet your needs. The continuums and the support materials are therefore included on the accompanying CD-ROM so that you can make modifications based on your particular state standards, curriculum, group of students, and specific needs. Another unique feature is that the K–8 reading and writing continuums in this book each fit on one piece of paper. Using a one-page document to guide your teaching, assess students, and report to parents is far more manageable than using multi-page continuums or sets of books.

Like the First Steps and the British Columbia Resource materials, this book contains narrative portraits (Chapter 2) and a glossary (Chapter 3). In addition, this book also include case studies (Chapter 2), a database (CD-ROM) and list of books by stages (Chapter 4), hyper-linked list of assessment tools (Chapter 5), student self-evaluation versions of the continuums (CD-ROM), and materials for ESL/EAL students (Chapter 9). These materials are also included on the accompanying CD-ROM. Without these support materials, using the continuums would indeed be daunting.

Modifying the Continuums

Initially, there were eight stages on the K–5 reading and writing continuums developed by the Bainbridge Island teachers. As the teachers and students used the continuum, a ninth stage was added, and the descriptors were reordered and revised. At the point when the continuums were first published in *Practical Aspects of Authentic Assessment* (Hill and Ruptic, 1994), there were nine developmental stages: Preconventional, Emerging, Developing, Beginning, Expanding, Bridging, Fluent, Proficient, and Independent. In 1995, the Bainbridge teachers added a significant number of descriptors to the last four stages on the continuums. The increased level of specificity helped teachers, parents, and students describe growth more clearly.

Further Modifications: Broadening the Base

Teachers in other schools and districts have continued to revise and refine the continuums in order to make them clearer and more precise. In 1996, a group of educators from four universities joined with teachers from around the state of Washington who had used the Bainbridge Island continuums for several years. They brought concerns and suggestions about additional descriptors or changes. The continuums were also revised to match the state standards (Washington State Essential Academic Learning Requirements). (On the CD-ROM, you can see the version of the continuums in which the fourth, seventh, and tenth grade benchmarks are indicated in circles by the matching descriptors.) In the process of aligning the continuum with the state standards, we cut and pasted the descriptors to show the horizontal progression of skills and strategies, using icons to represent each standard/strand. The icons and strands helped teachers clearly see the developmental progression of skills and the connection to standards. In 1996, we also added the seventh grade benchmarks for reading and writing and added a tenth stage (Connecting), then modified the descriptors to make the continuums applicable through middle school.

At the same time, six-trait writing from the Northwest Regional Educational Laboratory in Portland, Oregon had been incorporated into the Washington State standards. We again cut apart the continuum in order to include the language from six-trait writing. We embedded descriptors for ideas, organization, word choice, sentence fluency, voice and conventions into the writing continuum. (For more information about six-trait writing, see the phone number and web site for the Northwest Regional Educational Laboratory listed in the References.) As new ideas about curriculum and teaching emerge, you can use the CD-ROM to modify the continuums.

Fine-Tuning the Descriptors

Over the past ten years, I have had meetings, conversations, and email exchanges with hundreds of teachers as I have added, moved, or modified the descriptors. For instance, a year and a half ago, teachers suggested I add a descriptor about phonemic awareness. I emailed all the early years experts I knew about adding a continuum descriptor at the Developing stage. I discovered that no one could agree. Are all students able to blend phonemes and break words into discrete sounds? Should all students be expected to "clap syllables" and create nonsense words based on onset/rime patterns? How do these behaviors look different at the Emerging and Developing stages? Are these truly developmental benchmarks all children will exhibit? As I wrestled with those questions, I created a tentative definition. However, I found it nearly impossible to translate the descriptor into "kid language" for the student version of the continuum. The closest approximation was "I rhyme and play with words," which was already a descriptor in the Emerging stage.

As I finished this book, the same question arose again and emails once again flew back and forth. Some wanted a more technical definition ("Manipulates the individual sounds, syllable, phonemes, and word chunks in the spoken word by segmenting, blending, or deleting), while others argued that not all children will exhibit all of these behaviors and some may use phonics in a more visual than auditory way. Others questioned what it meant to "manipulate" sounds. They felt I would therefore have to define "segmenting," "blending," and "deleting." One teacher wrote, "By adding phonemic awareness descriptors, we're trying to satisfy a need to be current. In my opinion, from all my reading and all the different definitions and interpretations that exist, I'm not sure anyone knows enough yet. You're entering a quagmire!" In the end, one descriptor was added at the Developing stage on the reading and writing continuums: "Uses growing awareness of sound segments (e.g., phonemes, syllables, rhymes) to read/write words." This is one example of conversations that shaped many of the descriptors on the continuum. One of the reasons for including the continuum on the CD-ROM is so that you can modify the descriptors.

Each of the 10 continuum stages contains 7–15 descriptors. The descriptors provide the specificity that makes the continuums useful as assessment and reporting tools. Some schools and districts have tried to simplify the continuums by including fewer descriptors. What soon becomes apparent is that with fewer descriptors, it becomes much harder to differentiate between stages. On the other hand, if more descriptors are added, the continuums soon become two- or three-page documents and quickly lose their usefulness and clarity. For instance, one district in Colorado created a 14-page continuum which teachers found overwhelming. As drafts of the continuums have evolved, we learned that 15 descriptors per stage and 10 stages on one piece of paper was the most manageable, yet informative length. Additional information can always be included in supplementary support materials.

The Challenge of a Math Continuum

Since we had a continuum for reading and writing, why not create one for mathematics? For many years I gathered math experts together and tried to create a math continuum to parallel the literacy continuums. In each discussion, three major challenges arose. The first was that there are so many continuum stages and so many NCTM (National Council of Teachers of Mathematics) standards that we inevitably ended up with a wall chart, rather than one piece of paper. Second, changes in mathematics instruction are still unfolding. Rather than viewing mathematics as primarily computation or discrete units such as geometry or measurement, experts suggest that an integrated approach is the most meaningful method of instruction. Would each NCTM standard become a continuum strand, or would they be interwoven? Finally, a spiral curriculum implies that skills are not taught once, but woven into increasingly challenging tasks that build upon each other. When we tried to create a math continuum, we kept slipping back into the old paradigm of discrete skills.

In 1997, teachers at Brighton School in Lynnwood, Washington did develop a draft of a K–8 math continuum. Revisions were made over the next two years based on the 1998 NCTM standards and the continuum was included on the Brighton report card in 1999. The first five stages were on one piece of 11 x 17 inch paper and the second five stages on a second page. In the original draft of the math continuum, the problem-solving strand was omitted from the continuum and was included in a separate section on the report card, since this ability applies as much to science and social studies as it does to mathematics. Without problem solving as the anchor strand, however, the descriptors looked more like a scope and sequence document and began to lose the developmental and cognitive aspect of mathematics.

Interesting differences between development in mathematics and literacy acquisition also emerged as teachers used the continuums. Reading and writing develop in a somewhat linear fashion, with one skill building upon another, but math seems more dependent on what has been taught. For instance, students do not naturally progress from algebra into geometry. If student learning is more dependent on what is taught, is a continuum the most appropriate format, or would the document be better as a curricular guide? Along the same lines, if a particular strategy is not demonstrated, is it because the student is not able to demonstrate that strategy, or because it has not yet been introduced? Another challenge is that as the Brighton teachers have changed their math programs, they have had to revise the math continuums several times. It is important for instruction to match the curriculum, yet the continuum should not be program-specific. These are the sorts of issues that must be resolved before the math continuum is ready to be published. This year Brighton teachers are currently revising the continuum based on discussions about these issues, feedback from teachers in other schools, and the more recent NCTM standards.

I originally intended to include a chapter in this book about the math continuum and support materials, but the documents are still in their infancy and need many more drafts before they are ready to publish. Once the math continuum has been through several more revisions and has been used by teachers in various states and other countries, it will then be possible to create the support material to parallel those in this book. Eventually, the Brighton teachers hope to create narrative portraits, a glossary, a list of assessment tools, a student version of the continuum, checklists, and a family support document for mathematics. You may want to contact the principal, Cliff Nelson, through their web site (www.brightonschool.com) for a copy of the current draft, or if you are interested in piloting and providing feedback on the math continuums and support materials.

Marking the Continuums

Continuum Descriptors

No child's behaviors fall neatly into one stage. Teachers find that most students' skills fall primarily into one stage, with some items still not mastered in the earlier stage and evidence of a few others from the stage ahead. In many ways, this is one of the strengths of a continuum. By looking at the strands, you can show that a student may struggle with decoding, yet demonstrate strong comprehension during literature discussions. Another advantage of the continuum is that even for students with special needs, the continuum still reflects what the student *can* do. Rather than being discouraged by low grades, struggling students and their families can celebrate growth and set concrete goals for students' next steps in reading and writing.

Reporting at the Ballpark Level

How you mark the continuum will depend on your purpose and audience. Some teachers simply use the continuum as a general guideline for reading and writing growth and do not mark specific descriptors. Using the continuum in this way, you would indicate the "ballpark" for a student's reading and writing development by placing a date in the broad arrow above the descriptors for each grading period to note the child's general continuum stage. The arrow emphasizes the fact that reading and writing do not occur in discrete stages, but in a continuous developmental progression. There are no lines inside the arrow so that you can place the date (month and year) anywhere along the continuum. If a student can demonstrate some of the descriptors, you could place the date to the left side of the stage. You can indicate when students exhibit half of the behaviors at a particular stage by marking the date in the middle of the stage. Similarly, the date can be placed toward the right side of the continuum when a student shows evidence of most of the skills and strategies at a particular skill.

Reporting at the Descriptor Level

Other teachers prefer to mark the continuum at the descriptor level. They use a different color highlighter each grading period to mark each skill that students demonstrate. For instance, some teachers use colored markers to denote fall, winter, and spring quarters:

Autumn = YELLOW

Winter = BLUE

Spring = PINK

Parents, teachers and student appreciate the visual way in which the colors show growth over time. Other teachers place a date by the descriptor (9/00) or use a symbol (A = autumn). In some schools, the continuums are on the computer and teachers simply click the mouse to indicate a skill that has been mastered or use a pull-down menu of choices (A = autumn, W = winter, S = spring).

Deciding how to mark the continuum will depend on several factors. If you are the only teacher in your building using the continuum, determining whether to use dates, symbols, or color highlighters may depend on your teaching style and personal preference. If you are using the continuum as a grade level or as part of a school or district pilot, you will want to agree upon a common marking system. Your decision will also be impacted by whether the continuum will be shared with parents as part of the report card or during conferences. If you decide to use the continuum on your report card, you will have to determine if you will mark the continuum by hand using colored highlighters or put the continuums on a computer.

If you mark the continuum at the descriptor level, you would still want to add the date on the arrow at the end of each grading period. Rather than placing the date by looking at the student's general literacy behaviors, you can be much more specific. For instance, Stacia demonstrated six of the reading skills and strategies in the Bridging stage. Her teacher, Anne Klein, placed the date during the first grading period about one third of the way along the arrow under the Bridging stage. By the next report card, Stacia's work reflected 8 of the 15 descriptors, so Anne placed the second date in the middle of the stage. By June, Stacia had mastered all but one of the descriptors in the Bridging stage and showed evidence of two descriptors in Proficient, so Anne placed the date just above the line between the two stages (Figure 1.4). By dating the continuums three times a year, Anne, Stacia, and her family can visually see growth over time.

WARNING! It is very important to only mark a descriptor when you see evidence on a consistent basis. As teachers, you love your students and enjoy celebrating growth. When you first use the continuum, it's tempting to start marking skills too quickly, rather than waiting until the skill is demonstrated consistently. Only mark the skill or strategy when it's being used consistently. For instance, if you mark that Mario "uses a range of strategies for planning writing," you would expect him to be able to show you several types of prewriting in his writer's notebook. Since the continuum will be marked over time, it's better to err on the side of caution in order to show growth and provide consistency between grade levels.

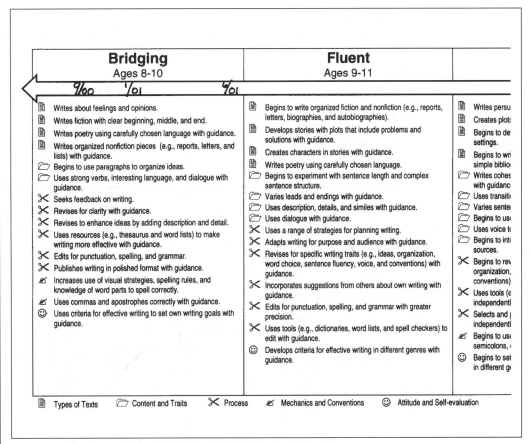

Figure 1.4 Marking the Continuum

Using the Continuums for Reporting

In some schools, the continuums are part of the report card and student-led conferences. The continuums provide a focus point for conversations about the student as a reader and writer, supported by evidence from the student's portfolio.

> Teachers and parents can never know all that a child knows. A report card is merely a snapshot, a tiny slice of a child's learning over a period of time. It is through talking with the child, looking at what the child creates, and watching the child in action that we gain a clearer, more comprehensive understanding of a child's progress. (Ministry of Education, British Columbia, 1992, p. 9)

If you decide to use color highlighters to mark the continuums, you will have to determine how to make copies for families. One solution is to send the student version home with the student and place the teacher version in the student's permanent record. Some schools prefer to photocopy the continuums to send home each grading period. Depending on your copier, the shades of gray do appear and you can then place the color version in the student's permanent folder. Teachers at Brighton School, in Lynnwood, Washington, experimented with using symbols for each grading period. They found that the color highlighters were a far more effective way to show growth. The continuums are marked in January with a yellow highlighter. Parents sign the report card envelope and return the continuums, which are marked again in June, using a pink highlighter. A copy is made for parents and sent home the week after school is over and the original is placed in the Learner Profile that travels with the student from year to year. Making a second copy does not take much time, especially the second semester when there are only a few new descriptors to highlight.

Organizing Continuum and Assessment Information

Throughout this book, I will describe how information about continuums and assessment can be organized and stored for teachers (Figure 1.5), students (Figure 1.6), and families (Figure 1.7). If you are writing a grant or planning a budget that includes materials for implementing continuums, you may want to build in funds for notebooks, sections dividers, clear acetate slip-sheets, clipboards, and plenty of Post-it notes. I'll first describe the four types of notebooks for teachers.

Teacher Information

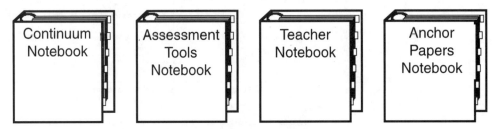

Figure 1.5: Teacher Notebooks

Continuum Notebooks

It is helpful to create a Continuum Notebook in a three-ring binder to store all of the continuum information that you plan to use. You can keep a copy of the continuums in the back of the notebook for reference. The continuum information that you plan to use can be printed from the CD-ROM and stored in the Continuum Notebook, using dividers for the following eight sections:

1. Narrative Portraits
2. Glossary
3. Charts
4. Book Lists by Stages
5. Student Self-Evaluation Checklists
6. Family Support
7. English as an Additional Language (EAL)
8. Data Collection

Assessment Tools Notebooks

You can keep all the assessment forms you may want to use in an Assessment Tools Notebook. In the front of this notebook, you may want to keep a copy of your Organizational Grid, which is your assessment plan and calendar for the year (Chapter 5). You may want to insert six dividers in this notebook:

1. General Assessment Tools
2. Spelling Assessment
3. Writing Assessment
4. Reading Assessment
5. Content Area Assessment
6. References

As you read through this book, you will probably find some assessment forms that you want to use. For instance, you may want to use the Parent Survey (Form 8.2), the Reading Conference Form 9.6) and the Fiction Rubric (Form 7.17). Using the CD-ROM, you can print the forms, then place a copy in the appropriate section of your Assessment Tools Notebook. Many teachers use clear acetate slip-sheets to store the forms. When you are ready to use a particular form, you can then simply slip the form out of the plastic sleeve and make copies for your students. If you find other useful assessment forms at conferences or workshops, you can add those pages into the appropriate section of your Assessment Tools Notebook. You can also store a copy of useful professional journal articles about assessment in this notebook.

Teacher Notebooks

The third notebook contains all the assessment information you collect about your students. (Detailed information about organizing a Teacher Notebook is described in Chapter 5.) The three-inch three-ring binder contains section dividers for each of your students, so that all of your assessment information about your students is located in one place. For example, in each student's section, you may have a copy of the parent survey, your anecdotal notes, a spelling dictation from the fall and spring, a retelling, and several reading conference forms.

Anchor Papers Notebooks

The fourth notebook would be created together by your staff. The Anchor Papers Notebook includes samples of student work at each continuum stage as anchors or benchmarks. Grade-level teams can work together to decide upon representative samples for reading and writing. For instance, you may want to include exemplary writing samples in various genres and examples of students' revision at different levels. In the reading section, you can include samples of written response to literature and retellings. You will need 20 section dividers for your Anchors Papers Notebook, 10 for each of the continuum stages for reading and writing. These anchor papers help ensure consistency in filling out the continuums.

Student Information

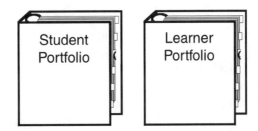

Figure 1.6 Student Portfolios and Learner Profiles

Student Portfolios

Students can become part of the evaluation process by keeping portfolios of their work. Representative samples of work in various content areas can be included in student portfolios, along with reflections about why the particular pieces were chosen. As students complete the student versions of the continuums, they use samples from their portfolios as evidence of particular skills or strategies. The continuums and portfolios then provide the structure and focus for student-led conferences.

Learner Profiles

Each student at Brighton School in Lynnwood, Washington, also has a Learner Profile that is passed on from year to year. The Learner Profiles include representative slices of the students' work from preschool through grade eight (see Chapter 5). The binder contain a checklist and dividers for ten sections:

1. Student Goals
2. Self-Portraits
3. Art Samples
4. Writing Samples and Reflections
5. Photocopies of Reading Samples and Reflections
6. Reading Logs
7. Math Samples and Reflections
8. Content Area Samples and Reflections
9. Letters to Next Teacher
10. Report Cards

Each Learner Profile also contains a videotape of the student reading aloud in the fall and spring of every year. The Learner Profiles are presented to the students and their families when students leave or graduate from Brighton as a record of their learning over time.

Parent Information

Figure 1.7 Parent Handbook

Parent Handbook

You may want to share information about continuums with families at a Curriculum Night about reading and writing development. You may also want to create a Parent Handbook with copies of the reading and writing continuums, the Narrative Portraits (Chapter 2), the Glossary (Chapter 3), and the Family Support documents (Chapter 8). In some schools, the Parent Handbook also includes the Book Lists by

Continuum Stages (Chapter 4). At Brighton School, this information is also included on the school's web site (www.brightonschool.com). By including copies of the continuums and appropriate support materials in the notebooks, you can provide a common language and framework for teachers, students, and families.

Continuum Versions

There are several versions of the 11 x 17-inch continuums included on the CD-ROM.

Black and White Checkboxes

The CD-ROM contains a version of the continuums with check boxes by each descriptor where you can place a date or symbol for the grading period. If you are using the continuum on a computer, you may want to create a pull-down menu that allows you to place a letter in the checkbox to indicate the trimester that the skill or strategy was mastered (F = fall, W = winter, S = spring).

Black and White Icon Versions

If you plan to use color highlighters to mark the continuums, you may want to use the continuum version that includes icons to represent the five strands on the continuum listed below.

Reading Continuum
Types of Texts and Oral Reading (📖)
Attitude (☺)
Reading Strategies (☑)
Comprehension and Response (👆)
Self-Evaluation (∿)

Writing Continuum
Types of Texts (📄)
Content and Traits (📁)
Process (✂)
Mechanics and Conventions (✎)
Attitude and Self-Evaluation (☺)

These strands for reading and writing match the state standards in Washington State. By using the continuum version with the icons, you can clearly see patterns to students' skills as readers and writers. For instance, a student may write clear nonfiction and imaginative poetry, yet struggle with conventions and spelling. The black and white versions of the continuums are also included at the end of this book.

Color Icon Versions

For those of you who are visual learners, I also created a version of the reading and writing continuums using different colors for each of the strands. Many teachers find that the color version helps them understand the continuum strands and the horizontal flow of the descriptors more clearly. For instance, by looking at the blue "Content and Traits" strand on the writing continuum, you can see how the expectations increase from stage to stage:

Writes with a central idea. (Expanding)

Begins to use paragraphs to organize ideas. (Bridging)

Writes cohesive paragraphs, including reasons and examples with guidance. (Proficient)

Writes cohesive paragraphs, including supportive reasons and examples. (Connecting)

Uses a clear sequence of paragraphs with effective transitions. (Independent)

As you read Chapter 5 and Chapter 6 and decide which assessment tools you plan to use, you may want to be sure that you have included at least one assessment tool for each of the continuum strands. For instance, as a primary teacher, you may want to use a reading log to assess the types of text students read, a survey to assess attitude, running records to assess reading strategies, retelling to assess comprehension, and the continuum checklists from Chapter 7 for student self-assessment. You may want to laminate a copy of the color versions of the reading and writing continuums to keep by your desk.

Washington State Standards Versions

As described earlier, Washington State has standards for reading and writing, with benchmarks and new criterion-referenced tests for grades four, seven, and ten. The CD-ROM includes a version of the continuums that indicates which descriptors match the state standards at each of the three grade levels.

Student Self-Evaluation Versions

Student versions of the reading and writing continuums are included at the end of this book and on the CD-ROM. Many teachers, especially at the intermediate and middle school levels, ask students to complete the continuums, using their class work and portfolios as evidence. For instance, Anne Klein's fourth and fifth graders in Edmonds, Washington fill out the student versions of the continuums. Anne reminds her students that if they highlight a particular skill, she expects them to show her evidence. This also means that Anne must have explained each descriptor clearly. For instance, Devon marked that he "uses transitional sentences to connect paragraphs." He was able to pull three samples from his writing folder to show Anne where he demonstrated this skill. If one of our goals is to help students learn to evaluate their own work, it makes sense to include them in the assessment and evaluation process. More specific information about using the continuums for self-evaluation can be found in Chapters 7 and in Chapter 10.

Continuum Descriptor Versions

Several copies of the continuums are included on the CD-ROM which show connections between the continuum descriptors and specific assessment tools. Two versions of the reading and writing continuums show which descriptors can be assessed using anecdotal notes and checklists (Chapter 6). Another version shows which descriptors on the reading and writing continuum that social studies teachers in middle school can assess (Chapter 10).

English as an Additional Language (EAL) Versions

In Chapter 9, I describe how Cecilia Vanderhye, Anna Marie Amudi, and Kathryn Blatch created the listening/speaking continuum for students who are learning English. The CD-ROM includes the English as an Additional Language (EAL) continuum, and three other versions (color, checkboxes and student self-evaluation).

Spanish Versions

Enrique Mejía and Cecilia Vanderhye helped translate the reading and writing continuums into Spanish. Both the black and white versions with icons and the color versions of the Spanish continuums are included on the CD-ROM.

Versions in Other Languages

The most surprising aspect of developing the continuums has been the way their use has spread around the world. Ten years ago as I worked with teachers on Bainbridge Island, I never dreamed these documents would be used by teachers in Grand Forks, North Dakota, in Winnipeg, Canada, and in Denver, Colorado. The continuums are being used in international schools in Mexico, Belgium, Sri Lanka, Bangladesh, Saudi Arabia, Bahrain, and the United Arab Emirates. Figure 1.8 shows the reading continuum translated into Arabic. The widespread use of continuums highlights the universal nature of literacy acquisition.

Figure 1.8 Arabic Continuum

Many of these schools have begun translating the materials from this book into other languages. If you translate the continuums or support materials into other languages, please send me a copy so that they can be shared with other teachers and families.

Continuum Support Materials: Chapters 2–12

Unless the continuums are directly connected to instruction and classroom-based assessment, they may remain buried in a notebook or lost in a pile on your desk. The remainder of the book contains support materials and provides specific information about using the continuums in your classroom.

Chapter 2: Narrative Portraits and Case Studies

What are some examples of student work at various stages on the continuums? Chapter 2 includes narrative vignettes of students at each stage on the reading and writing continuums. These narrative portraits are also included on the CD-ROM and could be included in a Parent Handbook. In the second half of the chapter, the case studies include examples of student work at each of the ten continuum stages.

Chapter 3: Glossary

What do the descriptors on the continuums mean? A glossary of terms is included in Chapter 3 and on the CD-ROM, which can help ensure a common language as you and your colleagues begin using the continuums.

Chapter 4: Books by Continuum Stages

In the reading continuum, you may notice the use of phrases such as "pattern books," "medium chapter book," or "challenging children's book." What do these terms mean? The types of texts students read provide the anchor for reading assessment. Chapter 4 includes a chart of the characteristics of books at each continuum stage, as well as a sample book lists for each stage. The CD-ROM also contains a database of over 2,000 titles, leveled according to continuum stages.

Chapter 5: Assessment Tools

What assessment tools can I use to collect assessment information in order to fill out the continuums? In Chapter 5, I provide a chart of useful assessment tools for each descriptor on the continuums. This assessment information is also summarized by stages. On the CD-ROM, the list of assessment tools is hyper-linked so that you can print the assessment forms you want to use.

Chapter 6: Anecdotal Notes and Checklists

How can I gather specific information about each of my students? How can anecdotal notes be connected to the continuum descriptors? This chapter explores practical ways to take anecdotal notes by linking your instruction and assessment directly to the continuum descriptors. Lists of anecdotal note focus questions and checklists are included in the chapter and on the CD-ROM.

Chapter 7: Student Self-Evaluation

Can students use the continuums for self-evaluation? How do the continuums connect to student portfolios? When students are asked what they do well as readers, they often shrug and say, "I don't know." As educators, we rarely show students the steps along the way to becoming independent readers and writers. The continuums provide students with the language for self-evaluation. Chapter 7 includes examples of how teachers at various grade levels have used the reading and writing continuums with students. The chapter includes examples of student self-evaluation, self-evaluation checklists, and charts of the continuums. The checklists, charts, and student versions of the continuums are also included on the CD-ROM.

Chapter 8: Family Support

What can families do to support reading and writing at home? How can the continuums be shared with parents? In this chapter, I examine ways in which various schools have used the continuums as the focus for parent education and reporting. A list of ways in which families can support literacy at home is provided for each continuum stage at the end of the chapter and on the CD-ROM.

Chapter 9: English as an Additional Language

How can the continuums be used for students who are just learning English? Chapter 9 includes a listening and speaking continuum for non-English speaking students. The chapter also includes narrative portraits, a glossary, a list of assessment tools, checklists, and a family support document for EAL/ESL students. These materials are also included on the CD-ROM.

Chapter 10: Middle School Challenges

How can the continuums be used in middle school? How can you help students learn to assess their own skills and set goals independently? Chapter 10 explores how continuums can provide the language students need for self-evaluation, along with examples of how a middle school teacher uses the continuums to teach the process of student self-evaluation.

Chapter 11: Data Collection and Staff Development

What is the normal developmental range for readers and writers at my grade level? How do I answer parents' questions about how their child compares to other students the same age? Chapter 11 includes information on collecting information about the patterns of growth in your classroom. You may want to share this information with your colleagues in order to look at developmental patterns within and across grade levels.

How can I convince my colleagues to use the continuums? What are some staff development activities that are helpful as we adopt the continuums as a school? Staff development activities are provided at the end of each chapter. In addition, Chapter 11 outlines typical questions that arise over a five-year period as teachers incorporate continuums into their instruction, assessment, and reporting methods. Teachers from around the world describe the positive impact that continuums have had in their schools.

Chapter 12: Conclusion

The book concludes with a discussion of the advantages of using developmental continuums. Some of the remaining challenges will be explored in the next two books in the *Corner Pieces Assessment Series* on student portfolios and reporting student growth.

The CD-ROM

How do I find time to create forms and support materials? The biggest obstacle to implementing new ideas in education is time. You scarcely have enough time to sip your coffee or make a phone call during the day, much less create forms on a computer. For that reason, much of the material in this book is included on the accompanying CD-ROM. Rather than creating continuums and assessment forms yourself, you can modify the ones from the book to match your specific needs, grade level, and group of students. The CD-ROM contains the continuums, support materials, assessment tools, and a database of over 2,000 books leveled by continuum stages.

STAFF DEVELOPMENT

One of the most effective and memorable ways to introduce a continuum is to present a visual demonstration of the concept. I often begin a workshop by asking ten volunteers to come up to the front of the room. I choose a topic, such as "singing" and we arrange ourselves in a continuum from left to right. For instance, those on the left are people who can't carry a tune, those in the middle like to sing in the car or shower, and those on the right can read music and perhaps sing in a choir. The volunteers move to where they would be on the "singing continuum." As we change topics (how much we like chocolate, how well we cook, ski, garden, etc.) people move to where they fit on each continuum. When I ask what people notice, they point out that there is a great deal of movement. They recognize that everyone has some topics where they would be far on the left and others where they would be far to the right. This visual activity serves as a memorable introduction to continuums. I then discuss how reading and writing can also be presented as a developmental continuum.

With your colleagues, create a list on chart paper or an overhead of the benefits and challenges of using developmental continuums. You may want to compare your list with the chart in this chapter. After using the continuums for a year, you may want to revise your list.

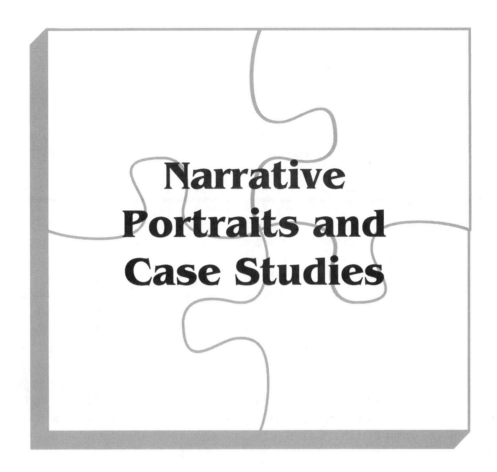

Narrative Portraits and Case Studies

Chapter 2

To live a rich, full and satisfying life at each stage of growth is the
best possible preparation for the next stage.

Dorothy Butler and Marie Clay, 1979, p. 22

The amount of information on the reading and writing continuums can be overwhelming to some parents. How can you share information about literacy growth in a more accessible format? The Narrative Portraits were first developed by Sandi Sater, Carrie Holloway, and Patti Kamber on Bainbridge Island. The Portraits evolved over to years to match the changes in the continuums. In the Narrative Portraits of Readers and Writers, each stage of the continuums is described in a short paragraph. The Narrative Portraits that are included in this chapter and on the CD-ROM were created to help teachers and parents understand reading and writing development. This chapter also includes Case Studies of Readers and Writers in which I describe actual students at each continuum stage and provide examples of their reading and writing. The final section of this chapter includes chart versions of the reading and writing continuums. The Narrative Portraits, the Case Studies, and the Charts can be used for parent education and for staff development.

Narrative Portraits

Several years ago, teachers at Brighton School in Lynwood, Washington, filled out continuums three times a year, in September, January, and June. They found, however, that it was very challenging to collect enough information about students in the first two or three months of school in order to complete the continuums accurately. In addition, it felt redundant and time consuming to be sharing information both in writing, as well as orally during fall conferences. So last year, Brighton teachers decided to hold parent conferences in the fall and spring (November and March) and fill out report cards (including the continuums) in the winter and at the end of the year (January and June).

At the November conference, teachers show parents the reading and writing continuums and describe where their child's behaviors generally fall. Teachers also share the Narrative Portraits as they chat with parents about their child. Together, they set goals—what the child hopes to learn, what the teachers will work on at school, and what families can do to support literacy development at home (see Chapter 8). Teachers continue to assess students and to collect evidence of learning and growth; then in January, the students' completed continuums are sent home.

In March, teachers meet with each family to discuss what students have learned and to set goals for the rest of the year. In several classrooms, these spring conferences are student led. This second conference is particularly meaningful as the teacher, student, and family examine evidence of learning and celebrate growth. A report card with the updated continuums is sent home at the end of the year. Teachers find that the Narrative Portraits are a valuable parent education component and a way to provide a common language for teachers and families to talk about reading and writing development. (The Narrative Portraits for English as an Additional Language are included in Chapter 9.)

Continuum Notebook

You may want to create a Continuum Notebook that would include the reading and writing continuums, the Narrative Portraits from this chapter, as well as some of the other support pieces described in the next few chapters. Some teachers use clear acetate slip-sheets to store pages they may want to photocopy during the year.

Parent Handbook

Teachers at Dhahran Academy in Saudi Arabia created a Parent Handbook that includes copies of the continuums and the Narrative Portraits. You can give families a copy of the Narrative Portraits at parent conferences, at Back to School Night, or at a Curriculum Night as you explain the continuums. At Brighton School, this same information is also included on their website (www.brightonschool.com). Once parents read the descriptions of reading and writing at each stage, it's pretty easy to spot the general stage where their child's behaviors fall.

Case Studies

The Narrative Portraits paint a picture of how reading and writing develop using broad brush strokes, but I also wanted to bring the portraits to life by using actual children as case studies. Teachers at Brighton School identified one student at each stage on the continuums and collected their reading and writing samples, logs, journals, and surveys. I interviewed the students, their teachers, and their families, then wrote several pages about each student, including samples of their work. I want to offer a special thanks to the Brighton students, families, and teachers who helped with the collection of work and multiple revisions of the Case Studies.

For the Case Studies, Brighton teachers chose "typical" students who represented the types of literacy behaviors often seen at each stage. They also selected students who were at the same stage for both reading and writing, which is not always the case. One of the challenges of choosing one student at each stage was that even as we identified the children and began collecting work samples, many had already progressed on to the next stage. The Case Studies are presented in ten sections, one for each of the continuum stages. There are three parts to each section: a chart of the characteristics of readers and writers, a narrative description of students at that stage, and a case study. Chapter 4 contains more specific information about the types of texts that students read at each stage.

Charts

I created Charts of each of the ten continuum stages for reading and writing by simply enlarging the continuums. In some schools, the complete reading and writing continuums are hung in a central location in the school to visually display the developmental nature of literacy acquisition. You could display either the teacher version (which is included at the end of this chapter) or the student version of the charts (Chapter 7 and CD-ROM). Both versions are included on the CD-ROM but not in this chapter. You could print the charts on $8 \frac{1}{2}$ x 11-inch paper or enlarge them to poster size, then laminate the charts. Some schools post the charts outside the library or in the front hallway as another form of communication with parents. You may also want to send home information about the continuums in parent newsletters or at a family evening about reading and/or writing development.

Continuum Wall

Many schools use the continuum charts for staff development. At the Saudi Arabian International School (SAIS) in Jeddah, Jill and Jack Raven and the other first grade teachers turned their Team Room into a continuum room. On each of the four walls, they hung the spelling, reading, writing, and math continuums. Below each stage, they glued samples of student work as anchor papers. What a visual way to capture growth in mathematics, reading, and writing (Figure 2.1). You can create the charts by hand, as the teachers did in Jeddah, or you can enlarge the "stage by page" adult version of the continuum charts included on the CD-ROM.

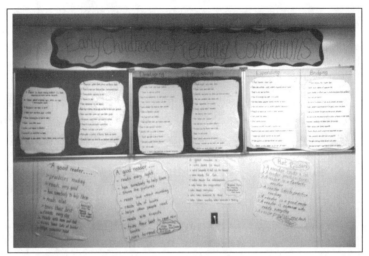

Figure 2.1 Continuum Wall

Anchor Papers Notebook

You may want to create a three-ring binder with sections for each stage (ten for reading and ten for writing). As you collect student work, the samples displayed under each stage of the continuums can be copied and placed in your Anchor Papers Notebook. You may want to have teachers bring student work samples to a faculty meeting and sort them into continuum stages. The continuums, the continuum wall and anchor pieces, along with the Narrative Portraits and Glossary (which will be described in Chapter 3), can provide a shared framework for literacy instruction and assessment. Now let's take a look at the Narrative Portraits and Case Studies for each of the ten continuum stages.

Preconventional (Ages 3–5)

Characteristics of Preconventional Readers

- Begins to choose reading materials (e.g., books, magazines, and charts) and has favorites.
- Shows interest in reading signs, labels, and logos (environmental print).
- Recognizes own name in print.
- Holds book and turns pages correctly.
- Shows beginning/end of book or story.
- Knows some letter names.
- Listens and responds to literature.
- Comments on illustrations in books.
- Participates in group reading (books, rhymes, poems, and songs).

Preconventional learners display curiosity about books and reading. They enjoy listening to books and may have favorites. Children focus mostly on illustrations at this stage as they talk about the story. They love songs and books with rhythm, repetition, and rhyme. Students participate in reading by chiming in when adults read aloud, and children at this age often enjoy hearing the same stories read aloud over and over. Preconventional readers are interested in environmental print, such as restaurant and traffic signs, labels, and logos. Children hold books correctly, turning the pages as they look at the illustrations. They know some letter names and can read and write their first name.

Characteristics of Preconventional Writers

- Relies primarily on pictures to convey meaning.
- Begins to label and add "words" to pictures.
- Writes first name.
- Demonstrates awareness that print conveys meaning.
- Makes marks other than drawing on paper (scribbles).
- Writes random recognizable letters to represent words.
- Tells about own pictures and writing.

At the Preconventional stage, children rely on their pictures to show meaning. They often pretend to write by using scribble writing. Children sometimes make random letters and numbers to represent words. Some children add "words" to their pictures to share meaning. They often tell stories about their pictures.

Case Study: Ryan

Ryan Clausen is an outgoing four-year-old boy with a happy disposition (Figure 2.2). He loves books and language and attends preschool three days a week.

Figure 2.2 Preconventional Reader and Writer—Ryan

Preconventional Reader

Ryan is an active child, but manages to settle down easily to listen to books. He particularly enjoys listening to books with patterns and refrains, like *Have You Seen My Cat?* (Eric Carle, 1988) or *I Went Walking* (Sue Williams, 1989) that invite participation. He also likes nonfiction books about trains and tractors and frequently points to the pictures to ask questions. As he listens to books, Ryan talks about the illustrations and makes predictions. He often joins in as his parents read familiar books aloud and can retell his own version of familiar stories. He plays with magnetic letters on the refrigerator and sings the alphabet song. Ryan knows the names of most letters and calls attention to letters on signs and stores. He loves to play rhyming games with his mother in the car.

Preconventional Writer

Ryan is hovering on the brink of writing conventionally. In Figure 2.3, he used scribble writing when he wrote a letter to Santa.

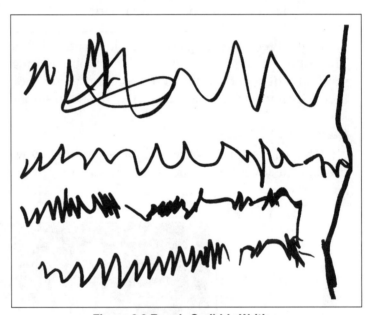

Figure 2.3 Ryan's Scribble Writing

Ryan is able to write his first name, "mom," and "dad," but does not yet have a bank of other familiar words he can write. In Figure 2.4, he used random strings of letters to write, "You can be nice if you say 'yes'" after a discussion with his mother about being polite. Ryan is just beginning to ask, "How do you make that letter?" as he writes. The word play and literacy activities he experiences at home pave the way for a smooth transition into kindergarten for this budding reader and writer.

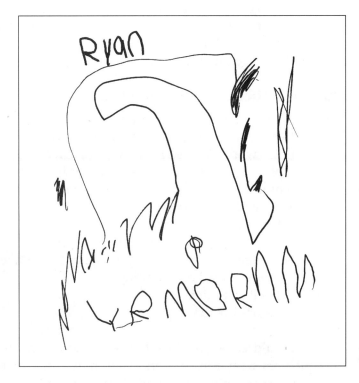

Figure 2.4 Ryan's Writing with Random Strings of Letters

Emerging (Ages 4–6)

Characteristics of Emerging Readers

- Memorizes pattern books, poems, and familiar books.
- Begins to read signs, labels, and logos (environmental print).
- Demonstrates eagerness to read.
- Pretends to read.
- Uses illustrations to tell stories.
- Reads top to bottom, left to right, and front to back with guidance.
- Knows most letter names and some letter sounds.
- Recognizes some names and words in context.
- Begins to make meaningful predictions.
- Rhymes and plays with words.
- Participates in reading of familiar books and poems.
- Connects books read aloud to own experiences with guidance.

At the Emerging stage, children are curious about print and see themselves as potential readers. They may pretend to read familiar poems and books. Children rely on the illustrations to tell a story but are beginning to focus on the print. They participate in readings of familiar books and often begin to memorize favorites, like *Brown Bear, Brown Bear, What Do You See?* (Bill Martin, Jr., 1967). Children begin to make connections between books read aloud and their own lives and experiences. They enjoy rhyming and playing with words. Emerging readers know most letter names and some letter sounds. They recognize some names, signs, and familiar words. These children are often highly motivated to learn to read and may move through this stage quickly.

Characteristics of Emerging Writers

- Uses pictures and print to convey meaning.
- Writes words to describe or support pictures.
- Copies signs, labels, names, and words (environmental print).
- Demonstrates understanding of letter/sound relationship.
- Prints with upper case letters.
- Matches letters to sounds.
- Uses beginning consonants to make words.
- Uses beginning and ending consonants to make words.
- Pretends to read own writing.
- Sees self as writer.
- Takes risks with writing.

These children begin to see themselves as writers. Some students begin to label their pictures with a few letters. They may write their name and some familiar words in a way that others can read. Students may write just the beginning or the beginning and ending sounds they hear. At the Emerging stage, children often write everything in upper case letters. They may pretend to read their own writing, often elaborating to embellish their stories.

Case Study: Sami

Sami Schneider's green eyes sparkle under her bangs as she looks through books (Figure 2.5). She is an eager participant in her kindergarten class.

Figure 2.5 Emerging Reader and Writer—Sami

Emerging Reader

She chimes in when her teacher, Linda Johnson, reads stories with rhymes and patterns. Sami sees herself as a reader as she memorizes familiar stories that she's heard several times at home and at school. As an Emerging reader, she looks through books, often making up stories to go along with the illustrations. She is able to read books with one or two words on a page, like *Carrot, Parrot* (Jerome Martin, 1991). Like many children at this stage, she recognizes her name and familiar signs in her world, such as "McDonalds" and "Stop."

Sami knows all her upper and lower case letters as well as the sounds they make. For instance, she can think of several words that begin with a particular letter. She rhymes and plays with words at home and at school. Her mother notes that Sami delights in new words (such as "possible," "encourage," and "exciting") and tucks them into her conversation. Although Sami doesn't yet have a word bank of sight words she recognizes, her interest in words and reading are sure signs that this skill is right around the corner. As she learns to sound out three- and four-letter words, she is increasing in her confidence as an Emerging reader.

Her parents read to her at least 15 minutes each night before bedtime. Sami's favorite books are the *Arthur* series by Marc Brown and books about animals. As she snuggles up with her parents on the couch or her bed, Sami makes connections between the books they read together and her life. She also "pretends to read" at home and at school. She uses the illustrations from books to tell the story and can make meaningful predictions about what will happen next. At home, she asks her parents to tell stories from their childhood over and over, then retells them in her own words. Stories are very much an important part of Sami's life.

Emerging Writer

Early in the year, Linda Johnson takes dictation from students in their journals. You can see how in September she transcribed Sami's description of her drawing of a scientist (Figure 2.6).

My Scientist is a statue. She has her arms out to think about the whole world.

Figure 2.6 Sami's Dictation

A month later, Linda still took dictation for most of the words, but Sami copied Robert Munsch's name from the board (Figure 2.7). This scaffolding provides support as Sami builds her confidence and knowledge of letter names and sounds. She used a "reading voice" as she pretended to read what she had written.

Most students represent words with two or three letters for several months. Sami, however, plunged right into using phonetic spelling by including many of the sounds she could hear in words. She wrote some sight words that she knew automatically and copied other words from around the room or on the board. She intermixed upper and lower case letters as she began to add text to her pictures.

In November, she wrote "I ws trick or treting" in her journal. She included the beginning and ending sounds in "was," and copied most of the letters in "trick or treating" correctly from the board. With her teacher's help, she wrote short words and phrases in her kindergarten journal and in the journal the students kept about their weekly author study. At home, Sami wrote short two- and three-word notes to her parents and to her teacher.

Figure 2.7 Sami's Author Journal—Copying Words

By January, Sami was writing in her author journal independently (Figure 2.8). When they studied books by Joanne Ryder, she wrote, "TheBaBrWpanenoTra." (The baby bear was playing on the rainbow.) She intermixed upper and lower case letters. Sami included some beginning and some ending sounds with no spaces between words. Notice her first attempt at using a period.

Figure 2.8 Sami's Journal—Independent Writing

Sami wrote words, lists, and letters at home. She sometimes copied the names of books or words from the text. Her mother commented that Sami was constantly drawing and writing words and carried a pen and pad of paper everywhere. Sami saw herself as a writer and was eager to write about her pictures and ideas. She took risks with her writing by sounding out words on her own. Sami could usually tell an adult what she had written at the time, but was sometimes not be able to read her writing a day or two later. The next steps for this Emerging writer would be to include vowels and consonant blends, and to write one or two sentences.

Linda uses Marie Clay's (1993) technique of asking students to write all the words they know in the fall, and again at the end of the year. In October, Sami listed 11 words, including her name, "Mom," "Dad," and the names of two friends. By the end of the year, Sami wrote 40 words in the same amount of time. She had moved into the next stage as a Developing writer. One of the delights of teaching students at this age is watching how rapidly their writing flourishes with immersion in print, intentional instruction, practice, and praise.

Developing (Ages 5–7)

Characteristics of Developing Readers

- Reads books with simple patterns.
- Begins to read own writing.
- Begins to read independently for short periods (5–10 minutes).
- Discusses favorite reading material with others.
- Relies on illustrations and print.
- Uses finger-print-voice matching.
- Knows most letter sounds and letter clusters.
- Recognizes simple words.
- Uses growing awareness of sound segments (e.g., phonemes, syllables, rhymes) to write words.
- Begins to make meaningful predictions.
- Identifies titles and authors in literature.
- Retells main event or idea in literature.
- Participates in guided literature discussions.
- Sees self as reader.
- Explains why literature is liked/disliked during class discussions with guidance.

These children see themselves as readers. They can read books with simple patterns, like *Dear Zoo* (Rod Campbell, 1982) or *Mrs. Wishy-Washy* (Joy Cowley, 1999) or simple texts, like *Go Dog Go* (P. D. Eastman, 1961). Later in this stage, they can read books with patterns that vary more, such as *Just for You* (Mercer Mayer, 1975), or *Cookie's Week* (Cindy Ward, 1988). They begin to look at books independently for short periods of time (5–10 minutes) and like to share books with others. Developing readers know most letter sounds and can read simple words (such as "dog" and "me") and a few sight words (such as "have" and "love"). Recognizing patterns and word families helps readers generalize what they know about one word to similar new words. They use both print and illustrations to make meaning as they read. Children often read aloud word-by-word, particularly with a new text. They gain fluency with familiar books and repeated readings. These young readers can retell the main idea of a story and participate in whole-group discussions of literature. This is another stage that children may pass through quickly.

Characteristics of Developing Writers

- Writes 1–2 sentences about a topic.
- Writes names and familiar words.
- Generates own ideas for writing.
- Writes from top to bottom, left to right, and front to back.
- Intermixes upper and lower case letters.
- Experiments with capitals.
- Experiments with punctuation.
- Begins to use spacing between words.
- Uses growing awareness of sound segments (e.g., phonemes, syllables, rhymes) to write words.
- Spells words on the basis of sounds without regard for conventional spelling patterns.
- Uses beginning, middle, and ending sounds to make words.
- Begins to read own writing.

Students at the Developing stage write names and familiar words. They begin to write one or two short sentences, such as "MI DG PLS" ("My dog plays"). Developing writers use beginning, middle and ending sounds to make words. For example, *learn* might be written "LRn." This developmental reliance on the sounds of letters is called "invented spelling," "phonetic spelling," or "temporary spelling." At this stage, students spell some high frequency words correctly. Students often interchange upper and lower case letters and experiment with capital letters and simple punctuation. Their writing goes from left to right and begins to include spacing. Students are able to read their own compositions aloud immediately after writing, but later may not remember what they wrote.

Case Study: Ellie

Ellie McMahon is a petite, soft spoken, thoughtful participant in class (Figure 2.9). She loves school and her mother says she takes her "job" of learning very seriously. She has an older brother and younger sister.

Figure 2.9 Developing Reader and Writer—Ellie

Developing Reader

Ellie loves to read class poems and charts. She can read books with simple patterns and one or two lines of texts, such as *The Good Bad Cat* by Nancy Antle (1985). At school, she reads from the *Reader Rabbit* series, the *Hello Reader* series (Level 1), and *School Zone* series (Level 1). She keeps a reading log of the books she reads with her teacher or other adults at school (Figure 2.10).

At home, Ellie's parents read to her most school nights before bed and during the afternoons on weekends. She also reads aloud to her parents each school night. Ellie meticulously keeps track of the books she reads at home on the monthly reading log she keeps for school. She loves books with colorful pictures, which she studies carefully. One of her favorite illustrators is Jan Brett and she enjoys reading new books, as well as re-reading old favorites. Ellie likes listening to chapter books about ballet and about young girls, such as *The American Girl* books and the *Little House* series by Laura Ingalls Wilder. Her mother says that Ellie identifies strongly with the female characters in the books they read together.

Developing Writer

At home, Ellie draws or writes every day and likes to "play school" with her younger sister. She writes grocery lists, notes, and letters to friends on her personalized stationery. In Ellie's first grade class, students write in their weekly journals, field trip journals, author journals, science logs, and literature response logs. They also write poetry, letters, lists, and class books.

READING LOG

Name Ellie _____ Month/Year _____

Date	Title	How much did you like it? A Little Some A Lot
9-16-98	THE CAT IN THE HAT	1 2 3 ④ 5
9-18-98	TOO BIG for ME	1 2 3 ④ 5
Maurine Giles 9.21.98	This IS NOT SAM	1 2 3 ④ 5
9-22-98	LOOK AT THIS BOOK	1 2 ③ 4 5
9-22-98 Mrs. X.	One FrOg One Fiy	1 ② 3 4 5
Mrs. m. 9-23-98	LOOK AT ME	1 2 ③ 4 5

Figure 2.10 Ellie's Reading Log

Ellie enthusiastically began her weekly journal in September with, "I like everything" (Figure 2.11). In her phonetic spelling of "everything" (avethng), you can see how she is writing the sounds she hears in the word. In another entry, she writes, "football game" as "fblg" and "lots of fun" as "lisovfn."

Figure 2.11 Ellie's September Journal

In her October entry (Figure 2.12), notice her invented spelling of "trick-or-treat" and "I am Dorothy!" She spells some high frequency words correctly. Like many children at this stage, Ellie intermixes upper and lower case letters. She includes the beginning, middle, and ending sounds and uses spacing between words. Her entries using invented spelling are quite readable and usually consist of one or two short phrases or sentences. She can usually read what she has written.

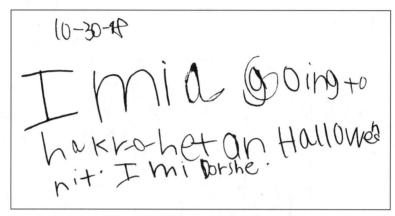

Figure 2.12 Ellie's October Journal

Ellie is actively figuring out how written language works. In one journal entry, she places a period at the end of every line as she overgeneralizes the concept of a period. In the next entry, she places the period after every word. Two weeks later, the period appears correctly at the end of the sentence.

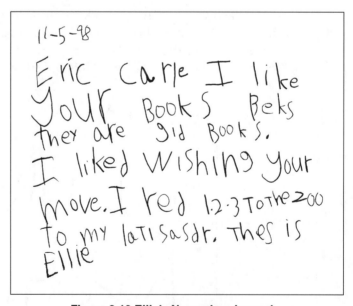

Figure 2.13 Ellie's November Journal

By November, her letter to Eric Carle is longer and she's using periods correctly (Figure 2.13). ["Eric Carle, I like your books because they are good books. I liked watching your movie. I read *1–2–3 to the Zoo* to my little sister. This is Ellie."]. Of the 28 words in her letter to Eric Carle, 20 are spelled correctly. Notice the correct word endings of "-ed" and "-ing." Ellie's next few journal entries are neither as neat, as long, nor as conventionally spelled as the letter to Eric Carle. For many students, writing growth is uneven as they try new strategies and forms of writing and solidify their skills. As you can see from these samples over several months, Ellie is building her confidence and fluency as she grows from a Developing into a Beginning writer.

Beginning (Ages 6–8)

Characteristics of Beginning Readers

* Reads simple early-reader books.
* Reads harder early-reader books.
* Reads and follows simple written directions with guidance.
* Identifies basic genres (e.g., fiction, nonfiction, and poetry).
* Uses basic punctuation when reading orally.
* Reads independently (10–15 minutes).
* Chooses reading materials independently.
* Learns and shares information from reading.
* Uses meaning cues (context).
* Uses sentence cues (grammar).
* Uses letter sounds and patterns (phonics).
* Recognizes word endings, common contractions, and many high frequency words.
* Begins to self-correct.
* Retells beginning, middle, and end with guidance.
* Discusses characters and story events with guidance.
* Identifies own reading behaviors with guidance.

Beginning readers rely more on print than on illustrations to create meaning. They understand basic punctuation when they read aloud, such as periods, question marks, and exclamation marks. At first, they read simple early readers, like *Sammy the Seal* (Syd Hoff, 1959) and picture books with repetition, like *The Napping House* (Audrey Wood, 1984). Students take a big step forward when they learn to read longer books, like *The Cat in the Hat* (1957) or *Green Eggs and Ham* (1960) by Dr. Seuss.

Later in this stage, they can read more difficult early readers, like *Frog and Toad Together* (Arnold Lobel, 1971) and more challenging picture books, like *A Bargain for Frances* (Russell Hoban, 1970). They often enjoy simple series books, such as the *Little Bear* books by Else Minarik or the humorous *Commander Toad* series by Jane Yolen. Many of these books are labeled "I Can Read" books on the covers. Beginning readers take a developmental leap as they begin to integrate reading strategies (meaning, sentence structure, and phonics cues). They are able to read silently for 10–15 minutes. These children know many words by sight and occasionally correct themselves when their reading doesn't make sense. They are able to discuss the characters and events in a story with the teacher's help. When they read simple nonfiction texts, such as *Mighty Spiders* (Fay Robinson, 1996) or *Dancing with the Manatees* (Faith McNulty, 1994), they are able to talk about what they learn. It may take significantly longer for children to move through this stage since there is a wide range of text complexity at this level.

Characteristics of Beginning Writers

- Writes several sentences about a topic.
- Writes about observations and experiences.
- Writes short nonfiction pieces (simple facts about a topic) with guidance.
- Chooses own writing topics.
- Reads own writing and notices mistakes with guidance.
- Revises by adding details with guidance.
- Uses spacing between words consistently.
- Forms most letters legibly.
- Writes pieces that self and others can read.
- Uses phonetic spelling to write independently.
- Spells simple words and some high frequency words correctly.
- Begins to use periods and capital letters correctly.
- Shares own writing with others.

At the Beginning stage, children write recognizable short sentences with some descriptive words. They can write several sentences about their lives and experiences or simple facts about a topic. Students sometimes use capitals and periods correctly. Many letters are formed legibly and adults can usually read what the child has written. Students spell some words phonetically and others are spelled correctly. They usually spell simple words and some high frequency words correctly as they become more aware of spelling patterns. Beginning writers often start a story with "Once upon a time" and finish with "The End." Children may revise by adding details with the teacher's help. They enjoy sharing their writing with others. Students may stay at this stage longer than the previous ones as they build fluency.

Case Study: Leah

Leah Flegenheimer is full of enthusiasm about school, friends, and life. (Figure 2.14).

Figure 2.14 Beginning Reader and Writer—Leah

Beginning Reader

Leah's mother is a teacher, so reading is a high priority at their house. Leah has enjoyed listening to her parents read Beverly Cleary books and the *Boxcar Children* series by Gertrude Chandler Warner, as well as more challenging books, such as *Bunnicula* (James Howe, 1979) and *Maniac Magee* (Jerry Spinelli, 1990).

Leah uses several effective strategies when she's reading. She says that when she gets to a hard word, she asks her mom, reads ahead to see what would make sense, or looks at the letters a word starts with. She has a good bank of sight words she recognizes quickly. She sometimes makes miscues when she reads without going back to self-correct, even when the sentence doesn't make sense. Her teacher, Donna Kerns, is working to help Leah learn to crosscheck using all three cueing systems (meaning, grammar, and phonics). Another goal for Leah is to watch for punctuation in order to increase her fluency and read more smoothly.

At the end of first grade, Leah read simple picture books that had the support of patterns, like *Hop on Pop* (Dr. Seuss, 1963) and *Just Me and My Puppy* (Mercer Mayer, 1985). By the fall of second grade, she moved into reader books like *Arthur's Halloween* (Marc Brown, 1983) and the *Poppleton* and *Henry and Mudge* series by Cynthia Rylant. She is now just beginning to self-correct for meaning, usually with adult guidance. She no longer relies on the support of predictable books, as you can see by her reading log from October (Figure 2.15). The first five books on this log are all fiction, but the last nonfiction book was quite a bit more challenging. Note that Leah didn't care for this book very much. Leah is able to choose books easily and reads either independently or with friends during silent reading time at school.

READING LOG

Name Leah **Month/Year** oct. 98

Date	Title	How much did you like: A Little / Some / A Lot
21, 10 1998	Little eagle learns to Fly	1 (2) 3 4 5
26, 10 1998	Horrible Harry and the Kickball Wedding	1 2 (3) 4 5
26, 10 1998	Pinocchio	1 (2) 3 4 5
28, 10 1998	Parents night fright	1 2 (3) 4 5
2 11 1998	Arthur's Halloween	1 (2) 3 4 5
11-4 98	Puzzle maps U.S.A.	(1) 2 3 4 5

Figure 2.15 Leah's Reading Log

During literature discussions, Leah shares her ideas and makes thoughtful observations. She is able to retell stories and discuss story events and characters. One of Leah's strengths as a reader is her awareness of her own growth as a reader. Her teacher noted, "She is aware of the strategies she uses and self-monitors in a way that I don't often see in children this age." Leah's goal is to "read long chapter books."

One of the challenges of this project was that children often zip through these early stages of reading and writing. By January, Leah had moved into the Expanding stage as she started reading the *Jewel Kingdom* (Jahnna N. Malcolm) and *Clue Junior* (Parker C. Hinter) series. She's just begun reading the Level 4 texts in the *Hello Reader* series by Scholastic and picture books with more challenging vocabulary.

Beginning Writer

Leah loves to write at home and at school. In her response log, Leah writes about her favorite parts of the books she reads in literature circles. She can write several sentences about what she reads or what she likes and notices. Leah loves to write poetry (Figure 2.16).

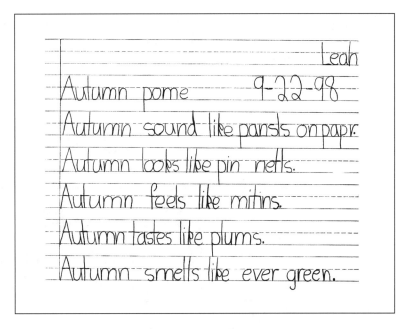

Figure 2.16 Leah's Poetry

She can also write persuasively, as you can see in her journal entry about why she thought the class should get a gecko (Figure 2.17). She sums up the reasons by saying, "It's science. Most kids would like it."

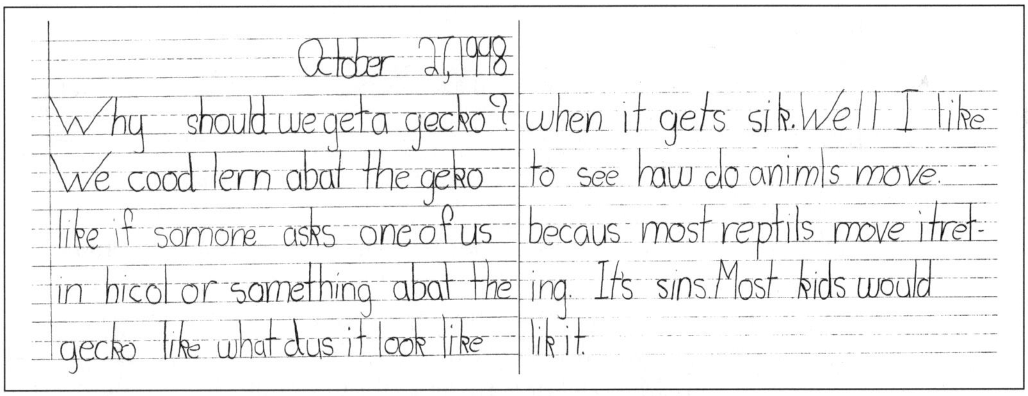

October 27, 1998

Why should we get a gecko? We cood lern abat the geko like if somone asks one of us in hicol or something abat the gecko like what dus it look like when it gets sik. Well I like to see haw do animls move. becaus most reptils move itreting. It's sins. Most kids would lik it.

Figure 2.17 Leah's Nonfiction Writing

Leah's most fluent writing is in her "weekend window" journal in which students write about what they did over the weekend (Figure 2.18). Like many children this age, she simply lists what she did at a birthday party, but adds, "We danced to music—Third Eye Blind I think." On the second page of this entry, she wrote, "Sarah H. is writing the same thing and probably Lianne is too. Kelsey, Caroline, and Hannah were there, too." In fact, the other girls' journals did look remarkably similar. In this entry, she's omitted punctuation, although she used periods correctly in the previous entry and in all the ones that follow. That's why it's so important to look at several writing samples before marking the continuum.

Donna Kerns is teaching Leah to check her work for capitals and periods. She checks the students' weekend windows and helps the children with spelling and punctuation as they read their entries aloud. With this kind of individual support, Leah will internalize this self-monitoring and editing strategy.

Figure 2.18 Leah's Journal

Leah likes to write with her friends after school. They make up schedules and compose ongoing stories. At home, Leah also writes letters and notes. During an interview, she told me that she writes notes to her mom when she's on the phone and that her mom reads them and just nods! She loves to share her writing at home and at school. Most of her writing is about her family and personal experiences and she sometimes keeps a journal. Leah's next steps as a writer will be to write longer pieces and to begin adding interesting language in different forms of writing. As Donna provides focus lessons about adding details (who, when, why, where, how, and what), she notices that Leah adds more such information each week.

Leah is becoming a visual speller and beginning to notice common spelling patterns. For instance, she spelled "bright" as "brite" and "train" as "trane," which are both reasonable approximations. Leah spells many words conventionally ("little," "when," "should," "showed," and "things"), while at other times she uses her invented spelling in order to write independently. Her writing is easy to read, since she uses spacing between words, writes in complete sentences, often uses periods correctly, and prints neatly. When she shares her writing at Author's Chair, she sometimes catches misspellings or words she's omitted. Leah also likes to write poems and chose to include one in her portfolio, along with her prewriting web using the five senses. Just as I finished collecting and scanning Leah's writing samples, her teacher and her mother both commented that Leah's writing had suddenly taken off. She's now writing chapter stories at home with complicated plots that incorporate some dialogue and description. Lately, she's been working on her own plays, complete with lists of characters, sparked by the *Jewel Kingdom* series (Jahnna Malcolm). Leah's reading clearly influences her writing. For instance, she wrote, "They looked all over the green wood, the white winter land, the red mountains, and the blue lake, but they could not find her at all." Leah is starting to move into the Expanding stage as a writer.

When asked during an interview, Leah replied that a good author, "makes the book interesting or funny, has a problem in the book, and uses big words that mean more than one thing." She commented, "I want to read more, so I can learn more words, so I can write more!"

Expanding (Ages 7–9)

Characteristics of Expanding Readers

> * Reads easy chapter books.
> * Chooses, reads, and finishes a variety of materials at appropriate level with guidance.
> * Begins to read aloud with fluency.
> * Reads silently for increasingly longer periods (15–30 minutes).
> * Uses reading strategies appropriately, depending on the text and purpose.
> * Uses word structure cues (e.g., root words, prefixes, suffixes, word chunks) when encountering unknown words.
> * Increases vocabulary by using meaning cues (context).
> * Self-corrects for meaning.
> * Follows written directions.
> * Identifies chapter titles and table of contents (text organizers).
> * Summarizes and retells story events in sequential order.
> * Responds to and makes personal connections with facts, characters, and situations in literature.
> * Compares and contrasts characters and story events.
> * "Reads between the lines" with guidance.
> * Identifies own reading strategies and sets goals with guidance.

At the Expanding stage, students solidify skills as they read beginning chapter books. Many children read series books and re-read old favorites while stretching into new types of reading. In the early part of this stage, they may read short series books, like *Pee Wee Scouts* (Judy Denton) or picture books like the *Arthur* series by

Marc Brown. As they build fluency, students often devour series books, like *Cam Jansen* (David Adler), *Bailey School Kids* (Debbie Dadey and Marcia Thornton Jones), or *Amber Brown* (Paula Danziger). They may also read nonfiction texts on a topic, such as *The Titanic: Lost . . . And Found!* (Judy Donnelly, 1987). Students are learning how to choose books at their reading level and can read silently for 15–30 minutes. They read aloud fluently and begin to self-correct when they make mistakes or their reading doesn't make sense. They can usually figure out difficult words but are still building their reading vocabulary. At this stage, children use a variety of reading strategies independently. These students make connections between reading and writing and their own experiences. Expanding readers are able to compare characters and events from different stories. They can talk about their own reading strategies and set goals with adult help.

Characteristics of Expanding Writers

- Writes short stories and poetry with guidance.
- Writes a variety of short nonfiction pieces (e.g., facts about a topic, letters, lists) with guidance.
- Writes with a central idea.
- Writes using complete sentences.
- Organizes ideas in a logical sequence in fiction and nonfiction writing with guidance.
- Begins to recognize and use interesting language.
- Uses several prewriting strategies (e.g., web, brainstorm) with guidance.
- Listens to others' writing and offers feedback.
- Begins to consider suggestions from others about own writing.
- Adds description and details with guidance.
- Edits for capitals and punctuation with guidance.
- Publishes own writing with guidance.
- Writes legibly.
- Spells most high frequency words correctly and moves toward conventional spelling.
- Identifies own writing strategies and sets goals with guidance.

Students at this stage can write poems and stories about their experiences and interests, as well as short nonfiction pieces. They use complete sentences and their writing contains a logical flow of ideas. Their stories sometimes contain a beginning, middle, and end. Expanding writers can add description, detail, and interesting language with the teacher's guidance. They enjoy reading their writing aloud and are able to offer specific feedback to other students. Their editing skills begin to grow, although students may still need help as they edit for simple punctuation, spelling, and grammar. Their writing is legible, and they no longer labor over the physical act of writing. Students spell many common words correctly as they begin to grasp spelling patterns and rules.

Case Study: Tyler

Tyler Cox is a bright, creative, and highly involved third grader (Figure 2.19). His mom says that he loves his teachers and school. He's a perfectionist, which sometimes causes him frustration. On the other hand, Tyler's handwriting is beautiful and he always tries his best.

Figure 2.19 Expanding Reader and Writer—Tyler

Expanding Reader

Like many boys his age, Tyler loves the *Goosebumps* (R. L. Stine), *Wayside School* (Louis Sachar), and *The Magic Tree House* (Mary Pope Osborne) series. He zips through these books fluently and has good comprehension. His retelling in September of one of the *Bailey School Kids* books (Debbie Dadey and Marcia Thornton Jones) was strong. His next steps are to justify his opinions and make connections to other books and authors. These series books are helping Tyler build his oral fluency. His teacher, Cindy Flegenheimer, has been helping him pay more attention to punctuation in order to read with more expression. Tyler likes to read mysteries, adventures, and science fiction: "I like those kinds of books because they are interesting and exciting." He prefers short chapter books like *The Littles Take a Trip* (John Peterson, 1968) and *The Bailey School Kids* books like *Angels Don't Know Karate* (Debbie Dadey and Marcia Thornton Jones, 1996) that are relatively short, quick reads. He likes nonfiction books about topics like rocks and dinosaurs, as well as magazines like *Ranger Rick* and *Kid City*.

Tyler enjoys reading. He reads for 15–30 minutes in class and reads for longer periods at home. He generally picks books at his own level. Once in a while he reads aloud to one of his parents or his younger sister, but most often reads to himself. He usually monitors his own comprehension and asks for help when he has questions. When asked about his reading strategies, Tyler said he "sounds it out, reads the rest of the sentence and figures it out, asks, or skips the word and keeps reading." He makes reasonable predictions and inferences when he reads material at his reading level. His comprehension is equally strong during read alouds that are at a more challenging level. Tyler is an involved listener and participant in literature discussions and makes connections to his own experiences. He discusses characters and story events with ease.

Cindy's third grade class spent several months studying wolves. In his written response to *Return of the Wolf* (Dorothy Hinshaw Patent, 1995), you can see how Tyler is able to write about his favorite part of the book and he is beginning to justify his opinions (Figure 2.20). He also pointed out two new words that he liked ("rendezvous" and "perceptive"). Tyler says that reading and math are his two favorite subjects.

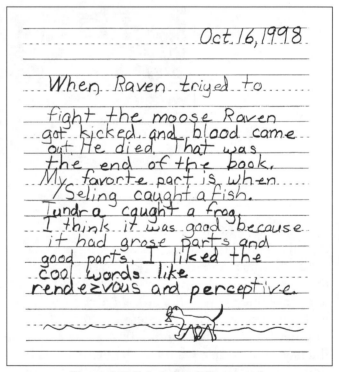

Figure 2.20 Tyler's Book Response

Expanding Writer

His mother says that drawing and painting are almost daily activities at home. She comments that "Tyler writes and draws in his notebooks all the time, making lists, writing letters and stories, and drawing creative pictures." For instance, his notebook includes a list of his favorite foods, neatly numbered, and another list of "Things I Like To Do." Tyler uses complete sentences with correct punctuation. His writing is very neat and his misspellings are close approximations. For instance, although he spelled "died" correctly, he wrote "triyed" for "tried." He spelled most high frequency words and a few challenging words correctly, such as "caught" and "because." He is definitely moving toward conventional spelling.

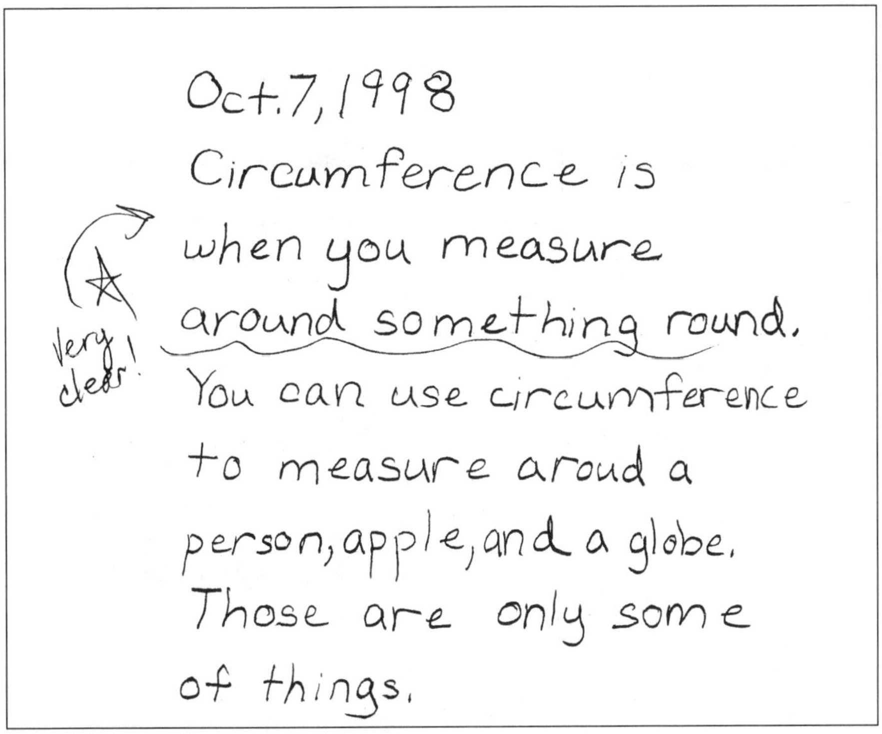

Oct. 7, 1998
Circumference is
when you measure
around something round.
You can use circumference
to measure aroud a
person, apple, and a globe.
Those are only some
of things.

Very clear!

Figure 2.21 Tyler's Writing in Math

In Cindy's class, students keep a math journal, in which they write about their mathematical reasoning and vocabulary. In Tyler's description of circumference, you can see that he is able to use writing to explain a concept using complete sentences (Figure 2.21) and writes a variety of forms and types of texts (Figure 2.22).

Tyler has a love of language and words. For instance, when the class was brainstorming similes, he suggested, "I felt as empty as a cloud with no rain." He asks about the meaning of new words and incorporates new vocabulary from the classroom "Wonderful Word Wall" into his writing. In September, he wrote, "Wolves are perceptive, too," using new vocabulary from the word wall. Cindy noted on Tyler's continuum at the Expanding level that he was able to recognize and use interesting language. Tyler says that he gets most of his writing ideas from the books he reads.

As you can see in a page from his scary story (Figure 2.23), Tyler is beginning to revise by adding details and description, as well as going back to replace "worn" words with more interesting ones. With his teacher's help, he is also beginning to edit his work for grammar, spelling, and punctuation. During the year, students publish several pieces of writing, which they share in class and with families during Portfolio Nights.

Sept. 21, 1998

My picture of a Scientist

1.   Scicentist try to come
     up with new ways.
2.   They experimet with chemicals.
3   They dissect bugs.
4.   Scicentist <u>Observe</u>.

Figure 2.22 Tyler's Writing in Science

I went out one night
to get ˢᵒᵐᵉfire wood from
the old lady ᵗʰᵃᵗ ˡⁱᵛᵉᵈ ⁱⁿᵃ ᶜᵃᵛᵉᵍᵃᵍᵉ·My friends
and ~~firends~~ ᴵ think she's a witch.
I walk up to her door I
thought she was going to
⌈I was scared, I a mouse, when it's being⌉
cook me for supper.She ᶜʰᵃˢᵉᵈ ᵇʸ ᵃ ᶜᵃᵗ·
ᵒᵖᵉⁿᵉᵈ
~~answered~~ the door, I ask
for wood ˢʰᵉgave me some.
I walk out I was glad
that I was not stew.

Figure 2.23 Tyler's Writing Sample—Simple Revisions

Tyler's next steps are to learn to use paragraphs and to create stories with a clear beginning, middle, and end. He says that good authors "use interesting words, have a problem in their story and a little adventure, and sometimes have scariness and mystery." Tyler's criteria for good writing reflects both his book preferences and his teacher's focus lessons.

Bridging (Ages 8–10)

Characteristics of Bridging Readers

- Reads medium level chapter books.
- Chooses reading materials at appropriate reading level.
- Expands knowledge of different genres (e.g., realistic fiction, historical fiction, and fantasy)
- Reads aloud with expression.
- Uses resources (e.g., encyclopedias, CD-ROMs, and nonfiction texts) to locate and sort information with guidance.
- Gathers information by using the table of contents, captions, glossary, and index (text organizers) with guidance.
- Gathers information from graphs, charts, tables, and maps with guidance.
- Increases vocabulary by using context cues, other reading strategies, and resources (e.g., dictionary and thesaurus) with guidance.
- Demonstrates understanding of the difference between fact and opinion.
- Follows multi-step written directions independently.
- Discusses setting, plot, characters, and point of view (literary elements) with guidance.
- Responds to issues and ideas in literature as well as facts or story events.
- Makes connections to other authors, books, and perspectives.
- Participates in small group literature discussions with guidance.
- Uses reasons and examples to support ideas and opinions with guidance.

This is a stage of consolidation when students strengthen their skills by reading longer books with more complex plots, characters, and vocabulary. They often choose well-known children's books, such as the *Ramona* books (Beverly Cleary) or the *Encyclopedia Brown* series (Donald Sobol). Students also enjoy more recent series, like *Goosebumps* (R. L. Stine), *Animorphs* (K. A. Applegate), and the *Baby-Sitters Club* books (Ann Martin). They may broaden their interests by reading a wider variety of materials, such as *Storyworks*, *Contact for Kids*, or *Sports Illustrated for Kids* magazines, or *The Magic Schoolbus* (Joanna Cole) nonfiction series. They begin to read aloud with expression and often memorize some of the humorous poetry by

Shel Silverstein and Jack Prelutsky. With adult guidance, Bridging readers can use resources, such as encyclopedias and the Internet, to find information. They can respond to issues and ideas in books, as well as facts and story events. Many students are able to make connections between their reading and other books and authors. Students at this stage begin to support their opinions with reasons and examples during small group literature discussions.

Characteristics of Bridging Writers

- Writes about feelings and opinions.
- Writes fiction with clear beginning, middle, and end.
- Writes poetry using carefully chosen language with guidance.
- Writes organized nonfiction pieces (e.g., reports, letters, and lists) with guidance.
- Begins to use paragraphs to organize ideas.
- Uses strong verbs, interesting language and dialogue with guidance.
- Seeks feedback on writing.
- Revises for clarity with guidance.
- Revises to enhance ideas by adding description and detail.
- Uses resources (e.g., thesaurus and word lists) to make writing more effective with guidance.
- Edits for punctuation, spelling, and grammar.
- Publishes writing in polished format with guidance.
- Increases use of visual strategies, spelling rules, and knowledge of word parts to spell correctly.
- Uses commas and apostrophes correctly with guidance.
- Uses criteria for effective writing to set own writing goals with guidance.

Bridging writers begin to develop and organize their ideas into paragraphs. Students at this stage are able to write about their feelings and opinions, as well as fiction, poetry, and nonfiction. However, this is a time of practice and their writing is often uneven. Writers may focus on one aspect of a piece and pay less attention to others. For example, a student may focus on strong verbs and descriptive language, while conventions and organization move to the back burner. Students still require a great deal of adult modeling and guidance at this stage. Bridging writers are learning that meaning can be made more precise by using description, details, and interesting language. Students experiment with dialogue in their writing. They are able to edit for spelling, punctuation, and grammar. They also experiment with different types of writing as they compose longer pieces in various genres. Bridging writers use the writing process to revise, edit, and publish their work with adult support.

Case Study: Amanda

Amanda Spohnholtz enjoys fourth grade, as well as watching TV, working on the computer, playing Nintendo, and "hanging out" with friends (Figure 2.24).

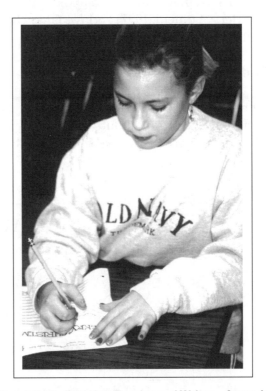

Figure 2.24: Bridging Reader and Writer—Amanda

Bridging Reader

Amanda likes to read medium level chapter books, such as horse stories, mysteries like *Dead Man in Indian Creek* (Mary Downing Hahn, 1990), biographies, and series books, like the *Ramona* (Beverly Cleary) books and *The Boxcar Children* (Gertrude Chandler Warner) series. She also likes "kind of gross stories," such as *How to Eat Fried Worms* (Thomas Rockwell, 1973). She reads books at this level with some expression and good comprehension.

At home, Amanda reads to herself a couple of times during the week. She mentioned that she enjoys when her parents read more challenging children's literature aloud, such as *Walk Two Moons* (Sharon Creech, 1994) and *The Phantom Tollbooth* (Norton Juster, 1961). She also liked *Tales of a Fourth Grade Nothing* (Judy Blume, 1972), which her teacher, Gabrielle Catton, read aloud. Amanda says that good authors "use good word choice and make good characters."

Although she prefers fiction, Amanda sometimes reads nonfiction. When the class studied the rainforest, her teacher and parents helped Amanda find facts about animals in the rainforest by using the glossary and index in several books. At school, she's an eager participant in literature discussions and easily discusses ideas and literary elements (such as plot, characters, and setting). One of her favorite books she read in literature circles was *Night of the Twister* (Ivy Ruckman, 1984). In her written response to literature, Amanda's teacher, Gabrielle Catton, sometimes jots notes in the margin asking for more information. Amanda includes her opinion of a book, but hasn't yet started to back up her ideas with specific examples or make connections to other authors and books. Her goal is to "read harder books," such as *Wringer* (Jerry Spinelli, 1997) and *The Giver* (Lois Lowry, 1993). Amanda is still consolidating her skills as a Bridging reader.

Bridging Writer

Amanda has written scary stories, personal narratives, letters, poems, and nonfiction research. She would rather write fiction than nonfiction and is willing to write more if it's a topic about which she is interested. One of her favorite pieces that she has written this year is a "chapter story" about Halloween (Figure 2.25).

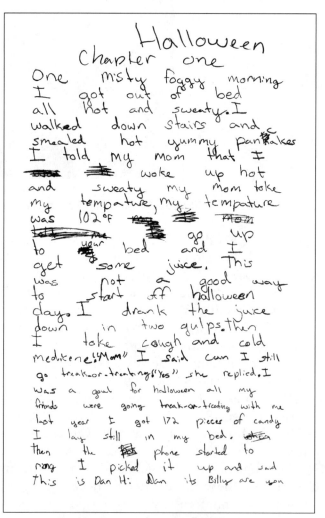

Figure 2.25 Amanda's Writing Sample

She also published a nonfiction report on the margay, a cat that lives in the rainforest (Figure 2.26). She produced an outline, notes, drafts, and final copy with adult support. Amanda used several resources to find information about her topic. She used her own voice in her report and lots of exclamation points. Gabrielle's feedback on drafts helped Amanda revise for clarity and organize her report into a logical flow using paragraphs.

Hi I'am doing my report on Margays. A Margay is type of cat that lives in the rainforest. The rainforest is a forest with: plants,animals,insects,and humidity. It has four layers: the Forest floor,Under story,Canopy,and the emergent layer.

The Margay grows up to be two,to four feet long. It has reddish or grayishfur with black spots and streaks. It sortof looks like a baby jaguar!

The margay is a carnivore. A carnivore is a meat eating animal. It has sharpteeth to eat all the meat up. **YUMMY!!** It eats: insects, monkeys, birds, rats,opposoms, reptiles, and more!

A Margay spends most of it's life in trees and hunting. Margays live in Central America, South America, and Bolivia.

Margays spend most of their time in the canopy trees. Margays have 1-2 cubs.

Margays are the only cat that can rotate their ankle joints when going down vertical trees. This animal has been listed endangered

Figure 2.26 Amanda's Research Report

Amanda's letter to a state representative about saving the rainforest shows her understanding of the topic and her growing ability to organize information (Figure 2.27).

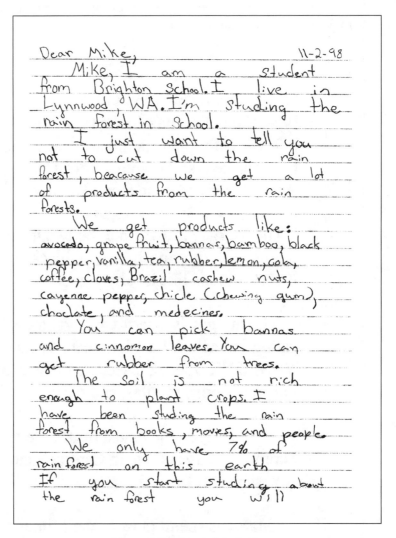

Figure 2.27 Amanda's Letter

Amanda spells most words conventionally. She sometimes misspells homonyms ("there" instead of "their" or "are" instead of "our"), but spells challenging words like "protection," "citizen," and "characters" correctly. She is usually able to catch her own misspellings. Her next step will be to use quotation marks and paragraphs consistently in her drafts. For now, Amanda's focus is on creating long stories with characters and an exciting plot. It's hard at age nine to do everything at once!

One of the differences between younger writers and those at the Bridging stage is the ability to revise and edit. You can see from Amanda's first draft (Figure 2.28) and her final published piece (Figure 2.29) that she is beginning to revise her writing. At this point, however, most of her changes are editing rather than revision.

She adds a few words to help with the flow of the piece, notes where paragraphs are needed, and checks for punctuation and spelling. She uses commas and apostrophes correctly and is beginning to use colons appropriately. Her writing would be strengthened by adding more details and interesting language.

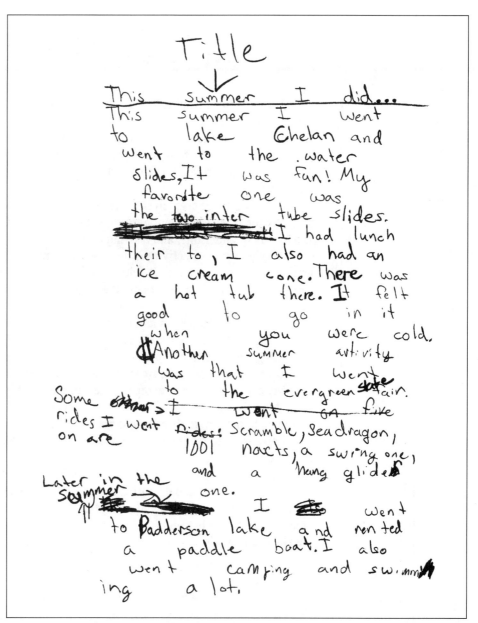

Figure 2.28 Amanda's Draft

Amanda's writes, "The thing that is hard is trying to find stories that are good to write." Most of her writing is sparked by assignments in school, such as her rainforest report and the diamantes that her teacher assigned. As a Bridging writer,

Amanda's goals are still very concrete, such as "putting in more similes." This is a stage for building the stamina of readers and writers as they read and write substantially longer texts.

This summer I did...

This summer I went to Lake Chelan and went to the water slides, I was fun!

My favorite ones were the to inter tube slides. There were cool!! I had lunch there and an ice cream cone. There was a hot tub there it felt good to go in it when you were cold.

I went to the Evergreen state fair I went on 5 rides these are the rides I went on: Scramble, Sea Dragon, 1001 knots, a hang glider one, and a swing one.

Another summer activity is that I went to my grandma's house. I went to Padderson lake and rented a paddle boat. I also went swimming and camping a lot!

I also went to the boys and girls club for two weeks of the summer. The first week I went to: A museum, I went swimming and to, and two parks
The second week I went to: two parks and swimming.

My cousins babysat me during the summer. While I got babysat I went
to: the mall, the movie theater, and the BP..

I also went to my grandma's house and made a fort at the beach. I also
went out to pizza with my grandma. It was fun!!

Ali and I were penpals during the summer and she spent the night at my house and I spent the day at her house. I got to see her pugs their names
are Daisy and Katie.

Figure 2.29 Amanda's Published Story

Fluent (Ages 9–11)

Characteristics of Fluent Readers

- Reads challenging children's books.
- Selects, reads, and finishes a wide variety of genres with guidance.
- Begins to develop strategies and criteria for selecting reading materials.
- Reads aloud with fluency, expression, and confidence.
- Reads silently for extended periods (30–40 minutes).
- Begins to use resources (e.g., encyclopedias, articles, Internet, and nonfiction texts) to locate information.
- Gathers information using the table of contents, captions, glossary, and index (text organizers) independently.
- Begins to use resources (e.g., dictionary and thesaurus) to increase vocabulary in different subject areas.
- Begins to discuss literature with reference to setting, plot, characters, and theme (literary elements) and author's craft.
- Generates thoughtful oral and written responses in small group literature discussions with guidance.
- Begins to use new vocabulary in different subjects and in oral and written response to literature.
- Begins to gain deeper meaning by "reading between the lines."
- Begins to set goals and identifies strategies to improve reading.

By the Fluent stage, students are well launched as independent readers. They read challenging children's literature in various genres for longer periods of time (30–40 minutes). Many readers begin to enjoy mysteries, like the *Nancy Drew* (Carolyn Keene) and *Hardy Boys* (Franklin Dixon) series and survival books, like *Hatchet* (Gary Paulsen, 1987) and *On the Far Side of the Mountain* (Jean Craighead George, 1990). Other children prefer fantasy books, like *James and the Giant Peach* (1961) or *Matilda* (1988) by Roald Dahl. The books they read contain fully developed characters and more challenging plots than in the previous stage. They can use resources, such as a dictionary and thesaurus, to learn new words and can find information in encyclopedias and on the Internet. Many readers enjoy magazines like *World: National Geographic for Kids*, *American Girl*, or *Time for Kids*. Students contribute thoughtful responses when they write or talk about books and begin to "read between the lines" to get at deeper levels of meaning. They are learning to evaluate their own reading strategies and set goals.

Characteristics of Fluent Writers

- Begins to write organized fiction and nonfiction (e.g., reports, letters, biographies, and autobiographies).
- Develops stories with plots that include problems and solutions with guidance.
- Creates characters in stories with guidance.
- Writes poetry using carefully chosen language.
- Begins to experiment with sentence length and complex sentence structure.
- Varies leads and endings with guidance.
- Uses description, details, and similes with guidance.
- Uses dialogue with guidance.
- Uses a range of strategies for planning writing.
- Adapts writing for purpose and audience with guidance.
- Revises for specific writing traits (e.g., ideas, organization, word choice, sentence fluency, voice, and conventions) with guidance.
- Incorporates suggestions from others about own writing with guidance.
- Edits for punctuation, spelling, and grammar with greater precision.
- Uses tools (e.g., dictionaries, word lists, and spell checkers) to edit with guidance.
- Develops criteria for effective writing in different genres with guidance.

This is a stage of increasing complexity. Students begin to write organized fiction and nonfiction pieces for different purposes and audiences. They write poetry, using carefully chosen language. Students write stories with problems and solutions, as well as multiple characters, with adult support. They experiment with leads, endings, and complex sentence structure. For example, they may start a sentence with an adverb ("Nervously, the boy sat at his desk, waiting for his turn to speak."). Students begin to revise for specific writing traits, such as ideas or word choice. Fluent writers are able to catch most spelling, punctuation, and grammatical errors independently as they edit their drafts. They begin to talk about the qualities of good writing in different genres.

Case Study: Tina

Tina Smith is an eager participant at school and particularly enjoys reading and writing (Figure 2.30).

Figure 2.30 Fluent Reader and Writer—Tina

Fluent Reader

Tina's love of reading is evident. She chooses to read whenever there is free time and always has a book to read in the car. Tina keeps a log of all her reading, both at home and at school (Figure 2.31).

She has solid comprehension as she reads challenging children's literature. She says that she is a quick reader and usually understands what she reads. Her teacher, Julie Ledford, notes that Tina's areas for growth are in the area of higher level or interpretive comprehension. Tina pushes herself for a balance in her reading and makes a conscious effort to read nonfiction. During her research project on polar bears, she found information using the Internet and several books on the topic at home and at school. Tina is able to use the table of contents, glossary, and index to find information, but she prefers reading fantasy, fiction, mysteries, and historical fiction.

At home, she reads to her parents or they read to her four or five nights a week for about 30 minutes. Some of the books they have read together recently are *Matilda* (Roald Dahl, 1988), *Bridge to Terabithia* (Katherine Paterson, 1977), and *Mary Poppins* (P. L. Travers, 1934). Some of her favorite authors are Roald Dahl, E. B. White, C. S. Lewis, Judy Blume, and Beverly Cleary. Tina also read two of the *Narnia* books by C. S. Lewis, *Dear Mr. Henshaw* (Beverly Clearly, 1983), a *Nancy Drew* mystery

(Caroline Keene), *Terror at the Zoo* (Peg Kehret, 1992), and *The BFG* (Roald Dahl, 1982). She reads aloud with fluency and expression.

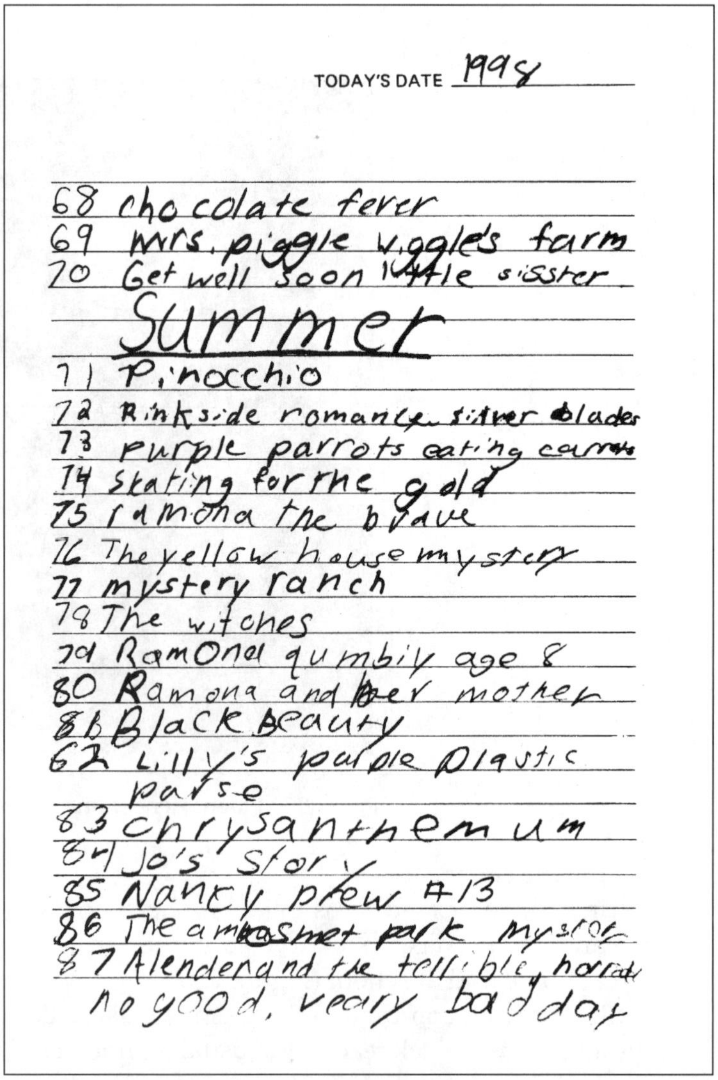
TODAY'S DATE 1998

68 chocolate fever
69 Mrs. piggle wiggle's farm
70 Get well soon little sisster
Summer
71 Pinocchio
72 Rinkside romance silver blades
73 purple parrots eating carrots
74 skating for the gold
75 ramona the brave
76 The yellow house mystery
77 mystery ranch
78 The witches
79 Ramona qumbiy age 8
80 Ramona and her mother
81 Black Beauty
82 Lilly's purple plastic purse
83 chrysanthemum
84 Jo's story
85 Nancy Drew #13
86 The amusment park mystory
87 Alendenand the terrible, horrible no good, veary bad day

Figure 2.31 Tina's Reading Log

Tina prefers fiction and says that she likes literature circles because "when you talk about the book with other people, it makes you think about what you read." She chose to put one of her responses to *The Lion, the Witch, and the Wardrobe* (C. S. Lewis, 1950) in her portfolio (Figure 2.32).

In this response, Tina did a good job of retelling the plot and describing the characters at a literal level. Her reflection states, "I chose this response because I think it's quality. It shows a good example of my handwriting and it is very organized." She creates thoughtful questions for literature circle discussions. She often takes the lead in these conversations and pushes her group to discuss meaningful topics.

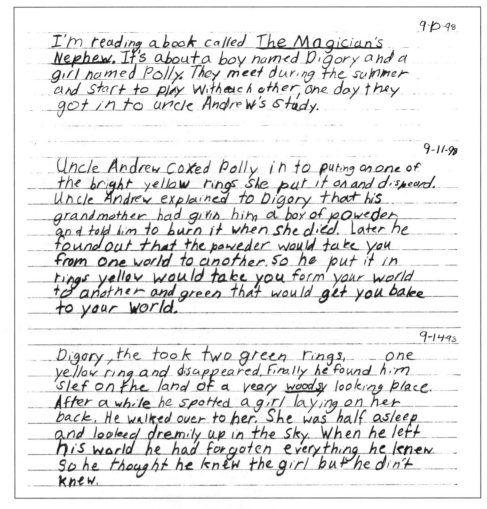

Figure 2.32 Tina's Reading Response

Tina's book projects show that she understands the challenging children's books she reads. The class uses a four-point rubric to assess journal responses and projects, and she usually receives three out of four points. She's trying to improve on her neatness, correct spelling, and sharing her opinion. Tina's goals as a reader are to "try to read more nonfiction books, use more examples to support my ideas, and write more in-depth responses."

Fluent Writer

Tina says that she likes to write because "I can make up my own worlds." She incorporates new vocabulary ("Window Words") into her stories. She uses lots of dialogue, although she still needs guidance about proper punctuation. She writes letters, fiction, and nonfiction (when required). She sometimes writes in her journal, but would like to do that more consistently. Her journal entry about her favorite place (Figure 2.33) shows her organization and voice.

My favorite place

When I'm sad mad or just bord I
go to my room. My favorite Spot in my
room is my bed. My bed is the top bunk
my brother sleeps on the bottem bunk.

Tina
11-13-98
writings
Age 10

I go there when I'm mad. Like when my
brother or sister gets me in trabble. I go
there when I'm sad. Like when we where
celebrating summer birthdays and we where
gone for my birthday and nabady whishes
me happy birthday.

My room has a   bunk bed on
the Right side of my room. A desk of the
left and a dresser on the right.

I'm glade I have my room if I didn't
I would belost.

Figure 2.33 Tina's Journal

Tina loves to share her writing and often shares previously published pieces. She is just beginning to incorporate description, dialogue, and humor into her stories. Free verse poetry has become a real area of strength for Tina. She likes the freedom to be creative without the constraints of conventional punctuation.

At school, Tina wrote an extensive research project on pandas, using several resources to gather information. She still needs to work on the organization of her narrative writing and needs guidance with paragraphs, transitional sentences between paragraphs, as well as sentence length and variety.

When Tina and her friend Kate were eight, they typed a series of stories called *The Adventures of Kate*, which they sent off to a contest. The girls find it harder to write together now that they have more after-school activities. Her mother says that at home, Tina still writes stories and illustrates them on her own. About once a month or so she gets quite dedicated to this sort of task. At school, Tina was one of the students in the class who really enjoyed keeping a writer's notebook. Her notebook in January was filled with newspaper articles, descriptions of field trips, programs from concerts, poems, dreams, and even an actual eraser. It's apparent that Tina reads like a writer. In her writer's notebook she wrote, "I found a really neat phrase: painted skies, lofty dreams, dare to reach on golden wings."

Tina's final drafts show how much work she puts into revising and editing her writing. She's beginning to revise for specific writing traits with her teacher's guidance. Spelling remains a challenge for Tina. She still misspells homonyms ("wright" instead of "write") and simple words ("metle" for "metal," "hart" for "heart," and "trobble" for "trouble"), but she doesn't let her spelling get in the way of her love of writing. She is learning to use a dictionary, word list, or spell checker to help with spelling. Rather than giving Tina one letter grade for writing, the continuum enabled her teacher to show that conventions were an area of concern but that Tina was a strong Fluent writer in terms of content, writing traits, writing process, and attitude. By using the continuum and several spelling assessment strategies (Chapter 5), Julie was able to document how Tina's spelling had improved by the end of the year.

Tina says that good writers create different plots and believable characters. As an example, Tina mentioned Beverly Clearly's memorable character, Ramona, and how the reader understands the character's feelings. She remarked how other good authors, like Roald Dahl, use humor and details. Tina also noted that good authors use interesting words, using *Ella Enchanted* (Gail Carson Levine, 1997) as an example. She said that her goal is "to learn how to include believable details like Roald Dahl so that readers can almost see what's happening in a story." She also wants to learn to create memorable characters who change, "like the main character, Gilly, in *The Great Gilly Hopkins* " (Katherine Paterson, 1978). She is beginning to develop criteria for effective writing. Tina's comments provide an example of how extensive reading can influence a student's writing.

Proficient (Ages 10–13)

Characteristics of Proficient Readers

- Reads complex children's literature.
- Reads and understands informational texts (e.g., maps, want ads, brochures, schedules, catalogs, and manuals, etc.) with guidance.
- Develops strategies and criteria for selecting reading materials independently.
- Uses resources (e.g., encyclopedias, articles, Internet, and nonfiction texts) to locate information independently.
- Gathers and analyzes information from graphs, charts, tables, and maps with guidance.
- Integrates information from multiple nonfiction sources to deepen understanding of a topic with guidance.
- Uses resources (e.g., dictionary and thesaurus) to increase vocabulary independently.
- Identifies literary devices (e.g., similes, metaphors, personification, and foreshadowing).
- Discusses literature with reference to theme, author's purpose, and style (literary elements), and author's craft.
- Begins to generate in-depth responses in small group literature discussions.

cont.

- Begins to generate in-depth written responses to literature.
- Uses increasingly complex vocabulary in different subjects and in oral and written response to literature.
- Uses reasons and examples to support ideas and conclusions.
- Probes for deeper meaning by "reading between the lines" in response to literature.

Proficient readers seek out complex children's literature and can choose books to read independently. They read a variety of genres, such as realistic fiction, historical fiction, biographies, nonfiction, and poetry. These books are sometimes set in other countries and time periods. Novels often deal with complex issues such as survival (e.g., *Island of the Blue Dolphin* by Scott O'Dell, 1960), death (e.g., *Bridge to Terabithia* by Katherine Paterson, 1977), or war (e.g., *Number the Stars* by Lois Lowry, 1989). Students are able to talk about the theme, author's purpose, style, and author's craft. Proficient readers begin to write and talk about literature at a deeper level and use reasons and examples to support their opinions. They delve into topics by reading both fiction and nonfiction materials and can locate information on a topic using several resources independently. Some students at the Proficient stage enjoy challenging magazines, such as *Zillions: Consumer Reports for Kids*.

Characteristics of Proficient Writers

- Writes persuasively about ideas, feelings, and opinions
- Creates plots with problems and solutions.
- Begins to develop the main characters and describe detailed settings.
- Begins to write organized and fluent nonfiction, including simple bibliographies.
- Writes cohesive paragraphs including reasons and examples with guidance.
- Uses transitional sentences to connect paragraphs.
- Varies sentence structure, leads, and endings.
- Begins to use descriptive language, details, and similes.
- Uses voice to evoke emotional response from readers.
- Begins to integrate information on a topic from a variety of sources.
- Begins to revise for specific writing traits (e.g., ideas, organization, word choice, sentence fluency, voice, and conventions).
- Uses tools (e.g., dictionaries, word lists, spell checkers) to edit independently.
- Selects and publishes writing in polished format independently.
- Begins to use complex punctuation (e.g., commas, colons, semicolons, quotation marks) appropriately.
- Begins to set goals and identify strategies to improve writing in different genres.

These are strong writers who can write persuasively about their ideas, feelings, and opinions. Their fiction and nonfiction writing is organized, and they can weave in information from several sources with some adult guidance. They use complex sentences, sophisticated language, and imagery independently and their writing is descriptive. Proficient writers are learning how to create fiction with detailed settings and well-developed plots and characters. Students revise, edit, and publish some of their work independently. They are beginning to set their own goals and identify ways in which to improve as writers.

Case Study: Melissa

Melissa Figel is a sixth grader who enjoys many activities outside of school, such as soccer, band, skiing, art, and gymnastics (Figure 2.34). Her mother says that Melissa likes to do things herself and is very independent. She's a good reader and writer, but one of her real strengths is mathematics.

Figure 2.34 Proficient Reader and Writer—Melissa

Proficient Reader

Melissa's reading log reflects her love of reading (Figure 2.35). Some of the complex children's literature she read this fall included *Running Out of Time* (Margaret Peterson Haddix, 1995), *Absolutely Normal Chaos* (Sharon Creech, 1990), and *Maniac Magee* (Jerry Spinelli, 1990). She also included a magazine (*Time for Kids*) on her log.

Melissa still likes *Nancy Drew* books (Carolyn Keene) and mentioned Gary Paulsen as one of her favorite authors. Several books on her fall reading log are mysteries. She writes, "I enjoy mysteries because it keeps you reading. I like all the clues that lead to the end." She also enjoys fantasy, realistic fiction, and adventure. Her least favorite genre is nonfiction. Her mother recently read aloud *The True Confessions of Charlotte Doyle* (Avi, 1990) and *My Life in Dog Years* (Gary Paulsen, 1998), although as she gets older, it's harder to find time to read at home. Melissa also enjoyed *The Giver* (Lois Lowry, 1993), which her teacher read aloud last year.

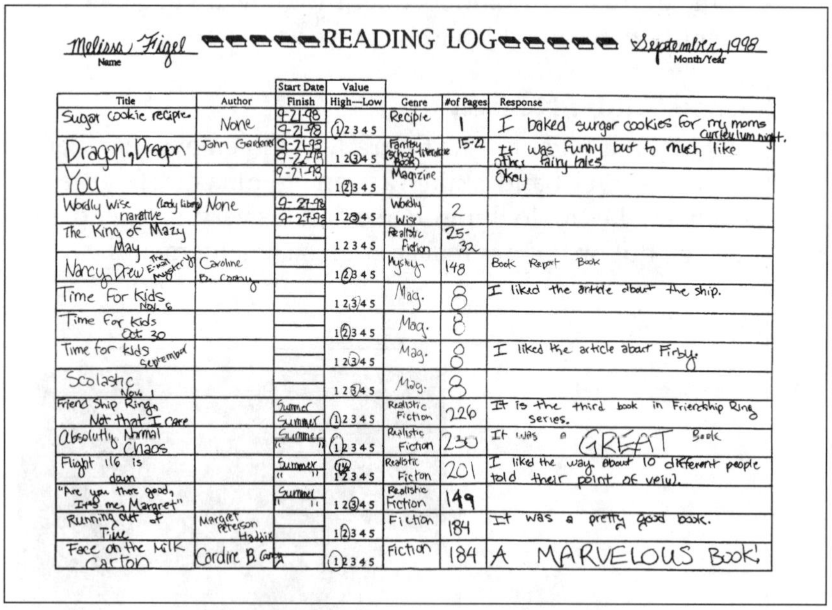

Melissa Figel — READING LOG — September, 1998
Name — Month/Year

Title	Author	Start Date / Finish	Value High—Low	Genre	#of Pages	Response
Sugar cookie recipie.	None	9-21-98 / 9-21-98	(1) 2 3 4 5	Recipie	1	I baked surgar cookies for my moms curriculum night.
Dragon, Dragon	John Gardener	9-21-98 / 9-22-98	1 2 (3) 4 5	Fantsy (school literature Book)	15-22	It was funny but to much like other fairy tales
You		9-21-98	1 (2) 3 4 5	Magizine		Okay
Wordly Wise (Lady liberty) narative	None	9-27-98 / 9-27-98	1 2 (3) 4 5	Wordly Wise	2	
The King of Mazy May			1 2 3 4 5	Realistic Fiction	25-32	
Nancy Drew The E-mail mystery	Caroline B. Cooney		1 (2) 3 4 5	Mystery	148	Book Report Book
Time For Kids Nov. 6			1 2 (3) 4 5	Mag.	8	I liked the article about the ship.
Time For Kids Oct. 30			1 (2) 3 4 5	Mag.	8	
Time for kids September			1 2 (3) 4 5	Mag.	8	I liked the article about Firby.
Scolastic Nov. 1			1 2 (3) 4 5	Mag.	8	
Friend Ship Ring Not that I care		Summer / Summer	(1) 2 3 4 5	Realistic Fiction	226	It is the third book in Friendship Ring series.
Absolutly Normal Chaos		Summer / " "	(1) 2 3 4 5	Realistic Fiction	230	It was a GREAT Book
Flight 116 is down		Summer / " "	(1½) 2 3 4 5	Realistic Ficton	201	I liked the way about 10 different people told their point of veiw.
"Are you there good, It's me, Margaret"		Summer / " "	1 2 (3) 4 5	Realistic Fiction	149	
Running out of Time	Margaret Peterson Haddix		1 (2) 3 4 5	Fiction	184	It was a pretty good book.
Face on the Milk Carton	Caroline B. Cooney		(1) 2 3 4 5	Fiction	184	A MARVELOUS Book!

Figure 2.35 Melissa's Reading Log

Melissa is a thoughtful participant in literature discussions. She is able to talk about the author's craft, as well as the characters and themes in a novel. Like her classmates, she is learning how to back up her opinions using the text. In her self-evaluation, Melissa says that she enjoys reading and is able to understand what she reads, but doesn't read very fast or at a very high level (Figure 2.36). One of her goals for the year is to read two chapter books each month. As she begins to read more sophisticated literature, Melissa's next steps as a reader will be to read for deeper levels of meaning in more complex texts.

Proficient Writer

When you look at the lead of Melissa's draft of her dog story next to the final copy, you can see that her revisions are more sophisticated than the changes students make at the Fluent stage. The lead on her first draft read, "After my dog T. J. died, my family looked at pet stores, PAWS, and at dogs people were trying to sell." She underlined the last phrase, using a key to show that an underline means "Find something else to say!" Her final lead was much stronger (Figure 2.37) as you can see from this portion of her story.

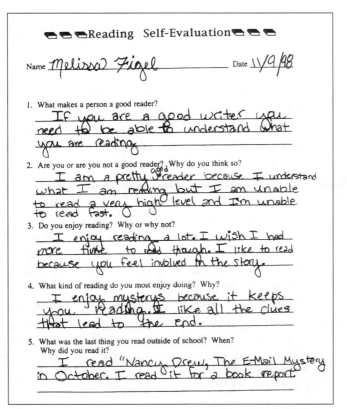

◼◼◼Reading Self-Evaluation◼◼◼

Name _Melissa Figel_   Date _11/9/98_

1. What makes a person a good reader?

   If you are a good writer you need to be able to understand what you are reading.

2. Are you or are you not a good reader? Why do you think so?

   I am a pretty good reader because I understand what I am reading but I am unable to read a very high level and I'm unable to read fast.

3. Do you enjoy reading? Why or why not?

   I enjoy reading a lot. I wish I had more time to read though. I like to read because you feel involved in the story.

4. What kind of reading do you most enjoy doing? Why?

   I enjoy mysterys because it keeps you reading. I like all the clues that lead to the end.

5. What was the last thing you read outside of school? When? Why did you read it?

   I read "Nancy Drew, The E-Mail Mystery in October. I read it for a book report.

Figure 2.36 Melissa's Reading Survey

Figure 2.37 Melissa's Writing with Strong Lead

Melissa Figel

November 1998

My Luck with Dogs

Ever since my dog T.J. died we had been looking at dogs. We would find a dog we liked but then something would be wrong. Like "He'll grow to big," or "She's to wild." We almost got a Beagle but the real owners claimed him. I was starting to think we would never find the right dog.

When I was skimming the paper for an article to bring to school for homework, a small add at the bottom caught my eye.

Black Lab puppies for sale!
2 Weeks old.
Call 635-4771 for details.

I knew my dad did not want a puppy so using my most grown up voice I dialed the number in the add.

"Hello," Said a woman's voice on the other line.

"Hi, my name's Morgan and I'm calling in regards to your add in the paper about the puppies, how much are they?" My mom always uses the word regarding.

"They're $10.00 each, but they still need their shots." She answered.

"Can I get your address in case I decide to buy one?"

She told me her address and said, "Hurry, there's only 2 left." Oh no, how am I ever going to talk Mom and Dad into it.

"Bye!" I said, and hung up the phone.

The next morning I checked the today's, Saturday's, bus schedule, 8:30, 9:00, 9:30, Bingo! I ate my eggs as quickly as possible. " I'm going to Amanda's house," I yelled as I grabbed my money and ran out the door. I checked my watch, 9:26, just enough time to run there.

I got to the bus stop just as the bus pulled up. I paid the driver and walked to the back of the bus. An old lady sat down next to me. "Aren't you a little young to be riding on the bus alone?" she annoyingly asked.

"My mom sent me on an errand." I answered in a rude voice. I didn't hear any more from her for the rest of the trip.

When I got to the woman with the puppies, house I started to get nervous. What if she wouldn't sell one to me? I slowly got of the bus and walked up and knocked on the door. A young woman wearing overalls and a plaid shirt answered …

Similarly, the last line in her original draft read, "My dog is very special to me and my family and we love her very much." Notice the improvement in the final draft which ties to her lead: "I picked up the puppy and knew I would never tell my little secret. I guess I'm not so unlucky when it comes to dogs." She is able to revise for specific writing traits with guidance. She often writes her stories at school and types them up at home. Outside of school, she often writes letters to friends.

Melissa enjoys writing poetry and included several examples in her portfolio. Other writing reflects her sixth-grade content area assignments, such as her colorful brochure on the Congo River. She is able to read several sources on a topic and synthesize information. Her notes are neatly arranged and her final products are organized and attractive. Her travel brochure for the Congo incorporated basic facts and an itinerary for the trip, using the information she had gathered, and a bibliography. Melissa uses paragraphs effectively and is a strong speller. She uses a dictionary and the spell checker on the computer to edit her work. Melissa is just beginning to use details and descriptive language on her own. Her next step would be to add fluency and voice to her nonfiction as she does in her stories.

Melissa and her friend, Elizabeth, published a mystery story with the flavor of a Nancy Drew book: "Shelby kept watching, her eyes getting bigger and bigger, almost as if she was getting hypnotized. Suddenly she woke from her trance as the tall skinny policeman put his hand on her shoulder. 'Kid, you did the right thing. We'll find the murderer,' he said and went over to the short, fat man". As you can see in this page from her story (Figure 2.38), Melissa has a solid plot with a problem, dialogue, suspense, and a clear ending.

As a Proficient writer, Melissa is just beginning to create multiple characters and detailed settings in her stories. For instance, in her mystery Melissa creates two protagonists (Shelby and Joe) who witness a murder. Although the characters are two dimensional, the plot hangs together and Melissa incorporates suspense, dialogue, and details. She's just beginning to incorporate powerful words like "sneered" and "stammered." In her writing reflection (Figure 2.39), she says that good writers describe characters so well that they seem like real people. Melissa's goals are to write more poetry, more persuasive letters, longer stories, and to start using more descriptive language.

It was a dark night. Moonlight shone into Shelby Thomas's window. She got up and looked out her window and saw a large man in a black suit and mask dart across the alley below toward a skinny little man. Shelby opened her window to hear what they were saying.

"Gi-me all your money our I'll blast ya'!" said the large man as he took out a cellular phone. "Opps, wrong thing," he said and replaced it with a gun.

"I-I d-d-don't have my m-m-money with m-me," stammered the skinny man. Shelby didn't want to see what would happen next so she quickly dove back into her bed. She heard a loud bang. For at least a minute Shelby lay still in her bed. Everything was quiet. Everything but the low groaning of the injured man outside. Shelby forced herself to get out of bed and see what had happened. When she got to her window sill she saw the blood stained clothes on the motionless body of the man that had been shot. Suddenly all the groaning stopped. Shelby was so scared she could not move. "Mom!" Shelby cried but she knew she wasn't there. Then she remembered her neighbors voice saying 'Now if you have any trouble while your parents are on vacation call me.' She slowly walked across the room to the kitchen where the telephone was, her knees still shaking from the experience. She slowly dialed the number. "Briiinnng...briiinnng...briiinnng... Hello!" said a voice with some rock-and-roll music in the background.

"Hi, this is Shelby," she said.

"Is everything O.K.?" asked her neighbor Joe.

"No everything is not O.K. Please come over here quick," Shelby said and hung up the phone. Soon there was a knock on the door. Shelby opened the door and her neighbor walked in. He was a lot older than she was. He was in collage and she was only 14. She led him to her bedroom window.

"Oh my Gosh!" he said "Did you see it happen?" Shelby nodded her head yes. "Tell me everything and don't leave anything out," said Joe.

Shelby told him about the man with the mask and the other man.

"Wait here while I call the police," Joe commanded.

Joe went into the kitchen and called the police. Shelby heard the whole terrible story over again.

"Come on Shelby, we're going downstairs to the lobby to wait for the police," Joe said and Shelby followed.

They zoomed down the elevator and sat down on the lobby couch. While Joe read the newspaper on the coffee table, Shelby just sat around. Time passed. Within a minute Shelby got bored. She twiddled her thumbs ...

Figure 2.38 Melissa's Mystery

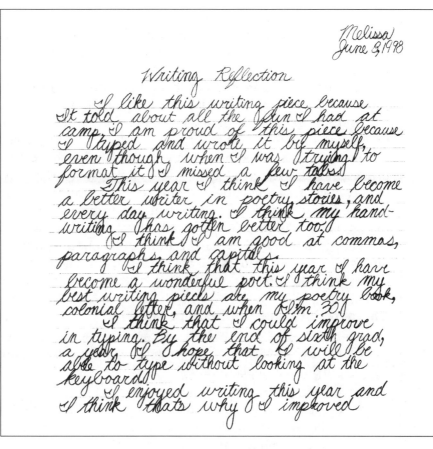

Figure 2.39 Melissa's Writing Reflection

Connecting (Ages 11–14)

Characteristics of Connecting Readers

- Reads complex children's literature and young adult literature.
- Selects, reads, and finishes a wide variety of genres independently.
- Begins to choose challenging reading materials and projects.
- Integrates nonfiction information to develop deeper understanding of a topic independently.
- Begins to gather, analyze, and use information from graphs, charts, tables, and maps.
- Generates in-depth responses and sustains small group literature discussions.
- Generates in-depth written responses to literature.
- Begins to evaluate, interpret, and analyze reading content critically.
- Begins to develop criteria for evaluating literature.
- Seeks recommendations and opinions about literature from others.
- Sets reading challenges and goals independently.

At the Connecting stage, students read both complex children's literature and young adult literature. These books include fully developed plots that often focus on complex issues, such as freedom, truth, good and evil, and human rights. Books like *Nothing but the Truth* (Avi, 1991) or *Slave Dancer* (Paula Fox, 1973) often require background knowledge and the ability to examine multiple perspectives on an issue. Many books include sophisticated language (such as the *Redwall* series by Brian Jacques) or complex plots (like *A Wrinkle in Time* by Madeleine L'Engle, 1962). Other books, like *The Giver* (Lois Lowry, 1993), *Wringer* (Jerry Spinelli, 1997), or *The Last Book in the Universe* (Rodman Philbrick, 2000), raise challenging issues. Characters in these novels are often approaching adolescence. Students at this stage read a variety of genres independently and are able to integrate information from fiction and nonfiction to develop a deeper understanding of a topic. They can contribute to and sustain discussions about what they read and start developing criteria for evaluating literature. They seek recommendations and opinions about books from others. Connecting readers are able to set reading goals and challenges for themselves independently.

Characteristics of Connecting Writers

- Writes in a variety of genres and forms for different audiences and purposes independently.
- Creates plots with a climax.
- Creates detailed, believable settings and characters in stories.
- Writes organized, fluent, and detailed nonfiction independently, including bibliographies with correct format.
- Writes cohesive paragraphs including supportive reasons and examples.
- Uses descriptive language, details, similes, and imagery to enhance ideas independently.
- Begins to use dialogue to enhance character development.
- Incorporates personal voice in writing with increasing frequency.
- Integrates information on a topic from a variety of sources independently.
- Constructs charts, graphs, and tables to convey information when appropriate.
- Uses prewriting strategies effectively to organize and strengthen writing.
- Revises for specific writing traits (e.g., ideas, organization, word choice, sentence fluency, voice, and conventions) independently.
- Includes deletion in revision strategies.
- Incorporate suggestions from others on own writing independently.
- Uses complex punctuation (commas, colons, semicolons, quotation marks) with increasing accuracy.

At the Connecting stage, students write in a variety of genres and forms for different purposes and audiences. Students use a variety of prewriting strategies to organize and strengthen their writing. They compose cohesive paragraphs, using reasons and examples for support. Connecting writers can integrate information from a variety of sources and can create graphs and charts to convey information. They write organized, fluent, and detailed nonfiction with bibliographies using correct format. In their fiction, students can create plots with a climax and believable characters. At this stage, writers use descriptive language, details, and imagery independently and may use dialogue to enhance character development. Connecting writers can revise for specific writing traits (such as organization or sentence fluency) independently. As they revise, students work through several drafts independently and may re-write or delete sections. They ask for feedback and incorporate others people's suggestions into their writing.

Case Study: Katy

Like her sister, Melissa, Katy Figel plays the flute, and enjoys reading, band, skiing, and gymnastics (Figure 2.40). Her mother says that Katy draws every day and loves art.

Figure 2.40 Connecting Reader and Writer—Katy

Connecting Reader

Katy enjoys reading realistic fiction and fantasy, but also reads a variety of other genres. She reads complex children's literature and young adult literature, such as *The True Confessions of Charlotte Doyle* (Avi, 1990), *King of Shadows* (Susan Cooper, 1999), and *The Giver* (Lois Lowry, 1993). By looking at the comments she writes in her reading log (Figure 2.41), you can see how Katy has developed criteria for evaluating literature.

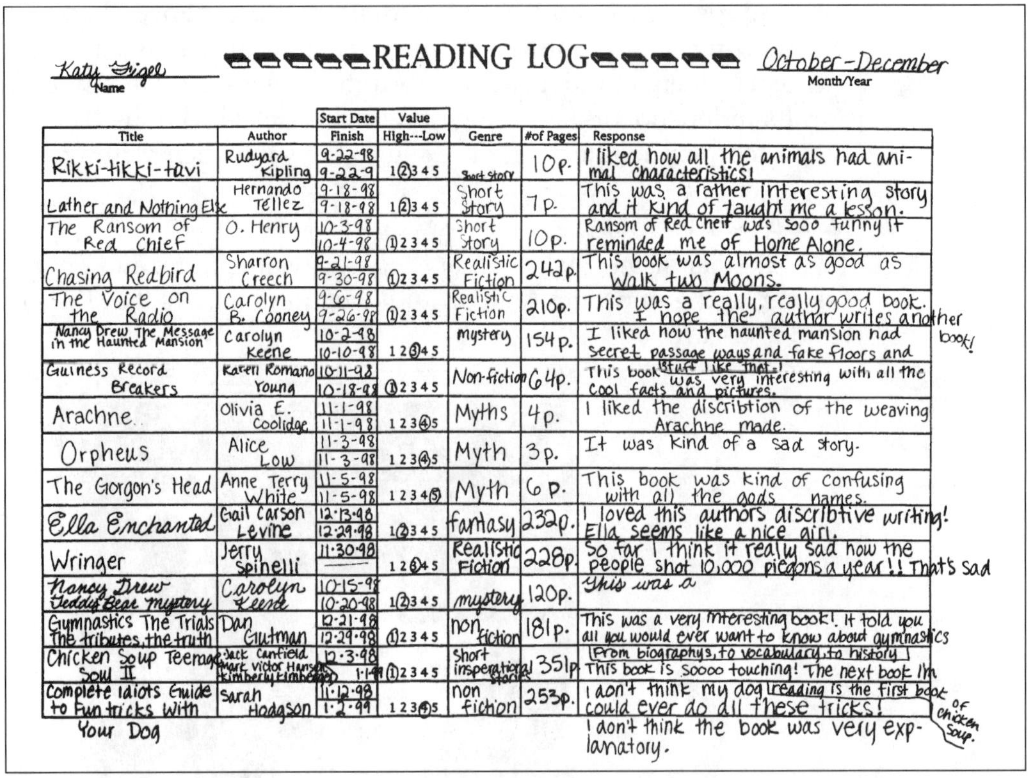
READING LOG

Name: Katy Frigel — Month/Year: October–December

Title	Author	Start Date / Finish	Value High---Low	Genre	#of Pages	Response
Rikki-tikki-tavi	Rudyard Kipling	9-22-98 / 9-22-9	1 (2) 3 4 5	Short story	10p.	I liked how all the animals had animal characteristics!
Lather and Nothing Else	Hernando Tellez	9-18-98 / 9-18-98	1 (2) 3 4 5	Short Story	7p.	This was a rather interesting story and it kind of taught me a lesson.
The Ransom of Red Chief	O. Henry	10-3-98 / 10-4-98	(1) 2 3 4 5	Short Story	10p.	Ransom of Red Cheif was sooo funny it reminded me of Home Alone.
Chasing Redbird	Sharron Creech	9-21-98 / 9-30-98	(1) 2 3 4 5	Realistic Fiction	242p.	This book was almost as good as Walk two Moons.
The Voice on the Radio	Carolyn B. Cooney	9-6-98 / 9-26-98	(1) 2 3 4 5	Realistic Fiction	210p.	This was a really, really good book. I hope the author writes another book!
Nancy Drew The Message in the Haunted Mansion	Carolyn Keene	10-2-98 / 10-10-98	1 2 (3) 4 5	mystery	154p.	I liked how the haunted mansion had secret passage ways and fake floors and (stuff like that.)
Guiness Record Breakers	Karen Romano Young	10-11-98 / 10-18-98	(1) 2 3 4 5	Non-fiction	64p.	This book was very interesting with all the cool facts and pictures.
Arachne	Olivia E. Coolidge	11-1-98 / 11-1-98	1 2 3 (4) 5	Myths	4p.	I liked the discribtion of the weaving Arachne made.
Orpheus	Alice Low	11-3-98 / 11-3-98	1 2 3 (4) 5	Myth	3p.	It was kind of a sad story.
The Gorgon's Head	Anne Terry White	11-5-98 / 11-5-98	1 2 3 4 (5)	Myth	6p.	This book was kind of confusing with all the gods names.
Ella Enchanted	Gail Carson Levine	12-13-98 / 12-29-98	1 (2) 3 4 5	fantasy	232p.	I loved this authors discribtive writing! Ella seems like a nice girl.
Wringer	Jerry Spinelli	11-30-98 / —	1 2 (3) 4 5	Realistic Fiction	228p.	So far I think it really sad how the people shot 10,000 piegons a year!! That's sad
Nancy Drew Teddy Bear mystery	Carolyn Keene	10-15-98 / 10-20-98	1 (2) 3 4 5	mystery	120p.	This was a
Gymnastics The Trials The tributes, the truth	Dan Gutman	12-21-98 / 12-29-98	(1) 2 3 4 5	non fiction	181p.	This was a very interesting book! It told you all you would ever want to know about gymnastics (From biographys, to vocabulary, to history)
Chicken Soup Teenage Soul II	Jack Canfield, Mark Victor Hansen, Kimberly Kimberger	12-3-98 / 1-1-99	(1) 2 3 4 5	Short insperational stories	351p.	This book is soooo touching! The next book I'm reading is the first book of Chicken Soup.
Complete Idiots Guide to Fun tricks With Your Dog	Sarah Hodgson	11-12-98 / 1-2-99	1 2 3 (4) 5	non fiction	253p.	I don't think my dog could ever do all these tricks! I don't think the book was very explanatory.

Figure 2.41 Katy's Reading Log

She contributes thoughtful responses during literature discussions and in her response journal. Katy's written description of the conflict in *The Ransom of Red Chief* (O. Henry, 1918) was organized, expressive, and humorous. Her book responses are colorful and creative. Katy is beginning to read for deeper meaning. She's able to appreciate author's craft and use of literary devices. For example, she wrote, "One of my all time favorite books that I've ever read is *Island of the Blue Dolphins* by Scott O'Dell. I like how the whole book had lots of similes and metaphors. When I read it I could always imagine that I was Karana (the main character). Since the setting is out in nature on an island and Scott O'Dell described it with such beautiful words, I was able to paint clear pictures in my head." She is able to provide specific examples to support her reactions to the book. Katy is also able to integrate information from multiple sources and incorporate the information into her nonfiction writing. She has strong comprehension of fairly complex material.

At home, her mother reads to both Melissa and Katy occasionally, although it's a challenge as the girls have become involved in sports and after-school activities. One of the books Katy enjoyed that her mother read aloud was *Lyddie* (Katherine Paterson, 1991). When asked what she wants to read next, Katy laughed and said she always has a stack of books to read. Katy is well read, and the next books she mentioned she wants to read, *Bloomability* (Sharon Creech, 1998) and *Wringer* (Jerry Spinelli, 1997), are both award-winning titles. In her written responses to literature, she is just beginning to make connections to her own experiences and other books she's read. Katy is able to assess her own strengths and set goals for herself. One of her goals is to push herself to read a variety of genres. Katy also listed improving her vocabulary as one of her goals this year: "I'd like to have a larger vocabulary so I can understand books better.

Connecting Writer

Her artistic talent and neat handwriting enable Katy to create beautiful final products. She creates polished poetry, reports, brochures, and books. In her narrative writing, she's beginning to incorporate dialogue and effective description. She effectively uses similes and metaphors in her poetry (Figure 2.42).

Depressed

Depressed is dark blue like the sky before a storm. It is flat and seems to not know what to do with itself.

Like a slug just slithering along.

It feels flat and unhelping like hands with wet nail polish on.

And tastes like stale air.

It walks through my stomach and makes it feel flat. As flat as cardboard.

Depressed smells like musty air.

It reminds me of the time when my guinea pig died.

I felt like I was a paper doll and someone was cutting right through me with scissors.

Depressed sounds like s carnival at night, in the winter, when no one is there. The rides sit there all alone, with the eerie buzzing sound in the air.

It makes me feel hopeless and then I wish the world could stop and let me rest awhile before going on.

Depressed

By Katy Figel

Figure 2.42 Katy's Poem

At other times, the metaphors are a bit overabundant as she experiments with descriptive writing (Figure 2.43). Katy is willing to seek feedback and incorporates the suggestions of others into her revisions. Katy writes letters and poetry at home. She gets her ideas for poetry by observing the world around her. At school, some of her poems are based on models provided by her language arts teacher, Judy Cromwell. In her self-evaluation, she comments, "I enjoy writing a lot. I like it because it lets me tell people how I am feeling. It also makes my mom happy when she reads poems I write."

Rachel watched the brown and orange curled leafs gracfully fall to the icey ground. The wind stroked the trees as they rocked back and forth, back and forth. The trees were almost skeletons by now. Their winter coats gone. Rachel pressed her little nose agaisnt the window causing a small smudge on the perfectly clear window frame.
The trees are getting tucked into bed thought Rachel. with the leaves as a colorful patchwork quilt and the wind rocking them to sleep.
Rachel had always been a deep, thoughtful, thinker. Almost as deep as her deep rich green eyes which were always sailing around gracfully taking all the scenery in. Her auburn hair with a redish tint lay flat and heavy against her head. Her lips light pink and in a cresent like the moon. Rice paper was the color of Rachel's skin and her eyelashes sprang from her eyes like springs.
Yes, thought Rachel the autumn trees and I are often alike with our faded colors.

By: Katy

Figure 2.43 Katy's Writing Sample—Adding Details

She has created several different forms of writing at school, including letters, a play, and research. Her letter to her parents about going skiing (Figure 2.44) was indeed persuasive. She anticipates her parents' concerns and lists the reasons they should let her take skiing lessons. Her prewriting strategy was a list, then she wrote three drafts before being satisfied with the final piece. In her drafts, she added information, deleted sentences, and added reasons.

She wrote, "I think this is one of my strengths, being able to write my opinion easily." Her research report on South Africa showed that she is able to integrate information from several sources and present the information using graphs and charts in an organized and interesting way.

Dear Mom and Dad,   October 26, 98
    I would really, really like to go up
on the ski bus and go skiing at Steven's
Pass. Almost everyone in my class goes
skiing and I would like to join them too,
and not be left out. It would be the
perfect way for me to get exercise and
and it's only for 6 weeks so it's not for
the whole year. As you already know, I
love to seeing and playing in the snow!
    Also, since Dad has a fire fighting
job he would be able to trade those
days so he could come skiing with
me and have tons of fun too. I know you would have fun Dad and
remember, it's great exercise!
    Hanging out with my friends would be
very special along with father, daughter
time.
    Although I know that I have gymnas-
tics on Friday nights starting at 5:15 pm
I will be willing to skip or arrive late
at gymnastics. I really wouldn't mind!
    I also know that after gymnastics
and skiing I will be very exhuasted and
promise that I will go straight to bed on
time or eairlier.
    Dad, you won't have to drive because
the ski bus will take us. That means you
can relax!

Figure 2.44 Katy's Persuasive Letter

Some of Katy's writing comes from her own experiences, such as her family's trip to the beach. One of the characteristics of a Connecting writer is the ability to write with personal voice instead of merely chronicling an event. As an example, Katy's title and lead have a sparkle that less sophisticated writers often lack:

A Refrigerator in the Car?

My Family's Fun Vacation

Last June, the week after school got out, my family jumped into a borrowed RV and hit the road towards Oregon. Now this wasn't an ordinary car trip with bathroom breaks every two hours, stops for food, and checking into hotels. Instead, we were riding in an RV!!

She says that many of her stories come from asking herself, "What would happen if . . .?" Katy says that good authors use descriptive writing so that readers form pictures in their heads. Her goal is to "use really descriptive language so that people are interested and want to read more."

Independent

Characteristics of Independent Readers

- Reads young adult and adult literature.
- Chooses and comprehends a wide variety of sophisticated materials with ease (e.g., newspapers, magazines, manuals, novels, and poetry).
- Reads and understands informational texts (e.g., maps, manuals, consumer reports, applications, and forms).
- Reads challenging material for pleasure independently.
- Reads challenging material for information and to solve problems independently.
- Perseveres through complex reading tasks.
- Gathers, analyzes, and uses information from graphs, charts, tables, and maps independently.
- Analyzes literary devices (e.g., metaphors, imagery, irony, and satire).
- Contributes unique insights and supports opinions in complex literature discussions.
- Adds depth to responses to literature by making insightful connections to other reading and experiences.
- Evaluates, interprets, and analyzes reading content critically.
- Develops and articulates criteria for evaluating literature.
- Pursues a widening community of readers independently.

Students at this stage read both young adult and adult literature. These books often focus on issues of growing up and entering adulthood. They include multiple characters who encounter complex issues and challenging obstacles. Some examples of young adult novels are *Ironman* (Chris Crutcher, 1995), *The Devil's Arithmetic* (Jane Yolen, 1988), *The Golden Compass* (Philip Pullman, 1995), *Shabanu* (Suzanne Fisher Staples, 1989), and the *Lord of the Rings* series by J. R. R. Tolkien. These students read a range of sophisticated materials for pleasure, to learn information, and to solve problems. For instance, they may read newspapers and magazines, download information off the Internet, or read longer biographies, such as *Eleanor Roosevelt* by Russell Freedman (1993). When they respond to literature during discussions or in writing, students add insightful comments as they make connections between other books and authors, their background knowledge, and their own lives. They stick with complex reading challenges and are able to evaluate and analyze what they read. Independent readers are interested in hearing other perspectives and sharing their opinions about what they have read.

Characteristics of Independent Writers

- Writes organized, fluent, accurate, and in-depth nonfiction, including references with correct bibliographic format.
- Writes cohesive, fluent, and effective poetry and fiction.
- Uses a clear sequence of paragraphs with effective transitions.
- Begins to incorporate literary devices (e.g., imagery, metaphors, personification, and foreshadowing).
- Weaves dialogue effectively into stories.
- Develops plots, characters, setting, and mood (literary elements) effectively.
- Begins to develop personal voice and style of writing.
- Revises through multiple drafts independently.
- Seeks feedback from others and incorporates suggestions in order to strengthen own writing.
- Publishes writing for different audiences and purposes in polished format independently.
- Internalizes the writing process.
- Uses correct grammar (e.g., subject/verb agreement and verb tense) consistently.
- Writes with confidence and competence on a range of topics independently.
- Perseveres through complex or challenging writing projects independently.
- Sets writing goals independently by analyzing and evaluating own writing.

Writers at the Independent stage create cohesive, in-depth fiction with carefully chosen language and strong characters, setting, plot, and mood. They use dialogue and literary devices (such as metaphors and imagery) effectively. They can also write accurate and fluent nonfiction on a variety of topics. Writing has become natural, and they have internalized the writing process. Independent writers seek feedback from others and work on multiple drafts. They begin to develop a personal voice and style of writing. In final drafts, there are very few spelling, punctuation, or grammatical errors. Students at this stage can analyze their own writing and set goals independently. They write with confidence and competence, and persevere through complex writing projects.

Case Study: Kim

Kim Jones is a self-confident middle schooler (Figure 2.45). She's very involved in dance, art, and activities with the Jewish and Korean communities. Her home is filled with books, music, and art.

Figure 2.45 Independent Reader and Writer—Kim

Independent Reader

Kim is reading adult novels and young adult novels, such as *Letters from Rifka* (Karen Hesse, 1992), *Roll of Thunder, Hear My Cry* (Mildred Taylor, 1976), and *Shabanu* (Suzanne Fisher Staples, 1989). She balances these challenging books with magazines and light reading. She has a strong understanding of other cultures and enjoys reading books that touch upon other ideologies. She is particularly interested in nonfiction about the Civil War and the Holocaust.

Kim reads a wide variety of genres and reads for the deeper meaning in complex literature. Her language arts teacher, Judy Cromwell, notes that "Kim brings insights to literature discussions that others don't see until she points them out." For instance, in her written response to *Chasing Redbird* (Sharon Creech, 1997), Kim writes, "You can look at this paragraph in two ways: the simple, standard, and logical way, or the deeper, more in-depth way of looking *into* it. I like to think of this as facing a path between two decisions: you could either take the path that is more daring and new, or you can stay at home and not bother to adventure at all. We all face life decisions, but to genuinely find those decisions, and make the right choice, you have to dig deeper into the soil to find what you're looking for, even if it isn't a straight answer."

In Figure 2.46, you can see another example of her ability to read books at a deeper level. She can step back, then analyze and evaluate what she reads.

> Like other Sharon Creech novels, it's hard to really know what is going on unless you've read the whole book. You can look at his paragraph two ways:
>
> The simple, standard and logical way, or the deeper, more in depth way of looking *into* it.
>
> This selection expresses a lot of emotions without saying that much. You have this Phoebe girl, who apparently gets her paranoia from her mother, and there is the other mysterious girl. I like to think of this as facing a path between two decisions:
>
> You could either take that path that is more daring and new, or you could stay at home and not bother to adventure at all. We all face life decisions, but to genuinely find those decisions, and make the right chose, you have to dig deeper into the soil to find what you're looking for, even if it isn't just a straight answer.
>
> Just to add some interesting tid bit about this book and my relationship with it.... I learned a new word from this book, when this experience with the "lunatic" was later referred to:
>
> Potential (lunatic). In my own words, it means this person has the *potential*, or motive to be a crazed psycho someday. Well, maybe not *psycho*, but maybe just a little off the edge from being sane.

Figure 2.46 Kim's Reading Response

Kim reads nonfiction with ease and frequently brings in extra credit work she has done researching a topic. She and her family read constantly and listen to books on tape in the car. Her father writes, "She reads to us, we read to her before bed, and we read together in the evening. We read in the car . . . everywhere!" At home, they've read books together, such as *Poetry Out Loud* (edited by Robert Rubin, 1993) and *Briar Rose* (Jane Yolen, 1992) about World War II. They also read two different editions of *The Odyssey* so they could compare and contrast the two versions.

Independent Writer

Kim says that writing is one of her favorite things to do outside of school. She incorporates dialogue, similes, and imagery naturally into her stories. Her writing is organized and fluent, in both fiction and nonfiction. She uses complex sentence structures to give her writing cadence. For example, in describing the challenges Christine Witty faced as an ice skater, she wrote, "The dues were set aside and Chris' Olympic dream was one step closer to reality." Rather than a chronological retelling of the skater's life, Kim's biography has fluency and voice (Figure 2.47).

When she did research reports, she collected information from books, articles, web sites, and online encyclopedias. She was able to integrate information from maps, graphs, and tables into her report. Even her nonfiction pamphlet about the Dead Sea has a touch of voice and humor (Figure 2.48).

Christine Witty

Christine Witty, strong not only in muscle and brain, but also in heart.

Being one of the strongest competitors the pressure is hard on her back.... But there is something else on her mind while competing.

Since Chris was a young 12 year old girl, raised in Milwaukee, her life long dream was to be a professional speed skater. The only problem was she couldn't afford the $35 in annual dues to be a member for the West Allis (Wisconsin) Speed skating Club.

Chris's family was in a hard time of lacking money. Her father, Walter, was a welder who had lost his job when the Allis Chalmers tractor factory went out of business. Her mother, Diane, unfortunately was also out of work. Chris's family of six could only live on Diane's unemployment check for a short period of a month.

While Chris and her family were worrying about costs, the people in charge of the speed skating club became interested in the young girl who wore her brothers black ice skates. The dues were set aside and Chris's Olympic dream was one step closer to reality.

To help her parents, Chris ventured around her neighborhood delivering newspapers with her brother, Mike. In her mind she knew the dues were paid, but that didn't mean traveling to competitions were also free. This is when she created a "skating fund" with her parents.

Figure 2.47 Kim's Biography

Her poetry is filled with imagery and descriptive language (Figure 2.49). In her reflection about a poem to her grandfather, Kim writes, "I don't think I would change a thing, because to me it flows very nicely. Every word just seemed to come to me. This year has been like a hammer breaking the ice for me. I'm very proud of every piece I have done." She is most proud of "That Feeling," a poem which was published in a Korean newspaper. Kim says that good writers are careful about their word choice, keep the reader interested, and enable readers to connect the story to their own life.

Dead sea in Israel is 1,312ft <u>below</u> <u>sea level</u>, I think that this sea might be that pit. Since I'm talking about the Dead sea, I might as well continue. I've been to a few lakes before, and they didn't exactly taste sweet. (Not to say I go around drinking sea water.) the water seemed awfully salty. now that I know the Dead is <u>nine times</u> saltier than the ocean, I don't think I'll be complaining to my mom about her cooking being too salty! People in Israel must never run out of salt! Companies use the natural recource by extracting the salt out of the sand around the ocean. cool, huh? Salt isn't the only product from the Dead sea. The mud from the sea has so many vitamins and minerals, it is a good cure for relaxing arthritis pain. The mud also makes a nice mud mask. I wonder what it would be like to take a plunge in the sea? That would be lovely!

THIS IS THE ONLY REMEMBRANCE OF THE JEWS SECOND TEMPLE DESTROYED BY THE ROMANS IN 70 C.E., JERUSALEM, ISRAEL

A KISS AT JERUSALEM'S ✡ WESTERN WALL ✡

Figure 2.48 Kim's Research Pamphlet

Grandpa Albert

Grandpa Albert has a voice that sounds like dead leaves blowing down the neighborhood street,
He walks in a slow, turtle like movement, taking baby steeps, creeping closer, and closer,
I hold his soft wrinkled hand that looks like an old bulldog pleading for food,
He smells like baby power, so very fragile, and calm,
I look into his eyes, but I see them somewhere else, yet full of happiness, and affectionate love,

Grandpa Albert reminds me of smoke, curling up my leg, because I know he's here, only sometimes you can't see him, and other times you can. Sometimes smoke creeps up on you like unexpected fires, but other times you're positive it's there!

Now he is gone. Carried away with the cool ocean breezes, to leave me with his memories, and what sweet memories they are!

by,
Kim Jones

Figure 2.49 Kim's Poem

Kim keeps a journal that she uses " to gather my thoughts when I'm in a difficult situation." She mentions how even in her journal, she's aware of effective writing. "If I only wrote about my day, then even I get bored. This just reminds me to keep what I write interesting. I guess what I'm saying is that my journal is one of my teachers. It guides me into becoming a good reader and writer and helps me through tough times." Her mother writes, "Kim uses journaling to solve emotional struggles. She was having difficulty writing a Torah commentary for her Bat Mitzvah. After weeks of avoidance, she wrote a poem that wove together and integrated the commentary and her struggle. In doing so, she makes the personal universal and solves her internal conflict. She recited the poem with poise and captured the heart of the congregation."

Kim revises independently, but also seeks feedback from other readers. She has learned to put herself in the place of her readers. She experiments with leads (Figure 2.50) and is able to revise independently.

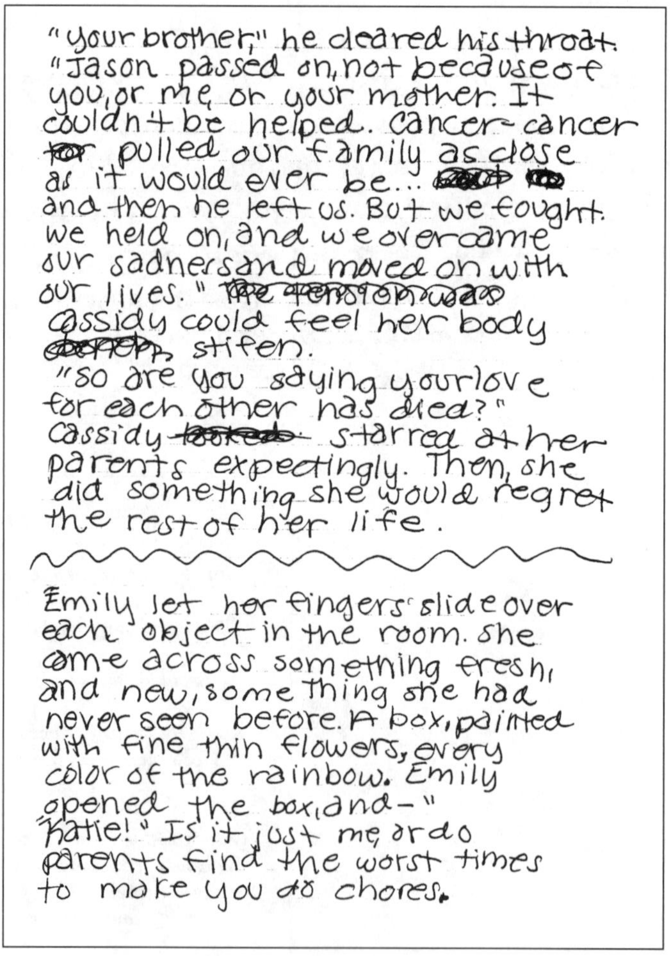
"your brother," he cleared his throat. "Jason passed on, not because of you, or me, or your mother. It couldn't be helped. Cancer-cancer ~~for~~ pulled our family as close as it would ever be... and then he left us. But we fought. we held on, and we overcame our sadners and moved on with our lives." ~~The tension was~~ Cassidy could feel her body stifen. "So are you saying your love for each other has died?" Cassidy ~~looked~~ starred at her parents expectingly. Then, she did something she would regret the rest of her life.

Emily let her fingers slide over each object in the room. She came across something fresh, and new, something she had never seen before. A box, painted with fine thin flowers, every color of the rainbow. Emily opened the box, and-" "Katie!" Is it just me, or do parents find the worst times to make you do chores.

Figure 2.50 Kim's Leads

Her stories have strong plots and characters. She publishes for different audiences, takes pride in polished projects and is beginning to develop her own writing style. For instance, instead of writing a typical lead for an autobiography, Kim wrote, "Born in the small town of Tongnae, South Korea, the lovely Miss Kim Young Mee is born. Okay . . . I can't take it any more. So if you want to know about me, then I've got to tell it my own way. As I was saying, I was just a little tyke in South Korea, battling the world of a foster home." She ends her autobiography with, "I like to interpret this as a symbol of beginnings and endings. Once you think you've just settled on something, you are truly just beginning another story in your life. I thought this was very appropriate for my autobiography. After I think I've finished writing this, I'll look back someday and realize I was just organizing my life, preparing for what lay ahead for me."

Judy Cromwell, her teacher, says that Kim's work always has the extra polish and additional depth of thought that distinguishes her work from students at the previous stages. She writes, "When I read Kim's work, I sometimes get chills or laugh out loud or cry. Her writing moves the reader." Kim does extra credit projects and sets her own time line for big projects. She is, indeed, an independent reader and writer.

The process of creating Case Studies was as valuable as the final product. I learned a tremendous amount both about these children and about the continuums as I created these vignettes. It's fairly easy to distinguish students at the first five or six stages on the continuum; however, it's far more challenging at the upper end. Middle school students are fairly fluent as readers and writers. Creating the Case Studies provided anchors for thinking about more proficient students. When I work with middle school students, I think of Melissa, Katy, and Kim. Even at Brighton School and at other schools where teachers have been using the continuums for years, many teachers have said that the specifics of the Case Studies have been extremely helpful in learning about the continuums. It seems appropriate to end the case studies of these ten young readers and writers with Kim's own words from her autobiography: "The only time you will ever truly get to know someone is when you can *see* their face, *hear* the way they talk, and *observe* their own language."

Staff Development

As a staff, you can create your own Case Studies of readers and writers. Identify one student at each stage on the continuum. Choose a fairly typical student who is at approximately the same stage for reading and writing. Interview the students and their families and collect samples of each child's reading and writing. Once you've identified one student at each stage, be sure to get written parental permission for this project. Set aside two or three months to collect information. Look at the continuums to be sure you have collected enough information about most of the descriptors. It's helpful to take a few photographs of the child at work and to videotape the child reading aloud. Once the information is collected, share the case studies at grade level or staff meetings. These students and their work can become anchors for the continuums in years to come. In addition, by creating the videotapes and case studies yourself, the Case Studies can reflect your school's unique population and character. The Case Studies can help new teachers understand the continuums and can be used for parent education at a Curriculum Night about continuums or reading and writing development.

Decide as a staff where to display the continuum charts. Do you want to post them in your classroom? Do you also want to hang the whole continuum in a central location in the building? Will you include student samples of work at each stage? Will the charts be used primarily for students, teachers, or families? Do you want to display the "student version" or "teacher version" of the charts? You may want to place a copy of both versions in your Continuum Notebook.

You may also want to display the writing continuum charts on the wall of your staff lounge or workroom as described at the beginning of this chapter. Ask each teacher to bring a sample of a typical student's piece of fiction writing to display under the appropriate stage. After all the samples have been added, ask grade level teams to select the most representative piece for each stage. If you include students' published work, be sure to include drafts as well as the final products. Obtain students' and parents' written permission, then attach the representative samples below the appropriate stages on the charts in the staff room. You may also want to photocopy the samples to add to your Anchor Papers Notebook. This collection of writing samples at each stage can help ensure consistency in marking the continuums and can become a useful resource for new teachers. The following month or the next term, repeat the same activity with nonfiction, poetry, or persuasive writing samples.

You can do a similar exercise with the reading continuum and the types of texts students read. Ask each teacher to select one student and photocopy a page from a fiction book that the student can read independently. Be sure to note the student's name, as well as the title and author of the book on each sample. At each grade level, choose one or two representative samples for each stage. Compare the samples with the Books by Stages list in Chapter 4. Attach one or two samples below each continuum stage. Copy the samples to include in the Anchor Papers Notebook. The same procedure could also be done for reading nonfiction and poetry. You could also collect written responses to literature that reflect students' level of comprehension at each stage on the reading continuum. You can add response journal samples for each stage on the continuum to the Anchor Papers Notebook in order to document students' increasingly sophisticated levels of comprehension.

Collecting and discussing student work can help your staff build a more consistent understanding of the reading and writing continuums. The Narrative Portraits, Case Studies, Continuum Wall, Charts, and Anchor Papers can provide a starting point for new levels of communication and staff development, as well as a way to visually capture reading and writing growth for students and their families.

Reading Continuum Charts
Student Version

Writing Continuum Key

▤ Types of Texts

🗁 Content and Traits

📖 Process

✎ Mechanics and Conventions

☺ Attitude and Self-Evaluation

Reading Continuum Key

📖 Types of Texts and Oral Reading

☺ Attitude

☑ Reading Strategies

☝ Comprehension and Response

👌 Self-Evaluation

Preconventional Reader

📖 Begins to choose reading materials (e.g., books, magazines, and charts) and has favorites.

📖 Shows interest in reading signs, labels, and logos (environmental print).

📖 Recognizes own name in print.

☑ Holds book and turn pages correctly.

☑ Shows beginning/end of book or story.

☑ Knows some letter names.

👍 Listens and responds to literature.

👍 Comments on illustrations in books.

👍 Participates in group reading (books, rhymes, poems, and songs).

Emerging Reader

📖   Memorizes pattern books, poems, and familiar books.

📖   Begins to read signs, labels, and logos (environmental print).

☺   Demonstrates eagerness to read.

☑   Pretends to read.

☑   Uses illustrations to tell stories.

☑   Reads top to bottom, left to right, and front to back with guidance.

☑   Knows most letter names and some letter sounds.

☑   Recognizes some names and words in context.

☑   Begins to make meaningful predictions.

👍   Rhymes and plays with words.

👍   Participates in reading of familiar books and poems.

👍   Connects books read aloud to own experiences with guidance.

Developing Reader

📖 Reads books with simple patterns.

📖 Begins to read own writing.

☺ Begins to read independently for short periods (5–10 minutes).

☺ Discusses favorite reading material with others.

☑ Relies on illustrations and print.

☑ Uses finger-print-voice matching.

☑ Knows most letter sounds and letter clusters.

☑ Recognizes simple words.

☑ Uses growing awareness of sound segments (e.g., phonemes, syllables, rhymes) to read words.

☑ Begins to make meaningful predictions.

☑ Identifies titles and authors in literature.

👍 Retells main event or idea in literature.

👍 Participates in guided literature discussions.

👓 Sees self as reader.

👓 Explains why literature is liked/disliked during class discussions with guidance.

Beginning Reader

📖 Reads simple early-reader books.

📖 Reads harder early-reader books.

📖 Reads and follows simple written directions with guidance.

📖 Identifies basic genres (e.g., fiction, nonfiction, and poetry).

📖 Uses basic punctuation when reading orally.

☺ Reads independently (10–15 minutes).

☺ Chooses reading materials independently.

☺ Learns and shares information from reading.

☑ Uses meaning cues (context).

☑ Uses sentence cues (grammar).

☑ Uses letter sounds and patterns (phonics).

☑ Recognizes word endings, common contractions, and many high frequency words.

☑ Begins to self-correct.

👍 Retells beginning, middle, and end with guidance.

👍 Discusses characters and story events with guidance.

👓 Identifies own reading behaviors with guidance.

Expanding Reader

📖 Reads easy chapter books.

📖 Chooses, reads, and finishes a variety of materials at appropriate level with guidance.

📖 Begins to read aloud with fluency.

☺ Reads silently for increasingly longer periods (15–30 minutes).

☑ Uses reading strategies appropriately, depending on the text and purpose.

☑ Uses word structure cues (e.g., root words, prefixes, suffixes, word chunks) when encountering unknown words.

☑ Increases vocabulary by using meaning cues (context).

☑ Self-corrects for meaning.

☑ Follows written directions.

☑ Identifies chapter titles and table of contents (text organizers).

👍 Summarizes and retells story events in sequential order.

👍 Responds to and makes personal connections with facts, characters, and situations in literature.

👍 Compares and contrasts characters and story events.

👍 "Reads between the lines" with guidance.

✍ Identifies own reading strategies and sets goals with guidance.

Bridging Reader

📖 Reads medium level chapter books.

📖 Chooses reading materials at appropriate reading level.

📖 Expands knowledge of different genres (e.g., realistic fiction, historical fiction, and fantasy)

📖 Reads aloud with expression.

☑ Uses resources (e.g., encyclopedias, CD-ROMs, and nonfiction texts) to locate and sort information with guidance.

☑ Gathers information by using the table of contents, captions, glossary, and index (text organizers) with guidance.

☑ Gathers information from graphs, charts, tables, and maps with guidance.

☑ Increases vocabulary by using context cues, other reading strategies, and resources (e.g., dictionary and thesaurus) with guidance.

☑ Demonstrates understanding of the difference between fact and opinion.

☑ Follows multi-step written directions independently.

👍 Discusses setting, plot, characters, and point of view (literary elements) with guidance.

👍 Responds to issues and ideas in literature as well as facts or story events.

👍 Makes connections to other authors, books, and perspectives.

👍 Participates in small group literature discussions with guidance.

👍 Uses reasons and examples to support ideas and opinions with guidance.

Fluent Reader

📖 Reads challenging children's books.

📖 Selects, reads, and finishes a wide variety of genres with guidance.

📖 Begins to develop strategies and criteria for selecting reading materials.

📖 Reads aloud with fluency, expression, and confidence.

☺ Reads silently for extended periods (30–40 minutes).

☑ Begins to use resources (e.g., encyclopedias, articles, Internet, and nonfiction texts) to locate information.

☑ Gathers information using the table of contents, captions, glossary, and index (text organizers) independently.

☑ Begins to use resources (e.g., dictionary and thesaurus) to increase vocabulary in different subject areas.

👍 Begins to discuss literature with reference to setting, plot, characters, and theme (literary elements) and author's craft.

👍 Generates thoughtful oral and written responses in small group literature discussions with guidance.

👍 Begins to use new vocabulary in different subjects and in oral and written response to literature.

👍 Begins to gain deeper meaning by "reading between the lines."

〰 Begins to set goals and identifies strategies to improve reading.

Proficient Reader

📖 Reads complex children's literature.

📖 Reads and understands informational texts (e.g., maps, want ads, brochures, schedules, catalogs, and manuals, etc.) with guidance.

📖 Develops strategies and criteria for selecting reading materials independently.

☑ Uses resources (e.g., encyclopedias, articles, Internet, and nonfiction texts) to locate information independently.

☑ Gathers and analyzes information from graphs, charts, tables, and maps with guidance.

☑ Integrates information from multiple nonfiction sources to deepen understanding of a topic with guidance.

☑ Uses resources (e.g., dictionary and thesaurus) to increase vocabulary independently.

👍 Identifies literary devices (e.g., similes, metaphors, personification, and foreshadowing).

👍 Discusses literature with reference to theme, author's purpose, and style (literary elements), and author's craft.

👍 Begins to generate in-depth responses in small group literature discussions.

👍 Begins to generate in-depth written responses to literature.

👍 Uses increasingly complex vocabulary in different subjects and in oral and written response to literature.

👍 Uses reasons and examples to support ideas and conclusions.

👍 Probes for deeper meaning by "reading between the lines" in response to literature.

Connecting Reader

📖 Reads complex children's literature and young adult literature.

📖 Selects, reads, and finishes a wide variety of genres independently.

☺ Begins to choose challenging reading materials and projects.

☑ Integrates nonfiction information to develop deeper understanding of a topic independently.

☑ Begins to gather, analyze, and use information from graphs, charts, tables, and maps.

👍 Generates in-depth responses and sustains small group literature discussions.

👍 Generates in-depth written responses to literature.

👍 Begins to evaluate, interpret, and analyze reading content critically.

👍 Begins to develop criteria for evaluating literature.

👍 Seeks recommendations and opinions about literature from others.

👓 Sets reading challenges and goals independently.

Independent Reader

📖   Reads young adult and adult literature.

📖   Chooses and comprehends a wide variety of sophisticated materials with ease (e.g., newspapers, magazines, manuals, novels, and poetry).

📖   Reads and understands informational texts (e.g., maps, manuals, consumer reports, applications, and forms).

☺   Reads challenging material for pleasure independently.

☺   Reads challenging material for information and to solve problems independently.

☺   Perseveres through complex reading tasks.

☑   Gathers, analyzes, and uses information from graphs, charts, tables, and maps independently.

👍   Analyzes literary devices (e.g., metaphors, imagery, irony, and satire).

👍   Contributes unique insights and supports opinions in complex literature discussions.

👍   Adds depth to responses to literature by making insightful connections to other reading and experiences.

👍   Evaluates, interprets, and analyzes reading content critically.

👍   Develops and articulates criteria for evaluating literature.

👓   Pursues a widening community of readers independently.

Writing Continuum Charts
Student Version

Preconventional Writer

📖   Relies primarily on pictures to convey meaning.

📖   Begins to label and add "words" to pictures.

📖   Writes first name.

📁   Demonstrates awareness that print conveys meaning.

✍   Makes marks other than drawing on paper (scribbles).

✍   Writes random recognizable letters to represent words.

☺   Tells about own pictures and writing.

Emerging Writer

📄 Uses pictures and print to convey meaning.

📄 Writes words to describe or support pictures.

📄 Copies signs, labels, names, and words (environmental print).

📁 Demonstrates understanding of letter/sound relationship.

✍ Prints with upper case letters.

✍ Matches letters to sounds.

✍ Uses beginning consonants to make words.

✍ Uses beginning and ending consonants to make words.

☺ Pretends to read own writing.

☺ Sees self as writer.

☺ Takes risks with writing.

Developing Writer

▤ Writes 1-2 sentences about a topic.

▤ Writes names and familiar words.

▱ Generates own ideas for writing.

✍ Writes from top to bottom, left to right, and front to back.

✍ Intermixes upper and lower case letters.

✍ Experiments with capitals.

✍ Experiments with punctuation.

✍ Begins to use spacing between words.

✍ Uses growing awareness of sound segments (e.g., phonemes, syllables, rhymes) to write words.

✍ Spells words on the basis of sounds without regard for conventional spelling patterns.

✍ Uses beginning, middle, and ending sounds to make words.

☺ Begins to read own writing.

Beginning Writer

📄 Writes several sentences about a topic.

📄 Writes about observations and experiences.

📄 Writes short nonfiction pieces (simple facts about a topic) with guidance.

📁 Chooses own writing topics.

✂ Reads own writing and notices mistakes with guidance.

✂ Revises by adding details with guidance.

✍ Uses spacing between words consistently.

✍ Forms most letters legibly.

✍ Writes pieces that self and others can read.

✍ Uses phonetic spelling to write independently.

✍ Spells simple words and some high frequency words correctly.

✍ Begins to use periods and capital letters correctly.

☺ Shares own writing with others.

Expanding Writer

- 📄 Writes short stories and poetry with guidance.

- 📄 Writes a variety of short nonfiction pieces (e.g., facts about a topic, letters, lists) with guidance.

- 📁 Writes with a central idea.

- 📁 Writes using complete sentences.

- 📁 Organizes ideas in a logical sequence in fiction and nonfiction writing with guidance.

- 📁 Begins to recognize and use interesting language.

- ✂ Uses several pre-writing strategies (e.g., web, brainstorm) with guidance.

- ✂ Listens to others' writing and offers feedback.

- ✂ Begins to consider suggestions from others about own writing.

- ✂ Adds description and details with guidance.

- ✂ Edits for capitals and punctuation with guidance.

- ✂ Publishes own writing with guidance.

- ✐ Writes legibly.

- ✐ Spells most high frequency words correctly and moves toward conventional spelling.

- ☺ Identifies own writing strategies and sets goals with guidance.

Bridging Writer

📄 Writes about feelings and opinions.

📄 Writes fiction with clear beginning, middle, and end.

📄 Writes poetry using carefully chosen language with guidance.

📄 Writes organized nonfiction pieces (e.g., reports, letters, and lists) with guidance.

📁 Begins to use paragraphs to organize ideas.

📁 Uses strong verbs, interesting language and dialogue with guidance.

✂ Seeks feedback on writing.

✂ Revises for clarity with guidance.

✂ Revises to enhance ideas by adding description and detail.

✂ Uses resources (e.g., thesaurus and word lists) to make writing more effective with guidance.

✂ Edits for punctuation, spelling, and grammar.

✂ Publishes writing in polished format with guidance.

✍ Increases use of visual strategies, spelling rules, and knowledge of word parts to spell correctly.

✍ Uses commas and apostrophes correctly with guidance.

☺ Uses criteria for effective writing to set own writing goals with guidance.

Fluent Writer

📄 Begins to write organized fiction and nonfiction (e.g., reports, letters, biographies, and autobiographies).

📄 Develops stories with plots that include problems and solutions with guidance.

📄 Creates characters in stories with guidance.

📄 Writes poetry using carefully chosen language.

📁 Begins to experiment with sentence length and complex sentence structure.

📁 Varies leads and endings with guidance.

📁 Uses description, details, and similes with guidance.

📁 Uses dialogue with guidance.

✂ Uses a range of strategies for planning writing.

✂ Adapts writing for purpose and audience with guidance.

✂ Revises for specific writing traits (e.g., ideas, organization, word choice, sentence fluency, voice, and conventions) with guidance.

✂ Incorporates suggestions from others about own writing with guidance.

✂ Edits for punctuation, spelling, and grammar with greater precision.

✂ Uses tools (e.g., dictionaries, word lists, and spellcheckers) to edit with guidance.

☺ Develops criteria for effective writing in different genres with guidance.

Proficient Writer

📄 Writes persuasively about ideas, feelings, and opinions

📄 Creates plots with problems and solutions.

📄 Begins to develop the main characters and describe detailed settings.

📄 Begins to write organized and fluent nonfiction, including simple bibliographies.

📁 Writes cohesive paragraphs including reasons and examples with guidance.

📁 Uses transitional sentences to connect paragraphs.

📁 Varies sentence structure, leads, and endings.

📁 Begins to use descriptive language, details, and similes.

📁 Uses voice to evoke emotional response from readers.

📁 Begins to integrate information on a topic from a variety of sources.

✂ Begins to revise for specific writing traits (e.g., ideas, organization, word choice, sentence fluency, voice, and conventions).

✂ Uses tools (e.g., dictionaries, word lists, spell checkers) to edit independently.

✂ Selects and publishes writing in polished format independently.

✍ Begins to use complex punctuation (e.g., commas, colons, semicolons, quotation marks) appropriately.

☺ Begins to set goals and identify strategies to improve writing in different genres.

Connecting Writer

- Writes in a variety of genres and forms for different audiences and purposes independently.
- Creates plots with a climax.
- Creates detailed, believable settings and characters in stories.
- Writes organized, fluent, and detailed nonfiction independently, including bibliographies with correct format.
- Writes cohesive paragraphs including supportive reasons and examples.
- Uses descriptive language, details, similes, and imagery to enhance ideas independently.
- Begins to use dialogue to enhance character development.
- Incorporates personal voice in writing with increasing frequency.
- Integrates information on a topic from a variety of sources independently.
- Constructs charts, graphs, and tables to convey information when appropriate.
- Uses pre-writing strategies effectively to organize and strengthen writing.
- Revises for specific writing traits (e.g., ideas, organization, word choice, sentence fluency, voice, and conventions) independently.
- Includes deletion in revision strategies.
- Incorporate suggestions from others on own writing independently.
- Uses complex punctuation (commas, colons, semicolons, quotation marks) with increasing accuracy.

Independent Writer

📄 Writes organized, fluent, accurate, and in-depth nonfiction, including references with correct bibliographic format.

📄 Writes cohesive, fluent, and effective poetry and fiction.

📁 Uses a clear sequence of paragraphs with effective transitions.

📁 Begins to incorporate literary devices (e.g., imagery, metaphors, personification, and foreshadowing).

📁 Weaves dialogue effectively into stories.

📁 Develops plots, characters, setting, and mood (literary elements) effectively.

📁 Begins to develop personal voice and style of writing.

✂ Revises through multiple drafts independently.

✂ Seeks feedback from others and incorporates suggestions in order to strengthen own writing.

✂ Publishes writing for different audiences and purposes in polished format independently.

✂ Internalizes the writing process.

✂ Uses correct grammar (e.g., subject/verb agreement and verb tense) consistently.

☺ Writes with confidence and competence on a range of topics independently.

☺ Perseveres through complex or challenging writing projects independently.

☺ Sets writing goals independently by analyzing and evaluating own writing.

Chapter 3

Glossary

> A continuum is a list of developmental stages. It's used to assess growth.
>
> —*Laura, Sixth-Grade Student*

The Glossary is primarily intended to provide a common language for teachers. What is the difference between "literary devices" and "literary elements?" What is "six-trait writing?" The Glossary defines terms like these from the continuums, which might be unclear. *The Literacy Dictionary*, edited by Theodore Harris and Richard Hodges (1995) was particularly helpful as I clarified the terminology on the continuums and created this Glossary. You may decide to operationalize some terms with even more specificity (e. g., for the descriptor, "knows some letter sounds," teachers may decide to determine how many letters a student should recognize). By using the CD-ROM, you can add terms or modify some of these definitions.

Using the Glossary

Since Cindy Flegenheimer and Julie Ledford were job sharing, they felt a strong need to communicate clearly with each other. With parent conferences looming ahead, they met to talk about each student's writing. For instance, Cindy and Julie looked at the students' wolf reports to see evidence of where these young writers had "added details and description with guidance." Both teachers had used the continuums for several years and had internalized the content, so they knew what to look for as they planned their focus lessons and assessed student work. The continuum descriptors guided Cindy and Julie as they taught specific writing focus lessons. For instance, the ability to revisit a piece of writing and add information is a monumental step for third graders. Throughout the year, both teachers modeled ways to re-read a piece of writing, stepping back to see what details could be added. Periodically, Cindy and Julie looked through their students' reports to see if these focus lessons had taken root. The information they collected helped the teachers decide which skills they needed to introduce, practice, or review next. Cindy and Julie used the continuums to share information and to ensure consistency, referring to the Glossary periodically.

As a new teacher to Brighton, Gabrielle Catton used the Glossary more frequently for clarification and for planning instruction. For instance, she looked at the definition for "literary elements" before she started her first literature circle on courage. For students in her fourth-grade classroom, she first focused on plot, then used her anecdotal notes to record when students discussed that particular literary element independently during literature discussions. She easily transferred this information to each student's reading continuum. Both the continuums and the Glossary guided Gabrielle's instruction and helped improve consistency within her classroom, as well as between her class and other classes and grade levels.

Key Phrases

There are three key phrases in the continuums that were used consciously to highlight the developmental nature of literacy acquisition: "with guidance," "begins to," and "independently." Skills and strategies are first introduced to students, then practiced *with adult guidance*. Over time, students *begin to* incorporate that strategy into their reading and writing, although they still may need occasional support or reminders. Eventually, we hope that students will use the strategy *independently*.

For example, very few second or third graders would edit their writing on their own. In fact, once students have finished writing, they often say, "I'm done" and have no desire to revisit that piece again. It's only with a great deal of modeling and practice that students learn how to improve their writing by re-reading it and adding information. Revision only occurs *with guidance*. By the intermediate grades, students *begin to* revise their work using revision guides or rubrics, but usually still need adult support. It isn't until middle school that students are usually able to revise their writing for specific traits *independently* in order to increase the power of their writing. As you introduce new skills, you gradually remove the scaffolding of teachers support as students become able to do more on their own. Here is a graphic presentation of these terms.

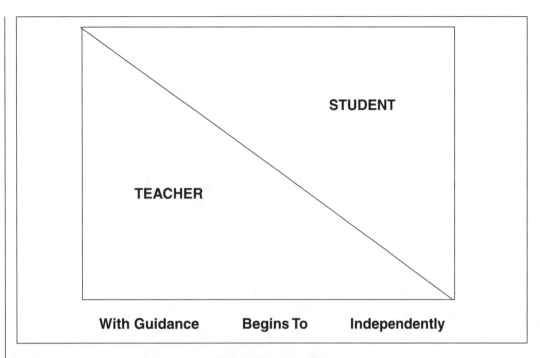

Figure 3.1 Scaffolding

Continuum Notebook, Anchor Papers Notebook, and Parent Handbook

The Glossary provides a clear common language for teachers and families. You may want to include the Glossary in your Continuum Notebook, along with copies of the continuums and the Narrative Portraits described in the last chapter. You may also want to include actual student samples in your Anchor Papers Notebook as evidence or as an explanation of specific terms, such as "complex sentence structure" or "literary devices." Some schools, like Dhahran Academy in Saudi Arabia, include the Glossary along with the reading and writing continuums in their Parent Handbook. The Glossary is also included on the CD-ROM so that you can modify the definitions or add new terms. The Glossary for English as an Additional Language is included in Chapter 9.

Staff Development

The following activity with the Glossary has been helpful as teachers first start using the continuums. Sit in grade-level teams, then hand each group one copy of either the reading or writing continuum and two colored highlighters. Each group should focus on the three continuum stages into which most of their students' behaviors fall. Ask teachers to use one color highlighter to mark all the descriptors that they find straightforward, easy to teach, and simple to assess. Use the second highlighter to note the descriptors that are more subjective, unclear, or challenging to teach or assess.

After the groups have finished this activity, start at the Preconventional stage, then discuss each descriptor that the teachers find unclear or challenging, moving through the ten stages. Inevitably, someone will describe how he or she assesses a particular skill or strand. The majority of teachers' questions are usually cleared up during the discussion. After the discussion, hand out the Glossary to see if the definitions clarify specific descriptors. If not, you may want to revise or add to the Glossary.

The continuums may look a little daunting to teachers who have not filled one out before. Looking at specific descriptors alleviates anxiety as teachers realize the descriptors usually describe skills and strategies that they already teach and expect from their students. You might want to repeat this activity every year as new teachers join the staff. The Glossary activity can help teachers build a common understanding and consistent use of terminology.

Glossary of Continuum Terms

analyze own writing: the student is able to step back from the writing in order to view it from a reader's perspective, consider changes or improvements, and make decisions about content, style, and effectiveness. This may lead to revising or editing the writing.

appropriate level: reading material that matches the reader's abilities and interests. The student should be able to read the text with 95 % accuracy and strong comprehension. Teachers often refer to this as a "just right" book for a student to read *independently*.

author's purpose: the author's intent or reason for writing (to entertain, to persuade, to inform, etc.).

basic punctuation: simple forms of punctuation, such as the period (.), question mark (?), and exclamation mark (!) used to clarify meaning.

begins to: indicates the first steps students take as they perform an activity or task on their own. Students still need help from an adult or peer. They may demonstrate a strategy some of the time, but not yet consistently.

brainstorm: a free-flowing offering of ideas or suggestions, often used as a prewriting, pre-reading, or problem-solving strategy.

challenging children's literature (Fluent Stage): chapter books with more characters and more challenging plots than medium level chapter books. Challenging children's literature includes mysteries (*Nancy Drew* books by Carolyn Keene) and nonfiction books on topics of interest (*Lightning* by Seymour Simon, 1997). Novels also include survival books (*Hatchet* by Gary Paulsen, 1987) and fantasy (*James and the Giant Peach* by Roald Dahl, 1961).

chapter books: novels written with multiple chapters (see "beginning chapter books" and "medium level chapter books").

characters: participants in a story.

children's literature: fiction, nonfiction, or poetry written for children (see "challenging children's literature" and "complex children's literature").

climax: high point or exciting part in the action of a story.

cohesive paragraph: a distinct section of text, usually indented, with a central idea and logical sequence and structure.

complex children's literature (Proficient and Connecting Stages): children's novels with several main characters who are often approaching adolescence. The texts include fully developed plots, frequently touching upon issues such as death, prejudice, poverty or war. These texts often require an understanding of other time periods, unfamiliar locations, or complex issues. Some examples include *Island of the Blue Dolphins* (Scott O'Dell, 1960), *Bridge to Terabithia* (Katherine Paterson, 1977), *Sign of the Beaver* (Elizabeth George Speare, 1983), and *Maniac Magee* (Jerry Spinelli, 1990). Many students also enjoy biographies, such as Diane Stanley's biography,

Leonardo Da Vinci (1996). Other books address broad themes, such as good versus evil, truth, and human rights. Examples of other complex literature include *The True Confessions of Charlotte Doyle* (Avi, 1990), *A Wrinkle in Time* (Madeleine L'Engle, 1962), and the *Redwall* fantasy series by Brian Jacques.

complex punctuation: more sophisticated punctuation marks, such as commas (,), colons (:), semicolons (;), and quotation marks (" ") used to clarify meaning.

complex sentence structure: sentences varying in length with multiple clauses and more sophisticated arrangement and punctuation.

context cues: the information available in surrounding words, illustrations, or sentences that helps the reader or listener make meaning. Teachers sometimes prompt readers to use context cues by asking, "Does that make sense?"

conventions: accepted practices in written language. As a writing trait, conventions include punctuation, spelling, capitalization, grammar, and use of paragraphs.

conventional spelling: correct spelling.

cueing system: sources of information (phonics, grammar, context, word parts, and text structure) that help readers construct meaning from print.

description: words used to evoke images in the reader's mind.

dialogue: conversation between people or characters.

draft: writing ideas down in a rough, unpolished form.

early-reader books (see "simple early-reader books" and "harder early-reader books").

easy chapter books (Expanding Stage): short books (60–100 pages) written in chapter format. Easy chapter books usually contain page numbers, a table of contents, and chapter numbers or titles. Nonfiction titles sometimes include a glossary. These books have significantly less controlled vocabulary and a smaller font than *I Can Read* books. Most books have only a few characters and a simple plot. Some easier examples include *Polk Street* books (Patricia Reilly Giff) and *The Magic Treehouse* series (Mary Pope Osborne). These books usually have illustrations every 2–6 pages. More challenging easy chapter books are *The Littles* (John Peterson), and the *Amber Brown* (Paula Danziger) series which may only have a few illustrations in each chapter and a smaller font.

edit: to correct or proofread for meaning, mechanics, and conventions (e.g., spelling, capitalization, and punctuation) in order to share or publish a piece of writing.

editing tools: resources used in the editing process (e.g., dictionaries, word lists, spell checkers, or editing handbooks) to check spelling, punctuation, or grammar.

environmental print: print and symbols connected to daily living (e.g., signs, restaurant menus, billboards, logos).

evaluate reading/writing: to examine students' work in order to determine their strengths as well as areas for growth. Reading and writing growth can also be examined by comparing recent and earlier reading or writing samples. Students can self-evaluate by stepping back to analyze their own work based on rubrics and criteria developed in class.

expand on others' ideas: to build on another person's comments by adding new information or relevant insights.

fiction: imaginative writing often designed to delight or entertain.

finger-print-voice matching: when young readers point to each word as they read, indicating that they have made the connection between spoken and written language.

genres: categories used to classify literature (e.g. mystery, biography, autobiography, poetry, historical fiction, fantasy, realistic fiction, science fiction, and nonfiction).

grammar: the structure of how language works (see "syntax"). Readers use the grammar of language to create meaning from written texts.

group reading: oral reading of a common text by several people, such as choral reading or Readers Theatre.

guided literature discussions: conversations about books which are facilitated by a teacher, older student, or other adult.

harder early-reader books (Later Beginning Stage): short books (20–75 pages) with fairly simple vocabulary, large font, and illustrations on every page or two. They are often marked on the cover as *I Can Read* books and may have sections that look like chapters but are not specifically labeled as "Chapter One." Some examples are the *Frog and Toad* (Arnold Lobel), *Henry and Mudge* (Cynthia Rylant) and *Little Bear* (Else Minarik) series.

high frequency words: common words that appear often in written or spoken language (e.g., "the," "of," and "because").

ideas: as a writing trait, the ideas include the content of a piece of writing, the theme, and the use of supporting details.

illustrations: pictures, artwork, or photography used to enhance, clarify, or extend the text.

imagery: mental pictures evoked by a piece of descriptive writing or through the use of similes or metaphors.

informational texts: functional data presented graphically or visually (e.g., want ads, brochures, schedules, catalogs, manuals, consumer reports, applications, and forms).

invented spelling: see "phonetic spelling."

irony: circumstances that are the opposite of what might normally be expected; an incongruous situation (e.g., "The cobbler's children have no shoes.").

knowledge of word parts: an understanding of common roots, prefixes, and suffixes (e.g., "un" usually means "not" and "ing" signifies an action verb).

lead: opening sentence of a paragraph or the beginning sentences of a longer piece of writing.

letter cluster: a sequence of two or more consonants (e.g., -nn- in "funny") or vowels (e.g., -ee in "bee").

letter/sound cues: sometimes referred to as "phonics" or "phonetics." The connection between a written letter or letter combination (such as "sp") and the spoken sound(s).

literature: fiction, nonfiction prose, and poetry.

literary devices: tools authors use to enhance the power of writing (e.g., simile, metaphor, personification, foreshadowing, irony, and satire).

literature discussions: small group discussions about a book students read in common (much like adult book clubs). During guided literature discussions, a teacher, older student, or another adult may provide modeling and support.

literary elements: essential features of a piece of writing (e.g., setting, plot, characters, mood, theme, and author's purpose).

meaning cues (see "context cues").

meaningful predictions: a reader's logical guesses about what will happen next, based on clues from the text and the reader's background knowledge.

medium level chapter books (Bridging Stage): relatively long novels (75–200 pages) with only a few illustrations. The books focus on everyday concerns of children growing up. Well-known medium chapter books include the *Ramona* (Beverly Cleary), *Encyclopedia Brown* (Donald Sobol), and *The Boxcar Children* (Gertrude Chandler Warner) series. More recent titles include popular series, such as *Goosebumps* (R. L. Stine), *Baby-Sitter's Club* (Ann Martin), *Animorphs* (K. A. Applegate), and *The Time Warp Trio* (Jon Scieszka).

metaphor: a literary device in which two different objects are compared by analogy (i.e., "The lake is a mirror.").

miscues: "mistakes" or deviations from text when reading aloud.

multiple strategies for spelling: varied ways of figuring out words (e.g., "sounding out" a word, drawing on knowledge of similar words, asking a friend, or using a dictionary)

nonfiction: prose other than fiction that is intended to inform, persuade, explain, or give directions (e.g., biographies, autobiographies, letters, lists, reports on a topic, technical manuals, and newspapers).

organization: as a writing trait, organization includes the internal structure and logical sequence of a piece of writing appropriate to a specific genre. It includes the sequence of ideas, transitions, and conclusion.

pattern books (Emerging and Developing Stages): picture books with predictable and repetitive phrases, structure, and/or plot, such as *Brown Bear, Brown Bear, What Do You See?* (Bill Martin, Jr., 167), *Just Like Daddy* (Frank Ash, 1981), *All By Myself* (Mercer Mayer, 1983), or *Quick as a Cricket* (Audrey Wood, 1990).

personification: a literary device in which inanimate objects are described with human-like qualities (i.e., "The sun was smiling down on me.").

persuasive writing: writing intended to convince, argue, or influence.

phoneme: minimal sound unit in speech made by a letter or combination of letters. For example, "cat" [k/ă/t] and "ship" [sh/ÿ/p] both have three phonemes. A phoneme is not the same as a syllable or a letter.

phonemic awareness: an awareness of the sounds (phonemes) that make up words.

phonetic spelling: spelling a word as it sounds (love = luv). Primary students often use phonetic spelling (sometimes called "temporary," "invented," or "creative" spelling) as they begin to construct an understanding of written language.

phonic cues: the speech sounds represented by a letter or letter combination. Readers use phonics cues to construct meaning from written texts. Teachers sometimes prompt students to use phonics cues by asking, "Does that look right?"

picture cues: illustrations in a book which help the reader figure out the printed text. For example, a picture of a cow might help the reader identify the word beneath an illustration. This is a temporary support during the early stages of reading. For older readers, an illustration in a social studies text may provide clarification and support for a new concept or term.

plot: the structure or sequence of events in a story, often including tension, a climax, and resolution.

point of view: the vantage point or perspective from which the author presents the action of the story. For instance, *Nothing But the Truth* (Avi, 1991) tells the same story from the perspectives of multiple characters.

predict: using the text structure, title, content, illustrations, and background knowledge to anticipate what might happen next.

prewrite: the initial writing stage of gathering ideas and information and planning writing. Students may sketch, brainstorm, or use webs, outlines, or lists to generate and organize ideas.

polished format: written material which has been carefully revised and edited to be precise and error free, then published to share with others.

publish: to prepare written materials to be shared with an audience, such as in a bound book or oral performance. This is the final stage in the writing process after the writer revises and edits.

range of strategies for planning writing: see "prewrite".

reading: the process of exploring, creating, and using meaning by interacting with written language.

"reading between the lines": the process of looking beyond the literal level of a text to achieve deeper understanding, also known as "inferring." Readers make inferences and draw conclusions by using the information in the text, as well as their own experiences and background knowledge.

reading materials and texts: a broader term than "books" which includes all reading materials, including literature (fiction, magazines, nonfiction, and poetry) and informational materials (manuals, guides, charts, newspapers, magazines, reference materials, and letters), as well as material on the computer (Internet and web sites).

reading strategies: the varied processes a reader uses to make meaning from written language (e.g., context, grammar, word patterns, and letter sounds). Students also use comprehension strategies by determining important information, using their background knowledge, asking questions as they read, visualizing, drawing inferences, making connections, and constantly checking for understanding.

resources to increase vocabulary: reference materials such as a dictionary, word list, or thesaurus.

resources to locate information: reference materials such as encyclopedias, the Internet, articles, or nonfiction texts.

response to literature: the ways in which students react to texts and demonstrate understanding and appreciation through oral discussions, writing, or the arts.

retell: a process in which the reader writes or orally describes what happened in a story after reading or hearing the text read aloud. A retelling is more detailed than a summary.

revision: making content changes in a text in order to make the meaning clearer or the writing more effective and powerful.

satire: the use of irony, ridicule, or sarcasm as a commentary on an event, person, or situation.

scaffolding: in education, the gradual withdrawing of adult assistance and support as students become able to accomplish a task more independently.

sentence fluency: as a writing trait, the sound and flow of sentences that contribute to readability.

sentence structure cues: the intuitive knowledge about grammar that helps the reader make meaning. Teachers sometimes prompt students to use sentence structure cues by asking, "Does that sound right?"

setting: the location and time period of a story.

similes: a literary device in which two unlike things are compared, using words such as "like" or "as" (e.g., "Her cheeks were as pink as roses.").

simple early-reader books (Early Beginning Stage): short books (10–50 pages) with simple vocabulary, large font, and illustrations on every page. Many students begin reading Dr. Seuss books at this stage, such as *The Cat in the Hat* (1960) or *Green Eggs and Ham* (1960). Some simple early readers contain rhyme (e.g., *Jamesberry* by Bruce Degan, 1983) or repetition (e.g., *I was so Mad* by Mercer Mayer, 1983) as support for beginning readers.

simple words: easily decodable words with consistent consonant-vowel-consonant patterns (e.g., "hot" or "cat"), simple sight words, Dolch words, or high frequency words (e.g., "the" or "me").

six-trait writing: the characteristics of effective writing developed by the Northwest Regional Educational Laboratory in Portland, Oregon. These traits include: ideas, organization, word choice, sentence fluency, voice, and conventions.

sound-symbol relationship (see "letter/sound cues").

strong verbs: specific and descriptive action words (e.g., "saunter" instead of "walk").

style: the author's choice of language, structure, and voice that makes the writing unique.

summarize: to state or write a brief statement about the essential ideas in a text.

syntax: the structure of sentences and word order and the grammar of English.

takes risks with writing: the writer is willing to explore new kinds of writing, techniques, or content. For new writers, this may include the use of invented spelling.

text: written or printed language.

text features: parts, other than the body of a text, that designate special features (e.g., the title, author, copyright information, and dedication).

text organizers: important features of texts that provide structure and help readers locate information (e.g., page numbers, table of contents, captions, glossary, and index).

theme: the underlying or implicit meaning, concept, or message embedded in a story.

traits: see "six-trait writing".

transitional sentences: sentences that link ideas or paragraphs together for fluidity and coherence.

visual cues: visual information (the way a word looks) used in connection with sound/symbol relationships and conventions of print (such as spacing and direction) to determine correct spelling and word identification. Teachers often ask, "Does it look right?" to help students focus on visual cues. Visual cues in a text may also include illustrations.

voice: the distinctive tone or style of a particular writer. Voice reflects the particular personality of the writer and often strikes an emotional chord in the reader.

web: a type of graphic organizer for planning or structuring writing. A web can also be used for supporting comprehension of texts during or after reading.

with guidance: the student performs an activity or task with direction or support from a teacher, another adult, or peer. Scaffolding (support) is gradually withdrawn, as the student becomes more independent. Students at this level still need adult help most of the time.

word choice: as a writing trait, the selection of precise and appropriate language and vivid vocabulary.

word family: a group of words with the same root word (e.g., "mailing" and "mailman") or phonic base or rime (e.g., "m-at," "f-at," and "h-at").

word structure cues: information available about word parts (prefixes, suffixes, root words, and word chunks) that help readers understand new vocabulary.

writing: the process of exploring, creating, and expressing meaning through written language.

writing process: the stages of writing (prewriting, drafting, revising, editing, and publishing). These stages are recursive, rather than linear. For example, the writer might brainstorm and draft, step back and make changes, then write more.

young adult literature (Connecting and Independent Stages): novels that address sophisticated and challenging issues and include complex characters who are often approaching adulthood. The style includes more complicated literary techniques (such as flashbacks, foreshadowing), as well as sophisticated language and vocabulary. These books require significantly more background knowledge on the part of readers. Some examples of young adult novels are *Roll of Thunder, Hear My Cry* (Mildred Taylor, 1976), *The Devil's Arithmetic* (Jane Yolen, 1988), *Shabanu* (Suzanne Fisher Staples, 1989), and *The Golden Compass* (Philip Pullman, 1995), as well as novels by Cynthia Voigt, Chris Crutcher, and Walter Dean Myers.

Chapter 4

Books by Continuum Stages

It's the sparks in the relationship between a child and a book that create the fire of literacy.

—*Mem Fox* (Radical Reflections, *1993, p. 138*)

One common question that parents and teachers ask about the reading continuum is the difference between terms such as "easy chapter books and "medium level chapter books." Without common definitions, determining a child's reading level on the continuum becomes completely subjective. I worked with many teachers over the past eight years to define terms and to develop the lists included in this chapter. At times, we argued passionately about where certain titles belong; however, there are no right answers. The database was created so that you can add new titles, make changes, or add comments for particular books. You can use your own teaching experience and knowledge about children's literature, together with the lists in this chapter and the database, to connect your students with just the right books.

There are three ways in which information about books is presented in this chapter: the database, the Book Lists, and the Key Benchmark Book list.

The Database

All of the titles mentioned in this chapter and in the rest of this book are listed in the database with full bibliographic information. The database on the CD-ROM

Database Fields

- Title
- Author
- Illustrator
- Publisher
- Publication Date
- Format
- Series
- Genre
- Time Period
- Literature Circles Themes
- Continuum Stage
- Guided Reading Level
- Annotation
- User Comments

included with this book makes it infinitely easier to locate book information, add new titles, sort by various categories, and print book lists based on a search. Books are recorded in the database using the fields listed in the chart to the left.

Many of the books in your classroom are probably already listed in the database. You may want to add other titles so that the database reflects your particular collection of children's books. As you read or purchase new books, you can enter the titles and bibliographic information, along with short annotations onto the database.

The database enables you to print various lists. For instance, if you want to add new titles for guided reading, you can sort the list by the *Fountas and Pinnell Guided Reading Leveling System*™ levels, then print the list for the levels you need. If you are collecting books for literature circles, you can sort by theme, then print the list of titles. If parents want to know the titles of books their child might enjoy, you could print a list of book titles for the appropriate continuum stage.

Book Lists by Continuum Stages

The Book Lists contain 50–75 books for each continuum stage. My goal was to keep each list no longer than one page, so I often listed only one sample book from a series or only one book by an author. Within each continuum stage, the books are arranged in order of complexity, with the simplest books listed first. The more challenging books can be found at the end of the list, thus forming a bridge to the next stage.

At conferences, teachers at Brighton School in Lynnwood, Washington, give parents the appropriate page from the Book Lists, based on each child's reading level. Most parents appreciate receiving book suggestions that match their child's abilities and interests. This year, Brighton School included the continuums and the Book Lists by continuum stages on their web site (www.brightonschool.com). Teachers add new titles periodically and include students' reviews of new books on this website.

You can use the Book Lists to level some of the books in your classroom, as well as to fill in missing gaps in your book collection as you purchase new books. For instance, if you have longed for an alternative to *Mouse Soup* (Arnold Lobel, 1977), you could glance at the Book Lists or database for other suggestions.

⚷ Key Benchmark Books Lists

The Key Benchmark Books list includes ten key books per stage that you can use as anchor books. For instance, when I think of "challenging children's literature" at the Fluent stage, I think of books such as *Charlie and the Chocolate Factory* (Roald Dahl, 1964), *Shiloh* (Phyllis Reynolds Naylor, 1991), and *Hatchet* (Gary Paulsen, 1987). In the complete Book Lists, I placed a key symbol (⚷) by these 10 titles from the Key Benchmark Books list. You might want to keep this Key Benchmark Books list by your desk and use it when you are purchasing new books for your class or filling out the continuums for your students.

Teachers in many schools have leveled hundreds of the books they use for guided reading and literature circles by continuum stages. Although initially time consuming, once the color codes and anchor books are in place, finding the right books for students becomes much easier. You may want to use colored dots or strips of electrician's tape to color code the books in your classroom by continuum stages. When you purchase new books, use the Key Benchmark Books list and the Book Lists in this chapter to level and color-code new titles before adding them to your collection

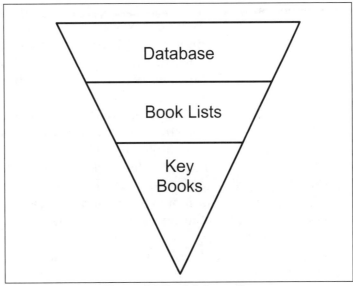

Figure 4.1 Book Information

Book Format

The descriptors on the reading continuum are based on the types of texts students can read independently. Therefore, it is very important to be consistent about the ways in which book levels are defined. The terms used for Book Format on the continuum were selected intentionally and are defined in the Glossary, which is included both in Chapter 3 and on the CD-ROM. The terms are also explained more clearly later in this chapter in the Book Characteristics charts for each continuum stage.

The types of texts that students read provide the anchor for the other reading continuum descriptors at that stage. For instance, when the continuum descriptor at the Expanding stage indicates that a student "Begins to read aloud with fluency," that descriptor is based on the types of texts at that stage. At the Expanding stage, students begin to read easy chapter books like the *Marvin Redpost* series by Louis Sachar. At the previous stage, they may have read books with simple patterns, like Dr. Seuss books, with *some* expression. It is more likely that Beginning readers are concentrating on decoding and making sense of what they read. The description of oral fluency is intended to link directly to the stage in which students begin to read short chapter books, like the *Cam Jansen* (David Adler) or *Amber Brown* (Paula Danziger) series with more fluency.

Progression of Text Difficulty
- wordless books
- label books
- highly predictable books
- pattern books
- simple early-reader books
- harder early-reader books
- easy chapter books
- medium chapter books
- challenging children's literature
- complex children's literature
- young adult literature
- adult literature

As I leveled books with teachers, I discovered that four of the stages had a huge range of texts. For instance, the books at the Beginning stage ranged from *I Was So Mad* (Mercer Mayer, 1983) to easy-reader books like *The Golly Sisters Go West* (Betsy Byars, 1985). Consequently, the Developing, Beginning, Expanding, and Bridging stages were each divided into an Early Stage and a Later Stage. Dividing the stages makes it easier for you to track your students' progress and show growth to parents.

As you look at the reading continuum, notice how the Types of Texts strand flows horizontally in a developmental progression. Theoretically, the books could be listed sequentially on one long continuum. For more practical purposes, however, books with similar characteristics were divided into continuum stages. You can track how students move from memorizing books to reading books with simple patterns, then transition from easy readers to progressively more challenging novels and nonfiction texts. You can use students' reading logs, your anecdotal notes during silent reading time, and your observations during reading conferences to mark the types of books that students can read on the continuum. (For more information about assessment tools, see Chapter 5.) Using the reading continuum is far easier when the types of texts students read is made explicit. If our goal is to help readers along the literacy continuum, we need to know how to find the right books at their level that will "spark the fires of literacy" (Mem Fox, 1993).

Picture Books

As children begin to read, they often start with wordless books and books with labels that match the pictures. They next memorize picture books with patterns, such as *Brown Bear, Brown Bear* by Bill Martin, Jr. (1967). These simple texts are designated as picture books on the database and are often written specifically for teaching emerging readers at the Preconventional, Emerging, and Developing stages on the continuum. The *Fountas and Pinnell Guided Reading Leveling System*™ levels for many of these simple texts are also included on the database.

Other picture books contain rich language and captivating illustrations or photographs. These picture books are usually 32 pages long and the illustrations support or extend the text. You may notice that very few picture books are listed on the lists of Key Benchmark Books or Books by Continuum Stages. The reason is that picture books are often too difficult to level. Where would you place *Wilfred Gordon McDonald Patridge* (Mem Fox, 1985) or *The Sunshine Home* (Eve Bunting, 1994)? Those of you who teach at the primary level know that both of these two picture books are far more difficult than an early chapter book such as *Poppleton* (Cynthia Rylant, 1997). A picture book may include more challenging vocabulary and concepts, or require more background knowledge. For instance, a second grader will respond to *The Sunshine Home* differently than an adult, since most young children have not had much experience with nursing homes. This certainly does not mean that picture books shouldn't be read to, with, and by students! This only means that these books are "everybody books," as they are called in some libraries. Only a few of these picture books are included in the list of Books by Stages, although over 500 picture books are listed on the database. These provide wonderful read alouds and springboards into writing. Picture books can be included in literature circles, during guided or shared reading, or as independent reading choices.

Picture Books for Older Readers

Illustrations also play an important role in picture books for older readers. These texts include more challenging vocabulary and content, and are often more appropriate to read with intermediate students. The database includes approximately 250 picture books for older readers, such as *Nettie's Trip South* (Ann Turner, 1987) and *Pink and Say* (Patricia Polacco, 1994). Picture books like these can be read aloud as an introduction to a theme or to spark conversations about a time period or historical event. They can also be used for focus lessons built around an author's use of language and imagery. Because you can use picture books for older readers with many ages in different contexts, I did not provide guided reading levels or continuum stages for these texts.

Early-Reader Books

Early-reader texts provide the bridge between simple predictable books and chapter books. These books still contain illustrations on every page, the print size is large and the vocabulary is limited. Early-reader books range from classic Dr. Seuss books like *Green Eggs and Ham* (1960) to the *Henry and Mudge* series by Cynthia Rylant or the *Little Bear* books by Else Homelund Minarik. The section in this chapter about Beginning readers contains further examples and information about these simple texts.

Easy Chapter Books

Easy chapter books are usually less than 100 pages and the text is divided into chapters. Some texts, like the *Pee Wee Scouts* series by Judy Denton, still use a large print and limited vocabulary. Students begin to read easy chapter books at the start of the Expanding stage. By the end of that stage, the easy chapter books have smaller print, with only ocassional illustrations, like the *Amber Brown* series by Paula Danziger. These books can provide more in-depth content for younger readers, as well as shorter, more accessible texts for older readers.

Books Between Stages: Transition Books

It is easy to identify when students memorize books as they begin to learn to read. It is also easy to tell when students are reading "medium level chapter books" at the Bridging stage or "young adult novels" at the Independent stage. It is far more difficult to label the types of shorter books that precede those longer texts. Where do you draw the line between *I Can Read* books and easy chapter books? The most challenging discussions have arisen as teachers leveled books in the Beginning and Expanding stages. In reality, it doesn't matter what you call these texts, as long as you can match readers with the right books.

It is not until you line up all the books that distinctions can really be made. The differences seem clear when I sort the books into tubs, yet I always find exceptions. For instance, the *Pinky and Rex* books by James Howe fall right between the line I have arbitrarily drawn between early readers and easy chapter books. Like the *Commander Toad* books by Jane Yolen, The *Pinky and Rex* books have a large print size and illustrations on every page, which would make the series more appropriate for students at the later half of the Beginning stage. On the other hand, the *Pinky and Rex* books have numbered chapters and more text on a page, more like the *Pee Wee* Scouts series by Judy Denton. For those reasons, I could have placed the books at the Expanding stage. I finally decided to put them in the Beginning stage because of length and vocabulary, but I placed the series last on the Book List to indicate that it serves as a bridge between books at the Beginning and Expanding stages. Leveling at this degree of specificity is only possible when you have samples of the books in front of you. This is why the book sorting activity described in more detail in the Staff Development section at the end of this chapter is so helpful for a grade-level team, committee, or school. The process of clarifying terms helps create a common language and ensure consistency as you talk about books with your colleagues.

Chapter Books

One third of the books in the database are chapter books. These texts are organized by chapters and are appropriate for independent readers in the intermediate and middle school grades, as well as for capable readers in the primary grades.

Young Adult Novels

Young adult novels contain more challenging vocabulary and/or more mature content. These books are usually only appropriate for middle school readers. Young adult novels often address controversial or sophisticated issues such as abuse, homelessness, or prejudice. The main characters in these novels are often adolescents. Many of these books require an understanding of other cultures, time periods, or perspectives. More information about the characteristics of these books is included in the sections on Connecting and Independent readers.

Factors In Leveling Books

How do you determine the reading level of a book? I remember using readability charts in education classes 25 years ago, carefully counting the number of sentences and syllables in 100-word passages. Published computer programs also exist that use a readability formula to level books, based strictly on the word count. Most teachers will tell you that it is not just the number of words or sentences on a page that determine the difficulty level of a book. How closely do the illustrations match the text? How large is the print? How much technical vocabulary is used? How much background knowledge is necessary for a young reader to understand the story? The chart below lists all of the factors that were considered as we leveled books. The first eight factors in the left column pertain to the physical layout of the texts, such as the print size and the number of words on a page. The remaining features address the content of a book, such as the complexity of the plot and the background knowledge required for understanding.

Factors in Leveling Books

- Print size
- Vocabulary
- Number of words on a page
- Sentence length/structure
- Line/page breaks
- Use of rhyme/repetition
- Length of text
- Supporting illustrations

- Subject matter
- Format
- Genre
- Plot complexity
- Background knowledge required
- Emotional content
- Historical setting
- Age of characters
- Number of characters
- Reader interest

For instance, books in *The Magic Schoolbus* series by Joanna Cole are far more challenging than many other straightforward, nonfiction texts about the same topics. Any primary teacher who has introduced Jon Scieszka's *Time Warp Trio* books can tell you that the setting and vocabulary make these slender books far more challenging than the humorous illustrations, book length, and large print would indicate. The Book Lists in this chapter are intended as a starting place. As you use the titles on the lists and become familiar with the formats and continuum stages, you can fine-tune your system of leveling. For those of you who have already leveled the books in your classroom, I hope these lists provide additional titles and a framework for fine-tuning your lists. In creating the database and lists, I relied heavily on the experience of many teachers who have used these books in their classrooms. Here are some of the factors we considered.

Format and Length

A great deal of artistry is involved in matching students to books. One factor to consider is the format of a text. For instance, *The View from Saturday* (E. L. Konigsburg, 1996) is written in alternating chapters, told from the different perspectives of the main characters. This challenging format can be difficult for younger readers to follow.

Length is also an issue for some readers. For example, the text of the *Redwall* series by Brian Jacques could probably be read by Proficient readers, but size of these novels (over 400 pages) would be fairly daunting. Although there is plenty of action to engage students, there is also a great deal of description and a huge cast of characters. Because of these factors, this fantasy series was placed at the Connecting stage. It is important to realize that length alone does not determine the level of a book. The length of a book is only one of a number of factors that contribute to the difficulty level of a text.

Emotional Content

Content is another critical factor in leveling books. Many fourth graders might be able to read the words in Chris Crutcher's young adult novel, *Ironman* (1995), but the book deals with adolescent issues and abuse and is inappropriate for younger students. The emotional impact of a book can be determined more easily after you have used a book with students. For instance, Cindy Flegenheimer selected *Bridge to Terabithia* (Katherine Paterson, 1977) as one choice in a fourth-grade literature circle set around the theme of courage. For many students, this was the first time they had ever read a book in which a main character dies, and they were all deeply affected. Students at the Fluent or even Bridging stage could read the book, if their reactions and comprehension were mediated by adult support and class discussions, as occurred in Cindy's class. This book would probably be more appropriate as an independent reading choice for students at the Proficient level. Similarly, although *Nightjohn* (1993) and *Sarny* (1997) are relatively short novels by Gary Paulson, they contain graphic details of what happened to slaves who were caught teaching others to read and would be most appropriate for independent reading in middle school.

Background Knowledge, Content, and Genre

Children's prior knowledge about a subject also plays a crucial role in their comprehension of texts. For instance, in fourth grade, Keith scored much higher on the *Qualitative Reading Inventory* (Leslie and Caldwell, 1995) passage about Pele, the soccer player, than he did on the selection about Andrew Carnegie because of his first-hand knowledge of soccer. Students also need additional support as new genres are introduced. Many students whose reading diet has consisted primarily of fiction may struggle with the informational texts presented in fourth and fifth grade. It is also difficult for students to understand a book like *The Devil's Arithmetic* (Jane Yolen, 1988) without some understanding of the history of World War II and concentration camps. *Number the Stars* (Lois Lowry,1989) is also a book about World War II that many teachers use with younger children. Students could probably read this book on their own, but they would understand the issues in the book at a deeper level if you provided some background information about the time period. Therefore, I placed the book at the Proficient stage, at which point students could better understand the book's context and content on their own.

Interest

Even more important than format or background knowledge is whether or not a book interests the student. Research shows that interest is a strong factor in reading achievement (Braunger and Lewis, 1998). Sometimes students surprise us by tackling challenging material if the topic is appealing. In order to match readers to books, you should know both the abilities and the interests of your students. Surveys, informal discussions, and reading conferences can reveal your students' hobbies, interests, and activities outside of school. For instance, if I had a pile of nonfiction books on a table about a wide

Children's Literature Web Sites

Children's Literature Web Guide: http://www.acs. ucalgary.ca/~dkbrown/index.html

Katherine Schlick Noe's Literature Circles Resource Center: http://fac-staff.seattleu.edu/kschlnoe/ LitCircles

Carol Hurst's Children's Literature Site: http:// www.carolhurst.com/

Database of Award-Winning Children's Literature: http://www2.wcoil.com/~ellerbee/childlit.html

Book Links (American Library Association): http:// www.ala.org/BookLinks/

International Reading Association: http://www.ira.org

National Council of Teachers of English: http://www. ncte.org/

range of topics such as secret codes, origami, penguins, and the digestive system, I know exactly which book my son, Bruce, would choose. He loves learning about penguins and reads every book he can find on the subject, irrespective of the reading level. In fact, that is one of the appealing qualities of nonfiction. Offering a wide range of topics provides a chance to connect readers and their passions with literature.

In addition, you also should be familiar with children's literature. One of the best ways to find good children's books is to talk to your students and your colleagues about books. Both *Booklinks* (American Library Association) and *The Reading Teacher* (International Reading Association) offer excellent book reviews. There are also valuable resources on the Internet with reviews of books, as well as sites where you can search for books on a particular topic or even write to authors.

Balancing the List

Nonfiction

I made a concerted effort to include nonfiction, as well as fiction, at each stage. Nonfiction includes autobiographies, biographies, and informational books. There has been a virtual explosion of appealing nonfiction in the last few years, from the colorful *Emergent Science Readers* (Scholastic) at the Emerging level, to the fascinating *Eyewitness* books at the Connecting stage. These books, however, are often not well known by title. Although you may recognize fiction titles like *Holes* (Louis Sachar, 1998) or *Jumanji* (Chris van Allsburg, 1981), it is harder to recognize a book about sharks just by looking at the title. Since you may recognize a series, I tried to include one book from several different nonfiction series. I encourage you to locate the books on this list at a library or bookstore. Once you read these engaging texts, you will probably want to add some of these titles to your classroom collection. A few representative nonfiction texts have been included at each stage to serve as examples. I also tried to list at least one or two books by some of the best nonfiction writers, such as Patricia Lauber, Milton Meltzer, Russell Freedman, Seymour Simon, and David Adler.

Magazines

Many children find magazines appealing since the text is not as dense as fiction. Like adults, they can read magazines flexibly, flipping back and forth, and reading articles that look interesting. The photographs and illustrations in some magazines are designed to attract young readers. Magazines also provide a link to students' interests. For instance, my three children each subscribed to different magazines. In fourth grade, Keith pored over each issue of *Sports Illustrated for Kids* when it arrived in the mail. At the same age, Bruce preferred *Zillions: Consumer Reports for Kids*, and Laura's favorite magazine was *Stone Soup*. The Book Lists and database include a few representative magazine suggestions for the Expanding through Independent stages. The levels are intended to reflect the stage at which a student can read the magazine *independently with strong comprehension*. You can use the same magazines at earlier stages as read alouds at home or for guided reading at school.

Poetry

Leveling poetry presents quite a challenge, since many of the books can be used at different grade levels for shared and guided reading, as well as in literature circles and for choral reading. The poetry books listed here are included in the stage at which students can read the text *independently*. For instance, Lee Bennett Hopkins, *I Can Read* book, *Weather* (1994), contains simple poems that students at the Beginning stage can read on their own. Some young adults at the Connecting and Independent stages might appreciate collections of romantic poetry, such as *Buried Alive: The Elements of Love* (Ralph Fletcher, 1996) or *I Feel a Little Jumpy Around You: A Book of Her Poems and His Poems Collected in Paris* (Naomi Shihab Nye and Paul Janeczko, 1996). Others might find Arnold Adoff's collection of sports poems (*Sports Pages*, 1986) more appealing.

In her books for teachers, *Awakening the Heart* (1999) and *For the Good of the Earth and Sun* (1989), Georgia Heard suggests that poetry belongs in the classroom all year long, rather than only during poetry month. She recommends innumerable ways in which poetry can be shared and woven into the everyday fabric of your classroom. You may want to read poetry aloud since students may not gravitate to this genre unless they have been exposed to engaging poems that connect with their lives and interests. Many children delight in the humorous poetry by Shel Silverstein and Jack Prelutsky, but it's important to expose students to other types of poetry as well. I included only a few representative samples at each stage, but hope you will add your own favorite collections of poetry to this list and the database.

Series Books (📖)

Many series books are included on the list, particularly at the Beginning, Expanding, and Bridging stages. In order to keep the list to a reasonable size, I only recorded one or two representative books in each series. For instance, *Redwall* (Brian Jacques, 1986) is listed on the Key Benchmark Books list, Book List, and in the database, although there are now 14 books in the series. A book symbol (📖) is used on the list to indicate when a title is part of a series, or if it has a prequel or sequel. If I included every fascinating biography by Russell Freedman, all the great Dorling Kindersley informational books, or even all the new Harry Potter books by J. K. Rowling, the list would have become huge. I kept reminding myself that this was a list of *Key Benchmark Books* rather than an all-encompassing list of every good book for children.

Classics and Recent Books

A few of the books on this list are older titles, such as *My Father's Dragon* (Ruth Gannett, 1948) and *Henry and Ribsy* (Beverly Cleary, 1954), which some of you may remember from your own childhood. Many students still enjoy these classics. The bulk of the list, however, is composed of new titles. Half of the titles, particularly nonfiction, were published in the last ten years. By using the database included with the book, you can keep adding new titles to the list.

When you look at the titles on the Key Benchmark Books lists, remember that my goal was to choose ten books at each stage that most teachers would recognize. Therefore, I selected many older titles, such as the *Nancy Drew* mysteries (Carolyn Keene) or *The Great Gilly Hopkins* (Katherine Paterson, 1978), rather than including newer titles that some teachers may not have read. More recent titles are included on the Book Lists and in the database.

Warnings!

Not All Books Should Be Leveled

I wrestled with several issues as I worked on this chapter. First, not every book in your room needs to be leveled. At a recent workshop, one of the teachers said, "But we can't use any of the books you brought because they aren't leveled!" Knowing the level of a book is only one piece of information; you also need to trust your own intuition and experience to match children to books. If you are familiar with children's literature and have taught for a while, you are probably pretty good at helping your students find the right books. The purpose of this chapter is not to level every book, but rather to develop broad guidelines that can help you meet the needs of students at a specific stage on the reading continuum. The purpose of reading should not be to pass a test and race to the next level in a published program. Rather, we want our students to become engaged and self-motivated life-long readers.

No Child Fits Neatly Into One Stage

I want to emphasize that these are not discrete stages, but a continuum. Not all the books a child reads fit neatly into one stage. Children's skills may vary, depending on the difficulty of the text, their interest, and their energy on a particular day. Children may also read easy books for relaxation and harder books to challenge themselves or because they are interested in a topic. The categories are merely intended to provide broad brushstrokes as you try to capture a picture of each student as a reader in order to chart growth over time.

Books Are Leveled According to Independent Reading

When some teachers look at the list, they exclaim, "Oh, but I've used that book in third grade" when they see it has been placed at the Developing level. It's important to keep in mind that these are books that students can read *on their own with good comprehension*. The levels were created based on a student's *independent reading*, which means that a student should have 95% accuracy rate and strong comprehension. If a student's accuracy rate is 90–94%, you may want to use the book for literature circles or guided reading.

How can you determine a child's reading level? For younger readers, running records (Clay, 2000) provide a research-based and informative way to assess each child's level of reading accuracy. With older students, you may want to use the Reading Conference form or Informal Miscue Analysis form described in Chapter 5. When Cindy Flegenheimer notes Patrick's reading level on the continuum, she records what types of books he reads independently by using her anecdotal notes taken during silent reading time. She also uses her reading conference notes, informal conversations, and Patrick's log for additional information.

The only discrepancies between the Book Lists by continuum stages in this book and the *Fountas and Pinnell Guided Reading Leveling System*™ (Fountas and Pinnell, 1999, 2001) occurred with novels for older readers. At first, I was concerned that the continuum levels and guided reading levels were one stage apart for approximately 50 of the 200 books for intermediate readers. I believe that this was due to the different criteria we used to level books. *The Fountas and Pinnell Guided Reading Leveling System*™ from *Matching Books to Readers* (1999) and *Guiding Readers and Writers Grades 3–6* (2001) was designed specifically for *guided reading*, in which adults provide background information or assist with vocabulary. Students are reading texts with 90–94% accuracy. Classroom discussions may also help students understand the texts. As mentioned earlier, I leveled books according to a student's ability to read the same book *independently* with 95–100% accuracy and solid comprehension.

As you select books to use with your students, you may want to consider whether the book will be used with the support of guided reading or literature circle discussions, or if the book will be used for independent reading. Rather than using full-length novels for guided reading in the intermediate grades, I prefer to use shorter texts, picture books, nonfiction materials, or poetry. Reading strategies and comprehension skills can be taught through your read aloud books and small group literature circles. Since many teachers level books, I decided to include both guided reading levels and continuum stages in the hope that you can then decide the most appropriate way to use a book with particular students.

Don't Push Students Into Books That Are Too Hard

Have you ever tried to edit for punctuation and read for content at the same time? It is difficult to read for two purposes at once. In the same way, students who read texts that are too difficult often struggle with comprehension. In his book, *What Really Matters for Struggling Readers* (2001), Richard Allington writes:

> The researchers found that success rates had a substantial impact
> on student learning. They produced strong, consistent evidence
> that tasks completed with high rates of success were linked to
> greater learning and improved student attitudes toward the sub-

ject matter being learned, while tasks where students were moderately successful were less consistently related to learning and hard tasks produced a negative impact on learning (p. 44).

If you want to improve students' reading skills, students need practice with *new* strategies using *easier* texts. Regie Routman notes, "Especially for our struggling readers who learn at a slower pace, daily practice reading accessible books is absolutely essential for developing confidence and success" (2000, p. 111). One of the key reasons for leveling books is to become better at choosing the right books with enough challenge so that new learning occurs, yet providing enough support so that students can concentrate on making meaning.

Books Can Be Re-Read for Deeper Understanding

Research shows that multiple readings of books is important for solidifying children's reading skills and strategies (Braunger and Lewis, 1998). Books can be introduced during shared or guided reading, then students can practice using the same texts independently as they build fluency. Although the book lists and database provide general reading levels for books, it is important to recognize that as students re-read books, the amount of support that you provide can decrease.

Books can also be read and re-read to peel back new layers of meaning. The more we bring to a text, the more we can glean from it. For example, when my daughter, Laura, was in second grade, I read aloud *A Wrinkle in Time* (Madeleine L'Engle, 1962) and we talked about the book. She then re-read the book in fourth grade. This year in middle school, she read it again and commented about how much she missed when she read the book earlier. Many books can be read aloud or in literature circles when a child's understanding is supported by the discussions. A book like *The Giver* (Lois Lowry, 1993) could be read aloud to students at the Bridging or Fluent stages. This thought-provoking book would also be perfect for literature circle discussions in which a group of students constructs meaning together. It may not be until the Connecting stage, however, that students will be able to follow the concepts and understand the novel on their own.

Trust Your Professional Instincts, Experience, and Judgment

It is sometimes hard to feel confident as a teacher. Although the standards movement has provided some benefits to education, it has also placed a disproportionate emphasis on test and test results. When program funding or teachers' or principals' jobs are linked to test results, an inordinate and inappropriate value is placed upon this sole (and questionable) measure of student learning. The result has been a dramatic undermining of many teachers' confidence in themselves as professionals. Successful teachers doubt themselves and sometimes resort to methods or materials that clash with their beliefs. It is important to remember that *we* are the experts. My hope is that the continuums, the Book Lists, and the database will validate what you know and provide some useful guidelines. Matching students to the right book is an art. You are the person best able to match a child's interests, abilities, and background knowledge with a particular book or story. You can also determine whether a text would best be used as a read aloud, for shared or guided reading, in literature circles, or as an independent reading choice.

Although I know that many of you will find the lists and database in this chapter extremely valuable, I still had many reservations while writing this chapter. I worry that teachers may become so caught up in leveling books that they disregard their experience and intuition. In some cases, factors such as interest may be more important to consider than text difficulty. The success of the *Harry Potter* series by J. K. Rowling is a perfect example of how excitement about a book can spark even young or struggling students to read such long and challenging fantasy novels. I trust that this chapter will be a catalyst for conversations about books and readers and that each of you will adapt and modify the lists and database. Rather than providing simple answers, I hope this chapter will contribute to ongoing professional conversations.

Continuum Stages, Guided Reading, and Other Connections

The task of leveling books by continuum stages was made tremendously easier with the publication of *Matching Books to Readers: Using Leveled Books in Guided Reading K–3* (1999) and *Guiding Readers and Writers Grades 3–6* (2001) by Irene Fountas and Gay Su Pinnell. These well-known educators have leveled approximately 8,500 titles for grades K–6. Both books include lists of books, ordered alphabetically by title. The second half of their lists include the same titles, organized by guided reading levels (A–Z). I would like to thank Irene Fountas, Gay Su Pinnell, and Heinemann Publishers for their generosity in allowing me to use the *Fountas and Pinnell Guided Reading Leveling System*™ levels in the lists in this book and on the database.

For years teachers have asked for a chart that shows the connection between continuum stages and materials for teaching and assessing readers. The Correlation Chart (Figure 4.2) shows how the continuum correlates to ages, grade levels, book format, guided reading levels (according to the *Fountas and Pinnell Guided Reading Leveling System*™), Reading Recovery levels, and the Developmental Reading Assessment (Beaver, 1997). It is important to remember that these are approximate levels and comparisons.

Ages

A continuum highlights the developmental nature of literacy acquisition. An eight-year-old could be at the Beginning, Expanding, or even Bridging stage on the continuum, although no child falls neatly into one stage or the other. Most children will exhibit skills and strategies across two, or even three stages. Notice that there are three-year age spans for elementary students. By middle school, growth occurs more subtly and the stages include four-year age ranges (more about this issue is addressed in Chapter 10). No age ranges are listed for the Independent stage, since many of these skills are ones that we are still fine-tuning as adults.

Grade Levels

A developmental philosophy is the foundation for multiage classrooms. Multiage classrooms with two-year or even three-year grade spans are far more common in other countries than they are in the United States, especially in Canada, Australia, and New Zealand. The continuums are a perfect match for those class-

Continuum Correlation Chart

Continuum Stage	Ages	Grade Level	Book Format	Guided Reading Level*	Recovery	DRA
Preconventional	3–5	PreK/K	Wordless Books, Label Books	A	1	A, 1
Emerging	4–6	K 1	Highly Predictable	A B C D	1–6	1–4
Developing (Early)	5–7	K 1	Pattern Books	E F	6–10	6, 8, 10
Developing (Later)	5–7	K 1 2	Pattern Books	F G	9–12	10, 12
Beginning (Early)	6–8	K 1 2	Simple Early-Readers	H I J	13–16	14, 16
Beginning (Later)	6–8	1 2 3	Harder Early-Readers	J K L	17–20	18, 20
Expanding (Early)	7–9	1 2 3	Easy Chapter Books	L M N		24, 28
Expanding (Later)	7–9	2 3 4	Easy Chapter Books	M N O		30, 34
Bridging (Early)	8–10	2 3 4	Medium Level Chapter Books	O P Q		34, 38
Bridging (Later)	8–10	3 4 5	Medium Level Chapter Books	P Q R		40
Fluent	9–11	4 5 6	Challenging Chapter Books	R S T U		44+
Proficient	10–13	5 6 7	Complex Chapter Books	T U V W		
Connecting	11–14	6 7 8	Complex Books Young Adult Books	V W X Y		
Independent		7 8+	Young Adult Books Adult Books	X Y Z		

* Fountas and Pinnell Guided Reading Leveling System™

Figure 4.2 Continuum Correlation Chart

rooms. Teachers can pinpoint where students are and can plan instruction based on students' needs and strengths, rather than on grade level. In the United States, multiage classrooms are becoming more rare, partly due to the enormous pressure for testing, particularly in fourth grade. The rhetoric espoused by politicians that "all students will read by third grade" is unrealistic given the range of students in our classrooms. What do politicians mean by "grade level"? What do they mean by "reads well"? What types of texts do they mean? How will they measure reading achievement? In addition, this often-quoted goal ignores the challenges faced by students coming to school with far fewer literacy interactions or those for whom English is not their first language. Expecting all students to read equally well at age 9 is as preposterous as expecting all infants to begin walking at 12 months. Learning to walk usually occurs between the ages of 9 and 15 months. If children are walking at 7 months or not walking by 18 months, parents become concerned. Passing a law that all children will walk by the age of 1 will not change the normal developmental time line unique to each individual child. Of course, we want children to walk and read and write well, but they will not all learn at the same time or in the same way. The educational system in the United States, however, is usually structured around the concept of grade levels. As teachers, you probably have almost a two-year age span within your own group of students. Figure 4.2 shows the connection between continuumn stages and grade levels. By editing the continuum on the CD-ROM, you can make changes based on your state and district standards, benchmarks, and population.

Guided Reading

The value of the guided reading work by Irene Fountas and Gay Su Pinnell was discussed earlier in this chapter. With their permission, I included general guided reading levels in Figure 4.2 using the *Fountas and Pinnell Guided Reading Leveling System*™. By including three guided reading levels at each of the continuum stages, I created an overlapping and rather broad range of books. In the Jefferson County School District near Denver, Colorado, the level of accountability is so high that the district has created clear benchmarks and exit levels for students at each grade level. The district chart in Jefferson County includes only two guided reading levels at each continuum stage. For instance, I have guided reading levels at the Early Beginning continuum stage as equivalent to the "H, I, J" levels in guided reading. In Jefferson County, the students at the same stage are expected to read texts at guided reading levels of only "H" and "I." I listed the broader developmental range in the figure and charts, but the narrower range is indicated in bold print. You may wish to modify the charts and Figure 4.2 to match your own district and state requirements. The figure was included here as a general frame of reference. The levels for books according to the *Fountas and Pinnell Guided Reading Leveling System*™ are included on the Book Lists by stages (in parentheses after the title) and for approximately 25% of the books in the database.

Reading Recovery

Many primary teachers use Marie Clay's Reading Recovery levels as they work with young readers. Publishers often include Reading Recovery levels for their primary texts. The levels (up through level 20) are particularly useful for the fine gradation of texts used in Reading Recovery programs, as well as for primary teachers. You can see from Figure 4.2 how Reading Recovery levels match the first four stages of the reading continuum.

Developmental Reading Assessment (DRA)

Many districts and states that are requiring standardized testing for K–3 students have decided to use the Developmental Reading Assessment (DRA) (Beaver, 1997). This individually-administered assessment provides practical diagnostic information for teachers. Based on the work in Jefferson County School District near Denver, Colorado, Figure 4.2 also shows how DRA levels match continuum stages.

Independent vs Guided Reading

It is important to recognize that the DRA levels and the books listed by continuum stages are based on students' *independent* reading levels. The difference between *guided reading* and *independent reading* is quite significant in the primary grades. In order to consolidate their skills as readers, children at the Emerging and Developing stages need to re-read books many times on their own that they may have been introduced to during shared or guided reading. In addition to considering the level of a book, you also need to decide the level of support you will provide.

I have learned a tremendous amount in the process of writing this chapter and creating these lists. I want to thank all the teachers who helped me fine-tune this list. I'm also deeply grateful that my colleagues, Katherine L. Schlick Noe and Nancy J. Johnson, generously allowed me to use and build upon the database we created for *The Literature Circles Resource Guide* (Hill, Schlick Noe, and Johnson, 2001). The database in this book would not have been possible without the endless days they spent leveling books, filling in missing information, and annotating books. I hope that this chapter sparks valuable conversations with your colleagues as you talk about reading development and children's literature.

Following the staff development suggestions, the next section of this chapter begins with the list of Key Benchmark Books. The remainder of the section is organized by continuum stages and contains a general description of readers at each stage. Each stage contains a chart that includes the continuum descriptors and book characteristics. The charts are followed by the book lists for each stage. The charts and book lists are also included on the CD-ROM in the section on Continuum Support for Reading. You may want to keep a copy of the Key Benchmark Books and Book Lists in your Continuum Notebook.

Staff Development

One of the best ways to help teachers become familiar with the reading continuum is to do a "book sort." Block out an hour during a staff meeting or after school. Gather a stack of books from the Book List included in this chapter. It is helpful to have approximately three or four books per person. Place a stack of books of varying levels on each table before teachers arrive, along with a copy of the reading continuum. Next, set out ten tubs, one for each of the ten stages on the continuum. Ask teachers to sit in mixed groups, rather than sitting by grade levels. The best conversations usually occur when there are teachers from several grade levels in each group. The teachers should then sort the books into continuum stages. For instance, at what stage do they think children can read *Shiloh* (Phyllis Reynolds Naylor, 1991) *independently*? Rember that this means that the student can comprehend the text *without* discussion, adult support, or the teacher providing background information. It is important to have copies of the reading continuum available so that teachers can refer to the descriptors at each stage. As teachers sort the books, they begin to understand the descriptors on the reading continuum more clearly.

Once the books are sorted, hand each table one tub of books, representing one stage on the continuum. Ask teachers to look through the books at that stage. If they feel any particular books are too hard or too easy, they must take the book to the stage where they feel that book belongs and explain their rationale to the teachers in that group. Then ask each group to list five or six key characteristics of the books in their tub. After these activities, distribute the Book Lists in this chapter and discuss their reactions. Did they put books in approximately the same stages? Were their lists of book characteristics similar to the ones in this chapter?

You may want to repeat the book sorting activity every year or two as new teachers join the staff and new titles are added to your collections. You might want to begin faculty meetings by asking different grade levels to take turns sharing new children's books they have just read or used in the classroom, along with where they would place each book on the continuum. Such conversations about books promote consistency within and between grade levels.

Figure 4.3 Book Sorting Activity

At another staff meeting, have teachers meet by grade levels to edit the list of Key Benchmark Books. Do you agree with the 10 anchor books listed for each stage? Which ones would they want to change? Once you have finalized the list, make copies for the staff. You will probably want to revise the Key Benchmark Books list every few years. Remember, there will always be a degree of subjectivity involved. It is not the list itself as much as the process that is most valuable.

During grade-level meetings, you may want to start leveling the books in your classrooms. You may want to begin with titles that are on the Key Benchmark Books or the Books by Continuum Stages lists, then level books that are not on the lists. You may also want to keep a "wish list" of titles you want to add to your collection. As you find gaps in your school or classroom collections, you might approach your principal, district, or PTA/PTO for funding to buy multiple copies of these books. Many teachers also use funds from book fairs or points from book orders to purchase new literature for their classrooms or the library.

⌐ KEY BENCHMARK BOOKS

⌐ PRECONVENTIONAL/EMERGING
Look! Look! Look! by Tana Hoban
Good Dog, Carl by Alexandra Day
School by Emily Arnold McCully
Dig, Dig by Leslie Wood
The Bath by Judy Nayer
A Party by Joy Cowley
A Toy Box by Andrea Butler
Look What I Can Do by Jose Aruego
A Zoo by Andrea Butler
Growing Colors by Bruce McMillan (NF)

⌐ EMERGING
Have You Seen My Cat? by Eric Carle
Have You Seen My Duckling? by Nancy Tafuri
Brown Bear, Brown Bear, What Do You See? by Bill Martin, Jr.
The Bicycle by Joy Cowley
I Went Walking by Sue Williams
The Chick and the Duckling by Mirra Ginsburg
I Like Books by Anthony Browne
Mary Wore Her Red Dress by Merle Peek
School Bus by Donald Crews
We Like the Sun by Ena Keo (NF)

⌐ DEVELOPING: EARLY
All By Myself by Mercer Mayer
Quick as a Cricket by Audrey Wood
Mrs. Wishy-Washy by Joy Cowley
Go, Dog, Go by P. D. Eastman
Where's Spot? by Eric Hill
Dear Zoo by Rod Campbell
A Dark, Dark Tale by Ruth Brown
Rosie's Walk by Pat Hutchins
My Puppy is Born by Joanna Cole (NF)
Our Sense by Brenda Parkes (NF)

⌐ DEVELOPING: LATER
Soccer Game! by Grace Maccarone
Cookie's Week by Cindy Ward
The Carrot Seed by Ruth Kraus
More Spaghetti, I Say! by Rita Gelman
Just Like Daddy by Frank Asch
Sheep in a Jeep by Nancy Shaw
I Like Me by Nancy Carlson
Mouse Paint by Ellen Stoll Walsh

Each Peach Pear Plum by Janet and Allan Ahlberg
Bread, Bread, Bread by Ann Morris (NF)

⚷ BEGINNING: EARLY (Early-Reader Books)
Put Me In the Zoo by Robert Lopshire
Whose Mouse Are You? by Robert Kraus
Just Me and My Puppy by Mercer Mayer
The Napping House by Audrey Wood
There's a Nightmare in My Closet by Mercer Mayer
Are You My Mother? by P. D. Eastman
Hop on Pop by Dr. Seuss
Green Eggs and Ham by Dr. Seuss
The Cat in the Hat by Dr. Seuss
Mighty Spiders by Fay Robinson (NF)

⚷ BEGINNING: LATER (Harder Early-Readers)
Mouse Soup by Arnold Lobel
Little Bear series by Else Holmelund Minarik
Oliver Button is a Sissy by Tomie de Paola
Poppleton series by Cynthia Rylant
Nate the Great series by Marjorie Weinman Sharmat
Frog and Toad series by Arnold Lobel
Henry and Mudge series by Cynthia Rylant
Pinky and Rex series by James Howe
Dancing with the Manatees by Faith McNulty (NF)
Keep the Lights Burning, Abbie by Connie and Peter Roop (NF)

⚷ EXPANDING: EARLY (Easy Chapter Books)
Polk Street series by Patricia Reilly Giff
Pee Wee Scouts series by Judy Denton
Cam Jansen series by David Adler
Junie B. Jones series by Barbara Park
Arthur series by Marc Brown
Magic Treehouse series by Mary Pope Osborne
Marvin Redpost series by Louis Sachar
Freckle Juice by Judy Blume
Bailey School Kids series by Marcia Thorton Jones and Debbie Dadey
Kate Shelley and the Midnight Express by Margaret Wetterer (NF)

⚷ EXPANDING: LATER (Easy Chapter Books)
The Littles series by John Peterson
Flat Stanley by Jeff Brown
Chalk Box Kid by Clyde Robert Bulla
Stories Julian Tells series by Ann Cameron
Pioneer Cat by William Hooks
Amber Brown series by Paula Danziger
All About Sam by Lois Lowry

Wayside School series by Louis Sachar
The Titanic: Lost . . . And Found by Judy Donnelly (NF)
Pompeii . . . Buried Alive! by Edith Kunhardt (NF)

⚬— BRIDGING: EARLY (Medium Level Chapter Books)
Ramona series by Beverly Cleary
Boxcar Children series by Gertrude Chandler Warner
Goosebumps series by R. L. Stine
How to Eat Fried Worms by Thomas Rockwell
Yang the Third series by Lensey Namioka
Baby-Sitter's Club series by Ann Martin
Superfudge series by Judy Blume
Koya DeLaney series by Eloise Greenfield
Bunnicula by Deborah and James Howe
Five Notable Inventors by Wade Hudson (NF)

⚬— BRIDGING: LATER (Medium Level Chapter Books)
Fantastic Mr. Fox by Roald Dahl
Soup and Me series by Robert Newton Peck
Encyclopedia Brown series by Donald Sobol
Bingo Brown series by Betsy Byars
The Time Warp Trio series by Jon Scieszka
Charlotte's Web by E. B. White
Babe: The Gallant Pig by Dick King-Smith
Sarah, Plain and Tall by Patricia MacLachlan
The Magic Schoolbus series by Joanna Cole (NF)
Amazing Poisonous Animals by Alexandra Parsons (Eyewitness Junior series) (NF)

⚬— FLUENT (Challenging Children's Literature)
Charlie and the Chocolate Factory by Roald Dahl
Shiloh series by Phyllis Reynolds Naylor
Nancy Drew series by Carolyn Keene
Little House series by Laura Ingalls Wilder
Hatchet by Gary Paulsen
The War with Grandpa by Robert Kimmel Smith
In the Year of the Boar and Jackie Robinson by Bette Bao Lord
The Lion, the Witch, and the Wardrobe by C. S. Lewis
My Side of the Mountain by Jean Craighead George
Muscles: Our Muscular System series by Seymour Simon (NF)

⚬— PROFICIENT (Complex Children's Literature)
The Watsons Go to Birmingham – 1963 by Christopher Paul Curtis
Julie of the Wolves by Jean Craighead George
The Boggart by Susan Cooper
Number the Stars by Lois Lowry
Bridge to Terabithia by Katherine Paterson
Holes by Louis Sachar

Island of the Blue Dolphins by Scott O'Dell
Maniac Magee by Jerry Spinelli
You Want Women to Vote, Lizzie Stanton? by Jean Fritz (NF)
Immigrant Kids by Russell Freedman (NF)

⚷ **CONNECTING (Complex Children's Literature/Young Adult Literature)**
A Wrinkle in Time by Madeleine L'Engle
The True Confessions of Charlotte Doyle by Avi
The Witch of Blackbird Pond by Elizabeth George Speare
Slave Dancer by Paula Fox
Roll of Thunder, Hear My Cry by Mildred Taylor
Redwall series by Brian Jacques
The Giver by Lois Lowry
The View from Saturday by E. L. Konigsburg
Nightjohn by Gary Paulsen
Children of the Dust Bowl by Jerry Stanley (NF)

⚷ **INDEPENDENT (Young Adult Literature)**
Shabanu by Suzanne Fisher Staples
Ironman by Chris Crutcher
The Hobbit series by J. R. Tolkien
The Devil's Arithmetic by Jane Yolen
The Golden Compass series by Philip Pullman
The Outsiders by S. E. Hinton
The Ear, the Eye, and the Arm by Nancy Farmer
Anne Frank: The Diary of a Young Girl (autobiography) by Anne Frank (NF)
Children of Topaz by Michael O. Tunnell and George Chilcoat (NF)
Lincoln: A Photobiography (biography) by Russell Freedman (NF)

Books for Preconventional Readers (Ages 3–5)

Children at the Preconventional stage take their first steps as readers with wordless books. Tana Hoban has written over two dozen wordless books, such as *Look! Look! Look!* (1992), that spark conversations and focus preconventional readers on details in the illustrations. These appealing texts encourage students to use their oral language to tell stories. Some children can also read simple "label books" with one or two words on a page that match the illustration or photograph. For instance, *Growing Colors* by Bruce McMillan (1988) includes pictures of objects from nature. The matching label is a color word (e.g., "yellow" for a sunflower). By matching pictures to a word, children begin to focus on print and mimic the reading behaviors of siblings and adults. Many of these simple texts are published by The Wright Group, Steck-Vaughn, Scholastic, Modern Curriculum Press, and Rigby.

| Preconventional Readers and Book Characteristics ||
Student Behaviors	Book Characteristics
• Begins to choose reading materials (e.g., books, magazines, and charts) and has favorites. • Shows interest in reading signs, labels, and logos (environmental print). • Recognizes own name in print. • Holds book and turns pages correctly. • Shows beginning/end of book or story. • Knows some letter names. • Listens and responds to literature. • Comments on illustrations in books. • Participates in group reading (books, rhymes, poems, and songs).	• Illustrations provide strong support. • Some texts are wordless. • Some texts have 1–2 words per page. • Some texts have one line of print per page. • Illustrations appear on every page. • Illustrations closely match the text. • Illustrations often show concrete and familiar objects or actions. • Print placement is consistent. • Simple text follows consistent structure. • Text includes clear spacing between words. • Print is large and clear. **Fountas and Pinnell Guided Reading Leveling System™: A**

Preconventional Book List

Fiction

⚿ *Look! Look! Look!* by Tana Hoban
   The Snowman by Raymond Briggs
   Sunshine by Jan Ormerod 📖
   In the Woods by Ermanno Cristini
⚿ *Good Dog, Carl* by Alexandra Day 📖
   The Trunk by Brian Wildsmith
   A Boy, a Dog and a Frog by Mercer Mayer
⚿ *School* by Emily Arnold McCully
   Of Color and Things by Tana Hoban
   Early Morning in the Barn by Nancy Tafuri
   Peter Spier's Rain by Peter Spier
   Who's Counting? by Nancy Tafuri
   I See a Song by Eric Carle
   Deep In the Forest by Brian Turkle
   We Hide, You Seek by Jose Aruego
   Animals A to Z by David McPhail
   Tabby by Aliki
   Change, Changes by Pat Hutchins
   One Hunter by Pat Hutchins

Tail, Toes, Eyes, Ears, Nose by Marilee Burton
Hiccup by Mercer Mayer
Going on a Lion Hunt by Harriet Ziefert and Mavis Smith
Goodnight Gorilla by Peggy Rathmann
One, Two, Three to the Zoo by Eric Carle
Pancakes for Breakfast by Tomie de Paola
Do You Want To Be My Friend? by Eric Carle (A)
Monster Muffins by Rosann Englebretson
⚬→ *Dig, Dig* by Leslie Wood (A)
⚬→ *The Bath* by Judy Nayer (A)
⚬→ *A Party* by Joy Cowley (A)
⚬→ *The Toy Box* by Andrea Butler (A)
⚬→ *Look What I Can Do* by Jose Aruego (A)

Nonfiction
I Read Signs by Tana Hoban
Family by Helen Oxenbury 📖
⚬→ *A Zoo* by Andrea Butler (A)
⚬→ *Growing Colors* by Bruce McMillan (A)

Books for Emerging Readers (Ages 4–6)

At the Emerging stage, students begin to attend to both the illustrations and print. Some of the first books that children learn to read are books with rhythm and repetition. For instance, *Have You Seen My Cat?* (Eric Carle, 1988) begins with the question in the title and the rest of the story is carried through the illustrations. Many of you have listened to students or your own children proudly "read" books like *Brown Bear, Brown Bear, What Do You See?* (Bill Martin, Jr., 1967), which they have memorized. Repeated reading and subsequent memorization provide the foundation upon which young readers can build.

Short books at this stage, like *Everyone Wears Wool* (Gare Thompson, 1997), have illustrations or photographs on each page that closely match the text. Some simple texts, such as *The Bicycle* (Joy Cowley, 1983), have only 8–10 pages. The new *Social Studies Emergent Readers* by Scholastic are examples of eight-page nonfiction books with interesting content and simple texts of two or three words. Books at the end of this list may include one or two lines of print on each page and sentences that may run onto the next page. These books can be 10–20 pages and may include simple dialogue and a few compound words.

| Emerging Readers and Book Characteristics ||
Student Behaviors	Book Characteristics
• Memorizes pattern books, poems, and familiar books. • Begins to read signs, labels, and logos (environmental print). • Demonstrates eagerness to read. • Pretends to read. • Uses illustrations to tell stories. • Reads top to bottom, left to right, and front to back with guidance. • Knows most letter names and some letter sounds. • Recognizes some names and words in context. • Makes meaningful predictions with guidance.	• Rhymes and plays with words. • Participates in reading of familiar books and poems. • Connects books read aloud to own experiences with guidance. • Texts reflect common experiences, familiar objects and actions. • Some texts include repetition of one or two sentence patterns. • Patterns change only slightly (1–2 words change). • Texts include 1–3 lines of print per page. • Texts include memorable, repetitive language patterns. • Texts include an increasing number of high frequency words. • Some texts are based on familiar rhymes and songs. • Some texts include varied opening and closing sentences. • Texts include predominantly oral language structures. • Illustrations appear on every page. • Illustrations clearly support the text. • Print placement is consistent. • Adequate spacing appears between words. • Early books are usually 8–10 pages. • Later books are 10–20 pages. **Fountas and Pinnell Guided Reading Leveling System™: A B C D**

Emerging Book List
Fiction
⚿ *Have You Seen My Cat?* by Eric Carle (B)
   Cat on the Mat by Brian Wildsmith (B) 📖
   Can You Find It? by Amy John Casey (B)
⚿ *Have You Seen My Duckling?* by Nancy Tafuri (B)
   Carrot Parrot by Jerome Martin
   Mitten, Kitten by Jerome Martin
   My Cat Muffin by Marjory Gardner (B)
   Bunny Opposites by Anne Meyers (B)
   Bo Peep's Sheep by Gare Thompson (C)

The Fox on the Box by Barbara Gregorich (C) 📖
Pigs Peek by Rhonda Cox (C)
⚷ *Brown Bear, Brown Bear, What Do You See?* by Bill Martin, Jr. (C)
⚷ *The Bicycle* by Joy Cowley (C)
The Painting by Joy Cowley (C)
Rain by Robert Kalan (C)
I Want a Pet by Barbara Gregorich (C)
Up Went the Goat by Barbara Gregorich (C)
⚷ *I Went Walking* by Sue Williams (C)
Every Monday by Gare Thompson (C)
Now We Can Go by Ann Jonas
Ben's Pets by Anne Miranda (C)
⚷ *The Chick and the Duckling* by Mirra Ginsburg (D)
⚷ *I Like Books* by Anthony Browne (D)
⚷ *Mary Wore Her Red Dress and Henry Wore His Green Sneakers* by Merle Peek (D)
Whistle Like a Bird by Sarah Vázquez (D)
Look Up, Look Down by Tana Hoban (D)
Going to the Pool by Ena Keo (D)
Hide and Seek by Roberta Brown and Sue Carey (D)
The Bear Escapes by Gare Thompson (D)
Bears on Wheels by Stan and Jan Berenstain (D)
What Is Big? by Shane Armstrong and Susan Hartley (D)
Me Too by Susan Winter
The Haircut by Susan Hartley and Shane Armstrong (D)
I Can by Susan Winter
The Good Bad Cat by Nancy Antle (D) 📖
Things I Like by Anthony Browne (D)

Nonfiction
Everyone Wears Wool by Gare Thompson (A)
Rainforest Colors by Susan Canizares and Betsey Chessen (B)
Dancing by Susan Canizares and Betsey Chessen (B)
Playground Opposites by Anne Meyers (B)
⚷ *We Like the Sun* by Ena Keo (C)
A Busy Week by Katherine Mead (D)
⚷ *School Bus* by Donald Crews (D)
It Sounds Like Music by Sarah Vázquez (D)
My Skin by Alan Whitaker (D)

Books for Developing Readers (Ages 5–7)

Developing readers encounter more challenging texts as the books become less predictable and readers must focus on the print and use their growing decoding skills. Children at the Developing stage read more challenging pattern books. In some texts, whole sentences may be repeated (e.g., *All by Myself* by Mercer Mayer, 1983). As books become more difficult, only a few phrases or words may be repeated (e.g., *I Like Books* by Anthony Browne, 1988). In *Cookie's Week* (Cindy Ward,

1988), the days of the week and the illustrations provide cues for young readers. Rhyming text and supporting illustrations can also help Developing readers read more demanding pattern books (e.g., *Quick as a Cricket* by Audrey Wood, 1990.

Books at this stage use more literary language and include some challenging vocabulary, although the text is still supported by the story line and the illustrations. Print placement can vary and sentences are longer. Books at the beginning of this stage are usually about children's everyday events and experiences. These books often have 2–4 lines of print on a page and range from 10–20 pages. At this stage, students rely on both the illustrations and the print to make meaning. Children read slowly and you can see their eyes move back and forth between the words and the pictures as they cross check for meaning. It is vital that students read texts at the appropriate level as they incorporate new reading strategies into their repertoire.

Later in this stage, texts are a bit longer (10–32 pages), with more challenging vocabulary. Some books still contain the support of rhyme (e.g., *Sheep in a Jeep* by Nancy Shaw, 1986) or repetition (e.g., *Just Like Daddy* by Frank Asch, 1981). Developing readers can read simple nonfiction books about a single topic, like *My Puppy is Born* (Joanna Cole, 1991) or *Bread, Bread, Bread* (Ann Morris, 1989).

Developing Readers and Book Characteristics (Early)	
Student Behaviors	**Book Characteristics**
• Reads books with simple patterns. • Begins to read own writing. • Begins to read independently for short periods (5–10 minutes). • Discusses favorite reading material with others. • Relies on illustrations and print. • Uses finger-print-voice matching. • Knows most letter sounds and letter clusters. • Recognizes simple words. • Uses growing awareness of sound segments (e.g., phonemes, syllables, rhymes) to read words. • Begins to make meaningful predictions. • Identifies titles and authors in literature (text features). • Retells main event or idea in literature. • Participates in guided literature discussions. • Sees self as reader. • Explains why literature is liked/disliked during class discussions with guidance.	• Texts reflect common experiences. • Texts include conventional story structure. • Some texts include simple patterns. • Some texts include varied sentence patterns or repetition of two or more sentence patterns. • Vocabulary reappears throughout text. • Illustrations appear on every page. • Illustrations provide strong support. • Texts include straightforward and simple vocabulary. • Print placement varies. • Texts usually include 2–4 lines of print per page. • Texts are usually 10–20 pages. **Fountas and Pinnell Guided Reading Leveling System™: E F**

Developing Book List (Early)

Fiction

    Inside, Outside, Upside Down by Stan and Jan Berenstain (E)

⌐ *All By Myself* by Mercer Mayer (E) 📖

⌐ *Quick as a Cricket* by Audrey Wood

⌐ *Mrs. Wishy-Washy* by Joy Cowley (E) 📖

⌐ *Go, Dog, Go* by P. D. Eastman (E)

    The Gum on the Drum by Barbara Gregorich (E)

⌐ *Where's Spot?* by Eric Hill (E) 📖

    When We Are Big by Marilyn Minkoff (E)

⌐ *Dear Zoo* by Rod Campbell (F)

    Five Little Monkeys Jumping on the Bed by Eileen Christelow (E)

⌐ *A Dark, Dark Tale* by Ruth Brown (F)

⌐ *Rosie's Walk* by Pat Hutchins (F)

    Teeny Tiny Woman by Jane O'Connor (F)

    Ear Book by Al Perkins (E)

    Foot Book by Dr. Seuss (E)

    Yummy, Yummy by Judith Grey (F)

    Are You There Bear? by Ron Maris (F)

    The Fishy Alphabet Story by Joanne and David Wylie (F)

    Have You Seen the Crocodile? by Colin West (F)

    Here Comes a Bus by Harriet Ziefert (F)

    Sam the Scarecrow by Sharon Gordon (F)

Poetry

    Play Day: A Book of Terse Verse by Bruce McMillan

Nonfiction Titles

⌐ *My Puppy is Born* by Joanna Cole

    Bear Facts by Gare Thompson (E)

    I Can Be Anything by Ena Keo (E)

    Schools Around the World by Donald Mitchell (E)

    Great White Sharks by Christine Price (F)

    Who Lives in the Woods? by Anne Meyers (F)

⌐ *Our Senses* by Brenda Parkes (F)

Developing Readers and Book Characteristics (Later)	
Student Behaviors	**Book Characteristics**
• Reads books with simple patterns. • Begins to read own writing. • Begins to read independently for short periods (5–10 minutes). • Discusses favorite reading material with others. • Relies on illustrations and print. • Knows most letter sounds and letter clusters. • Recognizes simple words. • Uses growing awareness of sound segments (e.g., phonemes, syllables, rhymes) to read words. • Begins to make meaningful predictions. • Identifies titles and authors in literature (text features). • Retells main event or idea in literature. • Participates in guided literature discussions. • Sees self as reader. • Explains why literature is liked/disliked during class discussions with guidance.	• Texts reflect common experiences. • Texts include conventional story structure. • Text is less predictable. • Some texts include varied sentence patterns or repetition of three or more sentence patterns. • Vocabulary reappears throughout text. • Illustrations provide support for text. • Illustrations appear on every page. • Texts include straightforward and simple vocabulary. • Print size and placement vary. • Texts usually include 2–4 lines of print per page. • Texts are usually 10–32 pages. **Fountas and Pinnell Guided Reading Leveling System™: F G**

Developing Book List (Later)

Fiction

⚬ *Soccer Game!* by Grace Maccarone (F)

⚬ *Cookie's Week* by Cindy Ward (F)

   Goldilocks Comes Back by Anne Meyers (F)

   Across the Stream by Mirra Ginsburg (F)

⚬ *The Carrot Seed* by Ruth Kraus (G)

⚬ *More Spaghetti, I Say!* by Rita G. Gelman (G)

⚬ *Just Like Daddy* by Frank Asch (F)

   Baby Bear's Present by Beverly Randall (F)

   The 100ᵗʰ Day of School by Angela Medearis

   Agree by Janet Craig (F)

   Amy Loves the Snow by Julia Hoban (F)

⚬ *Sheep in a Jeep* by Nancy Shaw (G) 📖

   Muffy and Fluffy: The Kittens Who Didn't

   Frog's Lunch by Dee Lillegard (G)

   Here Comes Winter by Janet Craig (G)

   The Fat Cat Sat on the Mat by Nurit Karlin (G)

   Steve's Room by Mindy Menschell (G)

   The Amazing Fish by Christine Price (G)

   Buzz Said the Bee by Wendy Cheyette Lewison (G)

   Benny's School Trip by Gare Thompson (G)

⚬ *I Like Me* by Nancy Carlson

   Just for You by Mercer Mayer (G)

⚬ *Mouse Paint* by Ellen Stoll Walsh

⚬ *Each Peach Pear Plum* by Janet and Allan Ahlberg (G)

Nonfiction Titles

⚬ *Bread, Bread, Bread* by Ann Morris (F)

   Lift Off! by Gare Thompson (G)

   Frogs by Tom Williams (G)

   Dinosaurs, Dinosaurs by Byron Barton (G)

   Dragonflies by Gary Torrisi (G)

Books for Beginning Readers (Ages 6–8)

Young readers take a big leap as they move into the Beginning stage. They begin reading early-reader books, which have illustrations on every page, often contain repetition, and yet are clearly not "chapter books." These books are labeled as *Early Readers* in the database.

Simple Early-Reader Books

Continuum Stage – Early Beginning; Fountas and Pinnell Guided Reading Leveling System™ Levels H, I, J; Reading Recovery Levels 13–16; DRA Levels 14,16; Length 10–50 pages.

At the start of the Beginning stage, students begin to read some simple picture books with a supporting pattern, such as *Is Your Mama a Llama?* (Deborah Guarino,

1989). The illustrations play an important role in these books and clearly match the text. Some early readers, such as Mercer Mayer's *Critter* books have one sentence on a page with pictures that provide clues to readers as they try to figure out new words.

Some texts are written specifically for beginning readers and contain simple story lines (e.g., *Hop on Pop* by Dr. Seuss, 1963) and bear labels with "I Can Read It All By Myself" or "Beginner Book." These books can range from 10–50 pages long and often contain some repetition in the text for support, (e.g., *Green Eggs and Ham* by Dr. Seuss, 1960). Picture books at this stage often contain repeated phrases or sentences, like *The Napping House* (Audrey Wood, 1984). Other early readers provide support through the use of rhyme (*Jamberry* by Bruce Degan, 1983). Print placement and size may vary, and the text is usually double-spaced and does not always run from margin to margin. Most stories include a simple plot with only a few characters. Books begin to include adjectives and descriptive language, which sometimes present a challenge for beginning readers.

In the last 10 years, more and more well-written books in a variety of genres have been published for readers at this level. Some of the nonfiction books at the early part of the Beginning stage impart information using narrative text, such as *Mighty Spiders* (Fay Robinson, 1996). Other books, such as the *First Discovery Books* by Scholastic with their attractive clear acetate pages, present several facts about a topic with more challenging vocabulary.

HARDER EARLY-READER Books

Continuum Stage – Later Beginning; Fountas and Pinnell Guided Reading Leveling System™ Levels J, K, L; Reading Recovery Levels 17–20; DRA Levels 18, 20; Length 20–75 pages.

Later in the Beginning stage, children begin to read the first books that look like chapter books, such as the *Henry and Mudge* series by Cynthia Rylant or the *Frog and Toad* series by Arnold Lobel. More difficult early readers often contain a few characters, a series of events, and more dialogue. The print is still large and the illustrations provide some support for the text. These books are often labeled "I Can Read," "Ready to Read," or "Easy to Read" on the cover and are less than 75 pages long. Some books are leveled by publishers, such as the *Hello Reader* series published by Scholastic. These books are identified as "harder early-readers" because they are divided into sections that are not clearly marked as "chapters." They often include page numbers and sometimes have a table of contents. Harder early readers are books with illustrations on every page or two, large print, and yet are not yet divided into numbered chapters. These books are also labeled as *Early Readers* in the database.

Some of the nonfiction books in the later half of the Beginning stage introduce new formats, such as directions (e.g., *Gifts to Make* by Barbara Burt, 1998) or recipes. At this stage, students often begin to read simple historical fiction that does not require much background knowledge, such as *Keep the Lights Burning, Abbie* (Peter and Connie Roop, 1985).

Another challenge in leveling books lies in understanding children's conceptual development. Have you ever read *Amelia Bedelia* books (Peggy Parrish) to second graders? Half of the class understands the puns, while the other students try to figure out why their friends are laughing. In addition, not all the *Amelia Bedelia* books are the same. The Avon Camelot editions use a smaller type than the Harper Trophy versions. This transitional series sparked many debates. The *Amelia Bedelia* books are therefore listed near the end of the Beginning list, since they serve as transition books into the next stage.

Beginning Readers and Book Characteristics (Early)	
Student Behaviors	**Book Characteristics**
• Reads simple early-reader books. • Reads and follows simple written directions with guidance. • Identifies basic genres (e.g., fiction, nonfiction, and poetry). • Uses basic punctuation when reading orally. • Reads independently (10–15 minutes). • Chooses reading materials independently. • Learns and shares information from reading. • Uses meaning cues (context). • Uses sentence cues (grammar). • Uses letter/sound cues and patterns (phonics). • Recognizes word endings, common contractions, and many high frequency words. • Begins to self-correct. • Retells beginning, middle, and end with guidance. • Discusses characters and story events with guidance. • Identifies own reading behaviors with guidance.	• Fewer texts provide rhyme and repetition as support • Many books contain simple story line with a few repeated phrases. • Fairy/folk tales are retold using simpler vocabulary and language structure. • Texts may include literary language (more formal). • Text includes some descriptive language and details. • Texts include simple plots and only a few characters. • Illustrations on every page provide support. • Illustrations often represent sequence of events. • Vocabulary primarily consists of familiar words. • Print size and placement vary. • Text is often double-spaced and does not always run to right margin. • Texts are usually 10–50 pages. • Nonfiction texts are often shorter. **Fountas and Pinnell Guided Reading Leveling System™: H I J**

Beginning Book List (Early)

Fiction

⌐ *Put Me In the Zoo* by Robert Lopshire (H)

How Do I Put It On? by Shigeo Watanabe (H)

⌐ *Whose Mouse are You?* by Robert Kraus (H)

Sammy the Seal by Syd Hoff (H)

Here Are My Hands by Bill Martin, Jr. and John Archambault (H)

⌐ *Just Me and My Puppy* by Mercer Mayer (H) 📖

A Different Tune by Bruce Witty

⌐ *The Napping House* by Audrey Wood (I)

⌐ *There's a Nightmare in My Closet* by Mercer Mayer (I)

⌐ *Are You My Mother?* by P. D. Eastman (I)

This is the Bear by Sarah Hayes (I)

I Was So Mad by Mercer Mayer (J)

⌐ *Hop on Pop* by Dr. Seuss (J)

One Fish, Two Fish, Red Fish, Blue Fish by Dr. Seuss

⌐ *Green Eggs and Ham* by Dr. Seuss (J)

⌐ *The Cat in the Hat* by Dr. Seuss (J) 📖

Wake Me in Spring by James Preller (J)

The Missing Tooth by Joanna Cole (J)

Moon Boy by Barbara Brenner (J)

Oscar Otter by Nathaniel Benchley (J)

I Can Read With My Eyes Shut by Dr. Seuss (J)

Is Your Mama a Llama? by Deborah Guarino

Miss McKenzie Had a Farm by Tim Johnson (J)

Danny and the Dinosaur by Syd Hoff (J)

Poetry

Jamberry by Bruce Degen (J)

The Popcorn Shop by Alice Low (J)

Nonfiction

Turtle Nest by Lola Schaefer (H)

Building a House by Byron Barton (H)

Tale of a Tadpole by Karen Wallace 📖

Rabbit (See How They Grow) by Barrie Watts 📖

Turtle Talk by Avelyn Davidson

⌐ *Mighty Spiders* by Fay Robinson

Endangered Animals by Faith McNulty

Going on a Whale Watch by Bruce McMillan

Beginning Readers and Book Characteristics (Later)	
Student Behaviors	**Book Characteristics**
• Reads harder early-reader books. • Reads and follows simple written directions with guidance. • Identifies basic genres (e.g., fiction, nonfiction, and poetry). • Uses basic punctuation when reading orally. • Reads independently (10–15 minutes). • Chooses reading materials independently. • Learns and shares information from reading. • Uses meaning cues (context). • Uses sentence cues (grammar). • Uses letter/sound cues and patterns (phonics). • Recognizes word endings, common contractions, and many high frequency words. • Begins to self-correct. • Retells beginning, middle, and end with guidance. • Discusses characters and story events with guidance. • Identifies own reading behaviors with guidance.	• Many books are part of a series. • Books include a developed story line with little or no use of pattern. • Plots often include a series of events. • Fairy/folk tales are retold using simpler vocabulary and language structure. • Simple historical fiction and biographies do not require background knowledge. • Texts may include literary language (more formal). • Texts include some challenging vocabulary. • Text often includes dialogue. • Text includes some descriptive language and details. • Texts include simple plots and only a few characters. • Illustrations appear on every page or two and provide less support. • Illustrations often reflect a sequence of events. • Vocabulary primarily consists of familiar words. • Texts include some challenging vocabulary. • Text is often double-spaced and does not always run to right margin. • Many books are divided into sections with page numbers and table of contents. • Length is usually 20–75 pages. **Fountas and Pinnell Guided Reading Leveling System™: J K** L

Beginning Book List (Later)

Fiction

🔑 *Mouse Soup* by Arnold Lobel (J) 📖

🔑 *Little Bear's Friend* by Else Holmelund Minarik (J) 📖

    Mr. Putter and Tabby Paint the Porch by Cynthia Rylant (J) 📖

🔑 *Oliver Button is a Sissy* by Tomie de Paola

    Fox Outfoxed by James Marshall (J) 📖

    Grandmas at Bat by Emily Arnold McCully (J) 📖

    Morris the Moose Goes to School by Bernard Wiseman (J) 📖

🔑 *Poppleton* by Cynthia Rylant (J) 📖

    Little Poss and Horrible Hound by William Hooks

    In a Dark, Dark Room by Alvin Schwartz (J)

    Owl at Home by Arnold Lobel (J)

    Aunt Eater Loves a Mystery by Doug Cushman (K)

    Little Eagle Learns to Fly by S. A. Cornell

    The Mystery of the Missing Dog by Elizabeth Levy (J)

🔑 *Nate the Great* by Marjorie Weinman Sharmat (K) 📖

    Ruby the Copycat by Peggy Rathmann (K)

🔑 *Frog and Toad Together* by Arnold Lobel (K) 📖

    Commander Toad and the Big Black Hole by Jane Yolen (K) 📖

    Peter's Chair by Ezra Jack Keats (J)

    A Bargain for Frances by Russell Hoban (K) 📖

🔑 *Henry and Mudge and the Wild Wind* by Cynthia Rylant (J) 📖

    Bony-Legs by Joanna Cole (K)

    Alison's Wings by Marion Dane Bauer (K)

    The Town Mouse and the Country Mouse by Ellen Schecter

    Diamonds and Toads by Ellen Schecter

    Owen Foote, Frontiersman by Stephanie Greene 📖

    The Golly Sisters Go West by Betsy Byars (K) 📖

    Snowshoe Thompson by Nancy Smiler (K)

    Wagon Wheels by Barbara Brenner (K)

    Meet M & M by Pat Ross (K) 📖

    Daniel's Duck by Clyde Robert Bulla (K)

    Clifford and the Halloween Parade by Norman Bridwell (K) 📖

    Sheila Rae, the Brave by Kevin Henkes (K)

    The Last Puppy by Frank Asch (K)

    Grasshopper on the Road by Arnold Lobel (L)

    The Dog That Stole Football Plays by Matt Christopher (L) 📖

    Sleeping Ugly by Jane Yolen

    Chang's Paper Pony by Eleanor Coerr (L)

    Goldsworthy and Mort in Spring Soup by Marcia Vaughan (L) 📖

    Carlita Ropes the Twister by Yanitzia Canetti (L)

    The Josefina Story Quilt by Eleanor Coerr (L)

    The Long Way Westward by Joan Sandin (L)

    The Long Way to a New Land by Joan Sandin (L)

    Dust for Dinner by Ann Turner

⚷ *Pinky and Rex Go To Camp* by James Howe (L) 📖
Amelia Bedelia and the Baby by Peggy Parish (L) 📖

Poetry
Weather by Lee Bennett Hopkins (L)

Nonfiction/Biographies
Toby the Tabby Kitten by Colleen Stanley Bare
Antarctica by Helen Cowcher
All About Bats by Jennifer Jacobson (J)
⚷ *Dancing with Manatees* by Faith McNulty (K)
Ibis: A True Whale Story by John Himmelman (K)
Fire Fighter! by Angela Royston 📖
The Amazing Panda Adventure by John Wilcox and Steven Alldredge
A Boy Named Boomer by Boomer Esiason (K)
Magic Secrets by Rose Wyler and Gerald Ames
Gifts to Make by Barbara S. Burt (K)
⚷ *Keep the Lights Burning, Abbie* by Connie and Peter Roop (K)
The Snow Walker by Margaret and Charles Wetterer

Books for Expanding Readers (Ages 7–9)

Books at the Expanding level are generally considered the first "real chapter books." In her article, "First Novels," Bonnie Graves (1988) defines these texts as "books with more words and fewer pictures than their younger cousins, the easy-to-reads, and they look like novels, albeit mininovels. They are also divided into chapters, hence the name *chapter books*." (p. 51). As an author of easy chapter books, Graves says that she focuses on "writing about topics, characters, and problems that are sensitive to today's six-, seven-, and eight-year-olds' needs and interests, stories that speak in a language they can understand, stories that reflect their own struggles and hopes" (p. 51).

Easy Chapter Books

Continuum Level – Early Expanding; Fountas and Pinnell Guided Reading Leveling System™ Levels L, M, N, O; DRA Levels 24, 28, 30, 34; Length 60–100 pages.

By the first part of the Expanding stage, students have launched into longer books with clearly numbered chapters, often with a table of contents. This includes many series books, such as *Pee Wee Scouts* (Judy Denton), *Marvin Redpost* (Louis Sachar), and *The Magic Treehouse* (Mary Pope Osborne) series. The distinguishing features of "easy chapter books" are that the text is divided into chapters, there are illustrations only on every 2–6 pages, and the illustrations provide only minimal support.

These books contain more challenging vocabulary and dialogue. The plot is more complex than in early readers and events often take place over a period of time. Many of these early nonfiction books are presented in a narrative voice, like *Sam, the Sea Cow* (Francine Jacobs, 1979) or *Kate Shelley and the Midnight Express* (Margaret Wetterer, 1990).

By the end of this stage, the books are usually 75–100 pages long, with only a few illustrations in a chapter. Series books like *The Littles* (John Peterson) and *Amber Brown* (Paula Danziger) series contain page numbers, a table of contents, and chapter numbers and/or titles. Unlike the Early Readers at the previous stage, these stories often take place over time and include more characters. The key for students reading easy chapter books is that the texts are short. At the Expanding stage, students often read several books in a series as they build stamina and fluency.

Nonfiction books may be shorter and contain more photographs or illustrations for support as new vocabulary, format, and content are introduced. These texts frequently include a table of contents, chapter headings, captions, and an index. Some books use a question-and-answer format (e.g., *Inventors: Making Things Better* by Andrew Clements, 1998). Other nonfiction texts have engaging illustrations and small bits of information presented in an uncluttered format about topics that young students find interesting (e.g., *The Titanic: Lost . . . And Found* by Judy Donnelly, 1987). Many Expanding readers also enjoy magazines like *Ladybug, Ranger Rick*, and *Kid City*. Much of the appeal and content of nonfiction books and magazines at this level is carried through illustrations and photographs.

Very few picture books are included in the Book Lists since they are so hard to level. It is important to note that by the Expanding stage, students can read more complex picture books like *Owl Moon* (Jane Yolen, 1987) as they learn to read more difficult words.

Expanding Readers and Book Characteristics (Early)	
Student Behaviors	**Book Characteristics**
• Reads easy chapter books. • Chooses, reads, and finishes a variety of materials at appropriate level with guidance. • Begins to read aloud with fluency. • Reads silently for increasingly longer periods (15–30 minutes). • Uses reading strategies appropriately, depending on the text and purpose. • Uses word structure cues (e.g., root words, prefixes, suffixes, word chunks) when encountering unknown words. • Increases vocabulary by using meaning cues (context). • Self-corrects for meaning. • Follows written directions. • Identifies chapter titles and table of contents (text organizers). • Summarizes and retells story events	• Many books are part of a series. • Plots often include a series of events. • Fiction often includes the everyday events and problems that children encounter. • Fiction includes a few developed characters. • Nonfiction texts include clear facts and information. • Texts include some challenging vocabulary. • Texts include descriptive language and details. • Illustrations provide minimal support and can occur once every 2–6 pages. • Illustrations often depict characters and settings and may convey mood. • Text may include vocabulary specific to genre or topic.

cont.

in sequential order.
- Responds to and makes personal connections with facts, characters, and situations in literature.
- Compares and contrasts characters and story events.
- "Reads between the lines" with guidance.
- Identifies own reading strategies and sets goals with guidance.

- Text in easy chapter books is often double spaced and does not always run to right margin.
- Books often contain page numbers, table of contents, and chapter numbers and/or titles.
- Length is usually 60–75 pages.

Fountas and Pinnell Guided Reading Leveling System™: L M N

Expanding Book List (Early)

Fiction

December Secrets (Polk Street series*)* by Patricia Reilly Giff (M)

Trash Bash (Pee Wee Scouts series) by Judy Denton (L)

No Copycats Allowed! by Bonnie Graves (L)

Hot Fudge by James Howe

The Best Worst Day by Bonnie Graves (L)

The Three Little Pigs by James Marshall (L)

The Terrible Thing That Happened at Our House by Marge Blaine

I Hate English! by Ellen Levine (L)

Cam Jansen and the Chocolate Fudge Mystery by David Adler (L)

Horrible Harry and the Green Slime by Suzy Kline (L)

Miss Nelson is Missing by Harry Allard (L)

Long Way to a New Land by Joan Sandin (L)

Through Grandpa's Eyes by Patricia MacLachlan (L)

Junie B. Jones and a Little Monkey Business by Barbara Park (M)

The One in the Middle is the Green Kangaroo by Judy Blume (M)

The Pain and the Great One by Judy Blume

Solo Girl by Andrea Davis Pinkney (M)

Arthur's Mystery Envelope by Marc Brown (M)

The Crane Wife by Ena Keo (M)

Mummies in the Morning (Magic Treehouse series) by Mary Pope Osborne (M)

Marvin Redpost, Alone in His Teacher's House by Louis Sachar (L)

The Quilt Story by Tony Johnston (L)

A Chair for My Mother by Vera B. Williams (M)

The Art Lesson by Tomie de Paola (M)

Milo's Great Invention by Andrew Clements (M)

Freckle Juice by Judy Blume (M)

A Case for Jenny Archer by Ellen Conford (M)

Molly's Pilgrim by Barbara Cohen (M)

My Father's Dragon by Ruth Gannett (M)

Angels Don't Know Karate (Bailey School Kids series) by Debbie Dadey and Marcia Thornton Jones (M)

Poetry

My Parents Think I'm Sleeping by Jack Prelutsky
Good Books, Good Times! by Lee Bennett Hopkins (Ed.)
Brown Angels: An Album of Pictures and Verse by Walter Dean Myers
Kinda Blue by Ann Grifalconi

Nonfiction/Biographies

Hungry, Hungry Sharks by Joanna Cole (L)
Sam the Sea Cow by Francine Jacobs
Very Unusual Pets by Howard Gutner
Buddy, the First Seeing Eye Dog by Eva Moore
Storms! by Rick Leslie (L)
Farm Life Long Ago by Tim Johnson (L)
The True Story of Balto: The Bravest Dog Ever by Natalie Standiford (L)
Michelangelo by Mike Venezia 📖
Diego Rivera: An Artist's Life by Sarah Vázquez (L)
⚷ *Kate Shelley and the Midnight Express* by Margaret Wetterer (M)
Buttons for General Washington by Peter and Connie Roop
Just a Few Words, Mr. Lincoln: The Story of the Gettysburg Address by
   Jean Fritz
The Drinking Gourd: A Story of the Underground Railroad by Ferdinand
   Monjo (M)
Dinosaur Hunters by Kate McMullan (L)
Soccer (A New True Book) by Bert Rosenthal 📖
Laura Ingalls Wilder: An Author's Story by Sarah Glasscock (L)
Gail Devers: A Runner's Dream by Katherine Mead (L)

Magazines

Click by Carus Publishing
Ladybug by Carus Publishing

Expanding Readers and Book Characteristics (Later)	
Student Behaviors	**Book Characteristics**
• Reads easy chapter books. • Chooses, reads, and finishes a variety of materials at appropriate level with guidance. • Begins to read aloud with fluency. • Reads silently for increasingly longer periods (15–30 minutes). • Uses reading strategies appropriately, depending on the text and purpose. • Uses word structure cues (e.g., root words, prefixes, suffixes, word chunks) when encountering	• Many books are part of a series. • Texts include developed plots. • Fiction often includes the everyday events and problems that children encounter. • Fiction includes a few developed characters. • Nonfiction texts include clear facts. • Texts include some challenging vocabulary. • Texts include descriptive language and details.

cont.

unknown words.
- Increases vocabulary by using meaning cues (context).
- Self-corrects for meaning.
- Follows written directions.
- Identifies chapter titles and table of contents (text organizers).
- Summarizes and retells story events in sequential order.
- Responds to and makes personal connections with facts, characters, and situations in literature.
- Compares and contrasts characters and story events.
- "Reads between the lines" with guidance.
- Identifies own reading strategies and sets goals with guidance.

- Illustrations provide minimal support and can occur once or twice in a chapter.
- Text is single-spaced.
- Illustrations often depict characters and settings and may convey mood.
- Texts may include vocabulary specific to genre or topic.
- Nonfiction texts may include page numbers, table of contents, captions, chapter headings, and an index.
- Length is usually 75–100 pages.

Fountas and Pinnell Guided Reading Leveling System™: M N O

Expanding Book List (Later)

Fiction

- ⚷ *The Littles Take a Trip* by John Peterson (M) 📖
   Ghost Town Treasure by Clyde Robert Bulla (M)
   Sable by Karen Hesse (M)
   Cherries and Cherry Pits by Vera B. Williams (M)
   Maybe Yes, Maybe No, Maybe Maybe by Susan Patron (M)
- ⚷ *Flat Stanley* by Jeff Brown (N)
   Don't Call Me Beanhead by Susan Wojchiechowski (N)
   The Case of the Christmas Snowman by James Preller (N) 📖
   Max Malone and the Great Cereal Rip-off by Charlotte Herman (N)
- ⚷ *The Chalk Box Kid* by Clyde Robert Bulla (N)
   Toad for Tuesday by Russell Erickson (N)
- ⚷ *Stories Julian Tells* by Ann Cameron (N) 📖
   Shoeshine Girl by Clyde Robert Bulla (N)
- ⚷ *Pioneer Cat* by William Hooks (N)
   Tornado by Betsy Byars (O)
- ⚷ *Amber Brown Wants Extra Credit* by Paula Danziger (N) 📖
   Next Spring an Oriole by Gloria Whelan (N)
   Hannah by Gloria Whelan (N)
   Aunt Flossie's Hats (and Crab Cakes Later) by Elizabeth Fitzgerald Howard (M)
   Blackberries in the Dark by Mavis Jukes (N)
   Lili the Brave by Jennifer Armstrong (N)
   Chicken Sunday by Patricia Polacco (M)
   The Kid Who Only Hit Homers by Matt Christopher (M) 📖
   It Takes a Village by Jane Cowen-Fletcher (N)

    Wild Willie and King Kyle, Detectives by Barbara Joosse (N)

⚷ *All About Sam* by Lois Lowry (O)

    The Legend of the Bluebonnet by Tomie de Paola (O)

    Socks by Beverly Cleary (O)

    The Legend of the Indian Paintbrush by Tomie de Paola (O)

⚷ *Sideways Stories from Wayside School* by Louis Sachar (O) 📖

Poetry

    It's Raining Laughter by Nikki Grimes

    Meet Danitra Brown by Nikki Grimes

    Owl Moon by Jane Yolen (O)

    You and Me: Poems of Friendship by Salley Mavor (Ed.)

    Dance With Me by Barbara Juster Esbensen

    Roald Dahl's Revolting Rhymes by Roald Dahl (N)

Nonfiction/Biographies

    I Can Read About Sharks by C. J. Naden 📖

    Andy Bear: A Polar Cub Grows Up at the Zoo by Ginny Johnston and Judy Cutchins

    Scruffy: A Wolf Finds His Place in the Pack by Jim Brandenburg

    The Return of the Wolf by Dorothy Hinshaw Patent

    Movie Magic: A Star is Born! by Anne Cottringer 📖

    How to Babysit an Orangutan by Tara and Kathy Darling

    Living in Space by Judy Nayer

    Digging Up Dinosaurs by Aliki

    Inventors: Making Things Better by Andrew Clements (M)

    Margaret Wise Brown, Author of Goodnight Moon by Carol Greene (N) 📖

⚷ *The Titanic: Lost... And Found* by Judy Donnelly (N)

⚷ *Pompeii... Buried Alive!* by Edith Kunhardt (N)

    To the Top! by Sydelle Kramer (N)

    The Trojan Horse: How the Greeks Won the War by Emily Little (N)

Magazines

    Spider by Carus Publishing

    Ranger Rick by National Wildlife Federation

    Kid City by Children's Television Workshop

Books for Bridging Readers (Ages 8–10)

Books at the Bridging stage are quite a bit longer (75–200 pages) and include different genres (e.g., realistic fiction, informational texts, poetry, and biography). Medium level novels have chapter titles and a table of contents. Some texts may have occasional black and white illustrations, while others have no pictures. Key Benchmark Books at the Bridging level include well-known realistic fiction by Judy Blume and Beverly Cleary about the everyday world of children.

Many books at this stage are part of a series, such as the popular *Baby-Sitter's Club* (Ann Martin), *Animorphs* (K. A. Applegate), *Goosebumps* (R. L. Stine), and the

Matt Christopher sports books. Although teachers and parents may not approve of these choices, these series books provide an important step in reading development. Like the John Grisham or Danielle Steele books that adults often read for relaxation, series books are enjoyable for third and fourth graders. Since the characters and plots are predictable, children can focus on the content as they build stamina and fluency. We can ask students to balance their reading diet of the "just right" series books with books in other genres and by other authors.

Later in this stage, students are able to read short fantasy books, such as *The Knights of the Kitchen Table* (Jon Scieszka, 1991) and *Babe: The Gallant Pig* (Dick King-Smith, 1985). Some children become interested in historical fiction, such as *On the Mayflower* (Kate Waters, 1996), and biographies like *Five Brave Explorers* (Wade Hudson, 1995). Others enjoy solving the mysteries in the *Encyclopedia Brown* series (Donald Sobol). Many of these books contain memorable characters who develop and change, as well as more literary language.

Poetry by Shel Silverstein and Jack Prelutsky is popular with almost all students at this stage. Of course, children delight in hearing and memorizing poetry at earlier ages, but by the Bridging stage, they can read the poems independently. There are also appealing *Zoobooks* and *Eyewitness* books for readers at the Bridging stage, as children begin to read more nonfiction. Some students enjoy magazines like *Contact Kids*, and *Sports Illustrated for Kids*. Although they may have enjoyed looking through the *Magic Schoolbus* books by Joanna Cole earlier, Bridging students can now read and understand the concepts and vocabulary independently.

Bridging Readers and Book Characteristics (Early)	
Student Behaviors	**Book Characteristics**
• Reads medium level chapter books. • Chooses reading materials at appropriate level. • Expands knowledge of different genres (e.g., realistic fiction, historical fiction, and fantasy). • Reads aloud with expression. • Uses resources (e.g., encyclopedias, CD-ROMs, and nonfiction texts) to locate and sort information with guidance. • Gathers information by using the table of contents, captions, index, and glossary (text organizers) with guidance. • Gathers and uses information from graphs, charts, tables, and maps with guidance. • Increases vocabulary by using	• Series books contain familiar format, story structures, and characters. • Texts include fully developed plots. • Fiction includes series of episodes, problems, and solutions. • Fiction includes fully developed characters. • Nonfiction texts present simple facts in an organized structure. • Texts include challenging and content- specific vocabulary. • Authors use descriptive and memorable language. • Some books include occasional illustrations (usually 1–2 per chapter). • Fiction may include chapter titles and table of contents. • Nonfiction may include table of

context cues, other reading strategies, and resources (e.g., dictionary and thesaurus) with guidance.
- Demonstrates understanding of the difference between fact and opinion.
- Follows multi-step written directions independently.
- Discusses setting, plot, characters, and point of view (literary elements) with guidance.
- Responds to issues and ideas in literature as well as facts or story events.
- Makes connections to other authors, books, and perspectives.
- Participates in small group literature discussions with guidance.
- Uses reasons and examples to support ideas and opinions with guidance.

contents, captions, a glossary, and index.
- Text runs margin to margin with a more dense print format.
- Length is usually 75–200 pages.

Fountas and Pinnell Guided Reading Leveling System™: O P Q

Bridging Book List (Early)

Fiction

☞ *Ramona Quimby, Age 8* by Beverly Cleary (O)📖
   The Twits by Roald Dahl (P)
   Ramona's World by Beverly Cleary (O) 📖
   George's Marvelous Medicine by Roald Dahl (P)
   Henry and Ribsy by Beverly Cleary (O) 📖
☞ *The Boxcar Children* by Gertrude Chandler Warner (O) 📖
☞ *Attack of the Jack-O'-Lanterns* (*Goosebumps* series) by R. L. Stine (O) 📖
☞ *How to Eat Fried Worms* by Thomas Rockwell
   Chocolate Fever by Robert Kimmel Smith (O)
   The Skates of Uncle Richard by Carol Fenner (P)
   The Canada Geese Quilt by Natalie Kinsey-Warnock (P)
   Stone Fox by John Reynolds Gardiner (P)
   One Day in the Tropical Rainforest by Jean Craighead George (P) 📖
☞ *Yang the Third and Her Impossible Family* by Lensey Namioka (P) 📖
   Best Enemies Again by Kathleen Leverich (P) 📖
   Frindle by Andrew Clements
   The Wall of Names by Judy Donnelly (O)
   Baseball Saved Us by Ken Mochizuki (O)
   The Boys Start the War and The Girls Get Even by Phyllis Reynolds Naylor 📖
   Pippi Longstocking by Astrid Lindgren 📖
   The Night Crossing by Karen Ackerman (O)
   Knights of the Round Table by Gwen Gross
   The King's Equal by Katherine Paterson (O)

Sideways Stories from Wayside School by Louis Sachar (O) 📖
⚷ *Mallory and the Ghost Cat* (*Baby-Sitter's Club* series) by Ann Martin (O)
The Mouse and the Motorcycle by Beverly Cleary (O) 📖
Tales of a Fourth Grade Nothing by Judy Blume (Q)
The Dragonling by Jackie French Koller (Q)
⚷ *Superfudge* by Judy Blume (Q) 📖
Soup and Me by Robert Newton Peck (Q) 📖
⚷ *Koya DeLaney and the Good Girl Blues* by Eloise Greenfield (Q)
⚷ *Bunnicula* by Deborah and James Howe (Q) 📖
Mr. Popper's Penguins by Richard and Florence Atwater (Q)
The Invasion (*Animorphs* series) by K. A. Applegate 📖

Poetry

School Supplies: A Book of Poems by Lee Bennett Hopkins (Ed.)
Through Our Eyes: Poems and Pictures About Growing Up by Lee Bennett
  Hopkins (Ed.)
Love Letters by Arnold Adoff
Ten-Second Rainshowers: Poems by Young People by Sandford Lyne (Ed.)
If I Were in Charge of the World and Other Worries by Judith Viorst
Twilight Comes Twice by Ralph Fletcher
A Light in the Attic by Shel Silverstein
The New Kid on the Block by Jack Prelutsky

Nonfiction/ Biographies

Pirates! Raiders of the High Seas by Christopher Maynard 📖
Going for the Gold! by Andrew Donkin 📖
I Didn't Know That Chimps Use Tools by Claire Llewellyn
Armies of Ants by Walter Retan (O)
Nights of the Pufflings by Bruce McMillan
Moonwalk: The First Trip to the Moon by Judy Donnelly (O)
Tornadoes! by Lorraine J. Hopping (P)
People of the Canyon by Suzanne Weyn
Flute's Journey: The Life of a Wood Thrush by Lynne Cherry
Five Brave Explorers (Great Black Heroes) by Wade Hudson (P) 📖
⚷ *Five Notable Inventors (Great Black Heroes)* by Wade Hudson (Q) 📖

Magazines

Storyworks by Scholastic

Bridging Readers and Book Characteristics (Later)

Student Behaviors	Book Characteristics
• Reads medium level chapter books. • Chooses reading materials at appropriate level. • Expands knowledge of different genres (e.g., realistic fiction, historical fiction, and fantasy). • Reads aloud with expression. • Uses resources (e.g., encyclopedias, CD-ROMs, and nonfiction texts) to locate and sort information with guidance. • Gathers information by using the table of contents, captions, index, and glossary (text organizers) with guidance. • Gathers and uses information from graphs, charts, tables, and maps with guidance. • Uses context cues, other reading strategies and resources (e.g., dictionary and thesaurus) to increase vocabulary with guidance. • Demonstrates understanding of the difference between fact and opinion. • Follows multi-step written directions independently. • Discusses setting, plot, characters, and point of view (literary elements) with guidance. • Responds to issues and ideas in literature as well as facts or story events. • Makes connections to other authors, books, and perspectives. • Participates in small group literature discussions with guidance. • Uses reasons and examples to support ideas and opinions with guidance.	• Series books contain familiar format, story structures and characters. • Texts include fully developed plots. • Fiction includes series of episodes, problems, and solutions. • Fiction includes fully developed characters. • Books at this level include poetry, straightforward fantasy, sports stories, nonfiction, and simple historical fiction. • Nonfiction texts present simple facts in an organized structure. • Nonfiction may include table of contents, captions, a glossary, and index. • Texts include challenging and content-specific vocabulary. • Authors use descriptive and memorable language. • Some books include occasional illustrations (usually 1–2 per chapter). • Some books have no illustrations. • Text runs margin to margin with a more dense print format. • Length is usually 100–200 pages. **Fountas and Pinnell Guided Reading Leveling System™:** P **Q** R

Bridging Book List (Later)

Fiction

⌐ *Fantastic Mr. Fox* by Roald Dahl (P)

⌐ *Soup and Me* by Robert Peck (Q) 📖

   Trouble for Lucy by Carla Stevens

   Night of the Twisters by Ivy Ruckman

   Justin and the Best Biscuits in the World by Walter and Mildred Pitts (P)

⌐ *Encyclopedia Brown Solves Them All* by Donald Sobol (P) 📖

   Mrs. Piggle Wiggle by Betty MacDonald 📖

⌐ *Bingo Brown and the Language of Love* by Betsy Byars 📖

   Stuart Little by E. B. White

   There's an Owl in the Shower by Jean Craighead George

   A Taste of Blackberries by Doris Buchanan Smith

   Bound for Oregon by Jean Van Leeuwen

   The Farthest Away Mountains by Lynne Reid Banks

   Bright Shadow by Avi

   The Kid in the Red Jacket by Barbara Park

   Black-Eyed Susan by Jennifer Armstrong

   Shannon: A Chinatown Adventure, San Francisco, 1880 (*Girlhood Journeys*
      series) by Kathleen Kudlinski 📖

⌐ *Knights of the Kitchen Table* (*Time Warp Trio* series) by Jon Scieszka (P) 📖

⌐ *Charlotte's Web* by E. B. White (Q)

⌐ *Babe: The Gallant Pig* by Dick King-Smith (Q)

   There's a Boy in the Girls' Bathroom by Louis Sachar (Q)

   The Trouble with Tuck by Theodore Taylor (R)

   Changes for Addy (*American Girls* series) by Connie Porter 📖

   Poppy and Rye by Avi (S) 📖

   The Whipping Boy by Sid Fleischman (R)

⌐ *Sarah, Plain and Tall* by Patricia MacLachlan (R) 📖

Poetry

   Hailstones and Halibut Bones by Mary O'Neill

   Celebrations by Myra Cohn Livingston

   Who Shrank My Grandmother's House? Poems of Discovery by Barbara
      Juster Esbensen

   The Earth is Painted Green: A Garden of Poems About Our Planet by Barbara
      Brenner

   Night on Neighborhood Street by Eloise Greenfield (P)

   This Big Sky by Pat Mora (P)

   Joyful Noise: Poems for Two Voices by Paul Fleischman (P)

Nonfiction/Biographies

   The Story of Laura Ingalls Wilder, Pioneer Girl by Megan Stine

   The Magic Schoolbus and the Electric Field Trip by Joanna Cole (P) 📖

⌐ *Magic Schoolbus: Inside the Human Body* by Joanna Cole (P) 📖

   Amelia Earhart by John Parlin (P)

Roberto Clemente: Young Baseball Hero by Louis Sabin
If You Traveled West in a Covered Wagon by Ellen Levine (P) 📖
Salvador Dali (*Getting to Know the World's Greatest Artists* series) by Mike Venezia 📖
Midori: Brilliant Violinist by Charnan Simon 📖
On the Mayflower by Kate Waters 📖
Out of Darkness: The Story of Louis Braille by Russell Freedman
Marching to Freedom: The Story of Martin Luther King, Jr. by Joyce Milton
A Picture Book of Thurgood Marshall by David Adler 📖
Safe Return by Catherine Dexter
New Questions and Answers About Dinosaurs by Seymour Simon
The Penguin: A Funny Bird by Beatrice Fontanel 📖
⌐ *Amazing Poisonous Animals* (*Eyewitness Juniors* series) by Alexandra Parsons 📖

Magazines
Zoobooks by Wildlife Education
Sports Illustrated for Kids by Time
Contact Kids by Children's Television Workshop

Books for Fluent Readers (Ages 9–11)

At the Fluent stage, children plunge into more challenging children's literature. Key Benchmark Books at this stage include *Hatchet* (Gary Paulsen, 1987), *Shiloh* (Phyllis Reynolds Naylor, 1991), and more complex books by Roald Dahl, such as *James and the Giant Peach* (1961) and *Matilda* (1988). Students still read books like the *Nancy Drew* and *Hardy Boys* series; however, more of the books at this stage are single titles or books with a sequel. Fluent readers discover favorite authors such as Gary Paulsen or Roald Dahl and often devour all the books the author has written.

Some students could probably read *The Little House* series by Laura Ingalls Wilder or the more recent continuation of the Wilder story by Roger Lea MacBride at the Expanding or even Bridging stages. These books are quite a bit longer than the Judy Blume or Beverly Cleary books. Fluent readers are often more willing to tackle longer books and may even attempt to read the whole series.

Although most books at the Fluent stage are straightforward narratives, some touch upon serious issues such as animal rights, abuse, divorce, and death. These books are quite different in content from the Judy Blume and Beverly Cleary books in the previous stage. Fluent readers venture into mysteries (e.g., *View from the Cherry Tree* by Willo Davis Roberts, 1975), fantasy (e.g., *James and the Giant Peach* by Roald Dahl, 1961), and survival tales (e.g., *Rescue Josh McGuire* by Ben Mikaelsen, 1991). Some books, such as *Save Queen of Sheba* (Louise Moeri, 1981) and *On My Honor* (Marion Dane Bauer, 1986) are shorter than others at this stage, but the content and issues are more demanding. Other books may contain sophisticated vocabulary.

Nonfiction books incorporate appealing photography and artwork. Information is sometimes displayed in graphs, charts, maps, and tables. The Eyewitness and Dorling Kindersley books, as well as the stunning books by Simon Seymour, often appeal to students who have not been as excited about reading fiction. This is a good age for children to subscribe to magazines such as *American Girl*, *Time Magazine for Kids*, and *National Geographic World*.

Fluent Readers and Book Characteristics (Later)	
Student Behaviors	**Book Characteristics**
<ul><li>Reads challenging children's literature.</li><li>Selects, reads, and finishes a wide variety of genres with guidance.</li><li>Begins to develop strategies and criteria for selecting reading materials.</li><li>Reads aloud with fluency, expression, and confidence.</li><li>Reads silently for extended periods (30–40 min.).</li><li>Begins to use resources (e.g., encyclopedias, articles, Internet, and nonfiction texts) to locate information.</li><li>Gathers information using the table of contents, captions, glossary, and index (text organizers) independently.</li><li>Begins to use resources (e.g., dictionary and thesaurus) to increase vocabulary in different subject areas.</li><li>Begins to discuss literature with reference to setting, plot, characters, and theme (literary elements), and author's craft.</li><li>Generates thoughtful oral and written responses in small group literature discussions with guidance.</li><li>Begins to use new vocabulary in different subjects and in oral and written response to literature.</li><li>Begins to gain deeper meaning by "reading between the lines."</li><li>Begins to set goals and identifies strategies to improve reading.</li></ul>	<ul><li>Texts include fully developed plots, often around a central theme.</li><li>Plots in fiction include climax and resolution.</li><li>Books touch upon challenging issues (e.g., animal rights, death, abuse, divorce).</li><li>Fiction includes multiple fully-developed characters.</li><li>Books at this level may include poetry, fantasy, humor, historical fiction, animal stories, and adventure as well as nonfiction.</li><li>Nonfiction texts present many facts in an organized structure.</li><li>Nonfiction includes table of contents, captions, a glossary, and index.</li><li>Nonfiction texts may include tables, graphs, maps, and charts.</li><li>Illustrations, photographs, and captions support text in nonfiction materials.</li><li>Texts include more challenging vocabulary.</li><li>Authors use vivid descriptive and memorable language.</li><li>Fiction includes few, if any illustrations.</li><li>Print size is smaller.</li><li>Text difficulty determined more by content than by length.</li></ul>**Fountas and Pinnell Guided Reading Leveling System™:** R S T U

Fluent Book List

Fiction

    Jeremy Thatcher, Dragon Hatcher by Bruce Coville

    James and the Giant Peach by Roald Dahl (Q)

⚫ *Charlie and the Chocolate Factory* by Roald Dahl (R) 📖

    Midnight Fox by Betsy Byars (R)

⚫ *Shiloh* by Phyllis Reynolds Naylor (R) 📖

    Saving Shiloh by Phyllis Reynolds Naylor 📖

⚫ *The Mystery of the 99 Steps* (*Nancy Drew* series) by Carolyn Keene 📖

    The Mysterious Caravan (*Hardy Boys* series) by Franklin W. Dixon 📖

    Anastasia Krupnik by Lois Lowry (Q)

    The Best School Year Ever by Barbara Robinson 📖

    Regular Guy by Sarah Weeks📖

    Cricket in Times Square by George Selden (R)

    Terror at the Zoo by Peg Kehret

⚫ *Little House on the Prairie* by Laura Ingalls Wilder (Q) 📖

    Little Town in the Ozarks by Roger Lea MacBride 📖

    The Castle in the Attic by Elizabeth Winthrop 📖

⚫ *Hatchet* by Gary Paulsen (R) 📖

    Rescue Josh McGuire by Ben Mikaelsen

    Bearstone by Will Hobbs 📖

    Weasel by Cynthia DeFelice

    Save Queen of Sheba by Louise Moeri

    Dear Mr. Henshaw by Beverly Cleary (Q)

    View from the Cherry Tree by Willo Davis Roberts

    Matilda by Roald Dahl (S)

⚫ *The War with Grandpa* by Robert Kimmel Smith (S)

⚫ *In the Year of the Boar and Jackie Robinson* by Bette Bao Lord (S)

    Morning Girl by Michael Dorris (S)

    On My Honor by Marion Dane Bauer (S)

    Sadako and the Thousand Paper Cranes by Eleanor Coerr (R)

    Afternoon of the Elves by Janet Taylor Lisle

⚫ *The Lion, the Witch, and the Wardrobe* by C. S. Lewis (T)

⚫ *My Side of the Mountain* by Jean Craighead George (U) 📖

    Mrs. Frisby and the Rats of NIMH by Robert C. O'Brien 📖

    The BFG by Roald Dahl (U)

Poetry

    Winter Poems by Barbara Rogasky (Ed.)

    Song and Dance by Lee Bennett Hopkins (Ed.)

    Brown Honey in Broomwheat Tea by Joyce Carol Thomas

    Inner Chimes: Poems on Poetry by Bobbye Goldstein (Ed.)

    Eric Carle's Dragons and Other Creatures That Never Were by Laura
      Whipple (Ed.)

    Once Upon Ice and Other Frozen Poems by Jane Yolen (Ed.) 📖

    Moonstick: The Seasons of the Sioux by Eve Bunting

The Earth Under Sky Bear's Feet by Joseph Bruchac
Extra Innings: Baseball Poems by Lee Bennett Hopkins (Ed.)

Nonfiction/Biographies
Pearl Harbor is Burning! A Story of World War II by Kathleen Kudlinski
Magic Johnson: Court Magician by Richard Levin
Whales by Seymour Simon
The Big Bug Book by Margery Facklam
Life in the Rainforest by Lucy Baker 📖
A Chorus of Frogs by Joni Hunt
⊶ *Muscles: Our Muscular System* by Seymour Simon 📖
Lightning by Seymour Simon 📖
Sharks (Eyes on Nature) by Jane Resnick 📖
Shark (Eyewitness) by Miranda MacQuitty 📖
Sports (Eyewitness) by Tim Hammond 📖

Magazines
American Girl by Pleasant Company
Time for Kids by Time
National Geographic World by National Geographic Society
Cricket by Carus Publishing

Books for Proficient Readers (Ages 10–13)

Proficient readers are able to handle relatively complex children's literature. These are often longer books with more complicated characters and plots. Many of these books contain memorable characters such as Gilly Hopkins, Maniac Magee, Lucy Whipple, Taran, the Assistant Pig Keeper, and Stanley Yelnats. This stage contains more fantasy novels, such as *Dealing with Dragons* (Patricia Wrede, 1990), *The Boggart* (Susan Cooper, 1993), and science fiction books like the *Tripod* series by John Christopher. Students often delve into other time periods and read more historical fiction such as *Number the Stars* (Lois Lowry, 1989) and *The Fighting Ground* (Avi, 1984). Many books touch upon topics such as death (e.g., *Mick Harte Was Here* by Barbara Park, 1995), prejudice (e.g., *Maniac Magee* by Jerry Spinelli, 1990), and war (e.g., *My Brother Sam is Dead* by James and Christopher Collier, 1974).

Notice that the list of nonfiction titles at this stage is almost as long as the list of fiction. Many intermediate and middle school students enjoy reading magazines such as *Kids Discover* or *Zillions: Consumer Reports for Kids*. Some students become interested in well-written biographies, such as *Leonardo Da Vinci* by Diane Stanley (1996). Other books present information on other cultures, such as the *Vanishing Cultures* series by Jan Reynolds or other time periods (e.g., *Immigrant Kids* by Russell Freedman, 1980). Almost half of the nonfiction books in the list are informational books about topics like space, earthquakes, and "how things work." These books require different reading strategies as students read captions, use the index, skim, and locate information independently.

| Proficient Readers and Book Characteristics ||
Student Behaviors	Book Characteristics
• Reads complex children's literature. • Reads and understands informational texts (e.g., want ads, brochures, schedules, catalogs, manuals) with guidance. • Develops strategies and criteria for selecting reading materials independently. • Uses resources (e.g., encyclopedias, articles, Internet, and nonfiction texts) to locate information independently. • Gathers and analyzes information from graphs, charts, tables, and maps with guidance. • Integrates information from multiple nonfiction sources to deepen understanding of a topic with guidance. • Uses resources (e.g., dictionary and thesaurus) to increase vocabulary independently. • Identifies literary devices (e.g., similes, metaphors, personification, and foreshadowing). • Discusses literature with reference to theme, author's purpose and style (literary elements), and author's craft. • Begins to generate in-depth responses in small group literature discussions. • Begins to generate in-depth written responses to literature. • Uses increasingly complex vocabulary in different subjects and in oral and written response to literature. • Uses reasons and examples to support ideas and conclusions. • Probes for deeper meaning by "reading between the lines" in response to literature.	• Texts include fully-developed plots, often touching upon complex issues such as death, prejudice, poverty, or war. • Settings are often in other time periods or unfamiliar locations. • Books at this level include an increasing variety of genres (e.g., survival stories, nonfiction, mysteries, more complex fantasy, biographies, and historical fiction). • Texts begin to include multiple perspectives on an issue. • Texts include complex sentence structure and literary devices (e.g., metaphor, simile). • Well-developed characters face complex issues and challenges. • Texts include sophisticated language intended to communicate mood, emotion, and atmosphere. • Nonfiction texts include substantial amount of information and detail. • Nonfiction includes table of contents, captions, a glossary, and index. • Nonfiction texts may include tables, graphs, maps, and charts. • Illustrations, photographs, and captions support text in nonfiction materials. • Nonfiction texts may include newspapers, magazines, and manuals. • Texts often include specialized vocabulary. **Fountas and Pinnell Guided Reading Leveling System™: T U V W**

Proficient Book List

Fiction

The Great Gilly Hopkins by Katherine Paterson (S)

Sounder by William Armstrong (S)

☞ *The Watsons Go to Birmingham-1963* by Christopher Paul Curtis (T)

Sing Down the Moon by Scott O'Dell (T)

Sees Behind Trees by Michael Dorris (T)

Ella Enchanted by Gail Carson Levine (U)

☞ *Julie of the Wolves* by Jean Craighead George (U) 📖

☞ *The Boggart* by Susan Cooper (U) 📖

The Summer of the Swans by Betsy Byars (U)

☞ *Number the Stars* by Lois Lowry (U)

☞ *Bridge to Terabithia* by Katherine Paterson (U)

The King of Dragons by Carol Fenner

Sign of the Beaver by Elizabeth George Speare (U)

Yolonda's Genius by Carol Fenner

Absolutely Normal Chaos by Sharon Creech

Wringer by Jerry Spinelli (U)

The Secret Garden by Frances Hodgson Burnett (U)

Mick Harte Was Here by Barbara Park

Journey to Jo'burg by Beverly Naidoo

The Egypt Game by Zilpha Keatley Snyder (U)

Toughboy and Sister by Kirkpatrick Hill 📖

Ghost Canoe by Will Hobbs

Jason's Gold by Will Hobbs

The Ballad of Lucy Whipple by Karen Cushman

Dealing with Dragons by Patricia Wrede 📖

Walk Two Moons by Sharon Creech 📖

Chasing Redbird by Sharon Creech

Bloomability by Sharon Creech

The White Mountains by John Christopher, 📖

The Book of Three by Lloyd Alexander (U) 📖

Running Out of Time by Margaret Peterson Haddix

Belle Prater's Boy by Ruth White

A Family Apart by Joan Lowry Nixon 📖

Tuck Everlasting by Natalie Babbitt (U)

Randall's Wall by Carol Fenner

Old Yeller by Fred Gipson (V)

The Incredible Journey by Sheila Burnford (V)

Stepping on the Cracks by Mary Downing Hahn

☞ *Holes* by Louis Sachar (V)

☞ *Island of the Blue Dolphins* by Scott O'Dell (V)

The Cay by Theodore Taylor (V) 📖

The Fighting Ground by Avi (V)

Shades of Gray by Carolyn Reeder

☞ *Maniac Magee* by Jerry Spinelli (W)

Missing May by Cynthia Rylant (W)

Poetry
   Baseball, Snakes, and Summer Squash: Poems About Growing Up by
      Donald Graves
   Sports Pages by Arnold Adoff

Nonfiction/Biographies
   Leonardo Da Vinci by Diane Stanley
☞ *You Want Women to Vote, Lizzie Stanton?* by Jean Fritz (W) 📖
   Thomas Jefferson: A Picture Book Biography by James Cross Giblin
   Sky Pioneer: A Photobiography of Amelia Earhart by Corinne Szabo
   Himalaya: Vanishing Cultures by Jan Reynolds 📖
   Volcano:The Eruption and Healing of Mount St. Helens by Patricia Lauber
   Hurricanes: Earth's Mightiest Storms by Patricia Lauber
   Discovering Jupiter: The Amazing Collision in Space by Melvin Berger
☞ *Immigrant Kids* by Russell Freedman
   Storms and Hurricanes by Kathy Gemmell
   Earthquakes and Volcanoes by Fiona Watt
   Knights in Armor (*Living History*) by John Clare (Ed.) 📖

Magazines
   Zillions: Consumer Reports for Kids by Consumer's Union

Books for Connecting Readers (Ages 11–14)

Students at the Connecting stage read both complex children's literature and young adult literature. In fact, the line between the two is often blurred. Many students read books like *A Wrinkle in Time* (Madeleine L'Engle, 1962) or *The Giver* (Lois Lowry, 1993) at an earlier age. It's not until this stage that most students can read these books *independently* and fully understand the issues and layers of meaning. This list includes more difficult fantasy novels, such as *The Dark is Rising* series by Susan Cooper and the *Redwall* series by Brian Jacques. Many books deal with adolescents growing up and facing complex issues such as freedom, truth, good versus evil, and human rights. Novels are frequently set in other time periods and require some understanding of history in order to fully appreciate the story, like *The Witch of Blackbird Pond* by Elizabeth George Speare (1958) or *Nightjohn* by Gary Paulsen (1993). These books are sometimes read in fourth and fifth grade, but teachers usually have to provide the context and historical background through class discussions, literature circles, or as a part of the social studies curriculum. It is not until the Connecting stage that most students are able to really understand these books on their own.

You may wonder why the *Harry Potter* books by J. K. Rowling are listed at the Connecting stage. Although the books are popular with adults as well as with children of all ages, readers must be fairly sophisticated in order to read the books with good comprehension. In the fourth book in particular, the text is remarkably long (over 700 pages!) and readers must make inferences and follow the turns of plot, as well as make connections back to the previous three books. Of course, as students read and re-read these books and discuss them with friends, their understanding grows.

As in earlier stages, there are engaging biographies and nonfiction texts at this level. Books at this stage focus on topics that are more removed from students' experiences and require more of an understanding of history and geography, such as *Ancient China* by Arthur Cotterell (1994) or *The Day Women Got the Vote* by George Sullivan (1994). Information is presented in graphs, charts, maps, and tables, as well as in the text. Nonfiction books at this stage often contain sophisticated vocabulary or challenging concepts. Young writers at this stage sometimes enjoy reading stories and poems written by other students in magazines, such as *Stone Soup*.

Connecting Readers and Book Characteristics	
Student Behaviors	**Book Characteristics**
• Reads complex children's literature and young adult literature. • Selects, reads, and finishes a wide variety of genres independently. • Begins to choose challenging reading materials and projects. • Integrates nonfiction information to develop deeper understanding of a topic independently. • Begins to gather, analyze, and use information from graphs, charts, tables, and maps. • Generates in-depth responses and sustains small group literature discussions. • Generates in-depth written responses to literature. • Begins to evaluate, interpret, and analyze reading content critically. • Begins to develop criteria for evaluating literature. • Seeks recommendations and opinions about literature from others. • Sets reading challenges and goals independently.	• Fiction includes fully developed plots, often around complex issue such as freedom, truth, goodness and evil, and human rights. • Books include a variety of genres (realistic fiction, biography, fantasy, survival stories, historical fiction, and nonfiction). • Settings are often in other time periods or unfamiliar locations that require some background knowledge. • Texts include multiple perspectives that reflect the multifaceted complexity of an issue. • Texts include literary devices (e.g., metaphor, simile) and some imagery and symbolism. • Characters face complex issues and challenges. • Texts include sophisticated language intended to communicate mood, emotion, and atmosphere. • Nonfiction texts include substantial amount of information and detail. • Nonfiction texts include table of contents, captions, a glossary, and index. • Nonfiction texts include tables, graphs, maps, and charts. **Fountas and Pinnell Guided Reading Leveling System™:** V **W** X Y

Connecting Book List

Fiction

Catherine, Called Birdy by Karen Cushman (U)

⚷ *A Wrinkle in Time* by Madeleine L'Engle (V) 📖

⚷ *The True Confessions of Charlotte Doyle* by Avi (V)

Where the Red Fern Grows by Wilson Rawls (X)

Under the Blood Red Sun by Graham Salisbury

Lyddie by Katherine Paterson (U)

Tangerine by Edward Bloor (U)

⚷ *The Witch of Blackbird Pond* by Elizabeth George Speare (W)

⚷ *Slave Dancer* by Paula Fox

⚷ *Roll of Thunder, Hear My Cry* by Mildred Taylor (W) 📖

⚷ *Redwall* by Brian Jacques 📖

The Maze by Will Hobbs

The Wanderer by Sharon Creech

A Long Way from Chicago by Richard Peck 📖

Freak the Mighty by Rodman Philbrick 📖

Music from a Place Called Half Moon by Jerrie Oughton

Crazy Lady! by Jane Conly

Crash! by Jerry Spinelli

When Zachary Beaver Came to Town by Kimberly Willis Holt

Child of the Owl by Laurence Yep

Chain of Fire by Beverly Naidoo

Echoes of the White Giraffe by Sook Nyul Choi

Baby by Patricia MacLachlan

My Louisiana Sky by Kimberly Willis Holt

Dave at Night by Gail Carson Levine

The Barn by Avi

Dicey's Song by Cynthia Voigt (W)

White Lilacs by Carolyn Meyer

Little Women by Louisa May Alcott 📖

⚷ *The Giver* by Lois Lowry (Y)

The Last Book in the Universe by Rodman Philbrick 📖

⚷ *The View from Saturday* by E. L. Konigsburg (U)

Esperanza Rising by Pam Munoz Ryan

The Westing Game by Ellen Raskin (V)

Harry Potter and the Sorcerer's Stone by J. K. Rowling (T) 📖

The Dark Is Rising by Susan Cooper (X) 📖

Nory Ryan's Song by Patricia Reilly Giff

My Brother Sam is Dead by James and Christopher Collier (Y)

Whirligig by Paul Fleischman

⚷ *Nightjohn* by Gary Paulsen (W) 📖

Year of Impossible Goodbyes by Sook Nyul Choi (W)

Journey of the Sparrows by Fran Leeper Buss with Daisy Cubias

A Jar of Dreams by Yoshiko Uchida

Grab Hands and Run by Frances Temple

Dragonwings by Laurence Yep (V)
Crazy Weekend by Gary Soto
Jip: His Story by Katherine Paterson (V)

Poetry

Buried Alive: The Elements of Love by Ralph Fletcher
I Am Wings: Poems About Love by Ralph Fletcher
Dream Keeper and Other Poems by Langston Hughes
A Suitcase of Seaweed and Other Poems by Janet Wong

Nonfiction/Biographies

Ancient China (Eyewitness) by Arthur Cotterell 📖
Medieval Life by Andrew Langley
The Day the Women Got the Vote by George Sullivan
The Oceans Atlas by Anita Ganeri
Gold Rush Women by Claire Murphy and Jane Haig
The Body Atlas by Steve Parker
Inventors from Da Vinci to Biro by Struan Reid and Patricia Fara
⌐ *Children of the Dust Bowl* by Jerry Stanley
Castle by David Macaulay
Homesick: My Own Story by Jean Fritz
Kids at Work: Lewis Hines and the Crusade Against Child Labor by
   Russell Freedman

Magazines

Stone Soup by Children's Art Foundation

Books for Independent Readers

At this stage, students read both young adult literature and adult novels. Some teachers and parents also want their middle school students to read "the classics," such as *Treasure Island* (Robert Lewis Stevenson, 1883). Unfortunately, the books on the traditional canon often fail to engage young readers. When they become mired in books that are over their heads, some young adults turn off to reading. Students who do choose to read independently often leap into adult literature, by reading authors like Stephen King or John Grisham. Although they can read the books, the content is often inappropriate for their age.

What many middle school and high school students miss are the young adult novels with characters close to their own age facing challenges with which they can connect. Although the reading level may look deceptively easy, the issues in these young adult novels are both meaningful and challenging to students at this age. Other books touch upon complex topics such as war (e.g., *The Devil's Arithmetic* by Jane Yolen, 1988), prejudice (e.g., *Spite Fences*, by Trudy Krisher, 1994), and politics (e.g., *Habibi* by Naomi Shihab Nye, 1997). Many of these books employ techniques such as time travel or flashbacks. The fantasy novels at this level are quite sophisticated, like *The Golden Compass* by Philip Pullman (1995) or *The Ear, the Eye, and the Arm* by Nancy Farmer (1994). Because some books, like Chris Crutcher's novels, deal with sensitive subjects such as sexuality, abuse, and alcoholism, you should read the books yourself before recommending them. Some parents may question your inclusion of these young adult books in your classroom. As you select books, it is important to know your community, making certain in advance that there is a materials selection policy and grievance procedure in place at your school in case a book is challenged. For more information about using young adult novels, you may want to refer to *Battling Dragons: Issues and Controversy in Children's Literature*, edited by Susan Lehr (1995) or *Censorship Goes to School* by David Booth (1992). The value of using young adult novels is that you can tap into students' interests and desire to talk about meaningful topics. At this stage, students can engage in powerful literature discussions and learn to analyze and evaluate what they read.

The lengthy biographies and historical nonfiction by authors such as Russell Freedman and Jim Murphy contain a great deal of information and would be challenging reading for adults as well as middle school students. Students may also want to subscribe to magazines for adults, such as *National Geographic, Consumer Reports,* or *Time Magazine.* Students should be encouraged to balance their reading diet with adult novels, nonfiction titles, and young adult novels. Research shows that many young people stop reading in middle school, which is even more reason for finding good books that engage independent readers.

Independent Readers and Book Characteristics	
Student Behaviors	**Book Characteristics**
• Reads young adult and adult literature. • Chooses and comprehends a wide variety of sophisticated materials with ease (e.g., newspapers, magazines, manuals, novels, and poetry). • Reads and understands informational texts (i.e., manuals, consumer reports, applications, and forms). • Reads challenging material for pleasure independently. • Reads challenging material for information and to solve problems independently. • Perseveres through complex reading tasks. • Gathers, analyzes, and uses information from graphs, charts, tables, and maps independently. • Analyzes literary devices (e.g.,	• Some texts focus on complex and controversial issues. • Settings may require an understanding of other cultures and perspectives. • Texts sometimes include complex structure such as flashbacks or time travel. • Texts include sophisticated language, imagery, and symbolism. • Texts may promote specific ideologies or biases. • Adolescent and young adult characters often confront challenges and issues. • Texts may contain ambiguity, requiring students to make inferences, and read for deeper meaning. • Texts may contain multiple layers of meaning, facts, and concepts.

cont.

metaphors, imagery, irony, and satire).
- Contributes unique insights and supports opinions in complex literature discussions.
- Adds depth to responses to literature by making insightful connections to other reading and experiences.
- Evaluates, interprets, and analyzes reading content critically.
- Develops and articulates criteria for evaluating literature.
- Pursues a widening community of readers independently.

- Nonfiction texts include substantial information and details that require background knowledge and deeper level understanding of a topic.

Fountas and Pinnell Guided Reading Leveling System™: X Y Z

Independent Book List

Fiction

The Root Cellar by Janet Lunn (V)
⌐ *The Devil's Arithmetic* by Jane Yolen
Briar Rose by Jane Yolen (X)
⌐ *The Golden Compass* by Philip Pullman (Z) 📖
Petey by Ben Mickaelson
Out of the Dust by Karen Hesse (X)
Stargirl by Jerry Spinelli
Rules of the Road by Joan Bauer
Phoenix Rising by Karen Hesse (W)
Toning the Sweep by Angela Johnson
⌐ *The Outsiders* by S. E. Hinton (Z)
Beauty by Robin McKinley
Dangerous Skies by Suzanne Fisher Staples
Tears of a Tiger by Sharon Draper
⌐ *The Hobbit* by J. R. R. Tolkien (Z) 📖
Scorpions by Walter Dean Myers (Z)
Treasure Island by Robert Louis Stevenson (Z)
Waiting for Odysseus by Clemence McLaren
The Adventures of Tom Sawyer by Mark Twain
Malcolm X by Walter Dean Myers
Good Night, Mr. Tom by Michelle Magorian (Z)
⌐ *Ironman* by Chris Crutcher
Staying Fat for Sarah Byrnes by Chris Crutcher
Make Lemonade by Virginia Euwer Wolff 📖
⌐ *Shabanu, Daughter of the Wind* by Suzanne Fisher Staples 📖
Tomorrow, When the War Began by John Marsden 📖

Stones in Water by Donna Jo Napoli
Z for Zachariah by Robert C. O'Brien
The Last Oasis by Sue Pace
⊶ *The Ear, the Eye and the Arm* by Nancy Farmer
The Thief by Megan Whalen Turner
The Goats by Brock Cole
Mary, Bloody Mary by Carolyn Meyer
Go and Come Back by Joan Abelove
Turnabout by Margaret Peterson Haddix
Local News by Gary Soto
Spite Fences by Trudy Krisher
Habibi by Naomi Shihab Nye 📖
A Woman of Her Tribe by Margaret Robinson

Poetry

Step Lightly: Poems for the Journey by Nancy Willard (Ed.)
I Feel a Little Jumpy Around You by Naomi Shihab Nye and Paul Janeczko (Eds.)
Rising Voices: Writings of Young Native Americans by Arlene B. Hirschfelder
    and Beverly R. Singer (Eds.)

Nonfiction/Biographies

Red Scarf Girl: A Memoir of the Cultural Revolution by Ji Li Jiang
⊶ *The Children of Topaz: The Story of a Japanese-American Internment Camp* by
    Michael O. Tunnell and George Chilcoat
The Day Pearl Harbor Was Bombed: A Photo History of World War II by George
    Sullivan 📖
Rosa Parks: My Story by Rosa Parks with Jim Haskins
The Day Fort Sumter Was Fired On: A Photo History of the Civil War by Jim
    Haskins 📖
The Boys' War: Confederate and Union Soldiers Talk About the Civil War by
    Jim Murphy
The Great Fire by Jim Murphy
⊶ *Anne Frank: The Diary of a Young Girl* by Anne Frank
Always Remember: The Story of the Vietnam Veterans Memorial by Brent
    Ashabranner
⊶ *Lincoln: A Photobiography* by Russell Freedman
The Life and Death of Crazy Horse by Russell Freedman
The Hidden Children by Howard Greenfield
We Remember the Holocaust by David Adler
The Forgotten Heroes: The Story of the Buffalo Soldiers by Clinton Cox
Now Is Your Time! The African-American Struggle for Freedom by Walter Dean
    Myers

Chapter 5

Assessment Tools

The Teacher Notebook and various assessment tools not only provide a complete and accurate picture of my students, but also help to identify critical areas that I need to target in order to move each student along the continuum to academic success.

—*Jan Formisano, 2nd/3rd Grade Teacher, Mercer Island, Washington*

If you had never seen a continuum before and were handed a copy and told to assess your whole class, you might feel a little daunted. The purpose of this book is to provide support documents that make using the continuums easier and more manageable. Your students' behaviors probably fall into three or four stages on the continuums. How can you possibly meet the varied needs of this range of students unless you use a variety of assessment tools? Unless you assess each student, how can you determine what to teach next? What assessment tools can you use to help fill out the continuums? How can you weave assessment into the fabric of your classroom life? These questions create the structure for this chapter.

Charts of Assessment Tools

This chapter is divided into seven sections. There is a separate section for each of the first five stages on the continuums (Preconventional, Emerging, Developing,

Beginning, and Expanding). Because of the similarities of the assessment tools in the next five stages, I combined the Bridging and Fluent stages for intermediate readers and writers and also combined the last three stages (Proficient, Connecting, and Independent) for middle school students.

Assessment Tool Charts

Each of the seven sections is divided into writing and reading. In each section, you will find a chart with two columns. On the left side are the specific descriptors from the reading and writing continuums. The right column contains a menu of assessment tools for each descriptor. Some of the assessment forms are included in this book and the specific form number is included with the abbreviation DC (*Developmental Continuums*). Other forms are from *Classroom Based Assessment* (Hill, Ruptic, and Norwick, 1998) and noted with the abbreviation CBA. You may want to refer to that book if you want more detailed explanations of those specific assessment tools. The forms from both this book and from *Classroom Based Assessment* are on the CD-ROM included with this book. You may want to place a copy of the charts of assessment tools that match your grade level and group of students in your Assessment Tools Notebook.

Of course, these are not the only assessment forms and tools available. You've probably collected or developed others that you've used successfully for years. My goal is to show how assessment can be aligned with the continuums. As you develop your assessment plan, you may want to refer to other books on the topic. I recommend five other practical books that contain assessment forms. *Literacy Assessment: A Handbook of Instruments* (Rhodes, 1993) is a spiral-bound handbook of assessment forms. The thick accompanying text, *Windows into Literacy: Assessing Learners K–8* (Rhodes and Shanklin, 1993) provides a rationale, a narrative description, and further references about each assessment strategy. Another book of forms is *The Whole Language Catalog: Forms for Authentic Assessment* (Bird, Goodman, and Goodman, 1994). The fourth book which teachers find extremely useful is Bill Harp's second edition (2000) of *The Handbook of Literacy Assessment and Evaluation*. He begins each section with a description of the assessment tool, a teacher's description of how he or she uses the tool, a list of its advantages and disadvantages, and further references on the tool. Finally, *Making Assessment Elementary* by Kathleen and James Strickland (2000) is a recent assessment book with forms and information, as well as a CD-ROM. I'd highly recommend purchasing a copy of each of these books for your professional library. As you examine the assessment ideas, it's important to keep in mind that assessment should inform and guide your teaching and learning. In *Conversations* (2000), Regie Routman writes, "Assessment must promote learning, not just measure it" (p. 559).

Assessment Tools Summary

Below each chart of assessment tools, I have provided a short summary of how many of the continuum descriptors can be assessed by using each of the assessment tools. For instance, there are 13 descriptors on the continuum for the beginning stage of writing. In the chart, I list seven assessment tools which could be used to assess Beginning writers. By looking at the summary chart, you can see that 10 of the 13 descriptors can be assessed simply by looking at student writing samples. Another four descriptors can be assessed by taking anecdotal notes. Three descriptors can be assessed by using the Writing Strategies I Use form. The summary chart was intended to help you ascertain which assessment tools are the most efficient and provide the most information. In addition, the Summary charts are included on the CD-ROM, where they are linked to each of the assessment tools in the chart. By clicking on the "Anecdotal Notes," you can open the Anecdotal Notes Focus Questions for primary students or click on "Writing Strategies I Use" to access that particular form. The forms can either be printed directly in pdf format or you can make modifications by using the Word version of the form. More information about downloading and printing these forms can be found in the directions on the CD-ROM.

Analyzing Assessment Tools

Each of the seven sections in this chapter also contains a summary and narrative description of the assessment tools teachers have found most useful at each stage of the continuum and examples of how assessment fits into their daily teaching. Special thanks to Anne Klein and Lisa Norwick who let me ask questions and emailed comments about this chapter. I also want to thank all the teachers at Brighton School in Lynnwood, Washington, who allowed me to corner each of them for an hour at the beginning of a very busy year for an interview about assessment tools and continuums. These teachers let me know which ideas look great on paper, but only work in theory. My goal in this section is to present manageable ideas that teachers have used successfully in classrooms.

Organizational Grid (Creating a Plan)

Once you've looked at the chart of assessment tools in this chapter and read about which tools are most effective at each continuum stage, you can create your own assessment plan. You may want to select five or six assessment strategies that would work for your particular grade level and group of students. How can you organize the assessment tools you decide to use? Have you ever created a lovely assessment plan over the summer that works for the first month of school? Do you find that by November you have fallen behind your schedule and by February, you can't even remember where you put the plan? The Organization Grid, developed by Cynthia Ruptic, can help you create an assessment plan that actually works. At the end of this chapter (and also on the CD-ROM), I have included a Primary (DC Form 5.1) and an Intermediate (DC Form 5.2) Organizational Grid, as well as a blank Organizational Grid for you to use (DC Form 5.3).

After reading through this chapter and using the CD-ROM to look at various forms, make a list of the assessment tools you could use in your classroom. Next, prioritize your list. Transfer your list onto the left column of the Organizational Grid. Fill in all the squares, leaving blank squares for the month when you plan to use each particular tool. Be careful to balance assessment tools for each month. For instance, you might want to balance a parent survey in September, which doesn't require much work on your part, with a more intensive assessment tool, such as running records. As you complete each assessment activity, place a check in the blank square for the appropriate tool and month.

Many teachers lose their assessment momentum when they start to feel overwhelmed. It's better to start with no more than five or six assessment tools and weave them into your routine before adding a new one. If you have already used several of these strategies, such as running records and anecdotal notes, your list might be a bit longer. If you are a first-year teacher or have recently changed grade levels, you might want to start with just two or three tools. Like reading and writing, knowledge and expertise in assessment is also a continuum. Jan Formisano, a teacher on Mercer Island, Washington, states that by collecting a range of assessment tools, "I get fully detailed, invaluable information which truly guides my teaching. This was the first year that I felt I truly knew my second-grade readers, inside and out; I am able to really target their unique needs."

Creating a Teacher Notebook

Once you decide which assessment tools you want to use and have created your Organizational Grid, you are ready to make your Teacher Notebook. You'll need a large three-inch, three-ring binder with enough dividers with tabs for each of your students. For instance, this year Anne Klein has a section for each of her 30 fifth-grade students. She places each child's assessment tools in his or her section of her Teacher Notebook. During the first month of school, Anne places the Parent Surveys and the Reading/Writing Surveys in each child's section of the Teacher Notebook. As the year progresses, she files each student's Spelling Words samples, Reading Conference forms, a photocopy of a reading sample, and the "Fix-it" samples. She fills out the reading and writing continuums in October and May and stores them in each student's section. Anne finds it easy to fill out her report cards since she has filed all the information about her students in her Teacher Notebook. Parents are inevitably impressed at Anne's organization when she flips to their child's section in her Notebook as she discusses the student's strengths and areas for growth.

Other teachers prefer to use hanging files instead of a Teacher Notebook. Teachers like Julie Langley, a fifth-grade teacher on Mercer Island, Washington, have a hanging files with a folder for each child that contains all of that student's assessment information. Since Julie believes strongly that her students are part of the assessment process, she wants them to show evidence of the continuum descriptors. Julie wants her students to have access to the files so that they can reflect upon their own learning and ultimately set meaningful goals for themselves. Each student's folder in her class contains their initial assessments (Informal Reading Inventories, spelling inventories, surveys, strategy sheets, etc.). Students also keep their ongoing reading and writing workshop folders in their files. When she meets to go over the continuums with her students, all the evidence is in one place. Since Julie's students do student-led conferences, they are able to pull out items from their files as evidence for the continuum descriptors that have been marked.

It's easier to bring a few files home overnight and you don't have to open a binder to insert information. On the other hand, I find that when teachers have to file information in a Teacher Notebook, they tend to look at entries more often than if they simply drop a note, rubric, or survey into a child's folder. Whether you use hanging files or a notebook, it's important to be intentional about what you collect and to look through the information on a regular basis. You can use your anecdotal notes to plan instruction, to assess students, and to fill out report cards.

You will have to decide what information will be stored in your Teacher Notebook and what pieces will be housed in students' portfolios. Julie Langley's hanging files contain both her assessments and student work. Other teachers, like Anne Klein, only include their teacher assessments (such as anecdotal notes, spelling assessments, reading conference notes, etc.) in their Teacher Notebook. In Anne's classroom, representative student work is kept in students' portfolios, along with reflections for why each piece was selected. Anne finds that keeping student work in portfolios keeps her Teacher Notebook from becoming too full.

Gathering information in an organized way helps you get to know each student. Veronica Golden, a kindergarten teacher on Mercer Island, Washington, writes, "I find the Teacher Notebook helpful because when I need to think about a student's abilities or skills, I have concrete reminders of what he or she did on a specific day. This collection of tools makes me confident that I know my students and that I am meeting their needs."

Collecting classroom-based evidence can also increase your confidence at parent conferences. Rather than vague assurances, you have concrete examples and stories to tell. At Dhahran Hills School in Saudi Arabia, Kerry Wollak writes about her Teacher Notebook: "It's a lifesaver. After seven weeks of school, I am totally prepared for parent/teacher conferences. I no longer rush around the weeks before conferences trying to put together student folders. Their work samples, assessment information, and anecdotal notes are all collected in one place. The parents love the specific anecdotal notes I share at conferences, and I am able to target my instructional activities and goals for each child based on the evidence I have collected. I love my Teacher Notebook!"

Ingrid Stipes teaches fourth and fifth grade on Mercer Island, Washington, and has been using a Teacher Notebook for several years. She also finds that a Teacher Notebook helps her organization and confidence. When I asked her to write me about how this organizational strategy has been useful, Ingrid wrote,

> When I first started looking at classroom based assessment several years ago, I wondered how I could keep all the pieces of student work, my own rubrics I had developed, my anecdotal notes, and my assessment forms all organized. It all seemed so scattered to me (and to my students). My Teacher Notebook has been the answer. It holds as many sections as I have students and evolves throughout the year. By November, student and parent surveys, anecdotal notes, and letters from families fill the sections. As January approaches, the reading and writing continuums appear, marked for the first time. With each new month, I gain insights about the youngsters with whom I share my days as my Teacher Notebook grows. It has become my portable file cabinet, grade book, and student file all wrapped into one. Whether I am preparing for an on-the-spot meeting, report cards, or student-led conferences, my Teacher Notebook is my key source of information. Everything I need is in one place.

Carol Wilcox, a teacher and staff developer in Denver, Colorado, asks herself three questions: What is my purpose for assessing students? What do I want to learn about my students as readers and writers? Which are the easiest and most efficient ways to gather that information? In this chapter, I will examine which specific assessment tools would be most effective at each stage of the reading/writing continuums. You may want to read only those sections that apply to your particular group of students. Remember that no one uses all these ideas! In order to stay sane and still have time to teach, you will probably want to select five or six assessment tools to use. You may want to pick one general assessment strategy (such as anecdotal notes), one specific tool for spelling assessment, one for writing, and one or two for reading. Some of these tools may be ones you're already using. Others may be new ideas you can add to your repertoire. Once you get your assessment program running smoothly, you may want to revisit this chapter and add one or two new tools to your Organizational Grid. Remember, it's best to start small so you don't become overwhelmed. Let's now take a look at how teachers use specific assessment tools for students at each of the continuum stages.

Preconventional Writing: Assessment Tools

Continuum Descriptor	Assessment Tools
▤ Relies primarily on pictures to convey meaning.	Writing Samples
▤ Begins to label and add "words" to pictures.	Writing Samples
▤ Writes first name.	Writing Samples Words I Know (CBA Form 6.1)
▭ Demonstrates awareness that print conveys meaning.	Writing Samples
✎ Makes marks other than drawing on paper (scribbles).	Writing Samples Spelling Development (CBA Form 5.2) Words I Know (CBA Form 6.1) Emergent Writing Development (CBA Form 6.2)
✎ Writes random recognizable letters to represent words.	Writing Samples Spelling Development (CBA Form 5.2) Words I Know (CBA Form 6.1) Emergent Writing Development (CBA Form 6.2)
☺ Tells about own pictures and writing.	Anecdotal Notes (DC Form 6.7) Emergent Writing Development (CBA Form 6.2)

Summary: Preconventional Writing Tools

Assessment Tool	7 Descriptors: Number Assessed	
Writing Samples	6	(86%)
Emergent Writing Development (CBA Form 6.2)	3	(43%)
Words I Know (CBA Form 6.1)	3	(43%)
Spelling Development (CBA Form 5.2)	2	(29%)
Anecdotal Notes (DC Form 6.7)	1	(14%)

Teachers who work with preschool and kindergarten students are special people. You have to be well organized since there's scarcely a moment to catch your breath. You must have a huge amount of patience and remain unflustered by the wiggling energy, as well as the daily catastrophes and mishaps that are a normal part of your classroom. As preschool and kindergarten teachers, you also have to keep a tremendous amount of information about your young students in your heads. Teachers of three-, four-, and five-year-old children face several other challenges. Those of you with a morning and an afternoon class have a huge number of students to get to know, as well as a very short amount of time with each group. In addition, anyone who has worked with energetic youngsters this age knows that you don't have time to run for supplies, make phone calls, or even sip your coffee before it gets cold. Finally, children change so rapidly at this age. A writing sample from two months ago looks like it was written by a different child than today's journal entry. So how can you keep track of these young children's growth as readers and writers?

Writing Samples and Anecdotal Notes

Most preschool and kindergarten teachers agree that the best way to document writing growth is to look at students' work over time. Six of the seven descriptors at the Preconventional stage can be evaluated by looking at a child's ongoing drawing and writing. A few years ago, Marilyn O'Neill started writing workshop in her kindergarten class on Mercer Island, Washington. She has been amazed at the amount of writing her young students can produce when she provides modeling and daily time to write. Students bring her their journals each day as they finish writing. Marilyn uses Post-it notes and checklists to record students' breakthroughs and memorable comments from a few students each day. She also records what students say about their pictures and writing (Figure 5.1). Students do many types of writing in her room and save their cards, poems, notes, lists, letters, and stories in their writing folders. It is easy to mark the continuums by looking through children's daily samples and her anecdotal notes. Once a month, students select one writing sample for their portfolio. The children help bind the portfolio to give to their parents at the end of the year.

Figure 5.1 Marilyn O'Neill Taking Anecdotal Notes

Spelling Development

The Spelling Development Form (CBA Form 5.2) shows how young writers progress from scribble writing, to using random strings of letters, to relying on the sounds of the letters they hear, to spelling words phonetically. The form provides room to document a student's writing development three or four times during the year. You can record the date, check the developmental stage, and write a few notes. The Spelling Development form enables you to easily show writing growth to parents, supplemented by a few selected writing samples.

Emergent Writing Development

Sue Ondriezek, a kindergarten teacher in Mukilteo, Washington, modified the Spelling Development form in order to look more closely at the progression of young writers in the Preconventional stage. The Emergent Writing Development form (CBA 6.2) has room to note whether children are writing squiggly marks, letter-like marks, or random strings of letters. In addition, the form has room to note whether children can only vaguely remember what the piece was about, if they pretend to read the writing, or if children can actually point to the words as they read. You might want to look at both the Spelling Development and the Emergent Writing Development forms and decide which works best for you.

Words I Know

In *Classroom Based Assessment* (Hill, Ruptic, and Norwick, 1998), we described Marie Clay's (1993) technique of asking children three times a year to write all the words they know (Words I Know CBA Form 6.1). At the Preconventional stage, children may simply scribble or write random strings of letters. Kindergarten teachers who use this assessment technique usually see remarkable growth between the beginning and the end of the year.

Preconventional Reading: Assessment Tools

Continuum Descriptor	Assessment Tools
📖 Begins to choose reading materials (e.g., books, magazines, and charts) and has favorites.	Anecdotal Notes (DC Form 6.9) Parent Survey (DC Form 8.1)
📖 Shows interest in reading signs, labels, and logos (environmental print).	Anecdotal Notes (DC Form 6.9) Parent Survey (DC Form 8.1)
📖 Recognizes own name in print.	Anecdotal Notes (DC Form 6.9)
☑ Holds book and turns pages correctly.	Anecdotal Notes (DC Form 6.9) Concepts About Print (Clay, 2000)
☑ Shows beginning/end of book or story.	Anecdotal Notes (DC Form 6.9) Concepts About Print (Clay, 2000)
☑ Knows some letter names.	Anecdotal Notes (DC Form 6.9) Letter Recognition (CBA Form 8.1)
✋ Listens and responds to literature.	Anecdotal Notes (DC Form 6.9) Parent Survey (DC Form 8.1)
✋ Comments on illustrations in books.	Anecdotal Notes (DC Form 6.9) Parent Survey (DC Form 8.1)
✋ Participates in group reading (books, rhymes, poems, and songs).	Anecdotal Notes (DC Form 6.9)

Summary: Preconventional Reading Tools

Assessment Tool	9 Descriptors: Number Assessed	
Anecdotal Notes (DC Form 6.9)	9	(100%)
Parent Survey (DC Form 8.1)	4	(44%)
Concepts About Print (Clay, 2000)	2	(22%)
Letter Recognition (CBA Form 8.1)	1	(11%)

The foundations for reading are laid long before children come to school. Our job as teachers is to build on the knowledge about print that these children bring into our classrooms. Preschool and kindergarten teachers have the privilege of witnessing children's early forays into reading. Some of your students come with more literacy experiences at home than others. Your job is to affirm what they know and provide thoughtful instruction, as well as warm smiles, hugs, and great books as children unlock the mysteries of print. Children at this age grow so rapidly that our assessments must be ongoing. In addition, the marvelous energy of the children combined with the short amount of time you are with them, means that you have to plan ahead and be very thoughtful and organized about your assessments. How can you weave assessment into your daily routine? How can you make time to do individual conferences with each student? Which tools provide the most helpful information?

Anecdotal Notes

One of the best ways to assess early reading behaviors is to take anecdotal notes during quiet reading time. It's easy to observe which children stay engaged with a book, which ones read along with a pointer on poetry charts, and which ones can "read" a book from memory. Some kindergarten teachers target two children in the morning and two in the afternoon to watch during quiet reading time. Within two or three weeks, you will have at least one Post-it note about each child's reading strategies and response. You can note when a student picks a book to read during choice time or if two children chose to read together snuggled under a table. If students make wonderful comments or join in during your read aloud, you can jot down an anecdotal note as the class heads out to recess. In the busy world of kindergarten classrooms, if you don't write it down, the thought is probably gone by the end of the day. The key is to make note-taking part of your routine and to set realistic goals. One or two Post-it notes per day for each class is manageable. As the year progresses, you will have quite a bit of information about each child. These specifics are useful during parent conferences and when writing report card comments. You can assess all nine of the reading descriptors using anecdotal notes.

Concepts About Print

In *An Observation Survey of Early Literacy Achievement* (1993), Marie Clay describes a technique using two booklets (*Sand* and *Stone*) that you can use with Preconventional readers to assess their emerging Concepts About Print. She just published two alternate texts (*Follow Me, Moon*, 2000b and *No Shoes*, 2000c), along with an easy-to-read instructional booklet, called *Concepts About Print: What Have Children Learned about the Way We Print Language?* (2000a). The technique takes about 7–10 minutes for each student. As you read the text, ask the child to point out the cover, the title, and the words you're reading. The tasks get more challenging as the children discover pictures and words that are upside down and sentences that are backwards. If you use this tool with preschoolers and asked children to point to where you are reading, it is fascinating to see how many three and four year olds pointed to the illustrations, not yet realizing that print carries meaning. This is a perfect assessment tool for the beginning of the year or to use with new students as they join your class. There's no form in this book for this technique, so you will want to look at the directions and form in *Concepts About Print*. The Wright Group and Rigby have similar texts for assessing students' early concepts about the conventions of written language.

Parent Survey

No one is in a better spot to observe a child's emerging reading than parents. The Parent Survey included in Chapter 8 (DC Form 8.1) invites families to share what they know about their children's attitudes and interests in reading. At Curriculum Night, encourage families to send you notes when children memorize their first book or discover an illustrator they like. We want parents to feel like partners in the important job of helping their children become readers.

Letter Recognition

Like most kindergarten teachers, you probably use a letter recognition form to individually assess each child's knowledge of letter names and sounds. You most likely assess each child in September and several times throughout the year. You probably have a form you've used before, but we included a variation that Roz Duthie from Bainbridge Island, Washington created in *Classroom Based Assessment* (1998). The form contains room to record a child's knowledge of letter names and sounds in the fall, winter, and spring for both upper and lower case letters. What is unique about Roz's form is that she organized the letters into three categories of difficulty. The first list includes the "straightforward letters." The middle chart contains letters with two sounds, such as the letter "c" and the vowels. The last list includes letters that start with the "eh" sound (such as "n") and the "duh" sound (such as "w"), which are often confusing to young children. Some of you might want to use Roz's form (CBA Form 8.1), called the "Duthie Index," while others may prefer to use the "Letter Identification" form from *An Observation Survey* (Clay, 1993, p. 46) or a letter recognition form you've developed yourself.

Emerging Writing: Assessment Tools

Continuum Descriptor	Assessment Tools
📄 Uses pictures and print to convey meaning.	Writing Samples Words I Know (CBA Form 6.1) Emergent Writing Development (CBA Form 6.2)
📄 Writes words to describe or support pictures.	Writing Samples Emergent Writing Development (CBA Form 6.2)
📄 Copies signs, labels, names, and words (environmental print).	Writing Samples Anecdotal Notes (DC Form 6.7) Words I Know (CBA Form 6.1)
📁 Demonstrates understanding of letter/sound relationship.	Writing Samples Spelling Development (CBA Form 5.2) Words I Know (CBA Form 6.1) Emergent Writing Development (CBA Form 6.2)
✏ Prints with upper case letters.	Writing Samples
✏ Matches letters to sounds.	Writing Samples Spelling Development (CBA Form 5.2) Words I Know (CBA Form 6.1) Emergent Writing Development CBA Form 6.2)

cont.

✍ Uses beginning consonants to make words.	Writing Samples Spelling Development (CBA Form 5.2) Words I Know (CBA Form 6.1) Emergent Writing Development (CBA Form 6.2)
✍ Uses beginning and ending consonants to make words.	Writing Samples Spelling Development (CBA Form 5.2) Words I Know (CBA Form 6.1) Emergent Writing Development (CBA Form 6.2)
☺ Pretends to read own writing.	Anecdotal Notes (DC Form 6.7) Words I Know (CBA Form 6.1) Emergent Writing Development (CBA Form 6.2)
☺ Sees self as writer.	Anecdotal Notes (DC Form 6.7) Parent Survey (DC Form 8.1)
☺ Takes risks with writing.	Writing Samples Anecdotal Notes (DC Form 6.7)

Summary: Emerging Writing Tools

Assessment Tool	11 Descriptors: Number Assessed	
Writing Samples	9	(82%)
Words I Know (CBA Form 6.1)	7	(64%)
Emergent Writing Development (CBA Form 6.2)	7	(64%)
Spelling Development (CBA Form 5.2)	4	(36%)
Anecdotal Notes (DC Form 6.7)	4	(36%)
Parent Survey (DC Form 8.1)	1	(9%)

Kindergarten and first-grade teachers can learn a tremendous amount by looking carefully at students' writing samples. However, a writing sample is not an assessment tool; it's what you do with the information that makes the samples useful in evaluating student writing and planning your instruction.

Writing Samples

Do you cancel all evening activities and stay up far too late the week before parent conferences or report cards? Do you lug home tubs of journals each night and spend the weekend writing comments on report cards? One way in which to make assessment and reporting less overwhelming is to assess students on an ongoing basis. By looking at children's writing samples, you can assess 9 of the 11 descriptors at the Emerging stage. Some kindergarten and first-grade teachers establish a routine of looking at two students' writing folders or journals at the end of each day, then recording their observations on anecdotal notes or on a checklist. They might also jot themselves a note about a child's next steps or an idea for a whole-class or small-group focus lesson. By looking through two journals each day, you will have several comments for each student. Filling out the continuums becomes much less daunting by collecting evidence over time, rather than completing the continuums for all of your students at once.

It can be overwhelming to show parents too many writing samples during a brief 20-minute parent conference once or twice a year. Some primary teachers help students periodically select a few representative samples for their portfolios. Another way to capture growth over time is to create an accordion booklet such as the one Pam Pottle uses in her first-grade classroom in Bellingham, Washington. Pam tapes five pieces of construction paper side by side in alternating colors. The first page is the cover sheet and the last page includes a letter to parents. The other pages include photocopies of a writing sample from each month (Figure 5.2).

Figure 5.2 Monthly Writing Samples

She involves her young students in the selection process by giving each child a bright three-inch Post-it note each month. With much support and modeling, Pam teaches her first graders to place the sticky note on their best piece of writing. She asks each student, "Why is this a good piece of writing?" and "Why are you a good writer?" She and a parent volunteer circulate through the room and record the reason for each child's selection (Figure 5.3). Most children are very concrete at this age. For instance, Sarah celebrated the fact that she's writing longer pieces by noting in April, "I wrote a lot." The parent volunteer photocopies each child's selection, then mounts it into the accordion booklet, along with the child's reflection. These eight or nine monthly samples and periodic reflections provide the first step in helping students learn how to evaluate their own writing.

Figure 5.3 Pam Pottle—Portfolio Selection

Words I Know

Students who are starting to add labels to pictures and write the sounds they hear in words usually enjoy the Words I Know technique by Marie Clay (1993), described in *Classroom Based Assessment* (Hill, Ruptic and Norwick, 1998). Simply ask students to list all the words they know. It's important to model how to find words in the room, words children know "in their heads," as well as words they can "sound out." Cut paper into half vertically (4 1/4 x 11 inches) so the paper looks like a list (CBA Form 6.1). You might suggest that children start with their names and the names of people in their family and friends. Some students fill up both sides of the paper and even ask for another piece in order to write more words.

Once students have listed the words they know (10 minutes is usually enough), ask them to draw a line under their last word and put their pencils down. If you then let them get out of their seats and add to their list by looking around the room, you can observe many of their literacy behaviors in action. While they write, you can take anecdotal notes about the skills that you see your students using. This is a good opportunity to assess whether or not a student "Copies signs, labels, names, and words (environmental print)" which is a descriptor for Emerging Writers.

Have your students write all the words they know in the fall, mid-year, and at the end of the year. You can assess 7 of the 11 descriptors at this level by using this simple technique. A major advantage of this activity is that it can be done with the whole class in less than half an hour. If you plan to take anecdotal notes, you may want to use this assessment strategy with small groups rather than with the whole class.

In Figure 5.4, you can see how Michelle's list included 14 words at the beginning of the year, consisting mostly of names and words copied from around the room.

Figure 5.4 Words I Know—Fall Sample

In June (Figure 5.5), she lists 26 words which she even categorized into names and words she knows automatically, months, words she has learned (including an attempt at "Mississippi"), and even the name from the form (Words I Know). Notice that she's using more lower case letters, although she's struggling with how to form the letters "u," "n," and "r" correctly. Her fall list was written across the page, while her spring sample was written as a list.

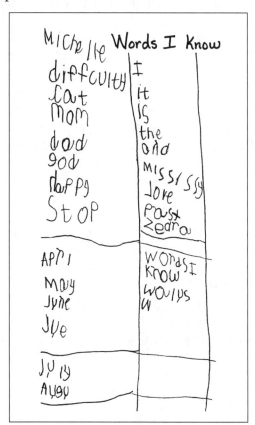

Figure 5.5 Words I Know—Spring Sample

Spelling Development and Emergent Writing Development

Once each grading period, you might also want to use the Spelling Development Form (CBA Form 5.2), which provides room to document a student's writing development. It's easy to record the date, check the developmental stage, and write a few comments. Others may prefer the Emergent Writing Development form (CBA 6.2). This form provides useful information about whether or not children can read their own writing. Marilyn O'Neill, a kindergarten teacher on Mercer Island, Washington, takes anecdotal notes as she asks her kindergartners to read her the plan they write for free choice each day. Once each trimester, she transfers the information from her notes to the Emergent Writing Development sheet (CBA Form 6.2) in order to record their emerging skills as readers and writers. Both forms are described in the Preconventional section of this chapter and provide room to record students' growing ability to use letters and words to express their ideas in writing and their growing concept of sound/symbol correspondence. At reporting time, it's easy to transfer the information from one of these forms to each student's writing continuum.

Anecdotal Notes

Four of the descriptors on the continuum at this stage cannot be assessed just by looking at writing samples. Some primary teachers take anecdotal notes using small $1^1/2$ x 2-inch Post-it notes during writing workshop to record whether students use the "words in the room" when they write. As students bring their writing to share with you or with the class, you can record which students merely talk about their writing and which ones pretend to read what they have written. You can also note if students see themselves as writers and if they take risks and are willing to try writing words. You might want to focus on two or three students each day to assess their early writing attitudes and behaviors.

Sue Elvrum, a kindergarten teacher at Brighton School in Lynnwood, Washington, finds that anecdotal notes and checklists are most useful when she decides on a specific focus for the month and records the focus in her plan book. After she and her assistant observe for a month, Sue takes an hour and transfers the Post-it notes to her Teacher Notebook and reflects on her observations.

Parent Survey

Many teachers find that a Parent Survey provides useful information at the beginning of the year. You may want to modify the survey from Chapter 8, which is also included on the CD-ROM (DC Form 8.1). This is another easy assessment tool since it doesn't take class time. The biggest challenge is getting all the surveys back! You can discover a parent's perceptions about their child as a writer, as well as clues about the student's interests and attitude toward writing. For instance, parents' views about spelling can have a significant impact on a child's willingness to take risks and use invented spelling. You can also discover which writing genres are familiar to children. The information from the survey is also useful as you help students select books or choose topics during writing workshop.

Emerging Reading: Assessment Tools

Continuum Descriptor	Assessment Tools
📖 Memorizes pattern books, poems, and familiar books.	Anecdotal Notes (DC Form 6.9) Parent Survey (DC Form 8.1)
📖 Begins to read signs, labels, and logos (environmental print).	Anecdotal Notes (DC Form 6.9) Parent Survey (DC Form 8.1)
☺ Demonstrates eagerness to read.	Anecdotal Notes (DC Form 6.9) Parent Survey (DC Form 8.1)
☑ Pretends to read.	Anecdotal Notes (DC Form 6.9)
☑ Uses illustrations to tell stories.	Anecdotal Notes (DC Form 6.9)
☑ Reads top to bottom, left to right, and front to back with guidance.	Anecdotal Notes (DC Form 6.9) Concepts About Print (Clay, 2000)
☑ Knows most letter names and some letter sounds.	Letter Recognition (CBA Form 8.1)
☑ Recognizes some names and words in context.	Anecdotal Notes (DC Form 6.9)
☑ Makes meaningful predictions with guidance.	Anecdotal Notes (DC Form 6.9)
☛ Rhymes and plays with words.	Anecdotal Notes (DC Form 6.9)
☛ Participates in reading of familiar books and poems.	Anecdotal Notes (DC Form 6.9) Parent Survey (DC Form 8.1)
☛ Connects books read aloud to own experiences with guidance.	Anecdotal Notes (DC Form 6.9) Parent Survey (DC Form 8.1)

Summary: Emerging Reading Tools

Assessment Tool	12 Descriptors: Number Assessed	
Anecdotal Notes (DC Form 6.9)	11	(92%)
Parent Survey (DC Form 8.1)	5	(42%)
Concepts About Print (Clay, 2000)	1	(8%)
Letter Recognition (CBA Form 8.1)	1	(8%)

As kindergarten and first-grade teachers, you see a tremendous amount of growth in your students as they take their first steps toward reading independently. You can see changes on a daily basis, but how can you share children's progress with each family? How can you record the specific skills each child is internalizing?

Anecdotal Notes
Eleven of the twelve reading descriptors can be assessed using anecdotal notes. You might want to focus on two or three students each day during silent reading time in order to assess their strategies and comprehension. It's easy to note when Antonio comes bursting in the door in the morning, eager to read a book he's just

memorized. You can record how Joseph and Monique used the intonation of reading in the restaurant in the play center when they "read" the menus and take orders. You might want to use anecdotal notes when Hong and Tacia chime in when you read *The Napping House* (Audrey Wood, 1984) aloud or when Carlos informs the class that his cat also fell in the toilet as you are reading *Cookie's Week* (Cindy Ward, 1988). Writing two or three such comments each day becomes manageable if you keep your clipboard handy and make note-taking part of your routine. Ongoing assessment means that the two weeks before parent conferences won't be quite so stressful!

Parent Survey

Sarah Otis, a first-grade teacher on Mercer Island, Washington, tells parents at Curriculum Night that memorizing books is one of the first stages of beginning to read. She stresses that parents (and siblings) should treat this stage as "real reading." You might want to modify the Parent Survey from Chapter 8 to include questions that would be appropriate for your particular group of students. What types of reading occur at home? Do families use the library and make time to read together? What books has the child memorized? Sarah sends the Parent Survey (DC Form 8.1) home in September. At parent conferences, she affirms what families are doing at home and uses the Family Support document from Chapter 8 to help parents choose a few new ways to support reading at home. Children are doubly blessed when their early reading is practiced and celebrated both at home and at school.

Concepts About Print and Letter Recognition

Marie Clay's (2000a) *Concepts About Print* technique and the Letter Recognition form (CBA Form 8.1) described in the Preconventional reading stage can still be useful in kindergarten and first grade for your Emerging readers. Do they know their letter names and sounds? Do they recognize some names and words in context? First-grade teachers may want to use these techniques with only those students still at the Preconventional and Emerging stages. The information you gather will be useful in planning the reading and writing activities that would be appropriate for children hovering on the brink of reading.

Developing Writing: Assessment Tools

Continuum Descriptor	Assessment Tools
📄 Writes 1–2 sentences about a topic.	Writing Samples
📄 Writes names and familiar words.	Writing Samples
📁 Generates own ideas for writing.	Anecdotal Notes (DC Form 6.7)
✍ Writes from top to bottom, left to right, and front to back.	Writing Samples
✍ Intermixes upper and lower case letters.	Writing Samples
✍ Experiments with capitals.	Writing Samples
✍ Experiments with punctuation.	Writing Samples
✍ Begins to use spacing between words.	Writing Samples

cont.

✍ Uses growing awareness of sound segments (e.g., phonemes, syllables, rhymes) to write words.	Writing Samples Anecdotal Notes (DC Form 6.7)
✍ Spells words on the basis of sounds without regard for conventional spelling patterns.	Writing Samples Spelling Development (CBA Form 5.2) Spelling Words (DC Form 5.5) Words I Know (CBA Form 6.1) Emergent Writing Development (CBA Form 6.2)
✍ Uses beginning, middle, and ending sounds to make words.	Writing Samples Spelling Development (CBA Form 5.2) Spelling Words (DC Form 5.5) Words I Know (CBA Form 6.1) Emergent Writing Development (CBA Form 6.2)
☺ Begins to read own writing.	Anecdotal Notes (DC Form 6.7) Emergent Writing Development (CBA Form 6.2) Parent Survey (DC Form 8.1)

Summary: Developing Writing Tools

Assessment Tool	12 Descriptors: Number Assessed	
Writing Samples	10	(83%)
Emergent Writing Development (CBA Form 6.2)	3	(25%)
Anecdotal Notes (DC Form 6.7)	3	(25%)
Words I Know (CBA Form 6.1)	2	(17%)
Spelling Development (CBA Form 5.2)	2	(17%)
Spelling Words (DC Form 5.5)	2	(17%)
Parent Survey (DC Form 8.1)	1	(8%)

Writing Samples

By the Developing stage, students are beginning to write short sentences. The same assessment tools that were described at the Emerging stage are appropriate here. Ten of the twelve descriptors for this stage can be assessed by examining students' writing samples. How can you document what you learn from looking at student work?

Anecdotal Notes

As mentioned for Emerging writers, you might want to look through two student journals each day and take anecdotal notes. You can also use your anecdotal notes to record if students are able to choose topics to write about, use their growing awareness of sounds to write independently, and if they can read what they have written. Sandy Figel at Brighton School commented that since her second graders write every day, she feels like she knows their writing skills very well. She uses anecdotal notes primarily to record new learning or breakthroughs. You may find that the Anecdotal Notes Focus Questions (DC Form 6.7) and Checklists (DC Form 6.15) described Chapter 6 are helpful as you use this assessment strategy.

Words I Know

When Roz Duthie used the Words I Know strategy with her first graders on Bainbridge Island, Washington, she found that most of her students knew too many words to list, especially by the end of the year. She "upped the ante" by modifying the technique. In the fall, students simply listed the words they knew. When they read *Samuel Eaton's Day* (Kate Walters, 1993) in November and studied Pilgrim daily life, she asked the children to list the things they do on a typical day. In the spring, Roz read *Frog and Toad Together* (Arnold Lobel, 1971) in which Toad keeps a list of "Things To Do Today" and Roz asked her first graders to create a similar list. These three lists show children's growing ability to spell words (e.g., their understanding of word endings, word families, silent leters) and provide a dramatic way to show early spelling and writing growth to students and families.

Spelling Development and Emergent Writing Development

The descriptors for spelling development were originally included on the Writing Continuum, but many teachers and parents wanted to examine spelling development more closely. Many primary teachers share the Spelling Continuum (DC Form 5.6) at Back to School Night in the fall as they show examples of the developmental spelling progression of young writers. The Spelling Development (CBA Form 5.2) and the Emergent Writing Development (CBA Form 6.2) forms are based on the Spelling Continuum. These two forms can help you document if students can read what they've written, as well as identify their early spelling strategies.

Spelling Words

A new technique that can be used at this stage is the Spelling Words (DC Form 5.5). This has been one of the most popular assessment tools with teachers around the world. Three times a year, give students a list of the same 10–15 words to spell. The first-grade list came from *Teaching Kids to Spell* (Gentry and Gillet, 1993). Lists for other grade levels are included at the end of this chapter and on the CD-ROM. These words are not ones you would expect children this age to spell correctly. Rather, they are challenging words that provide a window into a student's understanding of the conventions of English language and their strategies for spelling difficult words.

Because young children might find this task daunting, some kindergarten teachers tell the children that if they're not sure how to spell a word, "put a happy face on that line to show that you're happy to learn that word this year" (Figure 5.6). This positive approach helps all students feel successful. After Christy Clausen used the Spelling Words assessment with her first graders in the fall and again mid-year, she asked students to compare the two lists and write about what they noticed. Students commented about neater printing and the letters they left out in words at the beginning of the year. In this way, an assessment tool can also become a self-evaluation strategy, even with young children.

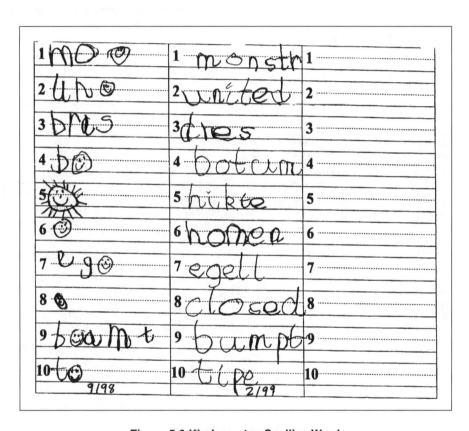

Figure 5.6 Kindergarten Spelling Words

Parent Survey

Finally, the Parent Survey (DC Form 8.1) can provide information about children's writing at home as well as their parents' goals. You may want to support families' interest in helping children at home by hosting a Family Night about writing development, sending parents home with copies of the Spelling Continuum (CBA Form 6.1), the Narrative Portraits (Chapter 2), and the Family Support document for writing (Chapter 8).

Developing Reading: Assessment Tools

Continuum Descriptor	Assessment Tools
📖 Reads books with simple patterns.	Anecdotal Notes (DC Form 6.9) Running Records (CBA Form 8.2) Parent Survey (DC Form 8.1) Photocopy of Reading Sample
📖 Begins to read own writing.	Anecdotal Notes (DC Form 6.9) Emergent Writing Development (CBA Form 9.6)
☺ Begins to read independently for short periods (5–10 minutes).	Anecdotal Notes (DC Form 6.9, 6.11)
☺ Discusses favorite reading material with others.	Anecdotal Notes (DC Form 6.9) Parent Survey (DC Form 8.1)
☑ Relies on illustrations and print.	Anecdotal Notes (DC Form 6.9, 6.11) Running Records (CBA Form 8.2)
☑ Uses finger-print-voice matching.	Anecdotal Notes (DC Form 6.9, 6.11)
☑ Knows most letter sounds and letter clusters.	Letter Recognition (CBA Form 8.1)
☑ Recognizes simple words.	Running Records (CBA Form 8.2)
☑ Uses growing awareness of sound segments (e.g., phonemes, syllables, rhymes) to read words.	Anecdotal Notes (DC Form 6.9, 6.11) Running Records (CBA Form 8.2)
☑ Begins to make meaningful predictions.	Anecdotal Notes (DC Form 6.9, 6.11) Running Records (CBA Form 8.2)
☑ Identifies titles and authors in literature (text features).	Anecdotal Notes (DC Form 6.9, 6.11) Running Records (CBA Form 8.2)
☝ Retells main event or idea in literature.	Anecdotal Notes (DC Form 6.9) Running Records (CBA Form 8.2)
☝ Participates in guided literature discussions.	Anecdotal Notes (DC Form 6.9, 6.12)
↪ Sees self as reader.	Anecdotal Notes (DC Form 6.9, 6.11) Parent Survey (DC Form 8.1)
↪ Explains why literature is liked/disliked during class discussions with guidance.	Anecdotal Notes (DC Form 6.9, 6.12)

Summary: Developing Reading Tools

Assessment Tool	15 Descriptors: Number Assessed	
Anecdotal Notes (DC Form 6.9, 6.11, 6.12)	13	(87%)
Running Records (CBA Form 8.2)	7	(47%)
Parent Survey (DC Form 8.1)	3	(20%)
Letter Recognition (CBA Form 8.1)	1	(7%)
Emergent Writing Development (CBA Form 9.6)	1	(7%)
Photocopy of Reading Sample and Reflection	1	(7%)

Anecdotal Notes

As in the two previous stages, the majority of descriptors of Developing readers can be assessed by using anecdotal notes. The biggest challenge is weaving anecdotal notes into your daily routine. It's helpful to target one particular descriptor, such as "Begins to read independently for short periods (5–10 minutes)." You can assess four or five students each day during silent reading time, looking primarily for their level of engagement with books. Sandy Figel at Brighton School, finds that when she looks closely with a zoom lens, she notices much more about her students than if she uses the wide-angle lens of observation. She may have to help Michael find a book and remind Stephanie to put away her yo-yo, but she can still look closely at four or five other readers. Rather than merely scanning the room and trying to watch everyone at once, you can focus your observations on specific behaviors, making your notes more intentional and informative. Sandy finds anecdotal notes particularly useful for assessing comprehension during small-group literature circles. She records her second graders' ability to retell the main events and to make predictions, as well as the contributions they make to the conversation.

Running Records

Perhaps the biggest change in reading in primary classrooms in the past five years has been the growing numbers of teachers who use running records. Running records are the best way to assess the reading strategies of Developing and Beginning readers. In fact, you can assess almost half of the reading descriptors at this stage by using running records. Running records are a technique in which you listen to a child read and record his or her mistakes or "miscues." A new book by Marie Clay, *Running Record for Classroom Teachers* (2000d), provides specific and clear directions for this technique. Most teachers analyze the errors to determine what strategies a child is using and what new skills to teach. You can mark the child's miscues directly on a photocopy of the text the student is reading, however, you probably don't have time to run to the office during the day to make copies of each child's text. In addition, you wouldn't have an organized way to analyze students' miscues. When she taught in Richmond, Washington, Lisa Norwick modified the traditional Running Record form (CBA Form 8.2) in order to have columns for tabulating cueing systems and self-corrections. For more information about this strategy and this particular form, see Chapter 6 on Assessing Emergent Readers in *Classroom Based Assessment* (Hill, Ruptic, and Norwick,1998).

Lisa takes running records on two students each day during silent reading time. This predictable schedule allows her to meet with students regularly to monitor their reading progress. It also gives her vital information about when a child is ready to read more challenging texts. The information you gather from running records about children's reading strategies can help you match students' needs with just the right book. (For more information about leveled books, see Chapter 4.) Other teachers take running records at the beginning or end of each guided reading group.

Parent Survey

You might want to send home the Parent Survey (DC Form 8.1) in order to learn parents' perceptions of their child as a reader. Children sometimes demonstrate different behaviors at school than at home. It is helpful to learn how much students read at home, as well as the types of books they prefer.

Letter Recognition and Emergent Writing Development

You may want to use the Duthie Index (CBA Form 8.1) from *Classroom Based Assessment* (1998) or your own letter recognition form with your Developing readers, as described in the previous stage. You can track when children begin to develop finger-voice-print matching, directionality, and a bank of words they can read. By the Developing stage, children should know most letter sounds and clusters as they begin reading books with simple patterns.

The Emergent Writing Development strategy (CBA Form 9.6) described in the Preconventional Writing section provides room to track when children first begin to be able to read their own writing.

Photocopy of Reading Sample and Reflection

If I told you that Christine had progressed from reading *Brown Bear, Brown Bear* (Bill Martin, Jr., 1967) to *Frog and Toad* (Arnold Lobel, 1971) in first grade, you would be impressed. However, most parents aren't as familiar with books and authors as you are. One of the most meaningful assessment tools for teachers and parents is simply to photocopy a sample page from a book the student can read independently in the fall, mid-year, and at the end of the year. Be sure to note the child's name, date, title, and author on the back of each sample. When you put those three samples side by side, families and the students themselves can visually recognize reading growth. At Brighton School, teachers at every grade level photocopy a reading sample for each student in the fall and spring of every year. These samples are placed in chronological order in a Learner Profile that travels with each child from year to year from kindergarten through eighth grade. This simple assessment tool provides a visual way to capture reading growth over time.

Beginning Writing: Assessment Tools

Continuum Descriptor	Assessment Tools
📄 Writes several sentences about a topic.	Writing Samples Writing Strategies I Use (CBA Form 7.4)
📄 Writes about observations and experiences.	Writing Samples Pieces I've Written (CBA Form 7.2)
📄 Writes short nonfiction pieces (simple facts about a topic) with guidance.	Writing Samples Pieces I've Written (CBA Form 7.2)
📁 Chooses own writing topics.	Anecdotal Notes (DC Form 6.7) Writing Topics (CBA Form 7.1) Pieces I've Written (CBA Form 7.2)
✂ Reads own writing and notices mistakes with guidance.	Anecdotal Notes (DC Form 6.7)

cont.

✂ Revises by adding details with guidance.	Writing Samples Anecdotal Notes(DC Form 6.7)
✍ Uses spacing between words consistently.	Writing Samples
	Writing Strategies I Use (CBA Form 7.4)
✍ Forms most letters legibly.	Writing Samples
✍ Writes pieces that self and others can read.	Writing Samples
✍ Uses phonetic spelling to write independently.	Writing Samples Spelling Words (DC Form 5.5) Spelling Analysis
✍ Spells simple words and some high frequency words correctly.	Writing Samples Spelling Analysis
✍ Begins to use periods and capital letters correctly.	Writing Samples
☺ Shares own writing with others.	Anecdotal Notes (DC Form 6.7) Writing Strategies I Use (CBA Form 7.4) Parent Survey (DC Form 8.1, 8.2)

Summary: Beginning Writing Tools

Assessment Tool	13 Descriptors: Number Assessed	
Writing Samples	10	(77%)
Anecdotal Notes (DC Form 6.7)	4	(31%)
Writing Strategies I Use (CBA Form 7.4)	3	(23%)
Pieces I've Written (CBA Form 7.2)	3	(23%)
Spelling Analysis	2	(15%)
Spelling Words (DC Form 5.5)	1	(8%)
Writing Topics (CBA Form 7.1)	1	(8%)
Parent Survey (DC Form 8.1, 8.2)	1	(8%)

Writing Samples

Students at the Beginning stage take a big step as writers as they begin to compose several sentences about a topic. You can assess 10 of the 13 descriptors at this stage by looking at students' writing samples. It's easy to check whether children are using spacing between words, writing short sentences, printing legibly, using periods and capital letters correctly, and spelling simple words and some high frequency words correctly. It is also easy to note their choices of topics and types of writing by looking through students' journals.

Anecdotal Notes

It's more challenging to record students' early revision strategies. You may want to take anecdotal notes during writing workshop and Author's Chair to record the kinds of changes your Beginning writers make. You can determine if children can choose their own topics, if they are willing to share their writing, and if they notice mistakes when they read their piece aloud. As you confer with students, you can record if they can add details with your help. As students become more independent during writing time, it becomes easier to move around the classroom to talk with students and to take anecdotal notes.

Spelling Words and Spelling Analysis

Note that by this stage, we've omitted the Emergent Writing Development and Spelling Development forms since students are now writing sentences rather than just words. Instead of using anecdotal notes to assess spelling growth, you may want to use the Spelling Words technique (DC Form 5.5) described in previous stages. The lists of 10 words for each grade level are included at the end of this chapter and on the CD-ROM. It's not just the number of words a child spells correctly that's important with this technique. You can learn a great deal by analyzing the strategies young writers uses as they spell unfamiliar and challenging words.

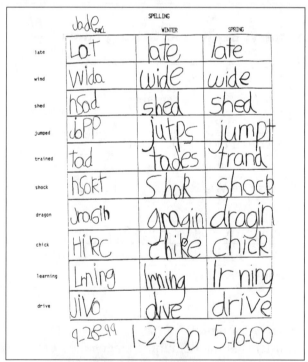

Figure 5.7 First Grade Spelling Words

Notice the difference between Jade's sample (Figure 5.7) from the fall when she was only using a few correct letters from a word and in June, when her approximations are much closer. For instance, "jumped" was written as "jopp" the fall, as "jutps" mid-year, and as "jumpt" by the end of the year. Diana Kastner, a first-grade teacher at Brighton School, uses the Words I Know assessment three times a year. She finds that it is a simple technique and another easy way to demonstrate growth to parents. She often shares a student sample at Back to School Night to show parents the rapid growth most of their young writers will make in first grade. The results from Spelling Words can help you tailor your instruction to the developmental needs of your students.

Another simple technique for assessing spelling is the Spelling Analysis. At the International School of Brussels, Cecilia Vanderhye reads a short story from one of the *Frog and Toad* books by Arnold Lobel aloud to her class. Students then retell the story in writing. Cecilia simply circles the misspelled words and at the bottom of the page, counts the number of words used, then calculates the percentage of words spelled correctly and the percentage using invented spelling. She uses the same story again in the spring. One of her ESL students from Finland, Joanna, used 85 words in the fall, with only 34% of the words spelled conventionally. Cecilia noted that she used the letter "k" instead of "c" in many of the words based on the sound in Finnish ("kame" instead of "came"). By the end of the year, Joanna's retelling used 99 words and 78% of her words were spelled correctly and she was using past tense correctly. This assessment strategy provides a powerful way to document spelling growth over time. There is no form for this technique, so you may want to record this idea on your Assessment Planning sheet (DCA Form 5.4).

You may also find that parents who have been fairly low key about their child's writing suddenly become more intense and concerned about correct spelling in second grade. Sharing a sample of a student's spelling growth using the Spelling Words or Spelling Analysis strategy at Back to School Night can help parents see the developmental nature of spelling and how much students at this age learn in one year. You may also want to share Richard Gentry's book, *My Kid Can't Spell* (1997) with families.

Pieces I've Written, Writing Strategies I Use, and Parent Survey

Two new assessment strategies have been added at the Beginning stage. When students begin to write longer pieces, many first- and second-grade teachers introduce the Pieces I've Written form (CBA Form 7.2) which serves as a table of contents for their writing folder. At a glance, you can determine if students can write simple facts about a topic and if they write about their own observations and experiences.

The second new form is Writing Strategies I Use (CBA Form 7.4), which includes a checklist for writing genres, strategies, and conventions that most teachers would expect of their first and second graders. The form was written in first person so students can begin to assess their own writing strategies. In the left column, you can date when a child can demonstrate the skill only with adult support and when the skill is used independently. The descriptors on the Writing Strategies I Use form were developed by primary teachers to match the descriptors in the first four stages of the writing continuum. The Pieces I've Written and Writing Strategies I Use forms can help students become part of the assessment process. You can add parents' perspectives of their child's writing at home by using the Parent Survey (DC Form 8.1 or 8.2). This triangulated information (from the teacher, the student, and the family) provides a rich portrait of Beginning writers.

Beginning Reading: Assessment Tools

Continuum Descriptor	Assessment Tools
📖 Reads simple early-reader books.	Anecdotal Notes (DC Form 6.9, 6.11) Reading Log (CBA Form 9.21–22) Parent Survey (DC Form 8.1) Photocopy of Reading Sample
📖 Reads harder early-reader books.	Anecdotal Notes (DC Form 6.9, 6.11) Reading Log (CBA Form 9.21–22) Parent Survey (DC Form 8.1) Photocopy of Reading Sample
📖 Reads and follows simple written directions with guidance.	Anecdotal Notes (DC Form 6.9)
📖 Identifies basic genres (e.g., fiction, nonfiction, and poetry).	Anecdotal Notes (DC Form 6.9) Reading Log (CBA Form 9.21–22)
📖 Uses basic punctuation when reading orally.	Reading Conference (CBA Form 9.6)
☺ Reads independently (10–15 minutes).	Anecdotal Notes (DC Form 6.9) Reading Strategies I Use (CBA Form 9.3)
☺ Chooses reading materials independently.	Anecdotal Notes (DC Form 6.9) Reading Strategies I Use (CBA Form 9.3) Reading Conference (CBA Form 9.6) Reading Survey (DC Form 7.4)
☺ Learns and shares information from reading.	Anecdotal Notes (DC Form 6.9) Reading Strategies I Use (CBA Form 9.3)
☑ Uses meaning cues (context).	Running Records (CBA Form 8.2) Reading Conference (CBA Form 9.6)
☑ Uses sentence cues (grammar).	Running Records (CBA Form 8.2) Reading Conference (CBA Form 9.6)
☑ Uses letter/sound cues and patterns (phonics).	Running Records (CBA Form 8.2) Reading Conference (CBA Form 9.6)
☑ Recognizes word endings, common contractions, and many high frequency words.	Running Records (CBA Form 8.2) Reading Conference (CBA Form 9.6)
☑ Begins to self-correct.	Running Records (CBA Form 8.2) Reading Conference (CBA Form 9.6)
✎ Retells beginning, middle, and end with guidance.	Reading Strategies I Use (CBA Form 9.3) Retelling (CBA Form 9.17–9.18)

cont.

☞ Discusses characters and story events with guidance.	Anecdotal Notes (DC Form 6.9, 6.11, 6.12)
	Reading Conference (CBA Form 9.6)
	Literature Discussions (CBA Forms 9.12, 9.13)
	Response Journals (CBA Form 9.14, 9.15)
	Retelling (CBA Form 9.17–9.18)
	Parent Survey (DC Form 8.1)
☞ Identifies own reading behaviors with guidance.	Anecdotal Notes (DC Form 6.9)
	Reading Strategies I Use (CBA Form 9.6) Reading Survey (DC Form 7.4)
	Reading Goals (CBA Form 9.4)

Summary: Beginning Reading Tools

Assessment Tool	15 Descriptors: Number Assessed	
Anecdotal Notes (DC Form 6.9, 6.11, 6.12)	9	(60%)
Reading Conference (CBA Form 9.6)	8	(53%)
Running Records (CBA Form 8.2)	5	(33%)
Reading Strategies I Use (CBA Form 9.3)	5	(33%)
Reading Log (CBA Form 9.21, 9.22)	3	(20%)
Parent Survey (DC Form 8.1)	3	(20%)
Photocopy of Reading Sample and Reflection	2	(13%)
Retelling (CBA Form 9.17, 9.18)	2	(13%)
Reading Survey (DC Form 7.4)	2	(13%)
Literature Discussions (CBA Forms 9.12, 9.13)	1	(7%)
Response Journals (CBA Form 9.14, 9.15)	1	(7%)
Reading Goals (CBA Form 9.4)	1	(7%)

Anecdotal Notes

Megan Sloan in Snohomish, Washington uses anecdotal notes to assess her second graders' reading range, comprehension, and attitude. She "clipboard cruises" during silent reading time and records what her students are reading and how long they can read independently. Megan also takes anecdotal notes during literature circle discussions. Her students meet in cozy groups of two or three students. She roams around the room recording their comments as they read a page, then pauses to talk about the characters and story events. Megan finds her notes to be extremely helpful in filling out the reading continuums. She uses the Anecdotal Notes Focus Questions for Reading (DC Form 6.9) and for Literature Circles (DC Form 6.12) to guide her observations.

Reading Conferences and Running Records

You could record students' reading strategies using anecdotal notes, but you would probably find that there's simply too much to write. It's more efficient to use a Reading Conference form (CBA Form 9.6) or the Running Records checklist (CBA Form 8.2) to assess reading strategies. Megan Sloan uses running records with two students each day during silent reading time. Megan places a check mark on the Running Record form (CBA Form 8.2) to represent each word the student reads correctly and also records any miscues. She uses the running record form to analyze which cueing systems the students rely upon and how often they self-correct. Her goal is to teach Beginning readers how to cross check by using more than one cueing system.

Lisa Norwick alternates between using running records and the Reading Conference checklist (CBA Form 9.6). She uses running records in September for baseline information. As students become more proficient and move into the Expanding stage, she switches to the Reading Conference form, which has room to record observations about a student's comprehension and fluency, as well as the specific strategy Lisa has taught. As students begin to read early-reader books, you can also record if they use basic punctuation as they read aloud. Running records provide more detailed diagnostic information, but requires some training and practice. You will have to decide which form works best for your teaching style and the reading abilities of your students.

Reading Survey, Reading Strategies I Use, and Reading Goals

By the time students can read harder early-reader books, you might want to involve them in the assessment process. The Primary Reading Survey (DC Form 7.4) can be a starting point for discussions in class about choosing books, favorite authors, where students prefer to read, as well as reading strategies. Lisa Norwick photocopies the Reading Survey on yellow paper in the fall and on pink paper in the spring. By asking the same questions over time, she can see clearly how much her students have grown as readers in one year.

You could include the Reading Strategies I Use form (CBA Form 9.3) in students' reading folders. As students read with you, with partners, and in literature circles, you can ask them to list the strategies they used. You can look over the form when you do reading conferences or running records and ask students to show you evidence of those strategies as they're reading. Using this form would help you assess the last descriptor at the Beginning reading stage: "Identifies own reading behaviors with guidance." Of course, you will need to explain the language, provide examples during focus lessons, and draw attention to the effective reading strategies that you see students using.

When Lisa Norwick introduced this form to her second graders, she talked about the first four strategies on Monday and students placed and "x" to show if they needed help or were independent in picking books and staying focused. The next day, Lisa modeled and discussed reading strategies as students evaluated these aspects of reading. She then discussed types of text and response and comprehension strategies on the following two days. Notice Mara's growing skills and honest self-evaluation between October (Figure 5.8) and April (Figure 5.9).

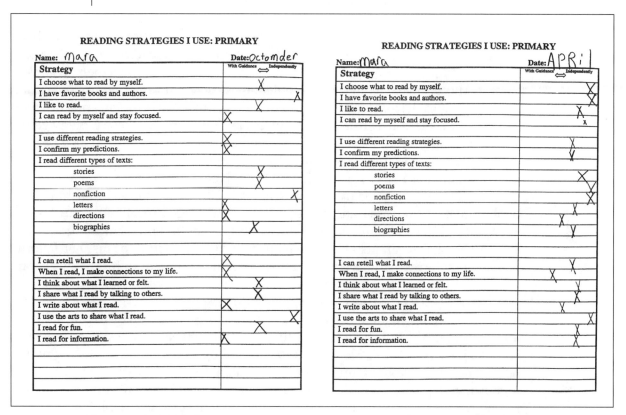

Figure 5.8 Fall Reading Strategies Self-Evaluation

Figure 5.9 Spring Reading Strategies Self-Evaluation

After a few months of listening to their second graders read, Sandy Figel and Donna Kerns at Brighton School brainstorm a class list of possible reading goals. Each student then selects a goal, which they write on a bookmark. The goal may be to read a longer book or read with more expression. The bookmark with each child's goal serves as a reminder to the student and to the teachers during reading conferences. You could also use the Goals form (CBA Form 9.4), which could be stapled to the front of students' reading folders.

Reading Logs, Parent Survey, and Photocopy of Reading Samples and Reflection

In Diana Kastner's first grade at Brighton School, her students keep track of the leveled books they read in class. They also keep a Reading Log (CBA Form 9.21–9.22) of the books that are read at home. By this stage, students should be reading fiction, nonfiction, and poetry. You can celebrate both the increasing difficulty of the books and the quantity of reading these students are doing. By photocopying a page from the books they read two or three times a year, it's easy to show growth to parents and to the students themselves. For instance, in September, Kyle could read simple books with a few words on a page as an Emerging reader. By the end of the year, he was reading harder early-reader books at the Beginning stage such as the *Henry and Mudge* series by Cynthia Rylant. These two samples, laid side by side, provided clear evidence of reading growth.

You may want to send Parent Survey (DC Form 8.1) home at the beginning of the year in order to learn more about your students' favorite books and authors. You can also glean information about how often parents read to their children at home. At Brighton School, each child has a videotape that follows them from year to year. The principal, Cliff Nelson, videotapes each child reading in the fall and again in the spring from kindergarten through eighth grade. Students practice their selection and mark it with a Post-it note. Their teachers photocopy the page the child read aloud, then the fall and spring samples are placed together in their Learner Profiles. Parents treasure these visual glimpses of reading growth.

A primary teacher at The Manhattan School in New York City, Pam Mayer, has her students vote on their five favorite books of the year. She reads each of these books into a tape recorder and makes a copy of the tape for each of her students to take home at the end of the year. What a special way to remember favorite books and teachers! You can also have each student draw a picture of his/her favorite book and make these into a collection for each student or a quilt for the classroom.

Retelling, Literature Discussions and Response Journal Self-Evaluations

During reading conferences, you can assess comprehension by asking students a few questions about the selection they read. Retelling a whole story, however, takes a bit longer. Megan Sloan introduces retelling as part of a storytelling unit in her second-grade classroom in Snohomish, Washington. Students read a picture book together, then practice retelling it to each other. Once her students understand that a good retelling should include information about the characters, plot, setting, and supporting details, she uses the Retelling form (CBA Form 9.17–9.18) as one way to assess comprehension.

Megan also takes anecdotal notes during literature circle discussions in order to assess comprehension. Once students are Beginning readers, Megan introduces a Literature Discussion Self-Evaluation form (CBA Form 9.12). The class brainstorms a list of what students could talk about during a discussion. For instance, the list usually includes "talk about your favorite part of the story" and "talk about the characters." Over the course of the year, the list becomes more sophisticated. After much modeling, the second graders are able to write what they did well during the literature circle discussion and how they could improve.

Some children may be quiet during discussions, but their written responses show strong comprehension. You can also provide examples of thoughtful journal entries on the overhead as your class constructs a list of the criteria for quality journal responses. From the list, you can generate your own rubric or modify the Response Journal Rubric (CBA Form 9.15). Once students are launched as readers, their retellings, discussions, and response journals reveal a great deal about their level of comprehension.

Expanding Writing: Assessment Tools

Continuum Descriptor	Assessment Tools
📄 Writes short fiction and poetry with guidance.	Writing Samples Pieces I've Written (CBA Form 7.2) Writing Genres (CBA Form 7.3) Writing Strategies I Use (CBA Form 7.4)
📄 Writes a variety of short nonfiction pieces (e.g., facts about a topic, letters, lists) with guidance.	Writing Samples Pieces I've Written (CBA Form 7.2) Writing Genres (CBA Form 7.3) Writing Strategies I Use (CBA Form 7.4)
📂 Writes with a central idea.	Writing Samples Six-Trait Guide (CBA Form 7.11)
📂 Writes using complete sentences.	Writing Samples
📂 Organizes ideas in a logical sequence in fiction and nonfiction writing with guidance.	Writing Samples Writing Strategies I Use (CBA Form 7.4) Guide (CBA Form 7.11) Primary Rubric (CBA Form 7.17)
📂 Begins to recognize and use interesting language.	Writing Samples Anecdotal Notes (DC Form 6.7, 6.8) Six-Trait Guide (CBA Form 7.11) Primary Rubric (CBA Form 7.17)
✂ Uses several prewriting strategies (e.g., web, brainstorm) with guidance.	Writing Samples/Drafts Anecdotal Notes (DC Form 6.7, 6.8)
✂ Listens to others' writing and offers feedback.	Anecdotal Notes (DC Form 6.7, 6.8)
✂ Begins to consider suggestions from others about own writing.	Anecdotal Notes (DC Form 6.7, 6.8)
✂ Adds description and detail with guidance.	Writing Samples/Drafts "Fix-it" Strategy Anecdotal Notes (DC Form 6.7, 6.8) Primary Rubric (CBA Form 7.17)
✂ Edits for capitals and punctuation with guidance.	Writing Samples/Drafts "Fix-it" Strategy Writing Strategies I Use (CBA Form 7.4) Six-Trait Guide (CBA Form 7.11) Primary Rubric (CBA Form 7.17)
✂ Publishes own writing with guidance.	Writing Samples/Drafts Pieces I've Written (CBA Form 7.2)
✍ Writes legibly.	Writing Samples
✍ Spells most high frequency words correctly and moves toward conventional spelling.	Writing Samples Spelling Strategies I Use (CBA Form 5.3) Spelling Words (DC Form 5.5) Spelling Survey (DC Form 7.1)
☺ Identifies own writing strategies and sets goals with guidance.	Writing Strategies I Use (CBA Form 7.4) Writing Survey (DC Form 7.2, 7.3) Portfolio Reflections and Self-Evaluation Writing Goals (CBA Form 7.5)

Summary: Expanding Writing Tools

Assessment Tool	15 Descriptors: Number Assessed	
Writing Samples	12	(80%)
Writing Strategies I Use (CBA Form 7.4)	5	(33%)
Anecdotal Notes (DC Form 6.7, 6.8)	5	(33%)
Primary Rubric (CBA Form 7.17)	4	(27%)
Six-Trait Guide (CBA Form 7.11)	4	(27%)
Pieces I've Written (CBA Form 7.2)	3	(20%)
Writing Genres (CBA Form 7.3)	2	(13%)
"Fix-it" Strategy	2	(13%)
Spelling Survey (DC Form 7.1)	1	(7%)
Spelling Words (DC Form 5.5)	1	(7%)
Spelling Strategies I Use (CBA Form 5.3)	1	(7%)
Writing Survey (DC Form 7.2, 7.3)	1	(7%)
Portfolio Reflections and Self-Evaluation	1	(7%)
Writing Goals (CBA Form 7.5)	1	(7%)

Writing Samples and Anecdotal Notes

Your eyes may widen as you look at the growing list of assessment tools at the Expanding stage! Don't be daunted by the longer list of assessment tools at this stage. Except for anecdotal notes, your students would fill out all the other forms—with your help, of course. Besides teaching focus lessons and sharing examples, your task would be to analyze writing samples, give the Spelling Words test (DC Form 5.5) three times a year, and take anecdotal notes. Take a look at this list of three spelling and eleven writing assessment tools for Bridging writers. Choose two or three that would best work for your teaching style and grade level and plan which months you will use each tool by using the Organizational Grid (Form 5.3).

By looking closely at a child's writing, you can still assess 12 of the 15 continuum descriptors at the Expanding stage. Students at the Expanding stage can write a page or two on a topic. They begin to revise and edit their writing and the best way to see growth is to look at their drafts and published pieces. Megan Sloan finds that by the end of second grade, the structure of writing workshop is in place and most of her students are able to work independently. This enables Megan to roam around the room with her clipboard, confer with individual children or small groups, and take anecdotal notes or use a checklist. She first teaches a particular technique, such as adding detail, then uses her anecdotal notes to assess which students have tried this new strategy. Her assessment is directly linked to her instruction, particularly as students begin to incorporate interesting language, description, and details. During Author's Chair, Megan also records a few of her students' suggestions to the author. You may want to ask students to attach their drafts to published work so that readers (especially parents and other teachers) can see the process as well as the final products. Learning to write longer pieces and to revise and edit is a huge leap for young writers and will take many years to internalize.

Writing Strategies I Use, Pieces I've Written, and Writing Genres

At the Expanding stage, how can you document the types of writing your students produce? Many of you have genre wheels for reading, but what about for writing? Students can record whether they write fiction, nonfiction, or poetry on either the Writing Strategies I Use (CBA Form 7.4) or Pieces I've Written (CBA Form 7.2) forms. By placing an asterisk (*) by the writing they publish on the Pieces I've Written form, you can also keep track of how much students have published. The Writing Strategies I Use form can also be used to note if students' writing is organized, interesting, and legible. A third option for assessing the range of student writing would be to have students use the primary Writing Genres graph (CBA Form 7.3). You might want to keep a copy of this chart by your desk or in your plan book as a reminder of the genres and forms of writing you need to model.

Six-Trait Writing Guide, Rubrics, and Checklists

If you are not familiar with the Six-Trait model of writing, you may want to contact the Northwest Regional Educational Laboratory (NWREL) in Portland (800-547-6339 or www.nwrel.org) for more information and a copy of their catalog. *Seeing with New Eyes* by Vicki Spandel (1997) provides teaching suggestions and *Picture Book* by Ruth Culham (1998) includes an annotated list of picture books you can use to teach each writing trait. Based on this model, writing instruction is organized around six traits: ideas, organization, sentence fluency, word choice, voice, and conventions.

Teachers often begin the year by discussing how writers choose topics and having students create their own topic list. The proper use of conventions is perhaps the most concrete skill to teach and can be woven into the editing process. Once students are writing longer pieces, organization becomes a major focus. You can teach organization as one of the six writing traits. By using examples from literature and from students, as well as modeling with your own writing, children can use the organization component of the Six-Trait Writing Guide (CBA Form 7.11) for self-evaluation. After showing examples and providing lots of practice, you can hold primary students accountable for having a central idea and a logical sequence in their writing.

A second trait that is developmentally appropriate for Expanding writers is word choice. Second and third graders can begin to use interesting language in fiction, nonfiction, and poetry. Megan Sloan uses her own writing on an overhead to model how she re-reads her writing and adds more interesting language. She then starts an Interesting Word Wall with her second graders. As students encounter unusual or intriguing words, they add them to the chart. Megan then periodically hands out "Wonderful Word" awards (making sure everyone eventually receives one) as she spots students using interesting language. She developed the Six-Trait Writing Guide (CBA Form 7.11) to help students learn to revise for both organization and word choice. Later in the year, students use the form for peer conferencing. Rather than just telling their writing partner they liked the story, the peer editors have to record what traits they helped with and the specific suggestions they made. All year long, Megan provides a great deal of practice and support as students begin these first steps in the revision process.

One of the benefits of teaching specific writing traits is that children begin to use that language in their portfolio reflections. Several years ago, Megan found that her students' reasons for selecting writing for their portfolio tended to be either, "I picked it because it's good." or "I picked it because I like it." After teaching a few of the traits, she started asking students to be more specific. For instance, Shannon wrote, "I chose this piece for my portfolio because I did a spectacular job." When she shared this brief reflection, Megan referred back to the traits she had taught and Shannon added, "I put an interesting word in it. My interesting word was *approached*." Megan also takes anecdotal notes when students talk about interesting language during literature discussions, and uses Post-it notes to record specific comments when students give each other feedback during Author's Chair. You can see the link between Megan's focus lessons, her assessment tools, and student portfolios.

One way to involve students in self-assessment is to create assessment checklists together. For instance, when Linda Horn's third-grade students at Brighton School wrote nonfiction reports about wolves, they first read several books about wolves. Together, the class then created a list of the qualities of good nonfiction. Linda then created a checklist specific to their nonfiction research. Katie's report was well organized and the reader can hear her voice as she describes facts she (and her peers) found interesting: "Let's talk about puppyhood! Did you know most of the wolf pups that are born are black? Most pups are very mischievous, curious, and adventurous. Can you believe that in the wild a mommy wolf licks the baby's tummy so it will know when to go to the bathroom?" Students used the checklist as a guideline as they drafted, as well as an evaluation for the final published report (Figure 5.10). Notice that the traits of organization, voice, and conventions are linked directly to the descriptors of the Expanding and Bridging stages of the writing continuum.

We created several Primary Rubrics (CBA Form 7.17) in *Classroom Based Assessment* as models; however, the most powerful rubrics are ones you create with your students. By using genre-specific checklists, rubrics, and the Six-Trait Writing Guide (CBA Form 7.11), you can help students learn to look more closely at the specific qualities of good writing.

Spelling Words, Spelling Strategies, and Spelling Survey

As in the two previous stages, the Spelling Words (DC Form 5.5) assessment strategy provides a simple way to document spelling growth three times during the year as students move toward conventional spelling. At the Expanding stage, you may also want to introduce the Spelling Strategies I Use (CBA Form 5.3) form which you can tuck into each child's writing folder. Rather than taking all 25 or 30 journals home before conferences, you can use the form to note effective spelling strategies and breakthroughs as you confer with students. Students can also use the form themselves to record new learning, as long as they can show evidence of a particular skill

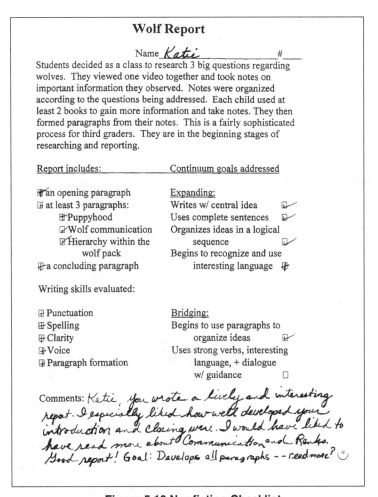

Figure 5.10 Nonfiction Checklist

in several writing samples. Even young children can use the Spelling Survey (DC Form 7.3) to assess their spelling skills. Notice the growth between Mara's reflection in the fall and her responses at the end of the year (Figure 5.11 and 5.12).

"Fix-it" Strategy

The "Fix-it" Strategy is new at this stage. Teachers find this simple technique useful in second through eighth grade. In October, give each student a Post-it note. Ask students to place the note on a piece of writing that shows who they are as a writer in October. You may want to include a clear acetate slip-sheet in each student's section of your Teacher Notebook. Place each child's fall sample in their section of your notebook (make sure the child's name and date is on the entry). In the spring, return the writing samples, telling them, "Re-write this piece, showing me what you've learned." You might want to refer to the charts you've created with the class about quality writing or remind students of the six traits you've been teaching. For instance, Lisa Norwick reminded her second graders about writing traits and their list of Quality Writing characteristics, then asked the students to write their piece again, showing her what they had learned during the year.

SPELLING SURVEY

Name: Mara   Date: Octoder

1. Are you a good speller? Why do you think so? __no__

2. What do you do when you don't know how to spell a word? __azcke__
   the techer

3. What are other ways to figure out how to spell a word? _____

4. What kinds of words are hard for you to spell? __a lot of wordz__

5. How do people get to be good spellers? _____

6. When is correct spelling important? __portfolio.__

Figure 5.11 Fall Spelling Survey

SPELLING SURVEY

Name: mara   Date: 4-29-99

1. Are you a good speller? Why do you think so? __yez__
   becase I tace my time.

2. What do you do when you don't know how to spell a word? __I will__
   replace the wcode withe another word. I uze my
   dictionary.

3. What are other ways to figure out how to spell a word? __I zound out__
   the word. I brake the word into partz.

4. What kinds of words are hard for you to spell? __namez, insiclopedea__

5. How do people get to be good spellers? __thay practiz. Read and__
   right a lot

6. When is correct spelling important? __a reportor whent pudlesh__
   my righting.

Figure 5.12 Spring Spelling Survey

Mara
he hum. I guess just because
Ilike mY Jat he is cool. becausehhem I ges gizi because.
Because, hum.. I guess just because

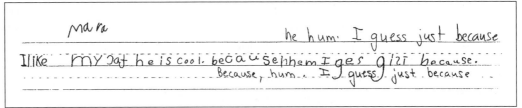

Figure 5.13 "Fix-it" Fall Sample

Figure 5.13 shows Mara's writing sample from the fall: "I like my cat. He is cool. Because, hum, I guess just because."

Look at the contrast in Mara's spring sample (Figure 5.14): "I love my cat. He is soft and gray and cuddly. We play catch the mouse and swing the yarn. I swing the yarn and he whacks the yarn. I have had my cat for two years. Sometimes he sleeps on my head. In the morning we play a game with my cup at breakfast. My cat tries to knock over my cup and get my chocolate milk. How do you play with your pet?" In addition to the length, notice all the areas in which Mara has improved (organization, details, conventions, word choice, sentence fluency, and voice). This simple assessment technique clearly captures growth over time.

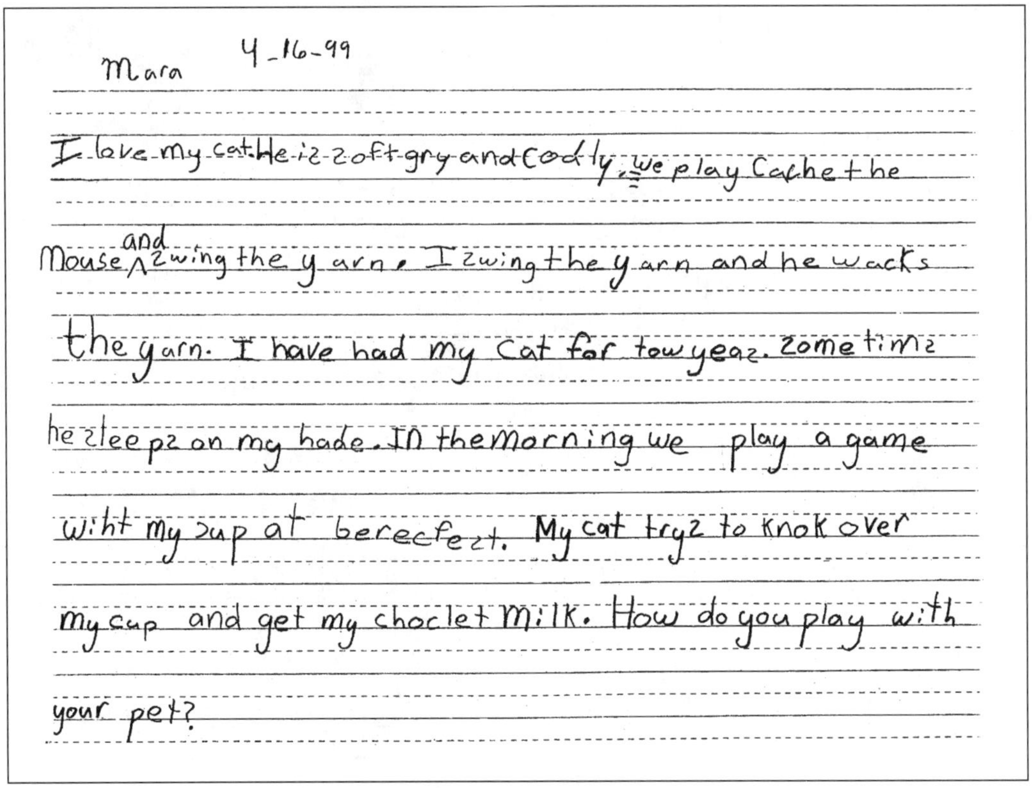

Mara 4-16-99
I love my cat.He iz zoft gry and Codly. We play Cache the
Mouse and zwing the yarn. I zwing the yarn and he wacks
the yarn. I have had my cat for tow yeaz. zometimz
he zleepz on my hade. In the Morning we play a game
wiht my zup at berecfezt. My cat tryz to knok over
my cup and get my choclet milk. How do you play with
your pet?

Figure 5.14 "Fix-it" Spring Sample

Writing Survey, Portfolio Reflection/Self-Evaluation, and Writing Goals

The Expanding stage is the first time students are expected to be able to identify their own writing strategies and set goals *with guidance*. Students can begin to reflect about what they do well as they complete the Writing Survey (DC Form 7.1 or 7.2). The quality of student reflection improves if you model the Writing Survey, Portfolio Reflections, and Writing Goals (CBA Form 7.5) on an overhead by thinking aloud about your own writing. The class could brainstorm a list of possible writing goals based on the continuum. With your guidance, each student can select one or two writing goals for each grading period. More information about student portfolios, reflections, and goal setting will be included in the forthcoming third book in the *Corner Pieces of Assessment* series, *Student Portfolios and Reflection*.

In Cindy Flegenheimer's third grade classroom at Brighton School, students write home each Friday with the week's classroom news, titled *Read All About It!* The weekly task provides a mental review of what they've learned during the week and helps students look for their next steps as learners. In Figure 5.15, you can see that one of Bruce's goals was to "write more in my writer's notebook." For children this age, setting small, concrete goals is developmentally appropriate so that they can see success. If you want to set writing goals each month or trimester, you may want to use Goals sheet (CBA Form 7.5) to record each student's goals for writing.

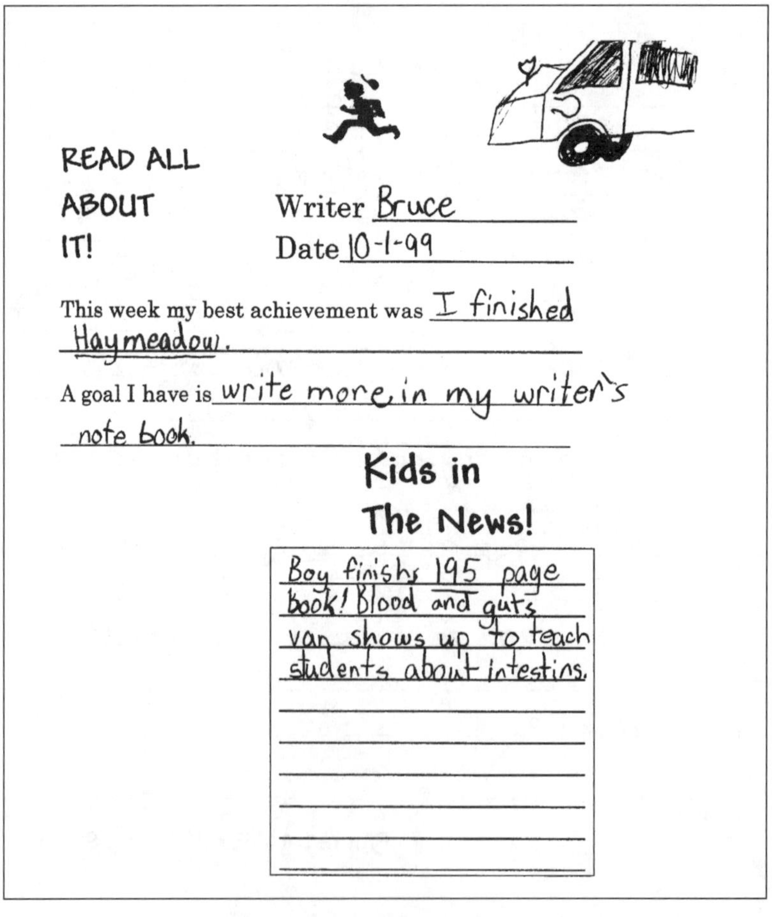
READ ALL ABOUT IT!

Writer Bruce

Date 10-1-99

This week my best achievement was I finished Haymeadow.

A goal I have is write more, in my writer's note book.

Kids in The News!

Boy finishs 195 page book! Blood and guts van shows up to teach students about intestins.

Figure 5.15 Student Goals

As a first-grade teacher in Woodinville, Washington, Christy Clausen created a simple T-chart that she staples inside each child's writing folder. The left side is labeled "I Am Learning to . . ." and the right side is labeled "I Can . . .". As each student reads what he or she has written to her, Christy ask the child to tell her one thing they do well. For instance, Michael noticed that he wrote one sentence about his picture in his journal. They decided Michael's next goal would be to write two or three sentences. Christy recorded, "write 2–3 sentences" on the left side of the chart. The next time Christy confers with Michael and notices he's writing more, she simply draws an arrow to the right side and places the date, then they set a new goal. This simple method enables you to help students build on what they do well and set their sights for their next incremental steps as writers. In Figure 5.16, you can see the evolving expectations for another student in Christy's class.

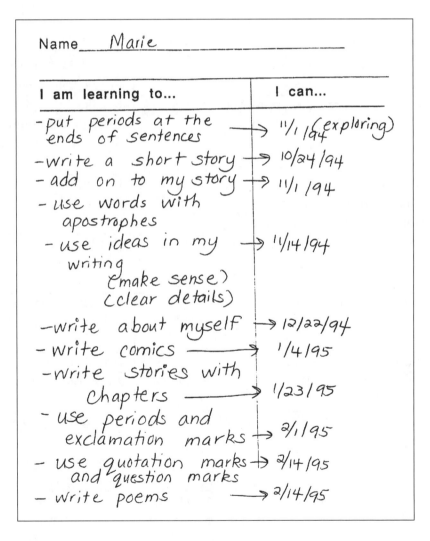

Figure 5.16 T-Chart Goals

Expanding Reading: Assessment Tools

Continuum Descriptor	Assessment Tools
📖 Reads easy chapter books.	Anecdotal Notes (DC Form 6.9, 6.10, 6.11) Reading Log (CBA Form 9.21–22) Photocopy of Reading Sample
📖 Chooses, reads, and finishes a variety of materials at appropriate level with guidance.	Anecdotal Notes (DC Form 6.9, 6.10) Reading Log (CBA Form 9.21–22) Reading Genres (CBA Form 9.23) Reading Strategies I Use (CBA Form 9.3) Reading Survey (DC Form 7.4)
📖 Begins to read aloud with fluency.	Anecdotal Notes (DC Form 6.9, 6.10, 6.11) Reading Conference (CBA Form 9.6) Informal Miscue Analysis (CBA Form 9.10)
☺ Reads silently for increasingly longer periods (15–30 minutes).	Anecdotal Notes (DC Form 6.9, 6.10) Reading Strategies I Use (CBA Form 9.3)
☑ Uses reading strategies appropriately, depending on the text and purpose.	Reading Strategies I Use (CBA Form 9.3) Reading Conference (CBA Form 9.6) Informal Miscue Analysis (CBA Form 9.10)
☑ Uses word structure cues (e.g., root words, prefixes, suffixes, word chunks) when encountering unknown words.	Reading Conference (CBA Form 9.6) Informal Miscue Analysis (CBA Form 9.10)
☑ Increases vocabulary by using meaning clues (context)	Reading Conference (CBA Form 9.6) Informal Miscue Analysis (CBA Form 9.10)
☑ Self-corrects for meaning.	Reading Conference (CBA Form 9.6) Informal Miscue Analysis (CBA Form 9.10)
☑ Follows written directions.	Anecdotal Notes (DC Form 6.9, 6.10)
☑ Identifies chapter titles and table of contents (text organizers).	Anecdotal Notes (DC Form 6.9, 6.10)
✍ Summarizes and retells story events in sequential order.	Literature Discussions (CBA Forms 9.12, 9.13) Reading Strategies I Use (CBA Form 9.3) Retelling (CBA Form 9.17–18)
✍ Responds to and makes personal connections with facts, characters, and situations in literature.	Anecdotal Notes (DC Form 6.9, 6.10, 6.12) Reading Strategies I Use (CBA Form 9.3) Literature Discussions (CBA Forms 9.12, 9.13) Response Journals (CBA Form 9.14, 9.15)

cont.

☝ Compares and contrasts characters and story events.	Anecdotal Notes (DC Form 6.9, 6.10, 6.12) Literature Discussions (CBA Forms 9.12, 9.13) Response Journals (CBA Form 9.14, 9.15)
☝ "Reads between the lines" with guidance.	Anecdotal Notes (DC Form 6.9, 6.10, 6.12) Literature Discussions (CBA Forms 9.12, 9.13) Response Journals (CBA Form 9.14, 9.15) Retelling (CBA Form 9.17–18)
ᏜᎭ Identifies own reading strategies and sets goals with guidance.	Anecdotal Notes (DC Form 6.9, 6.10, 6.11) Reading Strategies I Use (CBA Form 9.3) Reading Survey (DC Form 7.4, 7.5) Reading Goals (CBA Form 9.4)

Summary: Expanding Reading Tools

Assessment Tool	15 Descriptors: Number Assessed	
Anecdotal Notes (DC Form 6.10, 6.11, 6.12)	10	(67%)
Reading Strategies I Use (CBA Form 9.3)	6	(40%)
Informal Miscue Analysis (CBA Form 9.10)	5	(33%)
Reading Conference (CBA Form 9.6)	5	(33%)
Literature Discussions (CBA Forms 9.12, 9.13)	4	(27%)
Response Journals (CBA Form 9.14, 9.15)	3	(20%)
Retelling (CBA Form 9.17, 9.18)	2	(13%)
Reading Log (CBA Form 9.21, 9.22)	2	(13%)
Reading Survey (DC Form 7.4, 7.5)	2	(13%)
Reading Genres (CBA Form 9.23)	1	(7%)
Reading Goals (CBA Form 9.4)	1	(7%)
Photocopy of Reading Sample and Reflection	1	(7%)

Anecdotal Notes

Your eyes may widen as you look at the extensive list of assessment tools at the Expanding stage for reading. Notice, however, that you can assess two-thirds of the descriptors at this stage by taking anecdotal notes. As in the previous stage, anecdotal notes are more useful for documenting reading range, attitude, and comprehension than for assessing reading strategies. The Reading Conference form (CBA Form 9.6) provides a more efficient way to record students' miscues and oral fluency. Cindy Flegeheimer at Brighton School uses anecdotal notes to record students' comprehension during her Guided Reading lessons with small groups. For instance, as they read a nonfiction books about wolves, she may record instances where students were able to use the chapter titles and table of contents to locate information. You can also use your Post-it notes during silent reading to record the types of books students are reading, as well as their ability to read for more extended periods. By using the Anecdotal Focus Questions (DC Form 6.9, 6.10, and 6.12), you can assess students' growing ability to make predictions and personal connections to facts, characters, and events during literature discussions.

Reading Strategies I Use, Reading Conferences, and Informal Miscue Analysis

As children begin reading chapter books at the Expanding stage, they become more able to document their own reading strategies. Many of the descriptors from this stage on the continuum are on the Reading Strategies I Use form (CBA Form 9.3). By the Expanding stage, most students are able to fill out this form on their own. Of course, you would want students to be able to show you these strategies in action during literature discussions and individual reading conferences. Cindy Flegenheimer found that she needed to provide quite a bit of support for her third graders in the fall, but her students were able to complete the form without much help by the end of the year.

You may want to modify the Reading Conference form (CBA Form 9.6) to match the specific reading strategies that you have taught. Lisa Norwick uses the Reading Conference form to assess students' ability to use all three cueing systems as they decode new words and self-correct. She also records their fluency and comprehension. Lisa does two reading conferences each morning during silent reading time. She keeps the Reading Conference forms in the left pocket of a folder. As she reads with two students each day, she moves the two forms into the right folder pocket. When she has read with every student, she moves the whole stack back to the left side and starts again. This easy method and predictable schedule helps her build in time to read with every student on a regular basis. Lisa shares the Reading Conference forms with parents to celebrate growth and explain ways to help their child at home.

The running records described in the previous stages are powerful reading assessment tool for Developing and Begining readers, but what happens when students start reading longer chapter books and you can't make check marks fast enough? Lisa Norwick developed the Informal Miscue Analysis form (CBA Form 9.10) described in Chapter 9 of *Classroom Based Assessment* (Hill, Ruptic, and Norwick, 1998). Rather than merely recording miscues at the word level, this form has room to record whether students maintain meaning at the sentence level. Every time a child reads a sentence with a nonsense word or word that doesn't make sense, you put a tally in the "No" column. You record a tally in the "Yes" column when the sentence does make sense, and then calculate how much the reader is maintaining or losing meaning. You would also place a tally in the "No" column when a miscue causes the reader to lose the semantics of a story or text (e.g. when the child inserts a word like "not" that changes the meaning of the story). There's also room on the form to record fluency and comprehension. Although we want students in the previous stages to strive for oral fluency, much of their attention is focused on decoding. As they begin to read chapter books in the Expanding stage, we can expect students to begin to read with increasingly fluency and expression.

Retelling and Literature Discussion and Response Journal Self-Evaluations

As second and third graders begin to read chapter books, they become more proficient as literature circle participants. Cindy Flegenheimer takes anecdotal notes on her clipboard during literature circles and records students' abilities to discuss elements of literature, compare characters, make personal connections to the books, and "read between the lines." Students use one of the many Discussion Self-Evaluation forms (CBA Forms 9.12 and 9.13) to assess their strengths and areas for growth. Learning how to listen to each other, contribute appropriately, and stay focused on the book requires a great deal of modeling and practice. For example, Cindy models how to "piggyback" on other people's ideas, then uses her anecdotal notes to watch for instances when students apply the strategy. Her students then use the same language in their self-evaluations ("Today I piggybacked off what Quinn said about why Judd Travers was so mean in *Shiloh*."). Cindy alternates oral debriefings with written self-evaluations. She uses the students' insights to create classroom charts and rubrics about the criteria for quality discussions.

Lisa Norwick's students write about the books they read in reading response journals. Sometimes the entries are teacher directed, while at other times they are open-ended. She finds that some students who are quiet during discussions reveal a great deal more about their understanding through response journals. Lisa models how to write about books with her read aloud. She also shares student journal entries that exemplify a particular quality. Together, Lisa and her students develop a chart about the characteristics of quality journal entries. They then turn the list into a rubric such as the Response Journal Rubric (CBA Form 9.15). She then asks students to use a Post-it note to mark their best journal entry to assess using the rubric. At other times, Lisa uses the Assessing Response to Literature form (CBA Form 9.14), which provides a way to track developmental growth in students' ability to write about what they read. Both the assessment form and the rubric can help you evaluate students' comprehension.

Retelling is another effective way to assess comprehension. In Chapter 9 of *Classroom Based Assessment*, we created retelling forms for both fiction and nonfiction. You may want to copy a Retelling form (CBA Form 9.17) or Retelling Rubric (CBA Form 9.18) onto the back of each student's Reading Conference sheet.

Reading Log and Reading Genres

Sparked by new state standards and tests, teachers in Washington State have focused heavily on exploring a wider range of reading and writing genres. Reading Logs (CBA Form 9.21–9.22) and Reading Genre graphs (CBA form 9.23) both provide ways for students to record the amount and range of their reading. As an adult reader, Reading Logs are the only part of my personal portfolio I use almost every day. Before I put a book back on a shelf or return it to the library, I record the title, author, genre, and publication date, then rate the book. When people ask me for book recommendations (or I create a database), I have the information handy. I also like to look back at all the books I've read. Students are more motivated if they have an audience and purpose for keeping reading logs. They're often more diligent when they have a chance to share their logs with others or if they're periodically asked to look back over the books they've read and select their favorites to book talk or review.

Reading Survey, Reading Goals, and Photocopy of Reading Sample and Reflection

At the Expanding stage, students can begin to identify their own strategies and set reading goals. This can be done using the Reading Strategies I Use form (CBA Form 9.3) described earlier. Lisa Norwick also has her students complete the Reading Survey (DC Form 7.4 or 7.5) at the beginning of the year. They complete the same survey in June, and the differences between the two surveys can be quite dramatic. Rather than relying on "I don't know" or giving vague answers, her students are more articulate about what they like to read, as well as their goals. These changes not only show her students' reading growth, but also reflect the focus lessons that Lisa taught throughout the year.

By photocopying a representative sample from a book students can read independently in the fall and spring, you can see how reading growth becomes very apparent. This is the first stage on the continuum at which students are expected to set goals with adult support and modeling. Students can do some reflection about how they've improved as readers by looking at their fall and spring Reading Samples and Surveys, Reading Logs, and the Reading Strategies I Use form. The next logical step would be for students to identify what they want to learn next and how they can improve in reading. The student versions of the continuums and Student Self-Evaluation Checklists from Chapter 7 can help students set goals and identify their next steps as readers.

Over half of the assessment forms at the Expanding stage are ones that students can complete. You will have to provide a great deal of modeling and support at this stage, but students can become part of the assessment process. You will have to decide which of the 12 assessment tools described in this section will best help you document each child's reading range, strategies, comprehension, and attitude.

Bridging Writing: Assessment Tools

Continuum Descriptor	Assessment Tools
📄 Writes about feelings and opinions.	Writing Samples Pieces I've Written (CBA Form 7.2)
📄 Writes fiction with clear beginning, middle, and end.	Writing Samples Writing Strategies I Use (CBA Form 7.4) Six-Trait Guide (CBA Form 7.11) Fiction Rubric (CBA Form 7.17)
📄 Writes poetry using carefully chosen language with guidance.	Writing Samples Pieces I've Written (CBA Form 7.2) Writing Genres (CBA Form 7.3) Poetry Rubric (CBA Form 7.17)
📄 Writes organized nonfiction pieces (e.g., reports, letters, lists) with guidance.	Writing Samples Pieces I've Written (CBA Form 7.2) Writing Genres (CBA Form 7.3) Writing Strategies I Use (CBA Form 7.4) Nonfiction Rubric (CBA Form 7.17)

cont.

📁 Begins to use paragraphs to organize ideas.	Writing Samples Writing Strategies I Use (CBA Form 7.4)
📁 Uses strong verbs, interesting language, and dialogue with guidance.	Writing Samples Writing Strategies I Use (CBA Form 7.4) Six-Trait Guide (CBA Form 7.11) Rubrics (CBA Form 7.17)
✂ Seeks feedback on writing.	Anecdotal Notes (DC Form 6.8) Writing Strategies I Use (CBA Form 7.4)
✂ Revises for clarity with guidance.	Writing Samples/Drafts "Fix-it" Strategy Revising/Editing Forms (CBA Form 7.12, 7.13)
✂ Revises to enhance ideas by adding description and detail.	Writing Samples/Drafts "Fix-it" Strategy
✂ Uses resources (e.g., thesaurus and word lists) to make writing more effective with guidance.	Anecdotal Notes (DC Form 6.8)
✂ Edits for punctuation, spelling, and grammar.	Writing Samples/Drafts "Fix-it" Strategy Writing Strategies I Use (CBA Form 7.4) Revising/Editing Forms (CBA Form 7.12, 7.13)
✂ Publishes writing in polished format with guidance.	Writing Samples/Drafts Pieces I've Written (CBA Form 7.2)
✍ Increases use of visual strategies, spelling rules, and knowledge of word parts to spell correctly.	Writing Samples Spelling Strategies I Use (CBA Form 5.3) Spelling Words (DC Form 5.5)
✍ Uses commas/apostrophes correctly with guidance.	Writing Samples
☺ Uses criteria for effective writing to set own writing goals with guidance.	Writing Survey (DC Form 7.3) Portfolio Reflections and Self-Evaluation Writing Goals (CBA Form 7.5)

Fluent Writing: Assessment Tools

Continuum Descriptor	Assessment Tools
📄 Begins to write organized fiction and nonfiction (e.g., reports, letters, biographies, and autobiographies).	Writing Samples Pieces I've Written (CBA Form 7.2) Writing Genres (CBA Form 7.3) Writing Strategies I Use (CBA Form 7.4) Fiction/Nonfiction Rubrics (CBA Form 7.17)
📄 Develops stories with plots that include problems and solutions with guidance.	Writing Samples Fiction Rubric (CBA Form 7.17)
📄 Creates characters in stories with guidance.	Writing Samples Fiction Rubrics (CBA Form 7.17)
📄 Writes poetry using carefully chosen language.	Writing Samples/Drafts Poetry Rubric (CBA Form 7.17)
📁 Begins to experiment with sentence length and complex sentence structure.	Writing Samples/Drafts Rubrics (CBA Form 7.17)
📁 Varies leads and endings with guidance.	Writing Samples/Drafts Writing Strategies I Use (CBA Form 7.4) Revising/Editing Forms (CBA Form 7.12, 7.13) Rubrics (CBA Form 7.17)
📁 Uses description, details, and similes with . guidance	Writing Samples Writing Strategies I Use (CBA Form 7.4) Six-Trait Guide (CBA Form 7.11) Rubrics (CBA Form 7.17)
📁 Uses dialogue with guidance.	Writing Samples Writing Strategies I Use (CBA Form 7.4)
✂ Uses a range of strategies for planning writing.	Writing Samples/Drafts Anecdotal Notes (DC Form 6.8)
✂ Adapts writing for purpose/audience with guidance.	Writing Samples
✂ Revises for specific writing traits (e.g., ideas, organization, word choice, sentence fluency,	Writing Samples/Drafts "Fix-it" Strategy Six-Trait Checklist (CBA Form 7.11) Revising/Editing Forms (CBA Form 7.12, 7.13)
✂ Incorporates suggestions from others about own writing with guidance.	Anecdotal Notes (DC Form 6.8) Writing Strategies I Use (CBA Form 7.4) Revising/Editing Forms (CBA Form 7.12, 7.13)

cont.

✂ Edits for punctuation, spelling, and grammar with greater precision.	Writing Samples/Drafts "Fix-it" Strategy Writing Strategies I Use (CBA Form 7.4) Revising/Editing Forms (CBA Form 7.12, 7.13)
✂ Uses tools (e.g., dictionaries, checklists, and spell checkers) to edit with guidance.	Anecdotal Notes (DC Form 6.8) Spelling Survey (DC Form 7.1)
☺ Develops criteria for effective writing in different genres with guidance.	Rubrics (CBA Form 7.17) Writing Survey (DC Form 7.3) Portfolio Reflections and Self-Evaluation Writing Goals (CBA Form 7.5)

Summary: Bridging and Fluent Writing Tools

Assessment Tool	15 Descriptors: Number Assessed	
Writing Samples	12	(80%)
Rubrics (CBA Form 7.17)	6	(40%)
Writing Strategies I Use (CBA Form 7.4)	6	(40%)
Revising/Editing Forms (CBA Form 7.12, 7.13)	3	(20%)
Anecdotal Notes (DC Form 6.8)	3	(20%)
"Fix-it" Strategy	3	(20%)
Six-Trait Guide (CBA Form 7.11)	2	(13%)
Writing Genres (CBA Form 7.3)	2	(13%)
Pieces I've Written (CBA Form 7.2)	2	(13%)
Spelling Strategies I Use (CBA Form 5.3)	1	(7%)
Spelling Words (DC Form 5.5)	1	(7%)
Spelling Survey (DC Form 7.1)	1	(7%)
Writing Survey (DC Form 7.3)	1	(7%)
Portfolio Reflections and Self-Evaluation	1	(7%)
Writing Goals (CBA Form 7.5)	1	(7%)

Writing Samples and Ancedotal Notes

The assessment tools you would use for Bridging and Fluent writers are so similar that I have combined the charts and narrative descriptions for both stages. By looking at student work, you can assess 12 of the 15 writing descriptors in both stages. As students write longer pieces, however, it becomes more challenging to read everything they write. It makes sense to develop ways to assess as you confer and observe, as well as ways to involve students in the process.

Anne Klein ties her focus lessons in fourth and fifth grade directly to the six writing traits from the Northwest Regional Educational Laboratory. As she introduces each trait, she uses her own writing, student samples, and children's literature as models. She then takes anecdotal notes in order to assess writing strategies and traits during writing workshop, individual conferences, and Author's Chair. She frequently shares her observations with the class during discussions. For instance, Anne uses *The War with Grandpa* (Robert Kimmel Smith, 1984) as a class read aloud. She makes an overhead of the first page in which all the sentences are long and run together. She also makes an overhead of page 22 in which all the sentences are short and choppy, as the main character experiments with his writing style. The two samples provide a great contrast for Anne's lesson on sentence variation. As students read their writing aloud in class, they begin to listen for the rhythm and flow of their writing. Students often laugh at their own short, abrupt sentences, realizing that it sounds like "Peter's writing" from *The War With Grandpa*. Anne connects her teaching and assessing as she asks students to listen for sentence fluency in their own writing and in their literature circle books. She records further examples of students who understand the writing trait by using her anecdotal notes.

A few of the writing descriptors are best assessed through observation during writing time. For instance, you can use anecdotal notes as well as writing samples to note what prewriting strategies students use independently. By watching young writers, listening to their feedback during Author's Chair, and by looking at drafts, you can use Post-it notes to record if students merely listen to other people's suggestions or actually incorporate the changes into their writing. You might want to use anecdotal notes to record when writers ask you or their peers for feedback or when students use resources, such as word lists, dictionaries, spell checkers, or a thesaurus to improve their writing.

Spelling Strategies I Use, Spelling Words, and Spelling Survey

As students become stronger and more fluent writers, spelling assessment becomes a natural part of the editing process. Students at this stage are learning to rely on their knowledge of spelling rules and their understanding of word parts (such as root words, suffixes, and prefixes) as they move toward conventional spelling. Students can use the Intermediate Spelling Strategies I Use (CBA Form 5.3) form for self-evaluation.

Teachers find that the Spelling Words technique (DC Form 5.5) provides them with valuable information; although the change is more incremental at this stage than in the primary grades. In third grade, it's still informative to use the Spelling Words technique three times a year. Most teachers in fourth and fifth grade only use the Spelling Words strategy twice, once in the fall and again in the spring. Anne Klein has used this strategy for several years. This quick test gives her a lot of information about which children are still spelling phonetically and which are moving toward conventional spelling. For instance, many students spelled "pharmacy" with an "f" in the fall and with a "ph" by spring. Similarly, "receipt" was spelled as "reseat" by many students in September, but spelled correctly by several fifth graders by the end of the year. In June, Anne asked her students to look at both the fall and spring spelling lists and reflect on the changes. Yasim wrote,

> I can see that I am not spelling them right because both times I did not sound out the words. Example: (wrong) *im*baressed, (right) *em*barrassed. I say 'im' but that's the way I say it when I talk. I should say, 'em.' All of this goes for the other words. It is not anything with vowels or something like that. It is just sounding it out right. I think that when I read I pick up new words and remember them when I write.

By asking the students to look at samples over time, an assessment tool can become a powerful self-evaluation instrument.

The Spelling Survey (DC Form 7.1) also provides a window into students' spelling abilities. As you can see in Figure 5.17, it's easy to assess Emily's spelling strategies from her survey.

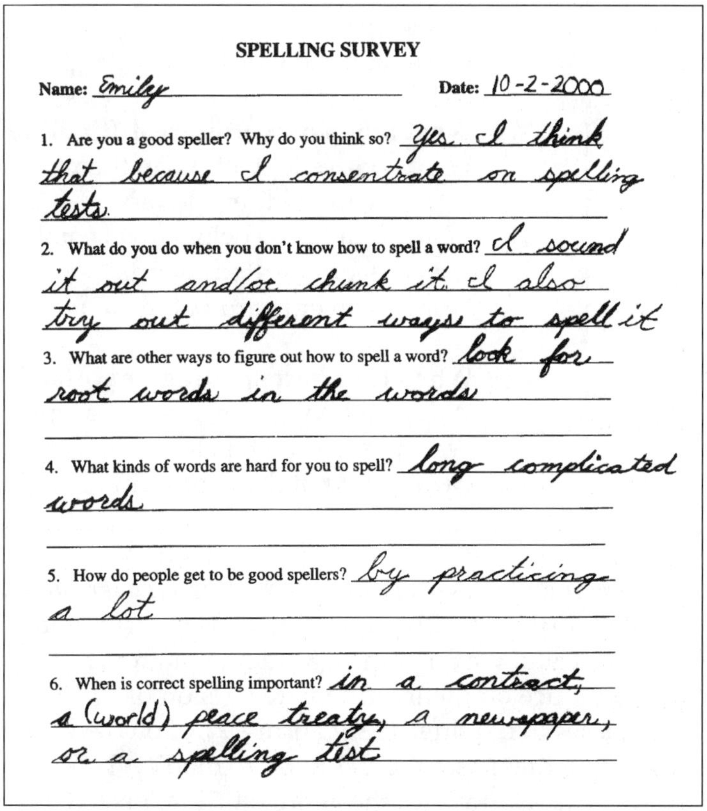

SPELLING SURVEY

Name: Emily   Date: 10-2-2000

1. Are you a good speller? Why do you think so? Yes, I think that because I consentrate on spelling tests.

2. What do you do when you don't know how to spell a word? I sound it out and/or chunk it. I also try out different ways to spell it

3. What are other ways to figure out how to spell a word? look for root words in the words

4. What kinds of words are hard for you to spell? long complicated words

5. How do people get to be good spellers? by practicing a lot

6. When is correct spelling important? in a contract, a (world) peace treaty, a newspaper, or a spelling test

Figure 5.17 Intermediate Spelling Survey

Do you consider yourself a good speller? In any group of teachers, I found that two-thirds spell well and the other third struggle with spelling. Poor spellers have learned to rely on the spell checker on their computer, use a dictionary when in doubt, ask a colleague to proofread parent newsletters, or even marry someone who spells well! Poor spellers need to know a variety of spelling strategies other than "look it up" or "sound it out!" One way to widen students' repertoire is to use the Spelling Survey (DC Form 7.1) as a springboard for discussions and by starting a chart of "What Do You Do When You Don't Know How to Spell a Word?" This fall, Anne Klein took assessment one step further by summarizing the results from her students' spelling surveys. She turned this information into a chart (see below) to use as teaching points for her next focus lessons.

Spelling Survey Information
Anne Klein's Fourth Grade

Ways to figure out how to spell words:
Spell it different ways and pick the one that looks right
Sound it out
Chunk it
Look it up in a dictionary or book
Ask someone
Work with the word

What kinds of words are difficult to spell?
Words with silent letters in them
Words with "hidden" letters
Words that have tricky vowel combinations
Longer (complicated) words
Words I never heard before

When is correct spelling important?
Writing a book report, story, or letter
Writing a contract, peace treaty, or article
On a test, final draft, or writing to turn in

Writing Strategies I Use, Pieces I've Written, and Writing Genres

By fourth and fifth grade, the focus in writing instruction shifts from quantity to quality and writing range. Students can record the range and genres of writing they produce on the intermediate version of Writing Strategies I Use (CBA Form 7.4), Pieces I've Written (CBA Form 7.2), or on the Writing Genres graph (CBA Form 7.3). Anne Klein uses the CD-ROM to modify the Writing Genres form to match the district expectations for the genres she is expected to emphasize at her grade level.

The Writing Strategies I Use Checklist (CBA Form 7.4) and Six-Trait Guide (CBA Form 7.11) become more useful as you discuss the qualities of good writing in each genre. Intermediate students can use these two forms to assess their persuasive writing, fiction, nonfiction, and poetry. Students can use the same forms to assess their use of paragraphs, strong verbs, interesting language, and dialogue. If students check that they have mastered a particular skill, they should be able to show you evidence from their writing folder or portfolio. Anne has her fourth and fifth graders complete the Writing Strategies I Use form right before the November parent conferences. She fills out a sample on the overhead, modeling the questions she might ask herself. Students evaluate their writing skills again at the end of the year.

Intermediate and middle school students can still use the Pieces I've Written (CBA Form 7.2) and Writing Genres (CBA Form 7.3) forms to show the amount and different types of writing they explore. The biggest difference between Bridging and Fluent writers is depth. Instead of writing fiction with only a beginning, middle, and end, Fluent writers are able to develop stories with problems and solutions. Fluent writers can create poetry with carefully chosen language *independently*, instead of *with guidance*. However, teacher support is still needed on 10 of the 15 descriptors. Students at the Fluent stage still require lots of modeling, many examples, and opportunities for practice.

Rubrics

A great deal of information can be gleaned from students' drafts, since so many of the writing descriptors at this stage are observable (e.g., varying leads, creating characters, using description and similes). At the Fluent stage, students can examine their own work and use forms to assess both their writing range and strategies. Of course, you would still need to model how to use each form and support students as they use these techniques. When you create rubrics *with* your students, it's important to begin with one or two traits and to provide student work or your own writing as examples. For instance, in middle school at Brighton, sixth graders write a persuasive piece, seventh graders compose a legend, and eighth graders create an animal folktale. Each of these genres requires a different set of criteria. Rubrics are far more useful when they are specific to the writing form or assignment and when they are created with your students. For instance, the Poetry Rubric (CBA Form 7.17F) can reveal if students write poetry using carefully chosen language, or the Fiction Rubric (CBA Form 7.17E) can show when writers create plots with problems and solutions. For more information about creating rubrics, you may want to refer to *Designing Rubrics for K–6 Classroom Assessment* (Debbie Rickards and Earl Cheek, Jr., 1999).

Six-Trait Guide and Revising/Editing Forms

In addition to writing widely, students at the Bridging and Fluent stages should be able to revise and edit their own work. This is one of the skills often measured on fourth-grade state tests. Revision at this stage still requires a great deal of teacher support. It's so easy to show writing growth at the primary level when the changes from the beginning to the end of the year are so dramatic. It's much harder to show progress with intermediate students, because it takes so many years to be able to revise and edit independently. Many of us are still working on those strategies as adults. Many parents are often unclear about the expectations for writing at various grade levels. Several intermediate teachers have shared the revision forms at Back to School Night and at student-led conferences. The increasingly challenging sequence of the Revision and Editing forms (CBA Form 7.12 and 7.13) in *Classroom Based Assessment* provides a way to show how expectations grow over time. The

Six-Trait revision forms (CBA Form 7.11) also capture how young writers learn to improve their writing by focusing on specific traits. When students learn to step back from their writing and make changes, they are taking a monumental step forward as writers. As Vicki Spandel and Richard Stiggins (1997) state, "self-assessment is the foundation of revision" (p. 5). Rubrics (CBA 7.17), the Six-Trait forms (CBA Form 7.11), the Revising/Editing forms (CBA Form 7.12 and 7.13), and the Writing Strategies I Use checklist (CBA Form 7.4) all provide students with the language they need to articulate their strengths and their next steps as writers.

"Fix-it" Strategy

The "Fix-it" Strategy is particularly powerful in the intermediate grades and in middle school as students learn how to revise and edit their work more independently. By saving a piece of students' writing from the fall (either from their writing folder or based on a prompt), then giving it back to students several months later to "fix-it" up and show you what they've learned, you can easily tell which focus lessons they have absorbed and internalized.

One of the differences between Bridging and Fluent writers is students' growing ability to revise and edit their work. The "Fix-it" strategy reflects their growth as writers from the beginning to the end of the year. It's also a quick assessment tool, especially in the fall when all you need to do is to collect a representative sample from each student. You can also involve students in the assessment process by placing the fall and spring samples side by side and asking students to write a reflection about the changes they notice. Self-evaluation is much easier for students when they have actual samples to compare.

Writing Survey, Portfolio Reflections/Self-Evaluation, and Writing Goals

The Writing Survey (DC Form 7.3), Portfolio Reflections, and Writing Goals sheet (CBA Form 7.5) can help students assess their own growth as writers, particularly in the last descriptor at the Bridging stage: "Uses criteria for effective writing to set own writing goals *with guidance.*" Note the last phrase. By the Fluent stage, writers are just *beginning to* set goals and identify goals for how to improve their writing in various genres. This metacognitive ability will require modeling and support throughout the intermediate grades and middle school. This is an age for building stamina and confidence in young writers. Students still continue to work on improving their writing fluency, quality, and range as they tackle multiple drafts. Notice that all of the assessment tools are the same at the Bridging and Fluent stages. What changes are our expectations for independence. Too often we set goals with students in the fall but never refer to them again. In Julie Ledford's fifth-grade class at Brighton School, students taped their reading and writing goals to the corner of their desks. As Julie conducted reading and writing conferences with students, the goals were there for a quick reference. In some classrooms, students write a letter home each trimester, describing what progress they have made toward their goals.

Bridging Reading: Assessment Tools

Continuum Descriptor	Assessment Tools
📖 Reads medium level chapter books.	Anecdotal Notes (DC Form 6.10, 6.11) Reading Log (CBA Form 9.21–22) Photocopy of Reading Sample
📖 Chooses reading materials at appropriate level.	Anecdotal Notes (DC Form 6.10, 6.11) Reading Strategies I Use (CBA Form 9.3) Reading Conference (CBA Form 9.6)
📖 Expands knowledge of different genres (e.g., realistic fiction, historical fiction, and fantasy).	Anecdotal Notes (DC Form 6.10) Reading Log (CBA Form 9.21–22) Reading Genres (CBA Form 9.23) Reading Strategies I Use (CBA Form 9.3)
📖 Reads aloud with expression.	Anecdotal Notes (DC Form 6.10, 6.11) Reading Conference (CBA Form 9.6) Informal Miscue Analysis (CBA Form 9.10)
☑ Uses resources (e.g., encyclopedias, CD-ROMs, and nonfiction texts) to locate and sort information with guidance.	Anecdotal Notes (DC Form 6.10) Reading Strategies I Use (CBA Form 9.3)
☑ Gathers information by using the table of contents, captions, glossary, and index (text organizers) with guidance.	Anecdotal Notes (DC Form 6.10)
☑ Gathers and uses information from graphs, charts, tables, and maps with guidance.	Anecdotal Notes (DC Form 6.10)
☑ Increases vocabulary by using context cues, other reading strategies, and resources (e.g., dictionary and thesaurus) with guidance.	Anecdotal Notes (DC Form 6.10)
☑ Demonstrates understanding of the difference between fact and opinion.	Anecdotal Notes (DC Form 6.10)
☑ Follows multi-step written directions . independently	Anecdotal Notes (DC Form 6.10)
✎ Discusses setting, plot, characters, and point of view (literary elements) with guidance.	Anecdotal Notes (DC Form 6.10, 6.11, 6.12) Reading Strategies I Use (CBA Form 9.3) Literature Discussions (CBA Forms 9.11–13) Response Journals (CBA Form 9.14, 9.15)
✎ Responds to issues and ideas in literature as well as facts or story events.	Anecdotal Notes (DC Form 6.10, 6.11, 6.12) Reading Strategies I Use (CBA Form 9.3) Literature Discussions (CBA Forms 9.11–13) Response Journals (CBA Form 9.14, 9.15)

cont.

✎	Makes connections to other authors, books, and perspectives.	Anecdotal Notes (DC Form 6.10, 6.11, 6.12) Reading Strategies I Use (CBA Form 9.3) Response Journals (CBA Form 9.14, 9.15)
✎	Participates in small group literature discussions with guidance.	Anecdotal Notes (DC Form 6.10, 6.12) Reading Strategies I Use (CBA Form 9.3) Literature Discussions (CBA Forms 9.11–13)
✎	Uses reasons and examples to support ideas and opinions with guidance.	Anecdotal Notes (DC Form 6.10, 6.11, 6.12) Literature Discussions (CBA Forms 9.11–13) Response Journals (CBA Form 9.14, 9.15)

Fluent Reading: Assessment Tools

Continuum Descriptor	Assessment Tools
📖 Reads challenging children's literature.	Anecdotal Notes (DC Form 6.10, 6.11) Reading Log (CBA Form 9.21–22) Photocopy of Reading Sample
📖 Selects, reads, and finishes a wide variety of genres with guidance.	Anecdotal Notes (DC Form 6.10) Reading Log (CBA Form 9.21–22) Reading Genres (CBA Form 9.23) Reading Strategies I Use (CBA Form 9.3) Reading Survey (DC Form 7.5)
📖 Begins to develop strategies and criteria for selecting reading materials.	Anecdotal Notes (DC Form 6.10) Reading Strategies I Use (CBA Form 9.3) Reading Survey (DC Form 7.5)
📖 Reads aloud with fluency, expression, and confidence.	Anecdotal Notes (DC Form 6.10, 6.11) Reading Conference (CBA Form 9.6) Informal Miscue Analysis (CBA Form 9.10)
☺ Reads silently for extended periods (30–40 min.).	Anecdotal Notes (DC Form 6.10) Reading Strategies I Use (CBA Form 9.3)
☑ Begins to use resources (e.g., encyclopedias, articles, Internet, and nonfiction texts) to locate information.	Anecdotal Notes (DC Form 6.10) Reading Strategies I Use (CBA Form 9.3)
☑ Gathers information using the table of contents, captions, glossary, and index (text organizers independently.	Anecdotal Notes (DC Form 6.10)
☑ Begins to use resources (e.g., dictionary and thesaurus) to increase vocabulary in different subject areas.	Anecdotal Notes (DC Form 6.10)

cont.

☝ Begins to discuss literature with reference to setting, plot, characters, and theme (literary elements), and author's craft.	Anecdotal Notes (DC Form 6.10, 6.11, 6.12) Reading Strategies I Use (CBA Form 9.3) Literature Discussions (CBA Forms 9.11–13) Response Journals (CBA Form 9.14, 9.15)
☝ Generates thoughtful oral and written responses in small group literature discussions with guidance.	Anecdotal Notes (DC Form 6.10, 6.11, 6.12) Reading Strategies I Use (CBA Form 9.3) Literature Discussions (CBA Forms 9.11–13) Response Journals (CBA Form 9.14, 9.15)
☝ Begins to use new vocabulary in different subject and in oral and written response to literature.	Anecdotal Notes (DC Form 6.10, 6.12) Literature Discussions (CBA Forms 9.11–13) Response Journals (CBA Form 9.14, 9.15)
☝ Begins to gain deeper meaning by "reading between the lines."	Anecdotal Notes (DC Form 6.10, 6.11, 6.12) Reading Strategies I Use (CBA Form 9.3) Literature Discussions (CBA Forms 9.11–13) Response Journals (CBA Form 9.14, 9.15)
✍ Begins to set goals and identifies strategies to improve reading.	Reading Strategies I Use (CBA Form 9.3) Reading Survey (DC Form 7.5) Reading Goals (CBA Form 9.4)

Summary: Bridging and Fluent Reading Tools

Assessment Tool	14 Descriptors: Number Assessed	
Anecdotal Notes (DC Form 6.10, 6.11, 6.12)	14	(100%)
Reading Strategies I Use (CBA Form 9.3)	8	(57%)
Literature Discussions (CBA Forms 9.12, 9.13)	4	(29%)
Response Journals (CBA Form 9.14, 9.15)	4	(29%)
Reading Survey (DC Form 7.5)	2	(14%)
Reading Log (CBA Form 9.21, 9.22)	2	(14%)
Reading Conference (CBA Form 9.6)	2	(14%)
Reading Genres (CBA Form 9.23)	1	(7%)
Informal Miscue Analysis (CBA Form 9.10)	1	(7%)
Reading Goals (CBA Form 9.4)	1	(7%)
Photocopy of Reading Sample and Reflection	1	(7%)

The biggest difference between readers at the Bridging and Fluent stages is the increased sophistication of the books at the Fluent level. Another distinction is that many of the reading strategies for Bridging readers occur *with guidance*. By the Fluent stage, students are beginning to incorporate these skills and use them more *independently*. Students still require support and modeling, but are increasingly able to write and talk about more challenging children's literature on their own.

Anecdotal Notes

At the Bridging and Fluent stages, virtually every descriptor can be assessed using anecdotal notes. Part of the reason for this is that the focus at these stages is on applying reading strategies to a variety of tasks. For instance, intermediate students should be able to gather information by using text organizers, such as a table of contents, index, and glossary, as well as resources like encyclopedias and the Internet. Anne Klein records this information as she watches her fourth and fifth graders work on research projects and discuss their weekly news magazine, *Time for Kids*. Anne also learns a great deal about their level of comprehension by listening in to their literature circle discussions and using the Anecdotal Notes Focus Questions (DC Form 6.12). She looks for their growing ability to discuss literary elements, such as plot, characters, point of view, and author's craft. Anne records when students make connections to other authors, books, or their own experiences in either discussions or in their response journals. Her observations help her complete the comprehension and attitude strands on the reading continuum.

Although most of Anne's students are at the Bridging and Fluent stages, she also takes notes when students demonstrate strategies from the next three stages. For instance, Anne helped students define "metaphors" and "similes" in their read aloud text, *The Loner* (Ester Weir, 1963). She divided the class into groups and each group looked through a different chapter, then recorded examples of these two literary devices, along with the page number. Anne typed up the list of metaphors and similes as a reference for her students. All of this was done with teacher guidance. A few weeks later, however, one of her fifth-grade students, Carole, demonstrated this skill independently as she read *The Golden Compass* (Philip Pullman, 1995). She came up to Anne and showed her several places where the author used a metaphor ("It was a mighty voice, a woman's voice, but a woman with lungs of brass and leather.") and a simile ("She could snap your backbone like a twig."). Anne recorded an anecdotal note on a Post-it note to record how Carole was beginning to identify literacy elements on her own. Anne will look for a few more examples before she marks this descriptor on Carole's continuum.

Reading Conferences and Informal Miscue Analysis

When possible, Anne Klein conducts one or two reading conferences a day, using the Intermediate Reading Conference form (CBA Form 9.6). She notes reading strategies, oral fluency, and comprehension and records one strategy she's taught. Anne lets students know what she's doing so that students understand that she is gathering information rather than "testing" them.

It's easy to show writing growth by looking at actual samples. It's far harder to show parents how their intermediate students are growing as readers. Anne shares her Reading Conference form with families at parent conferences. The form helps her document the types of books each child can read and the skills she is working on at school. If she needs more specific diagnostic information about a student, Anne may want to use the Informal Miscue Analysis form (CBA Form 9.10) described earlier in the Expanding section. These two assessment tools are particularly helpful to share with concerned parents or with colleagues at a staffing about a student.

Literature Discussion and Response Journal Self-Evaluations

Anne's intermediate students reveal much about their understanding of the books they read through their response journals. The Literature Discussion Self-Evaluation forms (CBA Forms 9.12 and 9.13) help students step back from their conversations and look at effective discussion strategies. With a great deal of modeling and discussion about quality, Anne's students move into student-led discussions in fourth and fifth grade. They are able to talk and write about literary elements, make connections to other books and authors, and use the text to support their opinions *with guidance*. The class creates rubrics for quality discussions and journal entries. The Literature Discussion (CBA Forms 9.12 and 9.13) and Response Journal (CBA Forms 9.14 and 9.15) forms and rubrics help Anne and her students strive for quality oral and written response to literature.

Reading Logs, Reading Genres Graph, and Photocopy of Reading Sample and Reflection

Bridging and Fluent readers can demonstrate how they explore new genres by using Reading Logs (CBA Form 9.21–9.22) and the Reading Genres Graph (CBA Form 8.23). Carol Wilcox, a teacher in Denver, notes, "The reading logs of the types and difficulty level of the books kids are reading are one of the most revealing pieces of data about readers." She notices what authors and what types of books students like, whether they are reading a variety of genres, if they are using a series to increase their fluency, whether or not they are picking books at the appropriate level, and if they are reading more challenging books over time.

At Brighton School, each student's Learner Profile contains sample Reading Logs and a photocopy of a page from a book the child can read from September and June. When collected each year from kindergarten through eighth grade, these samples paint a vivid picture of a student's growth as a reader. Each Learner Profile also includes a videotape of the student reading aloud in the fall and spring of each year. During running records, a teacher analyzes miscues on a challenging text. For the videotape, however, students choose a page to read that they have practiced and that represents their independent reading level.

Reading Strategies I Use, Reading Survey, and Reading Goals

By the intermediate grades, students can articulate what they do well as readers. Some intermediate teachers ask students to keep track of their growing skills by using the Reading Strategies I Use form (CBA Form 9.3). Bridging and Fluent readers can also complete the Reading Survey (DC Form 7.5) twice a year. Kary Brown at Brighton School photocopies the Reading Survey on yellow paper in the fall and green paper in the spring. She places these side by side in each student's section of her Teacher Notebook. By looking at the changes in their answers, Kary can easily see how much these students have grown as readers. Students could also reflect on their reading growth by looking at their fall and spring surveys.

How do students know what they do well as readers? What does a letter grade like a "C" mean in reading? Is it for strategies, fluency, the amount read, attitude, the amount of homework turned in, or the averaged scores from end-of-the-unit tests? How does getting an "A" in reading encourage a student to continue improving and to set goals? Intermediate students can use the student self-evaluation checklist version of the reading continuum (see Chapter 7) as a way of knowing exactly what they do well and what they need to learn next. By looking at the next stage on the continuum, it's easy for Bridging and Fluent readers to set realistic and specific goals using the Reading Goals form (CBA Form 9.4).

For intermediate teachers, the most informative assessment tools are anecdotal notes and a Reading Conference form (CBA Form 9.6). You can also gather information from the Reading Survey (CBA Form 7.5) and show growth over time by periodically photocopying representative Reading Samples. The other seven assessment tools are ones that students can complete with your guidance. Take a look at the assessment strategies described in this section. Are you already using some of these tools? Did you read about a few ideas you'd like to try? You may want to use the Organizational Grid (DC Form 5.3) to map out which assessment tools you plan to use each month. I've included Anne Klein's plan in Figure 5.18. The first page includes the tools she collects on a regular basis, some of which she shares at parent conferences.

ORGANIZATIONAL GRID

Assessment Tool/Strategy	SEPT	OCT	NOV	DEC	JAN	FEB	MAR	APR	MAY	JUN
Parent Survey	X									
Student Survey	X									
Reading Conference	X				X			X		
Fix-It		X							X	
Continuum				X					X	
Trimester Summary Forms			X				X			X
Spelling Strategies					X				X	
Reading Strategies								X		
Response to Lit. Journals	X	X	X			X	X		X	
Reading Logs →										
Anecdotal Notes →										

Klein 2000-2001

Figure 5.18 Anne Klein's Organizational Grid

The second page (Figure 5.19) includes the assessment tools required by her district. For instance, in fifth grade, she is required to focus on expository and persuasive writing. She teaches these writing forms, then uses the district rubric for assessment twice a year. By having a planned assessment time line, Anne can collect a few pieces of evidence each month without becoming overwhelmed.

Pg 2 (District)

Conferences   Springbrook Testing

ORGANIZATIONAL GRID

Assessment Tool/Strategy	SEPT	OCT	NOV	DEC	JAN	FEB	MAR	APR	MAY	JUN
Expository Writing		X			X					
Persuasive Writing			X			X				
Letters on-going	X	X	X	X						
Poetry									X	
Narrative	X						X			
Reports				X	X		X			
Math - District Tasks -										
Problem Solving					X					
Data Collection			X							
Number Sense		X								
Measurement						X				
Geometry					X					
Patterns & Functions									X	

Klein 2000-2001

Figure 5.19 Anne Klein's Organizational Grid—District Requirements

Proficient Writing: Assessment Tools

Continuum Descriptor	Assessment Tools
Writes persuasively about ideas, feelings, and opinions.	Writing Samples Pieces I've Written (CBA Form 7.2)
Creates plots with problems and solutions.	Writing Samples Fiction Rubric (CBA Form 7.17)
Begins to develop the main characters and describe detailed settings.	Writing Samples Fiction Rubrics (CBA Form 7.17)
Begins to write organized and fluent nonfiction, including simple bibliographies.	Writing Samples Pieces I've Written (CBA Form 7.2) Writing Genres (CBA Form 7.3) Writing Strategies I Use (CBA Form 7.4) Fiction/Nonfiction Rubrics (CBA Form 7.17)
Writes cohesive paragraphs including reasons and examples with guidance.	Writing Samples Writing Strategies I Use (CBA Form 7.4)
Uses transitional sentences to connect paragraphs.	Writing Samples Fiction/Nonfiction Rubric (CBA Form 7.17)
Varies sentence structure, leads, and endings.	Writing Samples/Drafts Writing Strategies I Use (CBA Form 7.4) Rubrics (CBA Form 7.17)
Begins to use descriptive language, details, and similes.	Writing Samples Writing Strategies I Use (CBA Form 7.4) Six-Trait Guide (CBA Form 7.11) Rubrics (CBA Form 7.17)
Uses voice to evoke emotional response from readers.	Writing Samples Six-Trait Guide (CBA Form 7.11) Rubrics (CBA Form 7.17)
Begins to integrate information on a topic from a variety of sources.	Writing Samples/Drafts Nonfiction Rubric (CBA Form 7.17)
Begins to revise for specific writing traits (e.g., ideas, organization, word choice, sentence fluency, voice, and conventions).	Writing Samples/Drafts "Fix-it" Strategy Six-Trait Guide (CBA Form 7.11) Revising/Editing Forms (CBA Form 7.12, 7.13) Rubrics (CBA Form 7.17)
Uses tools (e.g., dictionaries, word lists, spell checkers) to edit independently.	Anecdotal Notes (DC Form 6.8)
Selects and publishes writing in polished format independently.	Writing Samples/Drafts
Begins to use complex punctuation (e.g., commas, colons, semicolons, quotation marks) appropriately.	Writing Samples
Begins to set goals and identify strategies to improve writing in different genres.	Writing Strategies I Use (CBA Form 7.4) Rubrics (CBA Form 7.17) Writing Survey (DC Form 7.3) Portfolio Reflections and Self-Evaluation Writing Goals (CBA Form 7.5)

Connecting Writing: Assessment Tools

Continuum Descriptor	Assessment Tools
🗋 Writes in a variety of genres and forms for different audiences and purposes independently.	Writing Samples Pieces I've Written (CBA Form 7.2) Writing Genres (CBA Form 7.3)
🗋 Creates plots with a climax.	Writing Samples Fiction Rubric (CBA Form 7.17)
🗋 Creates detailed, believable settings and characters in stories.	Writing Samples Fiction Rubric (CBA Form 7.17)
🗋 Writes organized, fluent, and detailed nonfiction independently, including bibliographies with correct format.	Writing Samples Pieces I've Written (CBA Form 7.2) Writing Genres (CBA Form 7.3) Fiction/Nonfiction Rubrics (CBA Form 7.17)
🗀 Writes cohesive paragraphs including supportive reasons and examples.	Writing Samples Writing Strategies I Use (CBA Form 7.4)
🗀 Uses descriptive language, details, similes, and imagery to enhance ideas independently.	Writing Samples Rubrics (CBA Form 7.17)
🗀 Begins to use dialogue to enhance character development.	Writing Samples Writing Strategies I Use (CBA Form 7.4)
🗀 Incorporates personal voice in writing with increasing frequency.	Writing Samples Six-Trait Guide (CBA Form 7.11) Rubrics (CBA Form 7.17)
🗀 Integrates information on a topic from a variety of sources independently.	Writing Samples/Drafts Nonfiction Rubric (CBA Form 7.17)
🗀 Constructs charts, graphs, and tables to convey information when appropriate.	Writing Samples
✂ Uses prewriting strategies effectively to organize and strengthen writing.	Writing Samples/Drafts Anecdotal Notes (DC Form 6.8)
✂ Revises for specific writing traits (e.g., ideas, organization, word choice, sentence fluency, voice, and conventions) independently.	Writing Samples/Drafts "Fix-it" Strategy Six-Trait Guide (CBA Form 7.11) Revising/Editing Forms (CBA Form 7.12, 7.13) Rubrics (CBA Form 7.17)
✂ Includes deletion in revision strategies.	Writing Samples/Drafts
✂ Incorporates suggestions from others on own writing independently.	Anecdotal Notes (DC Form 6.8) Writing Strategies I Use (CBA Form 7.4)
✍ Uses complex punctuation (e.g., commas, colons, semicolons, quotation marks) with increasing accuracy.	Writing Samples Revising/Editing Forms (CBA Form 7.12, 7.13)

Independent Writing: Assessment Tools

Continuum Descriptor	Assessment Tools
📄 Writes organized, fluent, accurate, and in-depth nonfiction, including references with correct bibliographic format.	Writing Samples Pieces I've Written (CBA Form 7.2) Writing Genres (CBA Form 7.3) Nonfiction Rubric (CBA Form 7.17)
📄 Writes cohesive, fluent, and effective poetry and fiction.	Writing Samples Pieces I've Written (CBA Form 7.2) Writing Genres (CBA Form 7.3) Poetry/Fiction Rubrics (CBA Form 7.17)
📁 Uses a clear sequence of paragraphs with effective transitions.	Writing Samples Writing Strategies I Use (CBA Form 7.4)
📁 Begins to incorporate literary devices (i.e., imagery, metaphors, personification, and foreshadowing).	Writing Samples Rubrics (CBA Form 7.17)
📁 Weaves dialogue effectively into stories.	Writing Samples Writing Strategies I Use (CBA Form 7.4)
📁 Develops plots, characters, setting, and mood (literary elements) effectively.	Writing Samples Fiction Rubric (CBA Form 7.17)
📁 Begins to develop personal voice and style. of writing	Writing Samples Six-Trait Guide (CBA Form 7.11) Rubrics (CBA Form 7.17)
✂ Revises through multiple drafts independently.	Writing Samples/Drafts Revising/Editing Forms (CBA Form 7.12, 7.13)
✂ Seeks feedback from others and incorporates suggestions in order to strengthen own writing.	Anecdotal Notes (DC Form 6.8) Writing Strategies I Use (CBA Form 7.4)
✂ Publishes writing for different audiences and purposes in polished format independently.	Writing Samples/Drafts Pieces I've Written (CBA Form 7.2)
✂ Internalizes writing process.	Writing Samples/Drafts
✎ Uses correct grammar (e.g., subject/verb agreement and verb tense) consistently.	Writing Samples
☺ Writes with confidence and competence on a range of topics independently.	Writing Samples/Drafts Anecdotal Notes (DC Form 6.8) Pieces I've Written (CBA Form 7.2)
☺ Perseveres through complex or challenging writing projects independently.	Writing Samples/Drafts Anecdotal Notes (DC Form 6.8) Writing Survey (DC Form 7.3) Portfolio Reflections and Self-Evaluation
☺ Sets writing goals independently by analyzing and evaluating own writing.	Writing Strategies I Use (CBA Form 7.4) Writing Survey (DC Form 7.3) Portfolio Reflections and Self-Evaluation Writing Goals (CBA Form 7.5)

Summary: Proficient, Connecting, and Independent Writing Tools

Assessment Tool	15 Descriptors: Number Assessed	
Writing Samples	14	(93%)
Rubrics (CBA Form 7.17)	7	(47%)
Writing Strategies I Use (CBA Form 7.4)	4	(27%)
Pieces I've Written (CBA Form 7.2)	3	(20%)
Six-Trait Guide (CBA Form 7.11)	2	(13%)
Anecdotal Notes (DC Form 6.8)	2	(13%)
Revising/Editing Forms (CBA Form 7.12, 7.13)	2	(13%)
Writing Genres (CBA Form 7.3)	2	(13%)
"Fix-it" Strategy	1	(7%)
Writing Survey (DC Form 7.3)	1	(7%)
Portfolio Reflections and Self-Evaluation	1	(7%)
Writing Goals (CBA Form 7.5)	1	(7%)

There's quite a difference between students at the Fluent stage and those at the next three writing stages. You have to look carefully to notice that 10 of the 15 descriptors at the Fluent stage include the term, "with guidance." During the Fluent stage, many new strategies and concepts are introduced. You need to provide multiple examples from your own writing, as well as samples from other students and from literature. To use an analogy, this is much like the stage when children are using training wheels as they learn to ride a bicycle.

At the Proficient stage, only 1 of the 15 descriptors at the Proficient level states, "with guidance." You can take the training wheels off, but you can't quite let go. In fact, taking the analogy a bit further, it's more exhausting at this stage, because you have to run alongside the students, providing support as needed. Half of the descriptors at the Proficient level state that the student *begins to* use a strategy. The art of teaching in middle school is learning when to hang on and when to let go and allow students to wobble or even crash once in awhile. Your job is to provide both support as well as opportunities for independent practice in an environment that encourages risk-taking. For those of you who are visual learners, this chart might explain the progression more clearly:

	Fluent	Proficient	Connecting	Independent
with guidance	10	1	0	0
begins to	2	7	1	2
independently	3	7	14	13

Since there are so many among similarities the descriptors at the last three stages, it made more sense to put the tools on one list and just describe the progression in a narrative format. By middle school, students are completing all of the assessment forms except anecdotal notes. For example, Janine King at Brighton School provides more support and modeling for her sixth graders than she does for students in her eighth-grade classes since her younger students need more support. Like reading and writing, self-evaluation is also a developmental process.

Writing Samples, Rubrics, Six-Trait Guide, Writing Strategies I Use, and Revising/Editing Forms

In the primary grades, teachers focus on building writing fluency and guiding students to add information. By fourth and fifth grade, students have begun to revise and edit their work. As students move into middle school, the criteria for quality writing become more specific according to the form of writing, the purpose, and the audience. Janine King provides focus lessons on specific aspects of effective writing for particular genres or forms. Together, she and her classes create checklists and rubrics for various genres or assignments. Janine often uses the CD-ROM to tailor the forms to her group of students, and to the genres and skills she has taught. For instance, Janine focused on writing book reviews at the beginning of the year. She showed examples from educational journals, from her own reviews of books for a column in *The Reading Teacher*, and from other students. Each Friday, four or five students shared their book reviews. After discussing the key elements for a successful book talk, the class created a rubric, which they then used to evaluate their weekly reviews.

Judy Cromwell, a middle school social studies teacher at Brighton School, asks students to complete several research projects during the year. She assesses how well her students can integrate information from a variety of sources by looking at their drafts and watching students use resources at school. She also determines if they are able to back up their opinions with reasons and examples and use paragraphs correctly. Judy notes whether or not students' reports are organized and include bibliographies with correct bibliographic format. She uses her anecdotal notes to record how much support she needed to provide throughout the research process. For instance, she shows many more examples and provides more assistance for her sixth graders than she does with her eighth-grade students.

The most significant difference between writing in the intermediate grades and in middle school is students' ability to revise and edit more independently. Their writing becomes more powerful as they work through multiple drafts with clear criteria in mind. The two most powerful assessment tools for writing in middle school are the student's writing samples laid alongside the Writing Strategies I Use forms (CBA Form 7.4) and class-generated Rubrics (CBA Form 7.17). The Six-Trait Guides (CBA Form 7.11) and Revision and Editing forms (CBA Form 7.12 and 7.13) also help students recognize their growing ability to work through multiple drafts in order to improve their writing.

Pieces I've Written and Writing Genres

In addition to learning to write better, students are also learning to compose a wider range of texts for different audiences and purposes. Intermediate and middle school students can still use the Pieces I've Written (CBA Form 7.2) and Writing Genre (CBA Form 7.3) forms to show the range of what they've been writing.

Anecdotal Notes

Janine King takes anecdotal notes during writing workshop and during individual writing conferences. She specifically looks for incidents when students use prewriting strategies or use tools (e.g., spell checkers, dictionaries) to edit on their own. Janine also records when writers seek feedback and actually incorporate other people's suggestions. She jots notes as she looks through student's writing folders and portfolio entries. Since she knows her students well, Janine records breakthroughs, specific examples (such as an example of strong word choice), and ideas for future individual, small-group, or whole-class focus lessons. Since she has many more students than an elementary teacher would have, Janine may only have one or two Post-it notes per student for each grading period.

Janine also records peer comments which provide glimpses into students' writing process. For instance, as a sixth grader, Melissa provided feedback and asked a question in her written comment about Blaine's personal vignette: "Great descriptive words. The second draft was much better because you added more sentences that helped describe the story, like 'to my horror.' Now that was good! How old were you?" These comments reveal a great deal about the writing skills of both the "coach" and her writing partner.

Writing Survey, "Fix-it" Strategy, Portfolio Reflections/Self-Evaluation, and Writing Goals.

By middle school, much of the evaluation process belongs in the students' hands. Janine's middle school students fill out the Writing Survey (DC Form 7.3) and set individual Writing Goals (CBA Form 7.5). Her students also choose periodic writing samples for their portfolios. Each entry is accompanied by a reflection about why they chose that particular piece. The characteristics for each form of writing become the criteria for selecting portfolio samples and reflection. Janine's focus lessons, the assessment tools, and the continuum descriptors all match. Students at this level also fill out the continuums, using their writing folders and portfolios to provide evidence to back up their self-evaluation and to set goals. Growth can also been measured by using the "Fix-it" Strategy, described in the Bridging and Fluent sections, to look at changes from the beginning to the end of the year. Students can step even further back to look at their writing growth over time when they place their writing samples into their Learning Profile that contains a fall and spring writing sample from kindergarten through eighth grade. Growth can be viewed and celebrated by seeing nine years of writing samples side by side.

Proficient Reading: Assessment Tools

Continuum Descriptor	Assessment Tools
📖 Reads complex children's literature.	Anecdotal Notes (DC Form 6.10, 6.11) Reading Log (CBA Form 9.21–22) Reading Genres (CBA Form 9.23) Photocopy of Reading Sample
📖 Reads and understands informational texts (e.g., want ads, brochures, schedules, catalogs, manuals) with guidance.	Anecdotal Notes (DC Form 6.10)
📖 Develops strategies and criteria for selecting reading materials independently.	Anecdotal Notes (DC Form 6.10) Reading Survey (DC Form 7.5)
☑ Uses resources (e.g., encyclopedias, articles, Internet, and nonfiction texts) to locate information independently.	Anecdotal Notes (DC Form 6.10)
☑ Gathers and analyzes information from graphs, charts, tables, and maps with guidance.	Anecdotal Notes (DC Form 6.10)
☑ Integrates information from multiple nonfiction sources to deepen understanding of a topic with guidance.	Anecdotal Notes (DC Form 6.10)
☑ Uses resources (e.g., dictionary and thesaurus) to increase vocabulary independently.	Anecdotal Notes (DC Form 6.10)
👆 Identifies literary devices (e.g., similes, metaphors, personification, and foreshadowing).	Anecdotal Notes (DC Form 6.10, 6.12) Literature Discussions (CBA Forms 9.11–13) Response Journals (CBA Form 9.14, 9.15)
👆 Discusses literature with reference to theme, author's purpose and style (literary elements), and author's craft.	Anecdotal Notes (DC Form 6.10, 6.12) Literature Discussions (CBA Forms 9.11–13) Response Journals (CBA Form 9.14, 9.15)
👆 Begins to generate in-depth responses in small group literature discussions.	Anecdotal Notes (DC Form 6.10, 6.12) Literature Discussions (CBA Forms 9.11–13)
👆 Begins to generate in-depth written responses to literature.	Anecdotal Notes (DC Form 6.10, 6.12) Response Journals (CBA Form 9.14, 9.15)
👆 Uses increasingly complex vocabulary in different subjects and in oral and written response to literature.	Anecdotal Notes (DC Form 6.10, 6.12) Literature Discussions (CBA Forms 9.11–13) Response Journals (CBA Form 9.14, 9.15)
👆 Uses reasons and examples to support ideas and conclusions.	Anecdotal Notes (DC Form 6.10, 6.11, 6.12) Literature Discussions (CBA Forms 9.11–13) Response Journals (CBA Form 9.14, 9.15)
👆 Probes for deeper meaning by "reading between the lines" in response to literature.	Anecdotal Notes (DC Form 6.10, 6.11, 6.12) Literature Discussions (CBA Forms 9.11–13) Response Journals (CBA Form 9.14, 9.15)

Connecting Reading: Assessment Tools

Continuum Descriptor	Assessment Tools
📖 Reads complex children's literature and young adult literature.	Anecdotal Notes (DC Form 6.10, 6.11) Reading Log (CBA Form 9.21–22) Photocopy of Reading Sample
📖 Selects, reads, and finishes a wide variety of genres independently.	Anecdotal Notes (DC Form 6.10) Reading Log (CBA Form 9.21–22) Reading Genres (CBA Form 9.23) Reading Survey (DC Form 7.5)
☺ Begins to choose challenging reading materials and projects.	Anecdotal Notes (DC Form 6.10) Reading Log (CBA Form 9.21–22) Reading Survey (DC Form 7.5)
☑ Integrates nonfiction information to develop deeper understanding of a topic independently.	Anecdotal Notes (DC Form 6.10)
☑ Begins to gather, analyze, and use information from graphs, charts, tables, and maps.	Anecdotal Notes (DC Form 6.10)
☝ Generates in-depth responses and sustains small group literature discussions.	Anecdotal Notes (DC Form 6.10, 6.12) Literature Discussions (CBA Forms 9.11–13)
☝ Generates in-depth written responses to literature.	Anecdotal Notes (DC Form 6.10, 6.12) Response Journals (CBA Form 9.14, 9.15)
☝ Begins to evaluate, interpret, and analyze reading content critically.	Anecdotal Notes (DC Form 6.10, 6.11, 6.12) Literature Discussions (CBA Forms 9.11–13) Response Journals (CBA Form 9.14, 9.15)
☝ Begins to develop criteria for evaluating . literature	Anecdotal Notes (DC Form 6.10, 6.12) Literature Discussions (CBA Forms 9.11–13) Response Journals (CBA Form 9.14, 9.15)
☝ Seeks recommendations and opinions about literature from others.	Anecdotal Notes (DC Form 6.10, 6.12) Literature Discussions (CBA Forms 9.11–13)
ᕲ Sets reading challenges and goals independently.	Reading Survey (DC Form 7.5) Reading Goals (CBA Form 9.4)

Independent Reading: Assessment Tools

Continuum Descriptor	Assessment Tools
📖 Reads young adult and adult literature.	Anecdotal Notes (DC Form 6.10) Reading Log (CBA Form 9.21–22) Photocopy of Reading Sample
📖 Chooses and comprehends a wide variety of sophisticated materials with ease (e.g., newspapers, magazines, manuals, novels, and poetry).	Anecdotal Notes (DC Form 6.10) Reading Log (CBA Form 9.21–22) Reading Genres (CBA Form 9.23) Reading Survey (DC Form 7.5)
📖 Reads and understands informational texts (i.e., manuals, consumer reports, applications, and forms).	Anecdotal Notes (DC Form 6.10)
☺ Reads challenging material for pleasure independently.	Anecdotal Notes (DC Form 6.10) Reading Log (CBA Form 9.21–22) Reading Survey (DC Form 7.5) Reading Goals (CBA Form 9.4)
☺ Reads challenging material for information and to solve problems independently.	Anecdotal Notes (DC Form 6.10) Reading Log (CBA Form 9.21–22) Reading Survey (DC Form 7.5) Reading Goals (CBA Form 9.4)
☺ Perseveres through complex reading tasks.	Anecdotal Notes (DC Form 6.10) Reading Log (CBA Form 9.21–22) Reading Survey (DC Form 7.5) Reading Goals (CBA Form 9.4)
☑ Gathers, analyzes, and uses information from graphs, charts, tables, and maps independently.	Anecdotal Notes (DC Form 6.10)
✆ Analyzes literary devices (e.g., metaphors, imagery, irony, and satire)	Anecdotal Notes (DC Form 6.10, 6.12) Literature Discussions (CBA Forms 9.11–13) Response Journals (CBA Form 9.14, 9.15)
✆ Contributes unique insights and supports opinions in complex literature discussions.	Anecdotal Notes (DC Form 6.10, 6.12) Literature Discussions (CBA Forms 9.11–13)
✆ Adds depth to responses to literature by making insightful connections to other reading and experiences.	Anecdotal Notes (DC Form 6.10, 6.12) Literature Discussions (CBA Forms 9.11–13) Response Journals (CBA Form 9.14, 9.15)
✆ Evaluates, interprets, and analyzes reading content critically.	Anecdotal Notes (DC Form 6.10, 6.12) Literature Discussions (CBA Forms 9.11–13) Response Journals (CBA Form 9.14, 9.15)
✆ Develops and articulates criteria for evaluating literature.	Anecdotal Notes (DC Form 6.10, 6.12) Literature Discussions (CBA Forms 9.11–13) Response Journals (CBA Form 9.14, 9.15) Reading Survey (DC Form 7.5)
🖎 Pursues a widening community of readers independently	Anecdotal Notes (DC Form 6.10, 6.12) Reading Survey (DC Form 7.5) Reading Goals (CBA Form 9.4)

Summary: Proficient, Connecting, and Independent Reading Tools

Assessment Tool	13 Descriptors: Number Assessed	
Anecdotal Notes (DC Form 6.10, 6.11, 6.12)	12	(92%)
Literature Discussions (CBA Forms 9.12, 9.13)	5	(38%)
Reading Survey (DC Form 7.5)	4	(31%)
Response Journals (CBA Form 9.14, 9.15)	4	(31%)
Reading Log (CBA Form 9.21, 9.22)	3	(23%)
Reading Goals (CBA Form 9.4)	2	(15%)
Photocopy of Reading Sample and Reflection	1	(8%)
Reading Genres (CBA Form 9.23)	1	(8%)

By middle school, most students are strong readers. The greatest distinctions at the last three stages of the continuum are the difficulty of the texts and the depth of students' comprehension. Janine King tries to listen to all her middle school students at Brighton School read during the first month of school to identify any students who might be struggling. She asks students questions about their reading preferences and takes a few anecdotal notes about favorite genres, authors, and reading attitudes. It becomes more difficult to conduct individual reading conferences during the year due to the large numbers of students she meets with each week. Janine collects assessment information on her students' reading by using anecdotal notes, rubrics, logs, and surveys. Her students also take a significant role in the assessment process.

Anecdotal Notes and Rubrics

As a middle school social studies teacher at Brighton School, Judy Cromwell takes anecdotal notes about her students' research skills. By looking at their notes and bibliographies, she can observe who uses information from a variety of sources. During class activities, she can tell which students are able to gather and analyze information from charts, tables, and maps.

Janine King uses her Anecdotal Notes Focus Questions (DC Form 6.12) to record students' level of participation and comprehension during literature circle discussions. As she roams the room with her clipboard and Post-it notes, she can tell which students have read the book, as well as their level of understanding. She can also note when students discuss literary elements, such as theme or author's style, or make connections to their lives and to other books or authors (Figure 5.20). She shares general observations with the class during debriefings at the end of each discussion. Last year, her class generated a list of the criteria for good discussions that they used to create a Self-Evaluation Rubric (CBA Form 9.12 and 9.13). Since she is required to give grades in middle school, Janine uses a simple rubric (1 = not demonstrating, 2 = requires support, 3 = meets expectations, 4 = exceeds expectations) and jots a score at the bottom of the Post-it note as she listens to students during literature circles.

Figure 5.20 Janine King Taking Anecdotal Notes

Janine also takes anecdotal notes during her students' book talks. Each Friday, four or five students share the books they've been reading. They explain why they chose the book, summarize the plot, read a significant passage aloud, and give their opinion of the book. These weekly book talks provide a simple way for Janine to record information about all four of the Washington State reading standards (reading strategies, comprehension, range of text, and setting goals). By recording observations during literature circle discussions and book talks, Janine will usually have five or six notes for each student in reading for each grading period.

Occasionally you may have students who are very quiet during literature discussions, but whose journal writing reflects an ability to comprehend and analyze books at a deeper level than their conversations would indicate. In addition to listening to literature circle discussions, Janine also takes anecdotal notes as she reads through students' literature response journals. She periodically asks students' permission to share exemplary journal entries to help the class construct a chart of the qualities of good journal entries. They add to the chart throughout the year and use the criteria to create a Response Journal Rubric (CBA Form 9.15). Students can then use the rubric to assess the depth of understanding and clarity of their written response to literature. The rubrics, class discussions, and Janine's modeling help students learn to self-evaluate and to set their own reading goals.

Reading Logs and Reading Genres, and Photocopy of Reading Sample and Reflection

In middle school, students can use a Reading Log (CBA Form 9.21–9.22) or the Reading Genres Graph (CBA Form 9.23) to keep track of the books and other reading materials they read at home. At an age when students often quit reading, the logs and an expectation that students will read a certain amount outside of school can help adolescents make time for reading in their busy lives. The key is to help young adults find books that match their reading abilities and interests by keeping up with current young adult titles and sharing new books. Janine finds that the weekly book talks by their peers also help connect her students with good books.

In the fall and spring at Brighton School, students enter a sample Reading Log and a photocopy of a page from a book they are reading into their Learner Profile. Since by middle school students are usually fluent readers, each student is only videotaped reading aloud in the spring. The photocopied reading sample, the Reading Log, and the videotape in each student's Learner Profile provide a powerful glimpse of reading growth from kindergarten through eighth grade.

Reading Survey and Reading Goals

Janine's middle school students complete a Reading Survey (CBA Form 7.5) in the fall and spring. These surveys, which often show growth, are sent home at the end of the year in each student's portfolio. Janine has used the CD-ROM to include a question about goals on the Reading Survey. By using the class rubrics for literature circle discussions and response journal, the feedback on their book talks, their Reading Logs, and the Reading Continuum, most students are able to evaluate progress toward the goals they set at the beginning of the year.

Each spring, Janine also asks her eighth graders to create a portrait of themselves as readers. By talking with their parents and looking through their Learner Profiles, students create a time line of the key books for each year of their lives. What a wonderful way to celebrate the role of books in the lives of these readers!

Staff Development

Are you feeling overwhelmed at all the possible assessment tools you could be using? It's important to step back and first pat yourself on the back for all the strategies you *are* using. Use the Assessment Planning form (DC Form 5.4) to list all the assessment tools you already use under the "Now" column. I hope that as you've read this chapter, you feel affirmed for all the assessment ideas you're already using in your classroom.

Next, look at the continuum and notice the strands you already assess. Where are the gaps? Do you have more information about students' reading strategies, but less about the range of their reading? Do you assess writing strategies but not writing process? Now take a look through the reading and writing sections in this chapter that match the continuum stages for most of your students. List any assessment strategies or forms that you might want to try in either the "Next" or "Later" columns.

Finally, prioritize the "Next" column and choose two or three new assessment ideas to try. Transfer this information to the Organizational Grid (DC Form 5.3), mapping out which tools you plan to use each month. It's better to start small and feel successful, rather than to list too many ideas and then to feel overwhelmed. It's helpful to store your Organizational Grid in your Teacher Notebook so you can check off the assessment data that you have collected each month. As you create your yearly plan, be sure to balance one-shot strategies with the more time-consuming assessment tools, such as running records or reading conferences. You may next want to ask assistants or parent volunteers to photocopy the forms you'll need for the beginning of the year. Anne Klein also color-codes all of her assessment forms. She copies all the forms she plans to use in the fall on yellow paper, forms for the winter on blue, and the tools for the spring trimester on pink paper.

Once you've incorporated these new ideas into your classroom, revisit your list and see if you might want to modify any forms or add a new assessment technique. Creating a solid and manageable assessment plan is an ongoing and challenging task, but one which will improve your teaching, help you know your students better, and enable you to communicate more effectively with parents.

Nancy Emerson, the principal at West Mercer Elementary on Mercer Island, Washington, has a Principal's Notebook with a section for each teacher. Each teacher's Organizational Grid is kept in their section of her notebook, along with the teacher's professional goals. By referring to the grid, Nancy can provide positive feedback and support for the sound assessment practices she sees as she visits classrooms and evaluates teachers.

Once you and your colleagues have created individual plans, you can share the plans. Decide on five or six assessment strategies you all have in common, then create a generic Organizational Grid for your grade level. During grade-level meetings, you can refer to your Grade Level Organizational Grid as you remind each other of the assessment information you plan to collect each month. The collegial support can help you stay on track; and the monthly meetings create time to share questions, as well as assessment ideas and strategies. By requiring teachers to submit their individual and grade-level assessment plans in the fall and to meet in grade level teams on a regular basis to focus on assessment and continuums, Nancy has seen a new level of professional growth, confidence, and improved communication among her staff.

At the SAIS international school in Jeddah, Saudi Arabia, Jill and Jack Raven and their primary team offered Morning Coffee Circles in which they shared their Teacher Notebooks, the continuums, and samples of student work with colleagues at different grade levels. This informal and non-threatening sharing was well received by many staff members who had previously been reluctant to try using the continuums.

Wendy Evans, the Curriculum Coordinator at the American School in Monterrey, Mexico, held an optional Notebook Party the first year the staff piloted Teacher Notebooks. One veteran teacher set the tone for the meeting by stating, "I have my Teacher Notebook up and running, but I'm here to get some good ideas." The meeting became a forum for professional dialogue. For instance, a very young teacher shared her assessment tools and student work and explained how the Notebook provided her with confidence during parent-teacher conferences because she had so much information. The administrators continued this dialogue after the meeting and decided to ask all classroom teachers to keep a Teacher Notebook during the next school year. Wendy writes, "The Notebook Party was an opportunity to share ideas and information. It allowed for stimulating dialogue between teachers and became a vehicle that sparked change. Not bad for an hour session!" Teacher Notebooks and sound classroom based assessment can provide a powerful spark for staff development and professional conversations.

ORGANIZATIONAL GRID: PRIMARY GRADES

ASSESSMENT TOOL/STRATEGY	SEP	OCT	NOV	DEC	JAN	FEB	MAR	APR	MAY	JUN				
Parent Survey		▓	▓	▓	▓	▓	▓	▓	▓	▓				
Spelling 10 Words	▓	▓	▓	▓	▓	▓	▓	▓		▓				
Words I Know (Clay)	▓	▓	▓		▓	▓	▓		▓	▓				
Writing Continuum		▓	▓	▓	▓	▓	▓	▓	▓					
Running Records	▓	▓		▓		▓	▓	▓		▓				
Reading Continuum		▓	▓	▓	▓	▓	▓	▓	▓					
Photocopy Reading Sample		▓	▓	▓		▓	▓	▓	▓					
Anecdotal Notes (ongoing)														

ORGANIZATIONAL GRID: INTERMEDIATE GRADES

ASSESSMENT TOOL/STRATEGY	SEP	OCT	NOV	DEC	JAN	FEB	MAR	APR	MAY	JUN
Parent Survey		■	■	■	■	■	■	■	■	■
Student Surveys	■		■	■	■	■	■	■		■
Spelling 10 Words	■	■	■	■	■	■	■			■
"Fix-it" Strategy	■		■	■	■	■	■	■	■	■
Writing Continuum	■	■	■	■		■	■	■	■	
Reading Conference Form		■		■	■		■	■		
Reading Continuum	■	■	■	■		■	■	■	■	■
Photocopy Reading Sample	■	■	■							
Rubrics (ongoing)										
Anecdotal Notes (ongoing)										

ORGANIZATIONAL GRID

ASSESSMENT TOOL/STRATEGY	SEP	OCT	NOV	DEC	JAN	FEB	MAR	APR	MAY	JUN

ASSESSMENT PLANNING

NOW	NEXT	LATER

Spelling Words

FIRST GRADE (from Richard Gentry)
1. monster
2. united
3. dress
4. bottom
5. hiked
6. human
7. eagle
8. closed
9. bumped
10. type

SECOND GRADE
1. train
2. people
3. choice
4. porcupine
5. creature
6. somebody
7. huge
8. each
9. church
10. dressed

THIRD GRADE
1. usually
2. excellent
3. because
4. caterpillar
5. believe
6. watched
7. wouldn't
8. cucumber
9. cavities
10. bicycle
11. tomorrow
12. through
13. measure
14. experience
15. imagination

FOURTH GRADE
1. receive
2. business
3. difference
4. breakfast
5. surprising
6. knowledge
7. disappear
8. guess
9. experience
10. beneath
11. pressure
12. neighborhood
13. avenue
14. groceries
15. secretary

FIFTH GRADE
1. pharmacy
2. occasionally
3. engine
4. excitement
5. receipt
6. hypothesis
7. similar
8. gorgeous
9. apologize
10. accordingly
11. restaurant
12. committee
13. embarrassed
14. coincidence
15. license

SPELLING CONTINUUM

Pre-writing (Preconventional) Ages 3-5 WORD = ונ	Pre-phonetic (Preconventional) Ages 3-5 WORD = BMTYZ	Semi-phonetic (Emergent) Ages 4-6 WORD = WD or YD	Phonetic (Developing & Beginning) Ages 5-8 WORD = W9d	Transitional (Expanding & Bridging) Ages 7-11 WORD = Werd	Conventional (Bridging & Fluent) Ages 8+ WORD = WORD
• Experiments with drawing and writing. • Uses scribble writing	• Understands that print carries meaning. • Writes random recognizable letters to represent words.	• Begins to recognize that letters represent specific sounds. • Uses beginning consonants to write a word. • Uses beginning and ending consonants to write a word. • May use letter names (e.g., u for you) as words. • Begins to take risks and write independently.	• Matches letters to sounds. • Spells some words by the sounds heard. • Spells some words by sight. • Uses beginning, middle, and ending sounds to write words. • Uses phonetic spelling to write independently. • Begins to notice common spelling patterns. • Begins to ask for correct spelling of words.	• Moves beyond phonetic spelling toward conventional spelling. • Spells simple common words correctly. • Relies on visual spelling patterns. • Uses vowels in all syllables. • Uses letter combinations when writing words (e.g., clusters, blends, diagraphs). • Experiments with various ways to spell words. • Begins to use resources to spell challenging words. • Begins to edit for spelling.	• Uses visual patterns and other strategies to spell most words correctly. • Spells prefixes and suffixes correctly. • Spells contractions correctly. • Spells most compound words correctly. • Begins to learn correct spelling for irregular words. • Identifies misspelled words. • Uses resources when spelling challenging words. • Edits for spelling in final drafts. • Chooses words to learn to spell.

Form 5.1: Spelling Continuum

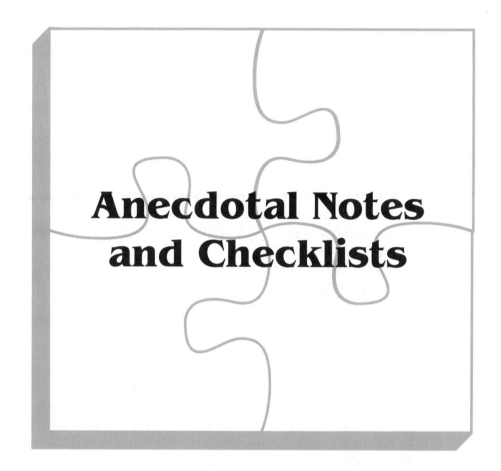

Anecdotal Notes
and Checklists

> I am struck again and again by the power of anecdotal notes. They are a powerful assessment tool we haven't begun to tap.
>
> —*Carol Wilcox, Staff Developer, Denver, Colorado*

In the field of anthropology, if you want to learn more about a group of people, you live among them, examining, questioning, and taking extensive field notes. Like anthropologists or ethnographic researchers, teachers continually collect information about students. Unlike anthropologists, however, teachers are also participants and not merely observers in the world of the classroom. Teachers need to collect data while interacting with students. In the last chapter, I described ways in which you can collect assessment information. In this chapter, I explain how anecdotal notes can add the stories and voice that enable you to portray each child's learning and unique personality.

In *Webster's Dictionary*, anecdotes are defined as "a short, entertaining account of some happening, usually personal." The word "short" is important here. In the busy world of teaching, you simply don't have time to write extensive descriptions of incidents that occur during the day, hence the term, anecdotal *notes*. The key phrases or verbatim comments that you record will trigger your memory of the incident when you look at your notes later.

The second part of the definition includes the term "entertaining," which is a word we don't usually connect with assessment. Some of the reasons why many of us enjoying teaching are the wonderful things children say and the classroom stories that we tell to our colleagues. Anecdotal notes are a perfect place to record those "Art Linkletter" comments students make. By recording students' words, you can gain insights into how they are constructing meaning. Their conversations enrich the information that you can gain through observation.

The final part of the definition implies that anecdotes are "personal." This is the significant difference between the plethora of assessment tools described in the last chapter and anecdotal notes. Anecdotal notes will help you become a better observer and researcher in your own classroom. In *Negotiated Evaluation* (1994), Helen Woodward states: "Observation in itself is not sufficient – to be useful, observations must be faithfully recorded" (p. 23). Anecdotal notes are one way to "faithfully record" learning in your classroom.

In *The Handbook of Literacy Assessment and Evaluation* (2000), Bill Harp defines anecdotal notes as "the written records a teacher keeps of his or her observations of children" (p. 19). He adds that these records are valuable for documenting progress, planning future instruction, and setting goals. For some of you, taking anecdotal notes may be a new strategy. Others may have used this strategy for several years. If you have tried taking anecdotal notes, do you change your method every year? Some years do you record your observations in a spiral notebook with tabs for each student and the next year take notes on index cards? Do you have trouble finding your notebook or index cards and end up writing on the back of a memo or envelope, fully intending to transfer your notes at a later date? Instead of simplifying life, do your notes pile up and add to your feeling of being overwhelmed? As you prepare for report cards and parent conferences, do you have a wealth of information about some students and embarrassingly little about others? If these scenarios sound familiar, this chapter may provide some practical strategies for streamlining your methods of recording observations about your students.

The first part of this chapter provides practical ideas about taking anecdotal notes. The second section contains focus questions to help you fine-tune your observations. In the last part of this chapter, I explore how checklists can also be an efficient way to document student learning. The Anecdotal Grids (DC Forms 6.1–6.6), the Focus Questions (DC Forms 6.7–6.14, and the Checklists (DCA Forms 6.15–6.20) are all included at the end of this chapter and on the CD-ROM.

Anecdotal Notes

At workshops, I present examples of many of the assessment tools described in the previous chapter. At the end of the session, I ask teachers to list one or two ideas they can use right away in their classrooms. Anecdotal notes are always at the top of the list. Teachers are delighted to find an organized and manageable way to record information about their students.

Why Take Anecdotal Notes?

Ten years ago, you probably kept a great deal of information about your students "in your head." Today the level of accountability is far higher. As professionals under intense scrutiny, it has become vital to support and document your observations. In addition, curriculum has changed. If students are involved in reading/writing workshop, literature circles, guided reading, cooperative learning, and inquiry studies, you need a method for keeping track of what students are learning. You have too many students and too many interactions to be able to remember everything. You may find that if you don't write something down, the thought has vanished by the end of the day. By taking anecdotal notes, you have more specific information when you get ready to write comments on report cards, fill out the continuums, and meet with parents.

As you take anecdotal notes, you may also become aware of instructional gaps and skills you need to teach or re-teach. If several students have a similar need, you may want to teach that specific skill in a small group. At other times, a whole group focus lesson may be more effective. Anecdotal notes enable you to teach more responsively based on students' needs.

Anecdotal notes can also be useful when you are concerned about a particular student. Your notes can be valuable during team meetings about a child, special services referrals, Child Protective Service reports, or meetings with concerned parents. Teachers sometimes see different behaviors than families see at home. For instance, Linda Johnson had a kindergarten student who was reading at a fourth-grade level. Although this student was quite advanced academically, she was not producing work in school that reflected the type of writing that Elizabeth's parents saw at home. As an only child, Elizabeth was able to write several pages at home without any distractions and with the help of two attentive adults. In the lively world of kindergarten, she was easily distracted and far more interested in what other children were doing than in writing in her journal. Her lack of maturity and social skills greatly affected her academic performance. Linda found it helpful to take daily anecdotal notes that she summarized in a weekly letter to Elizabeth's parents. The family became less critical and more supportive once Linda documented specific incidents and noted improvement. When you feel "on the spot," anecdotal notes can provide objective evidence to back up your educational decisions.

In another example, Lisa Norwick had a second grader who was struggling in all academic areas and diagnosed as having a learning disability. Brandon tested high in math, but his schoolwork did not reflect his abilities. During a resource team meeting, Lisa shared her anecdotal notes about Brandon's difficulty with the math work. Upon closer examination, the team discovered that many of the math pages dealt with two or three concepts at a time. For students like Brandon, leaping from one concept to another can cause difficulties. Lisa's anecdotal notes helped the referral team develop strategies to support Brandon's learning in the classroom.

Anne Klein uses her notes to share specific positive incidents with families of her fourth and fifth graders. For instance, Sam seldom contributed to literature discussions at the beginning of the year. By May, he had begun to ask thoughtful questions and demonstrated some leadership qualities. When Anne shared specific examples with Sam's father, he was extremely pleased, since he rarely heard positive comments about his son's behavior or performance at school.

Finally, anecdotal notes can be useful when you write comments on report cards. Janine King finds that 90% of her narrative report card comments came directly from her anecdotal notes. For instance, on Emily's sixth-grade report card, Janine wrote,

Emily thoughtfully contributes to literature circles and helps sustain the discussion. She is able to read between the lines, interpreting the deeper meaning of what she reads. Her written responses to literature are filled with interpretations of author's purpose, description, style, and use of language. Emily selects and finishes a wide variety of appropriate books independently. In writing, Emily is able to transfer what she has learned from so much reading to her own pieces. She makes great use of imagery and word choice to enhance her clever, creative ideas. She is developing her own strong voice and sense of style.

Janine's written observations enabled her to paint a portrait of Emily as a reader and a writer using very specific language.

Many teachers mention the following reasons why they feel that anecdotal notes are worth the time and effort:

Purpose for Anecdotal Notes
- provide documentation of each student's strengths and needs
- ensure that teachers gather data about every student
- provide additional documentation for students with special needs
- help teachers spot instructional gaps
- help teachers plan whole class, small group, individual instruction, or focus lessons based on needs
- provide immediate feedback to students
- give voice to narrative comments on report cards
- provide specific examples to share at parent conferences
- reflect how well you know each student

How Do You Take Anecdotal Notes?
Many teachers use a clipboard containing a grid with $1^1/2$ x 2-inch rectangles that fit 20 small Post-it notes on a page (DC Form 6.1 and 6.2). Since she has 30 students, Anne Klein uses two pages of grids on her clipboard. Other teachers prefer to use a legal size clipboard and grid that includes room for comments about 28 students. (The legal size $8^1/2$ x 14-inch grid for anecdotal notes is included on the CD-ROM.) Another variation (DC Form 6.6) contains room for six small ($1^1/2$ x 2-inch) and six large (3-inch square) Post-it notes that specialists or parent volunteers can use while working with small groups of students. You may want to place a copy of these grids in an acetate slip-sheet in either your Continuum Notebook or Assessment Tools Notebook so that they are easy to find and photocopy.

In the fall, Anne writes one student's name above each rectangle on the grid. She then makes several copies of the grid with students' names for her clipboard. At the beginning of a literature circle unit, for example, she places one blank Post-it note on the grid for each student. She chooses a focus, then writes the date and short observations on Post-it notes for a few students. Depending on her focus, she may write three or four notes each day. At the end of two weeks, she will have at least one anecdotal comment for each of her 30 students. The advantage of this system is that Anne can see by glancing at the grid on her clipboard which students she has missed. Once she has assessed all of her students, Anne transfers the notes into each child's section of her Teacher Notebook. All her notes about a child are then in one place, and she doesn't have to copy them over.

Of course, no one method works for everyone; you will want to adapt this strategy to fit your own needs and teaching style. For instance, Anne Klein used mailing labels instead of Post-it notes for many years. Linda Johnson prefers to take anecdotal notes in a spiral notebook with a page for each kindergarten student. It's helpful to have a single student's comments on one page without transferring notes; however, it's harder to be sure that you have recorded notes about every child. You may find that you have many comments about some students and relatively few for other children. By using the anecdotal grid, you can see at a glance which students you have missed. Whether you use Post-it notes, mailing labels, or a notebook, the key is to decide what to record and how to create an organized system for documenting your observations.

How Many Anecdotal Notes Do You Take Each Day?

Obviously, if you took notes on all of your students all day long, you wouldn't have time to teach. The number of notes you take will depend on your teaching style, your experience using this assessment strategy, the age of your students, and the context. For instance, Anne Klein usually takes notes on two or three groups of students as she moves around the room during literature circle discussions. At other times, she might only record two or three quick observations during Author's Chair or Writing Workshop. Start with a realistic goal. Taking notes on two or three students each day is manageable. At the end of two or three weeks, you will have assessed your whole class and can then choose a new focus. By middle school, students can also take anecdotal notes during literature discussions or peer conferences. Of course, this would require a great deal of modeling and support.

When Do You Assess?

When I asked teachers when they take anecdotal notes about reading and writing, their responses were very similar:

When to Take Anecdotal Notes
- silent reading time
- literature circles
- small reading groups
- guided reading
- writing workshop
- individual writing conferences
- Author's Chair

In the beginning, you may want to take anecdotal notes at one specific time during the day. For instance, you might want to observe whether students are engaged during silent reading. Do they read for only a few minutes at a time, for 10–15 minutes, or for 30–40 minutes? Janine King's middle school students have time for reading every Friday during language arts. Janine walks around the room and records the titles of the book each student is reading. When she goes to her desk to read her own book, she keeps her clipboard handy and glances up every 5–10 minutes and records which students are still engrossed in their books. This quick check makes it easy for Janine to assess the continuum descriptor at the Fluent stage that states, "Reads silently for extended periods (30–40 minutes)."

When she first tried this system several years ago, Janine thought that she could have predicted which students were able to read for long periods. When she observed more closely, she was surprised to learn that a few students that she thought could not sustain interest in a book were able to read for long stretches at a time. A few others had mastered the art of looking like they were reading but were not actually engaged with the text. Janine's intentional observations provided more precise information than simply scanning the room or relying on her general impressions of students.

Once you assess your students' ability to focus during reading time, you can start recording titles of books they read each day. You can note if they are reading books at an appropriate level, if they finish books, as well as the genres and types of books they read on their own. You can collect further information about the students' texts by looking at their reading logs, surveys, and self-evaluation checklists (Chapter 7). It will probably take two or three weeks to collect this information about all of your students. It is then quite simple to fill out the Types of Texts (📖) strand on the reading continuum.

Next, you might want to either assess reading comprehension or decide to spend a few weeks assessing writing behaviors. In order to assess reading and writing processes, it's easiest to take anecdotal notes when students are working independently. You can also jot down observations during whole group lessons. For instance, Anne Klein takes anecdotal notes when her students read their monthly *Time for Kids* magazine. She records information about students' oral fluency and their use of nonfiction reading strategies from the reading continuum.

The key is to create a structure in which your students are independent enough that you can take a few seconds to jot down a few notes. In her book, *Taking Note: Improving Your Observational Notetaking* (1996), Brenda Miller Power describes these as "in the midst" notes you can take while students are working. In *Negotiated Evaluation* (1994), Helen Woodward notes that "the closer to the time of observation the recording is done, the more accurate it will be" (p. 23).

Sometimes you're simply too busy teaching or solving problems to record your observations. The other types of notes Brenda Miller Power (1996) discusses are "after the fact" observations that you can write before school, when children are at P. E. or music, during planning time, after school, or at home. As a kindergarten teacher, Linda Johnson finds that the majority of her anecdotal notes are written "after the fact" at the end of the day, since her children are less independent and it's more difficult to jot down notes during the day. She prefers to record two or three anecdotal comments about students during lunch or after school. The key is to make this type of reflection a consistent part of your schedule and routine.

Lisa Norwick found that when she taught intermediate students, most of her note taking occurred "in the midst." When she moved to the primary grades, it became more challenging to take anecdotal notes. Lisa found that she could still take anecdotal notes during literature discussions, but it was much more difficult during Writing Workshop since her students were continually tapping her on the shoulder and asking for help. She decided to take anecdotal notes about writing "after the fact." Before she goes home each night, Lisa takes out two children's writing journals and looks through them, jotting down one or two anecdotal comments about what she notices. Over time, she accumulates several Post-it notes for each child with very specific information. These daily reflections also help Lisa plan her focus lessons based on the needs she sees in her students' writing. Rather than carting home a tub with all of her students' journals to look through the week before report cards, Lisa has built assessment into her daily routine.

Once her writing program was running smoothly, Lisa found three other times she could take anecdotal notes about writing. Lisa begins each writing workshop with a focus lesson and quick "status of the class," then students have 10 minutes of silent writing time. During that time, Lisa uses her writing clipboard and roams around the room, looking over students' shoulders and jotting down observations. Once the 10 minutes are over, students can talk as they write, or confer with peers or an adult. Lisa might write down an additional note or two as she conducts individual writing conferences. Her notes might be a few words or a phrase, almost like her own personal shorthand, that can jog her memory later about an interaction or a student's writing breakthrough. Finally, she takes a few more notes as students share their writing at Author's Chair.

As you become more comfortable with recording your observations, you might want to keep two or three separate clipboards for different subjects. For instance, Lisa has different clipboards for reading, writing, and math. If behavioral issues arise, Lisa places a Post-it note on the clipboard for the content area in which the problem occurred. Anne Klein keeps four clipboards; one for reading and writing, one for math/social studies/science, one for social and behavioral observations, and the fourth for parent volunteers to use. She uses her reading/writing clipboards in the morning and her math/science/social studies clipboard in the afternoon. Anne uses the third clipboard when behavioral or social issues arise or after a phone call or meeting with a parent. Other teachers, aides, or volunteers use the fourth clipboard during literature circles or when they help students edit their writing.

How Do You Organize Anecdotal Notes?

Anne Klein keeps a Teacher Notebook in a three-ring binder with section dividers for each of her 30 students. She keeps three blank anecdotal grids in each child's section of her Teacher Notebook. One grid is divided in half for comments about reading and writing (DC Form 6.3). The second grid has space for comments about math, social studies, and science (DC Form 6.4). Anne also uses a third blank grid where she places anecdotal notes about behaviors, social skills, work habits, and parent interactions. She copies the three grids on colored paper and uses matching Post-it notes for each trimester (yellow = fall, blue = winter, pink = spring). In the fall, Anne made 30 copies of the Reading/Writing grid on yellow paper and placed a copy in each student's section of her Teacher Notebook. She used yellow Post-it notes during literature circles, silent reading, writing workshop, and Author's Chair. Anne will have between eight and ten Post-it notes per child for reading and writing each trimester. She has three or four anecdotal notes for every grading period about each child's math, science, and social studies skills. Of course, when she first started to use the continuums, she had far fewer notes. She is able to record more as she has become familiar with the descriptors and has fine-tuned her methods and observations. In Figure 6.1, you can see an example of Anne's anecdotal notes about Brittany's reading and writing.

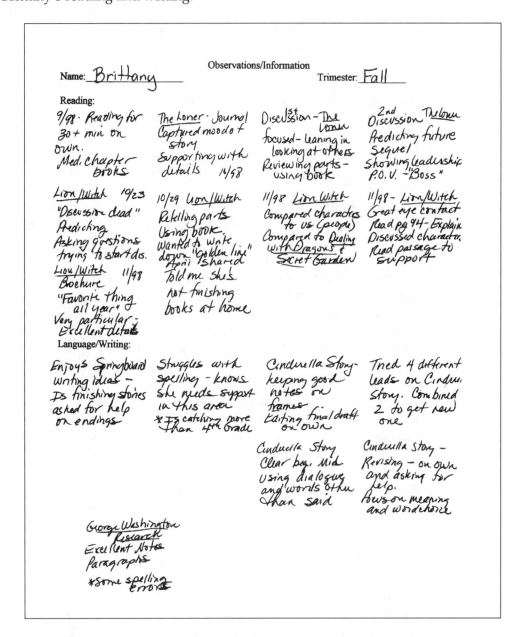

Figure 6.1 Sample Anecdotal Notes

Cindy Flegenheimer organizes her Teacher Notebook in a slightly different way. She records the date and observation on the Post-it notes until she has assessed her whole class. She then transfers the notes into her Teacher Notebook. In each fourth grader's section of her notebook, she has three blank grids that she copies on different colored paper. She transfers all her Post-it notes about reading onto the blue grid, writing notes onto the green grid, and math/science notes onto the yellow grid. Cindy will have about ten or twelve anecdotal notes per child in each subject area for the whole year. She may have more notes for children with special needs or concerns.

Lisa Norwick has two Teacher Notebooks, one for language arts and one for math. She keeps two blank grids in each student's section of her language arts notebook, one for reading and one for writing. The math notebook contains one blank grid in each child's section for Lisa's math observations. By the end of the trimester, she has a page of Post-it notes about each child's reading and writing and half a page for math. When it's time to fill out report cards, Lisa takes home her language arts Teacher Notebook in order to fill out the reading and writing continuums. She takes home her math Teacher Notebook another night in order to fill out the math section of her students' report cards.

Because she teaches three language arts classes in middle school, Janine King keeps three separate Teacher Notebooks, one for each of her sixth-, seventh-, and eighth-grade classes. In each student's section, she includes one blank grid for reading and another blank grid for writing. Janine will collect four or five anecdotal notes in reading and three or four notes in writing about each of her students for each grading period.

All four of these teachers have been keeping a Teacher Notebook and taking anecdotal notes using this method for several years now and have developed their own manageable system over time. If you are just starting to take anecdotal notes, you may want to start on a smaller scale. Some teachers place only one grid in each child's section of their Teacher Notebook. Since they only collect four or five Post-it notes per child per subject for the whole year, they simply place their notes in the appropriate row for reading, writing, math, and social/behavior. All of the variations of the anecdotal grids are included at the end of this chapter and on the CD-ROM (DC Form 6.1–6.6).

What Are The Challenges?

The biggest challenge is learning how to make anecdotal notes a habit. Teachers who have made note taking part of their teaching, automatically grab their clipboard at various times during the day. Another challenge is finding time to transfer the notes into your Teacher Notebook. Sandy Figel and Lisa Norwick transfer their notes into their Teacher Notebooks at the end of each day. Anne Klein finds it's easiest to do at the end of a unit or literature circle set. She also uses early release days, planning time, or an hour after school to transfer all her notes into her Teacher Notebook before report cards and parent conferences. Most parents are quite impressed with Anne's organization when she flips to their child's section, and they see how much information she has collected (Figure 6.2). Your Teacher Notebook can help your principal and parents see the time and effort that you put into teaching and assessing your students.

When I asked several teachers how their anecdotal note taking has changed over time, they all mentioned that their notes are more specific now and more closely connected to the continuums. Cindy Flegenheimer said, "I know the continuum better, so I know what I'm looking for and my anecdotal notes are more focused."

Figure 6.2 Anne Klein Organizing Anecdotal Notes

Rather than recording generic comments, these teachers now link their notes to skills and strategies they have taught and record specific examples or verbatim student comments. Teachers also remarked that organizing their clipboards and pages in their Teacher Notebooks by subject has been extremely helpful.

In order to be useful, taking anecdotal notes must become part of your daily teaching. For instance, Janine also admits that she has twice as many anecdotal notes for reading as she does for writing, since reading has been her focus this year in middle school. Next year she hopes to change the format of her writing program and to build in more time for taking anecdotal notes. It's important to be kind to yourself and not get overwhelmed by all the things you haven't done! Start small and team up with a friend as you try new ideas. Concentrate on your successes and set reasonable goals for incorporating anecdotal notes into your assessment plan.

Focus Questions for Anecdotal Notes

What Do You Record?

At the beginning of the year, anecdotal notes can help you get to know your students. As the year progresses, you can focus more on the specific strategies that you have taught. It's easy to become buried in piles of Post-it notes if you start writing down everything that goes on in your classroom. Anecdotal notes are most beneficial when you know exactly what you're looking for. A list of Primary and Intermediate focus questions is included at the end of this chapter and on the CD-ROM for both writing and reading. It's helpful to place a copy of the questions you plan to use in either your Continuum Notebook or your Assessment Tools Notebook. You may want to put the appropriate page with focus questions on the top of your anecdotal clipboards. You can highlight or place a date by the questions you have assessed. The focus questions become a framework for taking anecdotal notes.

In addition, since the focus questions were pulled from the reading and writing continuums, they provide the link between the continuums and anecdotal notes. (If you would like to see more about the connection, there is a copy of the reading and writing continuums on the CD-ROM with shading for each of the continuum descriptors that can be assessed by using anecdotal notes.) Each list includes about 20 focus questions. Sometimes the questions contain a developmental progression, such as questions 15 and 16 in the Anecdotal Notes Writing focus questions: "Can the student tell about his/her writing? Pretend to read his/her writing? Does the student read his/her own writing and notice mistakes?" You're observing one behavior (students reading what they have written), but looking for three developmental levels of sophistication.

You may want to pick one question and take notes for a week or two until you've assessed each student on that particular skill or strategy. When your grid is full, transfer the Post-it notes into your Teacher Notebook, then choose another focus for your observations. Your notes will be more effective if you tie your observations to a strategy you have just taught and if your focus lessons are linked directly to the continuums.

For instance, Anne Klein used an idea in *Craft Lessons* (Fletcher and Portalupi, 1998) to teach students about word choice, which is one of the descriptors on the writing continuum. Anne read aloud *John Henry* (1994) by Julius Lester, then asked students to find places in their own writing where they could add more vivid verbs. For the next few weeks, Anne conferred with students about their writing, recording specifically which students used this strategy. At the end of Writing Workshop, she asked one or two students to share examples of where they changed a passive or dull verb to a more interesting one.

It also helps to keep your anecdotal notes specific. A comment like "good writing" doesn't provide much useful information. Writing down direct quotes or specific examples from students keeps you objective and also provides the "voice" that makes your narrative comments on report cards or conversations with families show that you really know each student. As you listen to students talking about books or giving each other feedback during Author's Chair, you can also record gaps you see, books you want to share, and ideas for future focus lessons.

You can also involve parent volunteers, the ESL teacher, the reading specialist, or other adults in taking anecdotal notes by providing a clipboard with Post-it notes and a class seating chart, along with one of the focus questions. For instance, you might want to role play how readers can make connections between their book and other books, as well as to their own lives and experiences. The adults can then listen in to several literature circles, recording examples of when students discussed how their book reminded them of similar situations in their own lives.

The four lists of focus questions are based on the reading and writing continuums. I used italics to show which focus questions can be assessed most effectively by taking anecdotal notes. I've also included focus questions for adult volunteers to use. Primary teachers may want to use the next list of focus questions as a guide for recording social behaviors. The final list of focus questions is intended for principals to use as they observe and interact with teachers. In Chapter 9, you'll also find focus questions and checklists for teachers working with students who are learning English as an additional language. Note that the focus questions are numbered for quick reference. Rather than writing, "Mark made a personal connection to events in the book," you could simply write #21 from the primary Reading Focus Questions list, then jot down Mark's comment: #21: "I feel just like Marty in *Shiloh* when I spend the night away from my dog."

You may want to modify the list of focus questions on the CD-ROM to match your standards, report card, and particular grade level. For instance, third-grade teachers who hover in that gray zone between primary and intermediate may want to combine some of the focus questions from both the primary and intermediate lists. You may also want to revise the focus questions to match your curriculum and specific units. For example, after spending several weeks teaching poetry to her fourth graders, Anne Klein used two focus questions to record examples of students who used carefully chosen language in their poems (#5) and who revised their poems for clarity or word choice (#15).

Anecdotal Notes: Writing Focus Questions (Primary)

The Writing Focus Questions (Primary) (DC Form 6.7) can be used with K–2 students in the first four stages of the writing continuum (Preconventional, Emerging, Developing, and Beginning). The focus questions address approximately one fourth of the descriptors on the continuum for those first four stages. Anecdotal notes are most useful for assessing two continuum strands: Writing Process (✂) and Attitude (☺). Most teachers examine writing samples and use other assessment tools to assess Types of Texts (▤), Writing Content and Traits (▱), and Writing Conventions (✎).

Anecdotal Notes: Writing Focus Questions (Intermediate)

The Writing Focus Questions (Intermediate) (DC Form 6.8) address skills most commonly used by Expanding, Bridging, Fluent, Proficient, Connecting, and Independent writers in third through eighth grades. These questions cover approximately 20% of the descriptors in the last six stages of the writing continuum. Like primary teachers, teachers in the intermediate grades find anecdotal notes most appropriate for the Writing Process (✂) and Attitude (☺) strands, as indicated in italics on the list of focus questions. For instance, some intermediate teachers use anecdotal notes to record specific examples of writing process strategies (like prewriting), or a revision strategy they have taught (such as revising for word choice). You may want to record when a student becomes aware of using a convention or note when a child needs extra support. These types of anecdotal notes are particularly helpful if you write narrative comments on report cards, since they provide specific information about each child's writing skills. To assess Types of Texts (▤), Writing Content and Traits (▱), and Writing Conventions (✎), it's more efficient to examine writing samples and drafts and to use rubrics and revising/editing forms.

Anecdotal Notes: Reading Focus Questions (Primary)

The Reading Focus Questions (Primary) (DC Form 6.9) apply to the first five stages on the reading continuum (Preconventional through Expanding). Anecdotal notes seem to be far more powerful as a reading assessment tool than as a writing assessment strategy. In fact, over 75% of the descriptors in these stages are addressed in the reading focus questions. In writing, much can be learned from examining actual samples. Reading, on the other hand, is usually assessed at these early stages by watching students in action as they read and talk about books. At the primary level, you can use anecdotal notes during silent reading time or during guided reading groups to assess three strands: Types of Texts (▥) and Attitude (☺), and Self-Evaluation (〰). You can assess the Reading Comprehension (✋) strand using anecdotal notes during literature circle discussions and by examining students' response journals. Reading Strategies (☑) would be better assessed during individual reading conferences by using Concepts About Print (Clay, 2000a), Running Records (CBA Form 8.2), or a Reading Conference form (CBA Form 9.6). There is simply too much to write on a Post-it note as you listen to individual students read aloud and talk about books.

Anecdotal Notes: Reading Focus Questions (Intermediate)

The Reading Focus Questions (Intermediate) (DC Form 6.10) are particularly effective for assessing Bridging, Fluent, Proficient, Connecting, and Independent readers in third through eighth grades. These questions cover 95–100% of the descriptors in the last five stages of the reading continuum. Teachers at the intermediate level find anecdotal notes appropriate for all five of the continuum strands. Anecdotal notes can provide documentation about the strategies of more fluent readers. In order to discover which strategies they can do independently, you need to watch students "in action." You can use anecdotal notes as you listen to students talk about books during literature circle discussions and by looking at their response journals. Intermediate teachers like Anne Klein and Cindy Flegenheimer also use Reading Conference forms (CBA Form 9.6) for assessing comprehension, as well as reading strategies and fluency.

Anecdotal Notes: Reading Aloud Focus Questions

Sandy Figel has a pool of adults who read with children on a regular basis. Many of these parents, grandparents, and teaching assistants were unsure of what to record when they listened to students read. In response, Sandy developed the Reading Aloud Focus Questions (DC Form 6.11). Sandy asks adults to respond to one or two of these questions by writing their observations on larger 3 x 3-inch Post-it notes (DC Form 6.6). She sometimes gives volunteers a particular focus for their observations. For instance, she might ask, "Today, would you please note if the students are reading with expression?" Sandy often finds the perspective of another adult informative.

Anecdotal Notes: Literature Circles Focus Questions

When you listen to students talking about books during literature circles, you may want to keep the list of Literature Circles Focus Questions (DC Form 6.12) on the top of your clipboard. The focus questions serve as a reminder of what to observe and can be linked to your focus lessons. For instance, at the beginning of the year, Cindy Flegenheimer uses role playing to show both effective and distracting listening behaviors. Students brainstorm a list of ways Cindy will be able to tell that they are listening to each other during literature circle discussions. The next few times the students meet, Cindy uses her clipboard to record examples of effective listening skills. For example, during the debriefing after one discussion, she mentioned that Brandon's group was leaning forward and that their body language showed how focused they were on the discussion. She also noticed that Catherine asked Leah, "Why do you think that will happen?" which showed that she was listening to her group members.

Anecdotal Notes: Behavior Focus Questions (Primary)

The Reading and Writing Focus Questions for anecdotal notes have been useful for many K–8 teachers. Several kindergarten and first-grade teachers commented that at the beginning of the year, their focus is on classroom routines and behaviors. By November or December, they might start taking anecdotal notes on reading and writing behaviors. I therefore included a list of Behavior Focus Questions (DC Form 6.13) for students in kindergarten and first grade. You may want to modify the list to match your report card and curriculum. As described earlier, choose one or two questions and observe a few students each day until you have recorded information about your whole class. After transferring the Post-it notes to your Teacher Notebook, you may want to continue to observe students' social skills or begin focusing on early literacy behaviors.

Anecdotal Notes: Focus Questions for Principals

In one district in Washington State, the assistant superintendent keeps an Administrator's Notebook with a section for each principal. The principals, in turn, keep a Principal's Notebook with a section for each teacher. The principals keep a blank anecdotal grid in each teacher's section, along with the teachers' Organizational Grid (DC Form 5.3) and their professional goals for the year. Principals take anecdotal notes during staff meetings and when they informally visit classrooms. Their observations are directly linked to each teacher's goals and assessment plan. Principals also keep more extensive narrative records of formal classroom observations in the same notebook. In each teacher's section, the principal also places a grid with the names of all the students in that teacher's class for recording interactions with parents or with students. By scanning the class grid, principals can easily see which students they still don't know. Of course, just like students, teachers need assurance that principals are writing down all the great things they observe! If observations are stated positively and recorded objectively, principals will have specific data that can help support teachers' performance and professional growth. I've included Focus Questions for Principals (DC Form 6.14) for observing reading, writing, and assessment in classrooms. Principals may want to create additional questions as they observe other content areas. By keeping a Principal Notebook and taking anecdotal notes, principals can model these effective assessment techniques for their staff.

Checklists

Anecdotal notes are not necessarily the best assessment tool for all of the descriptors on the continuums. For instance, some very concrete skills, such as whether or not a student uses spaces between words, could be better documented by using a checklist. Many teachers have remarked that it would be useful to have checklists of the more specific descriptors on the continuums. In this chapter, I've developed six sample checklists for reading and writing. You may want to select the most appropriate checklist for your grade level, then keep the checklist tucked under your anecdotal note grid and focus questions on your clipboard. There are three checklists for writing and reading (Primary, Primary/Intermediate, and Intermediate/Middle School). All six checklists can be found at the end of this chapter and on the CD-ROM. You may want to keep a blank copy of the checklists you intend to use either in your Continuum Notebook or in your Assessment Tools Notebook.

Of course, not everything on the continuums can be assessed using a checklist. The checklists are intended as a starting point that can help you capture a picture of your whole class. (There is also a copy of the reading and writing continuums on the CD-ROM with shading for each of the continuum descriptors that can be assessed by using the checklists.) I included an abbreviation of the continuum stage for each descriptor in the left column of the checklists. Here is a chart of how the checklists match the continuum stages:

Writing Checklists

Writing Checklist	Continuum Stages	Percentage of Descriptors
Primary DC Form 6.15	Preconventional Emerging Developing Beginning	62%
Primary/Intermediate DC Form 6.16	Expanding Bridging	73%
Intermediate/Middle School DC Form 6.17	Fluent Proficient Connecting Independent	37%

Reading Checklists

Writing Checklist	Continuum Stages	Percentage of Descriptors
Primary DC Form 6.18	Preconventional Emerging Developing	69%
Primary/Intermediate DC Form 6.19	Beginning Expanding	74%
Intermediate/Middle School DC Form 6.20	Bridging Fluent Proficient Connecting	45%

Instead of listing skills by continuum stages, the checklists were organized in a developmental progression of skills, with similar skills listed together. For example, on the Primary Writing Checklist (DC Form 6.15), you can look at a child's writing and check whether the student included just a picture, pictures and print, or actual labels of the objects in the picture. Similarly, on the Intermediate/Middle School Writing Checklist (DC Form 6.17), you can record whether a student includes a plot with a problem and solution or actually creates tension and a climax in the story.

Are Anecdotal Notes or Checklists More Effective?

Linda Johnson said that checklists are particularly useful in kindergarten when students are less independent. The checklists for reading and writing help provide a portrait of her class and help her create groups based on similar needs. Cindy Flegenheimer also feels that checklists provide the "big picture" and help her track overall progress. She then uses anecdotal notes to provide more specific examples and to document changes and growth for individual students.

Lisa Norwick sometimes shares her checklists during parent conferences. When appropriate, she covers up the other students' names and shows parents how their child's skills fit in the normal range of reading and writing skills in her class. She finds that parents often have unrealistic expectations and lose sight of the developmental nature of literacy acquisition. The class checklist can help assuage parents' concerns and shows the normal developmental range within a particular grade level.

Anne Klein uses anecdotal notes first, then her checklists. She takes anecdotal notes in September as she gets to know her students. Anne then completes the checklists in November before filling out the continuums. She finds that the writing checklist is particularly easy to complete as she looks through her students' journals and writing folders. In Figure 6.3, you can see an example of a writing checklist for 15 students in Cindy Flegenheimer's third grade. She can use the information from the checklist to spot gaps for particular students, as well as to group students with similar needs for small group instruction. Cindy can also spot gaps in her instruction and plan focus lessons based on the needs she identifies as she fills out the checklists. Checklists are most effective in the intermediate grades since many of the skills can be observed by listening to students read aloud and discuss books and by looking at their writing samples.

Janine King said that she used checklists when she was new at using continuums and needed guidelines. She now prefers the more open-ended nature of anecdotal notes where she can record breakthroughs or student comments. Janine uses checklists only when she is looking for a specific behavior, such as a specific writing trait (i.e., sentence fluency). Looking at the percentages of continuum descriptors you can assess, you can see that checklists are a less effective tool in middle school. Since most strategies are still performed *with guidance*, it isn't until the Connecting stage that most skills can be checked off as mastered. As mentioned throughout this book, many strategies at the upper end of the continuum are not ones students do or do not demonstrate. Most high level literacy skills gradually become internalized and refined over many years of practice.

Should You Use Anecdotal Notes or Checklists?

A great deal will depend on your particular teaching and learning style, as well as your knowledge of the continuums. In some ways, checklists are like a photograph of your whole class. By stepping back, you get a quick image of your whole class. You can use the information in order to group students based on similar needs. The information can help you make instructional decisions about what students know and what needs to be taught or re-taught. Anecdotal notes, on the other hand, are more like video clips that can capture the voice and personality of individual students. Your notes contain particular examples of children's conversation and can show more detailed growth over time. Anne Klein says that when she looks back at her anecdotal notes, even ones written several years ago, she can vividly remember specific conversations, such as Brittany's tone of voice when she lamented to her group, "This discussion's dead!" Checklists are most helpful for grouping students and planning instruction; anecdotal notes provide specificity and details about each of your students.

WRITING CONTENT AND TRAITS CHECKLIST (INTERMEDIATE)

Skill	LB	AB	RB	BC	MD	LF	CF	NF	SH	BH	CL	SM	SCM	PM	BP
Central Idea	✓	✓	✓	✓	✓	✓	✓	✓	✓	✓	✓	✓	✓	✓	✓
Beginning/Middle/End	✓		✓	✓	✓	✓	✓	✓	✓	✓		✓	✓	✓	✓
Plot w/Problem and Solution	✓		✓	✓	✓	✓	✓	✓	✓	✓		✓	✓	✓	✓
Plot with Climax	✓		✓												
Multiple Characters	✓	✓	✓	✓	✓	✓	✓	✓	✓	✓	✓	✓	✓	✓	✓
Developed Characters															
Setting	✓		✓		✓	✓	✓	✓	✓	✓					
Developed Setting															
Dialogue	✓	✓	✓	✓	✓	✓	✓	✓	✓	✓		✓	✓	✓	✓
Effective Dialogue															
Poetry	✓	✓	✓	✓	✓	✓	✓	✓	✓	✓	✓	✓	✓	✓	✓
Poetry w/Chosen Language															
Varied Sentence Structure	✓		✓					✓							
Leads and Endings															
Details and Description						✓	✓	✓							
Strong Verbs			✓												
Interesting Language	✓														
Literary Devices															
Organized Nonfiction															
Reasons and Examples															
References															
Integrates Information															

Figure 6.3 Sample Checklist

In the last six chapters, I've presented ideas about connecting continuums to standards, children's literature, guided reading, and assessment. However, you shouldn't be doing all the work. In the next chapter, I'll suggest ways to also involve students in the assessment and evaluation process.

Staff Development

If your staff wants to learn more about anecdotal notes, you may want to use Brenda Miller Power's (1996) book, *Taking Note: Improving Your Observational Notetaking*, as a book study. She includes activities for teachers to try, including a creative budget for staff development (Chapter 8). As a staff, decide which content area to assess (either reading or writing). Meet a month later and share the ideas you have tried. What method worked for you? What types of comments or behaviors did you record? What worked well? Did your note-taking skills improve over time? What are your next steps? Anecdotal notes are powerful assessment tools, but learning how to manage this assessment strategy efficiently and how to make it a part of your everyday teaching takes time.

After you've become comfortable taking anecdotal notes, try using the primary or intermediate Writing Focus Questions for two weeks. Choose one of the questions and try to collect information about each of your students over the two-week period. For the next two weeks, use the Reading or Writing Checklist appropriate to your grade level. Were the anecdotal notes or checklists easier? Which was more informative? What types of things did you record using each method? How might you incorporate these assessment techniques into your classroom? Once you have tried both the focus questions and checklists, meet in grade-level groups and highlight the questions and descriptors that you found to be most informative. Use the CD-ROM to revise the lists to match your curriculum and grade-level expectations. Both the anecdotal focus questions and checklists can help you connect assessment with the reading and writing continuums.

Anecdotal Records for:

Form 6.1 Anecdotal Note Grid (Photocopy at 125%)

Anecdotal Records for:

Form 6.2 Anecdotal Note Grid (Photocopy at 133%)

Anecdotal Records for:

Reading

Writing

Form 6.3 Anecdotal Note Grid (Photocopy at 125%)

Anecdotal Records for:

Math		Science	Social Studies

Form 6.4 Anecdotal Note Grid (Photocopy at 125%)

Anecdotal Records for:

Reading				
Writing				
Math				
Social/Behavior				

Form 6.5 Anecdotal Note Grid (Photocopy at 125%)

Anecdotal Records for:

Form 6.6 Anecdotal Note Grid (Photocopy at 134%)

Anecdotal Notes: Writing Focus Questions (Primary)

✍ Writing Development and Conventions

1. Does the student rely on pictures to convey meaning? Pictures plus print?
2. Does the student label pictures and add words to the pictures?
3. Does the student copy names? Write names and familiar words?
4. Does the student use only upper case letters? Interchange upper and lower case?
5. Does the student use beginning/ending sounds to make words? Middle sounds?
6. Does the student use invented/phonetic spelling? Spell simple words correctly? Spell some high frequency words correctly?
7. Does the student write left to write? Use spacing between words?
8. Does the student experiment with capitals and punctuation? Use them correctly?
9. Does the student write legibly? Can others read the writing?

🗀 Content, Traits, and 2 Types of Texts

10. Does the student write 1–2 sentences about a topic? Several sentences?
11. Does the student write about observations and experiences?
12. Can the student write short nonfiction (simple facts about a topic)?
13. Does the student write pieces with a logical sequence?

✂ Writing Process

14. Is the student able to choose a topic?
15. Can the student tell about his/her writing? Pretend to read his/her writing? Match voice to print as reads own writing?
16. Does the student read his/her own writing and notice mistakes?
17. Does the student share his/her own writing? Offer feedback to others?
18. Does the student revise by adding details with guidance?

☺ Attitude and Self-Evaluation

19. Does the student engage promptly in and sustain writing activities?
20. Does the student see self as a writer? Show a positive attitude toward writing?
21. Does the student take risks with writing? Does student use writing for real purposes (cards, notes, etc.)?

Anecdotal Notes: Writing Focus Questions (Intermediate)

🗁 Content, Traits, and 📄 Types of Text

1. Does the student write fiction with a central idea? Beginning, middle, and end?
2. Does the student write plots that include problems and solutions? Climax?
3. Does the student create multiple characters? More developed characters? Setting? Detailed setting?
4. Does the student use dialogue? Effective dialogue for character development?
5. Does the student write poetry? Poetry with carefully chosen language?
6. Does the student use a variety of sentence structures? Leads? Endings?
7. Does the student use details/description? Strong verbs? Interesting language? Literary devices?
8. Does the student write organized nonfiction? Supporting reasons/examples? Simple bibliography? Correct bibliographic format? Integrate information from several sources?

✍ Conventions

9. Does the student spell most high frequency words correctly? Most words?
10. Does the student use simple punctuation correctly? Complex punctuation?
11. Does the student use complete sentences? Paragraphs? Paragraphs with support/examples? Transitional sentences to connect paragraphs?

✂ Writing Process

12. *Does the student use prewriting strategies? Which ones?*
13. *Does the student seek feedback on own writing? Incorporate suggestions?*
14. *Does the student listen to the writing of others and give appropriate feedback?*
15. *Does the student revise for clarity? For specific writing traits (organization, word choice, sentence fluency, voice and conventions)?*
16. *Does the student edit his/her writing for (punctuation, spelling, grammar?*
17. *Does the student use tools (dictionary, thesaurus) to help with writing? To revise and edit (dictionaries, checklists, spell checkers)?*
18. Is the final published product neat, legible, and free of most errors?

☺ Attitude and Self-Evaluation

19. Does the student engage promptly in and sustain writing activities?
20. *Can the student identify writing strategies? Criteria in different genres? Set goals? Create plan to achieve goals?*

Anecdotal Notes: Reading Focus Questions (Primary)

📖 Type of Texts and Oral Reading

1. *Does the student memorize books? Read pattern books? Own writing? Simple early-reader books? Harder early-reader books? Easy chapter books?*
2. *Does the student independently choose books? At appropriate reading level?*
3. *Does the student read aloud with fluency?*

☺ Reading Attitude and ✍ Self-Evaluation

4. *Does the student show a positive attitude toward reading? Share favorite books?*
5. *Does the student see him/herself as a reader?*
6. *Does the student read for pleasure? Information?*
7. *Does the student read silently? For 5–10 minutes? 10–15 minutes? 15–30?*
8. *Can the student explain why he/she likes or dislikes a book?*
9. *Does the student reflect on his/her reading and set goals with guidance?*

☑ Reading Strategies

10. Does the student pretend to read books? Memorize books?
11. Does the student use illustrations to tell a story? Rely on pictures and print? Use voice-print matching?
12. Does the student recognize some letter names/sounds? Most letters/sounds?
13. Does the student recognize some words in context? Simple words? Sight words?
14. Does the student use phonetic cues? Sentence structure cues? Meaning cues? Word structure cues (prefix, contraction)?
15. Does the student self-correct?

✤ Comprehension and Response

16. *Does the student focus during read alouds? Participate? Comment on illustrations?*
17. *Does the student rhyme and play with words?*
18. *Does the student listen to others' ideas during literature discussions?*
19. *Does the student make predictions?*
20. *Can the student summarize the main ideas of the text? Retell story events?*
21. *Does the student make personal connections to events/characters?*
22. *Can students discuss characters, setting, plot? Compare and contrast characters, setting, plot?*

Anecdotal Notes: Reading Focus Questions (Intermediate)

📖 Type of Text and Oral Reading

1.   *Does the student read medium chapter books? Challenging children's literature? Complex children's literature? Young adult literature? Adult novels? Informational texts?*

2.   *Does the student independently choose books at an appropriate reading level?*

3.   *Does the student read a variety of genres with guidance? Independently?*

4.   *Can the student read with fluency? Expression? Confidence?*

☺ Reading Attitude and ✍ Self-Evaluation

5.   *Does the student show a positive attitude toward reading?*

6.   *Does the student read silently for 30–40 minutes? Longer?*

7.   *Does the student set goals and make plans to improve reading?*

☑ Reading Strategies

8.   *Does the student use text organizers and resources to locate information? Integrate information?*

9.   *Does the student use resources to increase vocabulary? Use increasingly complex vocabulary in different subjects? In oral and written response to literature?*

10.   *Does the student gather and use information from charts, tables, and maps?*

11.   *Does the student develop strategies/criteria for selecting reading material?*

✆ Comprehension and Response

12.   *Does the student monitor his/her own comprehension? Adjust as needed?*

13.   *Can the student discuss plot and characters? Point of view? Theme? Author's style and purpose?*

14.   *Does the student support ideas with reasons and examples from the text?*

15.   *Does the student "read between the lines? Probe for deeper meaning?*

16.   *Does the student make connections to other books? Authors? Perspectives?*

17.   *Does the student participate during discussions? Contribute thoughtful responses? In-depth responses?*

   Does the student evaluate/analyze literature critically?

Anecdotal Notes: Reading Aloud Focus Questions

📖 Type of Text and Oral Reading

1. Is the student choosing books at an appropriate reading level? (not too hard and not too easy?)
2. Can the student identify whether the book is fiction or nonfiction?
3. Does the student read fluently?
4. Does the student read with expression? Confidence?
5. Does the student pay attention to punctuation marks when reading aloud?

☺ Reading Attitude and ∿ Self-Evaluation

6. Does the student seem to enjoy reading?

☑ Reading Strategies

7. When the student is unsure about a word, does he or she use phonics skills ("sounding out words")? (You can ask, "Does that look right?")
8. Does the student use grammar and the way English sounds to figure out unknown words? (You can ask, "Does that sound right?")
9. Does the student use meaning cues to figure out unknown words? (You can ask, "What word would make sense here?")
10. Does the student recognize most high frequency or common words by sight?
11. Does the student self-correct?

♦ Comprehension and Response

12. Does the student make meaningful predictions about what may happen next?
13. Can the student retell the main ideas of the story?
14. Can the student retell the beginning, middle, and end of the story?
15. Can the student identify the main characters?
16. If the book is nonfiction, can the student retell some of the main ideas or details?
17. Does the student respond and make personal connections to the book?

Anecdotal Notes: Literature Circles Focus Questions

1. Is the student prepared for the literature discussion?
2. Does the student use the text to share passages? To support ideas and opinions? How effectively?
3. Does the student listen actively to others?
4. Does the student ask questions? What kinds?
5. Do the questions get a thoughtful response? Which are most effective?
6. Does the student contribute thoughtful ideas?
7. Does the student make predictions? How effectively?
8. Does the student build on other people's comments?
9. Does the student keep the group on task?
10. Does the student discuss unknown or interesting words?
11. Does the student make personal connections to his/her life? At what levels?
12. Does the student make connections to other books, authors, and experiences?
13. Does the student discuss the author's craft and word choice?
14. Does the student discuss literary elements (plot, setting, character)?
15. Can the student reflect on literature circle participation and set goals?

Anecdotal Notes: Behavior Focus Questions (Primary)

1.   Does the student willingly follow simple directions?
2.   Does the student demonstrate a positive self-concept?
3.   Is the student curious and motivated to learn?
4.   Does the student interact appropriately with others? Parallel play? One-on-one? Small group? Whole class?
5.   Does the student respect other people's personal space?
6.   Does the student have one or more good friends?
7.   Does the student resolve conflicts appropriately?
8.   Does the student take care of and put away materials?
9.   Is the student on task during work time?
10. Does the student strive for quality and his/her personal best?
11. Does the student complete work? Use his/her time well?
12. Does the student listen during story time? Group time?
13. Does the student speak effectively in front of the group?
14. Does the student contribute appropriately during discussions?
15. Does the student give compliments to others?
16. Does the student verbally recognize and express feelings towards peers with respect and understanding?

Anecdotal Notes: Focus Questions for Principals

Assessment

1. What system does the teacher have for organizing assessment information?
2. Which familiar assessment tools does the teacher use? New tools?
3. How does the teacher use the assessment data to inform or modify instruction?
4. How does the teacher record interactions with students (anecdotal notes)?
5. How does the teacher communicate with parents?

Writing and Spelling

6. What is the teacher's structure for teaching writing?
7. How often do students write each day?
8. How often do teachers choose the topic/focus/genre? How often do students have a choice?
9. What focus lessons on writing have you observed? Does the teacher model writing strategies?
10. What evidence do you see that students are learning to revise and edit?
11. How is spelling taught?
12. What evidence do you see in the classroom of intentional writing instruction?
13. What evidence do you see of different types/genres of writing in the classroom?
14. How does the teacher assess spelling and writing?
15. What is the teacher's area of strength in teaching writing?

Reading

16. What is the teacher's structure for teaching reading?
17. What book is the teacher reading aloud?
18. How long do students read to themselves or a partner each day (SSR/DEAR)?
19. What whole group or small group focus lessons on reading have you observed? Does the teacher model reading strategies?
20. How does the teacher structure intentional reading instruction with small groups?
21. How does the teacher structure time for students to discuss literature?
22. How does the teacher structure individual reading conferences?
23. What evidence do you see of different types/genres of reading in the classroom?
24. How does the teacher assess reading?
    What is the teacher's area of strength in teaching reading?

PRIMARY WRITING CHECKLIST

Stage/ Skill														
Student														
Pre	Pictures													
Em	Pictures + print or labels													
Em	Copies names, signs, words													
Dev	Writes names and words													
Dev	Writes 1–2 sentence													
Beg	Writes several sentences													
Beg	Observations/experiences													
Beg	Short nonfiction about topics													
Beg	Chooses topic													
Em	Upper case													
Dev	Upper and lower case													
Em	Beginning sounds													
Em	Beginning/ending sounds													
Dev	Middle sounds/vowels													
Beg	Invented/phonetic spelling													
Beg	Spacing between words													
Dev	Experiments w/capitals													
Dev	Experiments w/punctuation													
Beg	Forms letters legibly													
Beg	Spells simple words correctly													
Beg	Spells sight words correctly													
Em	Pretends to read writing													
Dev	Reads own writing													
Beg	Shares at Author's Chair													

PRIMARY/INTERMEDIATE WRITING CHECKLIST

Student

Stage / Skill

Stage	Skill
Exp	Uses complete sentences
Exp	Fiction with guidance
Exp	Poetry with guidance
Bri	Poetry w/chosen language
Exp	Short nonfiction w/guidance
Bri	Feelings and opinions
Exp	Central idea
Bri	Uses paragraphs
Exp	Spells sight words correctly
Bri	Beginning/middle/end
Bri	Dialogue with guidance
Bri	Adds description/details
Bri	Strong verbs with guidance
Bri	Interesting lang. w/guidance
Exp	Uses prewriting with guidance
Bri	Revises with guidance
Bri	Edits for spelling/punctuation
Exp	Shares at Author's Chair
Exp	Offers feedback to others
Bri	Seeks and uses feedback
E/B	Publishes with guidance
Exp	Writes legibly
E/B	Sets goals w/guidance

INTERMEDIATE/MIDDLE SCHOOL WRITING CHECKLIST

Student

Stage / Skill														
Con	Uses prewriting strategies													
Flu	Organized nonfiction													
Con	Writes variety of genres													
Flu	Poetry w/chosen language													
Pro	Plot w/problem and solution													
Con	Plot with climax													
Pro	Multiple characters													
Con	Developed characters													
Pro	Setting													
Con	Detailed setting													
Con	Dialogue													
Ind	Effective dialogue													
Con	Details and description													
Con	Uses similes and imagery													
Ind	Literary devices													
Pro	Varied sentence structure													
Pro	Varied leads and endings													
Con	Bibliography w/correct format													
Con	Makes charts, graphs, tables													
Con	Revises for writing traits													
Con	Integrates information													
Ind	Incorporates personal voice													
Ind	Sets goals													

INTERMEDIATE/MIDDLE SCHOOL WRITING CHECKLIST (CONTINUED)

Student

Stage / Skill

Pro	Uses tools to edit															
Con	Uses complex punctuation															
Ind	Uses correct grammar															
Con	Cohesive paragraphs															
Con	Reasons and examples															
Pro	Transitional sentence															
Pro	Variety of sentence structure															
	Ideas and content															
	Word choice															
	Sentence fluency															
	Organization															
	Voice															
	Conventions															
	Prewrites															
	Draft															
	Seeks feedback															
	Offers feedback															
	Revise															
	Edit															
	Publish															

PRIMARY READING CHECKLIST

Stage / Skill												
	Student											
Pre	Has favorite books											
Pre	Reads own name											
Em	Rhymes and plays with words											
Em	Shows eagerness to read											
Em	Pretends to read											
Em	Memorizes books and poems											
Em	Uses illustrations to tell story											
Dev	Sees self as reader											
Dev	Reads simple words											
Dev	Reads own writing											
Dev	Reads simple pattern books											
Dev	Reads 5–10 minutes											
Pre	Holds book, turns pages right											
Pre	Shows beginning/end book											
Pre	Knows some letter names											
Em	Knows some letter sounds											
Dev	Knows letter sounds/names											
Dev	Uses finger-print-voice match											
Pre	Listens and responds to lit.											
Pre	Comments on illustrations											
Em	Connects books to own life											
Dev	Makes meaningful predictions											
Dev	Retells main idea/event											
Dev	Participates in discussions											

PRIMARY/INTERMEDIATE READING CHECKLIST

Student

Stage / Skill													
Beg	Reads simple early-readers												
Beg	Reads harder early-readers												
Exp	Reads easy chapter books												
Beg	Chooses books												
Beg	Shares info. from reading												
Beg	Uses punctuation w/reading												
Exp	Begins to read with fluency												
Beg	Uses meaning cues (context)												
Beg	Uses grammar cues												
Beg	Uses phonics cues												
Exp	Uses word structure cues												
Beg	Reads many sight words												
Beg	Identifies basic genres												
Exp	Follows written directions												
Beg	Reads 10–15 minutes												
Exp	Reads 15–30 minutes												
Exp	Self-corrects												
Beg	Retells beginning/middle/end												
Beg	Discusses charters/evens												
Exp	Summarizes, retells events												
Exp	Makes personal connections												
Exp	Identifies text organizers												
Exp	Compares characters/events												

INTERMEDIATE/MIDDLE SCHOOL READING CHECKLIST

Student

Stage / Skill																		
Bri	Reads med. chapter books																	
Flu	Reads challenging ch. books																	
P/C	Reads complex novels																	
C/I	Reads young adult lit.																	
Ind	Reads adult literature																	
Pro	Reads informational texts																	
Bri	Chooses books at right level																	
Con	Reads a variety of genres																	
Bri	Reads with expression																	
Flu	Reads w/confidence/fluency																	
Flu	Reads 30–40 minutes																	
Bri	Follows written directions																	
Pro	Uses resources for info.																	
Flu	Uses text organizers																	
Con	Uses info from charts/graphs.																	
Con	Integrates information																	
Bri	Connects to authors/books																	
Con	In-depth oral response																	
Con	In-depth written response																	
Pro	Identifies literary devices																	
Pro	Discusses literary elements																	
Pro	Uses reasons/examples																	
Pro	"Reads between the lines"																	
Con	Seeks recommendations																	
Con	Sets challenges/goals																	

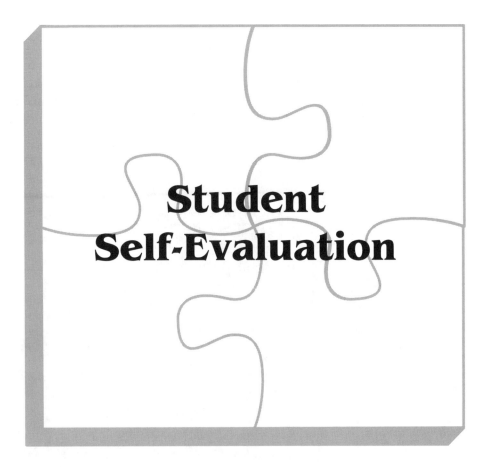

Student Self-Evaluation

The more you learn, the better you think.

—*Nicholas, First-Grade Student*

Our goal as educators is to create self-directed, lifelong learners. The more you can involve students in assessment and evaluation, the more ownership your students will have in their learning. The more ownership they have, the more effort students put forth, which results in higher quality work. How can you connect your instruction with the continuums in a way that will make sense for students? How can you involve students in assessing their own reading and writing?

Connecting to Instruction

Defining the Targets

The continuums would certainly be overwhelming if you simply handed out copies the week before parent conferences and asked students to fill them out! It makes more sense to familiarize students with the descriptors on a regular basis as you teach. In fact, each descriptor on the continuums should become at least one, if not a series of focus lessons. How can you begin?

In the fall, Anne Klein in Edmonds, Washington started the year by reading several books aloud, then asking her students, "What makes good writing?" and "What do good readers do?" She transferred the list onto two charts, labeled "What Makes a Good Reader?" and "What Makes Good Writing?" (Figure 7.1). Throughout the year, Anne and her students continually revise and add to the charts. Over time, her students' comments become more specific.

In the fall, two of the qualities her students mentioned were that good writers use "lots of details" and "detailed word choice." Anne looked at the Writing Content and Traits strand and found that at the Expanding and Bridging stages students should be able to recognize and use interesting language with adult support.

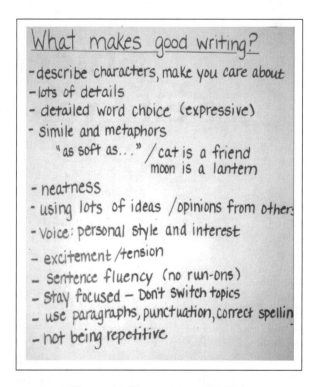

Figure 7.1 Chart of Good Writing

Her next step was to match the continuum description with the writing abilities of her particular group of fifth graders. She looked at what students could already do on their own and thought about each child's next steps. She provided guidance by using whole-class instruction and small-group focus lessons, as well as teaching tips during individual writing conferences.

Building Focus Lessons

Let's follow part of the series of focus lessons Anne developed about word choice. She began with a very tangible lesson on alternatives to the word, "said." She made a transparency of page 98 from *The Boxcar Children* (Gertrude Chandler Warner, 1977, 1942) in which the author used the word "said" several times. She also made a transparency of page 24 from *James and the Giant Peach* (Roald Dahl, 1961). Anne read from the two transparencies, then the class discussed how Roald Dahl's use of "screeched" and "ordered" and "snapped" provided clues about personalities of the main characters.

Anne then asked students to open their independent reading books and look for the words the writers used instead of "said." She recorded the words on the overhead and later transferred the list onto chart paper. The chart was posted in the room and students continued to add to the list throughout the year by recording new "said words" on Post-it notes which they later transferred to the chart. By the end of the year, the chart contained over 100 alternatives.

Anne has developed many effective focus lessons over time. Many of her ideas came from *After the End* (Lane, 1993) and *What a Writer Needs* (Fletcher, 1993). She has also found *Craft Lessons* (Fletcher and Portalupi, 1998) and *Nonfiction Craft Lessons* (2001) to be very helpful. Anne is also writing a book on focus lessons with Megan Sloan and Lisa Norwick that will be published next year with Scholastic.

The continuums provides the "bare bones" which your focus lessons can flesh out. Cindy Flegenheimer at Brighton School also creates focus lessons based on students' needs and the continuum descriptors. For instance, she used the focus lesson on "heavy sentences" from *Craft Lessons* (Fletcher and Portalupi, 1998, p. 52). Cindy brought in her daughter's clarinet case and opened it slowly, then talked about how a reader "unpacks" a heavy sentence throughout a chapter or book. The phrase quickly took hold in the classroom. For instance, when Bruce did his book talk on *The Last Book in the Universe* (Rodman Philbrick, 2000), he shared the first three sentences in the book: "If you're reading this, it must be a thousand years from now. Because nobody around here reads anymore. Why bother, when you can just probe it?" (p. 7). He explained, "The heavy sentences make you want to read more. You understand them better, the more you read of the book."

A week later, Catherine began her Halloween story with "In Enelville, everyone knows about Blackness Cave." She chose this story for her portfolio, and her reflection shows that she had internalized the idea of effective leads and "heavy sentences" (Figure 7.2). The same phrase cropped up during discussions of Cindy's read aloud, *Dovey Coe* (Frances O'Roark Dowell, 2000), and during their literature circle discussions about their theme of courage. These examples show how artfully Cindy Flegenheimer and Anne Klein connect instruction and assessment, as well as reading and writing.

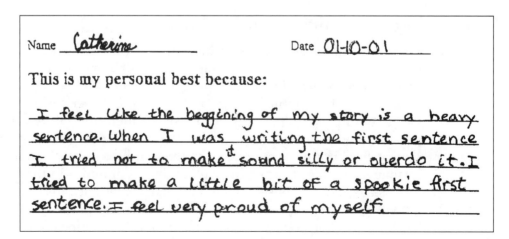

Figure 7.2 Portfolio Reflection

Providing Additional Evidence and Support

For several weeks, Anne Klien chose a student to record alternatives to "said" from the class read aloud on a piece of paper. Anne checked for correct spelling, then the student recorded the new words on the "Said Chart." Anne also shared part of a personal narrative she wrote about her adventures with her family in a cave. She asked the class to help her with her "said" words and read the revision aloud.

Anne also looked for strong examples in her students' writing. For example, she asked Frances for permission, then made a transparency of a page from her story:

> "Hey, kids. What should we do today?" Dad bellowed down to us.
>
> "Shopping, please!" my sister Megan begged.
>
> "You've said that every day since we got here," I reminded her.
>
> "I know what we can do today," said mom. "We can do whitewater rafting."
>
> "Yeah!" I yelled and ran upstairs.
>
> "I'd rather go shopping," Megan mumbled with a big sigh.

You may want to start your Anchor Papers Notebook with examples from your class. You can use these examples year after year as your collection grows and you exchange samples with colleagues.

As Anne conferred with her students about their writing, she pointed out instances when they incorporated interesting words into their dialogue. She also commented on this trait when students shared their stories at Author's Chair. Sometimes Anne focused the audience by asking students to listen specifically for the author's use of dialogue during Author's Chair, silent reading time, or literature circles. Once Anne presented the idea of interesting "said" words, she could incorporate that skill into the rubrics the class developed for particular forms of writing, such as personal narratives. As she conferred with her students, she also used her anecdotal notes to record the specific words students used in their writing.

Connecting to Student Self-Evaluation

Many of the descriptors on the student-evaluation checklists and student self-evaluation versions of the continuums will not be terms students know. It's our job as teachers to explain the terminology and to provide examples. You need to explain terms like "author's craft" and "reading between the lines." You should provide examples of "in-depth responses to literature" if you expect students to understand your high expectations. Notice that the terminology on the self-evaluation checklists and continuums in the last three stages is almost the same as the language on the "teacher version" of the continuums. In the first five stages, the language has been considerably simplified. For instance, instead of using the phrase, "with guidance," the student version includes the phrase "with help." By middle school, we should expect students to be able to describe their skills as readers and writers with more sophistication. The more we explain the terminology and show examples in our own reading and writing, as well as in student work, the more students will internalize this language. The continuum thus becomes an instructional, as well as an assessment, tool.

For instance, once students become aware of vivid verbs, they can use that quality of effective writing in their own self-evaluation. When Brittany selected a writing piece for her portfolio, she wrote, "I chose it because it's good writing." When Anne Klein asked her to be more specific and referred to the chart of Quality Writing, Brittany was able to add, "because it was organized and I used strong verbs, like 'zipped' and 'whispered.'" As students become aware of what specifically makes writing powerful, they begin to experiment with new strategies and also start to internalize the language in their self-reflections. As Anne's students learn to articulate the characteristics of effective writing, they can assess their own strengths and set specific goals.

Patti Kamber, a middle school teacher on Bainbridge Island, Washington, describes the cycle of developing criteria and using the standards of quality for self-evaluation:

> We consistently analyze learning activities in our classroom according to criteria we decide upon together. For example, when a writing assignment is given, we identify three or four criteria that we believe would make this a quality piece of writing. We put the criteria into writing. This is really where true learning about learning occurs. Putting the criteria in the open allows it to be analyzed by the learner and revised accordingly, while still meeting the teacher's responsibility. It removes the fuzziness from the learning process. Almost all the students can meet or exceed the criteria.
>
> After completing the assignment, students review their work using the selected criteria. They write a brief self-evaluation before conferring with me or a peer. Articulating the criteria for evaluating their work has been effective for all the children, particularly those of us who are not naturally intuitive.
>
> In order to evaluate students, we need to have clear criteria in mind, we must know each child in order to ascertain growth, and we must have some level of expectation in mind appropriate to the age of our students. We need to base our evaluation on clearly documented observations and student samples. Yet the amount of work students produce in a process-based classroom can be overwhelming. We can only assess and evaluate a small sample of what we *collect*. Evaluation requires that we *select* representative samples of a variety of types of products and processes to be evaluated. We also need to help children *reflect* on their learning. Ideally, this becomes a continuous process.

Student Surveys

How do your students view themselves as readers and writers? In addition to your anecdotal notes described in the last chapter, you can also use student surveys. The quality of students' answers will be much greater if you take the time to explain the questions and your purpose for giving the survey. You might begin by thinking aloud as you fill out a survey on the overhead. You may want to have adult volunteers or older students transcribe the answers for younger students. Lisa Norwick copies the fall survey on yellow paper and keeps the completed surveys in each child's section of her Teacher Notebook. At the end of the year, she copies the same survey on green paper. As she hands out the spring survey, Lisa reminds her class of their lists of the qualities of good readers and writers. She's always amazed at the growth even her primary students show over time.

Five student surveys are included at the end of this chapter (DCA Form 7.1–7.5). The surveys are also on the CD-ROM so that you can modify the forms to meet the needs of your particular group of students. You may want to keep copies of the surveys you plan to use in your Assessment Tools Notebook.

"Fix-it" Strategy

As explained in Chapter 5, the "Fix-it" strategy can also be an informative self-evaluation tool. Ask students to choose a piece of writing in September or October that shows who they are as writers. Be sure the sample includes the child's name and the date. If you keep the fall writing sample in clear acetate slip-sheets in each child's section of your Teacher Notebook, it will be easy to find in the spring. When you hand the samples back in May or June, ask students to "show you what you have learned" by writing another draft of the same story. This quick assessment strategy shows how many of your discussions about quality writing have taken root. For instance, in Sven's fall sample, he wrote, "It took us two hours to get there." His spring sample shows a better use of language when he wrote, "It took two hours to get to Birch Bay Village. The two hours went by like snapping your hands together." This technique, called the "Fix-it" strategy, is a quick, yet powerful way to document growth. You can use the same technique with math problem solving, reading journal responses, or work in content areas. By looking at actual samples of their work over time, it becomes much easier for students to evaluate their own growth.

Student Version of the Continuums and Charts

How can students use the continuums for self-evaluation? Although there are several different continuums published around the world, I couldn't find a single student version or information about how students could use continuums. With the help of many students and teachers, I created a version of the reading and writing continuums in first person for student self-evaluation. The process of trying to put each descriptor in "student language" led to several changes on the original "adult version." It didn't make sense to have strategies on the continuums that we couldn't explain to students! The resulting student version has now been used by many intermediate and middle school students around the world. The student versions of the continuums are included at the end of this book and on the CD-ROM. The continuums are written in first person and do not include ages, so that students focus on the descriptors. We want to emphasize growth, rather than competition.

As teachers present focus lessons to their students, they refer to the continuum charts they have posted in their rooms. The charts, written in first person "kid language" are included at the end of this chapter and on the CD-ROM. Some teachers laminate the charts, then use an overhead pen to check the descriptors they have introduced.

Ingrid Stipes, an intermediate-grade teacher on Mercer Island, Washington, uses the student version of the continuums with her students. Ingrid builds her focus lessons around the descriptors on the continuums. Each grading period, her students mark the Student Versions of the reading and writing continuums. They place an "F" for fall or "S" for spring by each skill or strategy they have mastered. In Figure 7.3, you can see Bryan, a fifth grader, filling out his continuum as he looks through his work for evidence. Anne also fills out the continuums for each student. During individual conferences, they compare the two versions, discuss any discrepancies, and set goals for the next grading period.

Figure 7.3 Student Using Continuum

Student Self-Evaluation Checklists

Linda Martin, a principal in Monroe, Washington, created individual checklists for each stage of the Reading and Writing continuums. With her permission, I adapted Linda's format to create the self-evaluation checklists included in this chapter and on the CD-ROM. The descriptors are listed by strands in the same order as on the reading and writing continuums. Some skills are listed in a series and students may want to just underline or circle the skills they can demonstrate. For example, a Proficient writer may note that she uses commas and quotation marks correctly, but not mark that she uses colons and semicolons correctly yet. You can also use rubrics to flesh out the expectations for particular descriptors for specific forms of writing.

Rather than handing students the whole 11 x 17-inch continuum, you can simply give each student the one checklist where most of their descriptors fall. For instance, Lisa Norwick gave Mara only the Expanding self-evaluation checklist for writing. The descriptors on the checklists provide clear benchmarks to indicate reading and writing growth. Students mark whether they use a particular skill or strategy "Not Yet," "Sometimes," or "Always."

Filling out one page for reading and one for writing self evaluation doesn't seem too overwhelming for most students in grades 2–8. You may want to use the CD-ROM and add graphics or symbols to the checklists for primary students. In any case, if you expect young students to use the language from the checklists, you'll have to provide quite a bit of guidance at first. Before asking students to complete the form, Lisa puts a copy of one of the checklists on the overhead and thinks aloud about her own skills as a writer as she models her thought process. Lisa had most of her class fill out the one-page student self-evaluation checklists while she walked around answering questions. There were five students, however, who found this task fairly challenging, so she met with each of them individually during Writer's Workshop to help them complete their checklists. Of course, it gets easier for students to use the self-evaluation forms with more experience. At Brighton School, some students have filled out these checklists for several years, so the self-evaluation process requires less time and adult support.

Student Portfolios and Goal Setting

The continuums are a powerful tool for bringing students into the assessment process. Cynthia Ruptic, a teacher at Osaka International School in Japan, writes, "The continuums supply the words that name learning so that students can look back and say, 'Here I am! Look what I can do!' They can celebrate what they have accomplished and look forward to what is coming next." She adds that students derive real pleasure in "ticking off" the skills that they do well. Using the continuums as guides, they can then write goals based on their next steps in the journey of literacy. Cynthia adds, "There is great power in choosing one's own goals and then noting that accomplishment before moving on to the next goal."

In *Creating Writers: Linking Writing Assessment and Instruction*, Vicki Spandel and Richard Stiggins (1997) state that, "self-assessment depends upon criteria: language that defines quality performance" (p. 5). Lisa Norwick used the continuum descriptors she had introduced as the criteria for quality work and portfolio selection. First with her own writing, then using student examples, she demonstrated how writers select pieces for their portfolios. Next, she showed how to write a portfolio reflection about her choice. For instance, she shared one of her own vignettes and wrote a reflection on the overhead, "I chose this piece because I used lots of details." Lisa intentionally links portfolio reflections to the continuum descriptors and to the class-generated charts of the qualities of good reading and writing.

Lisa also wanted to involve her students in the evaluation process. It would be very difficult for Mara, at age 7, to explain how she had grown as a writer during the year. By using specific writing examples and the continuum, however, this second grader could clearly see how she had improved. In her self-evaluation, Mara wrote, "Now I can organize my ideas in my head. I can describe things better and I use interesting words."

Many teachers use blank paper and an open-ended prompt, such as "How have you grown as a writer?" for student self-evaluations. If you have used portfolios and have provided a great deal of modeling and practice in self-evaluation, this can be a very powerful way to involve students in the assessment process. However, many students may look at you with a blank stare and blank piece of paper. Students may not know what to write unless you provide the language of reflection. If you want students to learn to evaluate their own work, you need to talk about the specific characteristics of quality work and provide many examples. Once children understand a particular trait or quality, they can use the criteria as they write portfolio reflections. Students' reflections move beyond, "I picked it because it's good," to more specific reflections that demonstrate their growing understanding of quality writing and reading.

Carol Wilcox, a staff developer in Denver, commented, "I got much better response from students when I gave them a writing piece from September and a sample from December and asked them to talk about how the two pieces were different." Having actual samples gives the conference a totally different quality than if you ask students, "How have you grown as a writer?" Students are able to point to specific places in their writing to show how they have changed and their comments tend to be much more precise. The continuum descriptors provide the specificity students need in order to describe both their strengths, as well as their next steps, as readers and writers.

Before students complete the continuums or checklists, it's important to tell them that they may only mark an item as mastered if they are able to provide evidence. If students know they have to provide examples, they're likely to mark the continuums more thoughtfully and honestly. When teachers find a discrepancy between their assessment of a child and what the child marked on the continuums, it's time for an individual conference. Sometimes students don't understand the descriptors clearly. At other times, they may be able to convince you of their skills by showing you three or four examples where they have demonstrated a particular strategy.

For instance, Anne Klein did not mark that Brittany read a variety of genres. During the conference, Brittany showed the increasing range of her reading on her most recent reading log. On the other hand, Anne had noted that Brittany used a variety of spelling strategies, but Brittany had not marked that particular descriptor. As they looked through Brittany's writing folder, they realized that when Brittany doesn't know how to spell a word, she uses a dictionary, asks a peer, uses the "guess and go" strategy, or uses the list of words in the room. These collaborative conferences provide insights and learning opportunities for both teachers and students.

The student self-evaluation checklists provide an easy segue into goal setting. In fact, each item on the checklist marked as "Not Yet" or "Sometimes" can become the student's next goals. For instance, Sarah's mother wrote, "I think Sarah did an accurate job in her self-assessment. This is a very useful tool for her and other students. They can learn to accurately self-assess and see areas in which they can improve." In many schools, continuums and goals are an integral part of the report card and student-led conferences. If you have talked about the continuum descriptors throughout the year and have shared quality work, your students will have the language they need for self evaluation and goal setting, and they can share that knowledge with their families (Figure 7.4).

Figure 7.4 Student-Led Conference

Ingrid Stipes, an intermediate teacher on Mercer Island, Washington, writes, "The bridge between my collection of notes, assessments, and continuums and my students is their portfolios. I no longer hold onto work samples. They reside in a hanging file where students may periodically select pieces for their portfolio. To help students keep focused on the continuum of reading and writing skills, I use the student self-evaluation checklists." For the past several years, Ingrid has used these checklists to clarify the skills she teaches and expects her students to learn in fourth grade. The students fill out the checklists during the conference with their parents and Ingrid present. Together, they discuss the student's areas of strength and "show off" samples of work included in the portfolio that provide support. The student creates one or two goals, which are recorded at the bottom of the checklist. Ingrid and her students review the goals and checklists alongside new portfolio entries throughout the year. Figure 7.5 shows Joanna's reading self-evaluation on an earlier version of the form. Her goal was listed at the bottom of the form. Notice Joanna's initialed "X" in January where she indicates progress toward her goal of using the dictionary to improve her vocabulary. In writing, Joanna noted, "My goal is to write neater, learn more types of genres, and to work on my punctuation." The checklists provide students with the language for self-evaluation.

Report cards are sent home in January and June at Brighton School. In the middle school, students fill out their continuums themselves, as described in Chapter 10. Students must use their work to provide evidence of what they can do. Teachers then check the continuums and confer when differences arise. In previous years at Brighton, Janine King's middle school students began the process by marking one continuum strand each day for the two weeks. For example, she began by asking students to use their reading logs to assess the types of books they read independently. She found that it was sometimes difficult for students to follow the strands since they are not lined up horizontally in the same order in each stage.

Name _Joanna_   Date _NOVEMBER 2000_

Things I Can Do in Reading

	Not Yet	Sometimes	Always
I read challenging children's books.			X
I choose, read and finish a wide variety of genres with help.		X	
I develop strategies for picking good materials to read.	X		
I read aloud with fluency, expression and confidence.			X
I read silently for extended periods (30-40 minutes).			X
I use tools (like a dictionary or thesaurus) to learn new words.		X	
I use tools (like an encyclopedia, articles, computer or non-fiction) to find information.		X	
I use the organization of non-fiction (titles, table of contents, index and glossary) to find information.			X
I use resources (dictionary and thesaurus) to increase my vocabulary.	X	X	
I discuss literature by talking about setting, plot, characters, theme and author's craft.		X	
I share thoughtful responses when I talk and write about literature with help.		X	
I use new vocabulary when I write and talk about what I read.		X	
I begin to gain deeper meaning by "reading between the lines."		X	
I begin to set goals and identify strategies to improve my reading.		X	

My goal:
My goal is to use the dictionary more to improve my vocabulary.

Comments:

Fluent

Figure 7.5 Self-Evaluation Checklist

This year, Janine has been experimenting with checklists that are organized by strands and include descriptors for the last five stages on the reading and writing continuums (Figure 7.6). Students then self-evaluate by using one of the checklists each day as Janine explains the different skills and strategies and shows examples. She has found that the checklists clarified and simplified the task of marking the continuum for her students since the developmental progression was easier to see. Students also focused on their behaviors, without worrying about the continuum stages, making the whole process a little more logical and less competitive. Janine notes, "I wouldn't recommend just handing out the lists for students to check without supporting their choices with dialogue and examples. It's not always clear how each step differs from the previous one. It was somewhat tedious doing all the checklists in a two-week time span. Ideally, each student would have a packet and they would go over it periodically, perhaps at the end of a big unit or writing assignment." Using the checklist, however, added an extra step in the process, since Janine had to transfer the information from the checklists onto each student's continuums. Like Janine, you may want to experiment with continuums and checklists in order to discover the best method for self-evaluation for your group of students.

Types of Text and Oral Reading

Name: Emily

Date: 11/17/99

DIRECTIONS: Place a √ next to the items that are true about you.

Choosing Books

Most of the books on my Reading Log are at the ___Connecting___ stage.

_____ I choose things to read that are at my reading level.

__√__ I *sometimes* use strategies for picking good materials to read.

_____ I can select reading materials *on my own*.

Genre

__√__ I understand the difference between different genres (realistic fiction, historical fiction and fantasy).

_____ I choose, read, and finish a wide variety of genres *with help*.

__√__ I select, read, and finish a wide variety of genres *independently*.

__√__ I read and understand want ads, brochures, schedules, catalogs, and manuals *with help*.

__√__ I choose and comprehend a wide variety of sophisticated materials with ease (e.g. newspapers, magazines, manuals, novels and poetry).

_____ I read and understand informational texts (e.g. manuals, consumer reports, applications and forms).

Reading Aloud

__√__ I read aloud with expression.

_____ I read aloud with fluency, expression and confidence.

Figure 7.6 Middle School Continuum Checklist

During March conferences, students lead their parents through a review of their work (e.g., portfolio, reader response journal, writer's notebook, computer slideshow) and discuss how the selected pieces demonstrate growth and progress toward the goals set in the fall. Ingrid Stipes notes, "I feel the value for the student in using the checklist is twofold. First, the discussion and awareness of specific behaviors empowers the learner. In addition, the consistent review of the portfolio entries and checklist throughout the year keeps goal setting alive for the learner. They learn that goal setting is a dynamic, ongoing process."

In fourth grade at Brighton School, Bruce wrote his goals for reading and writing in November (Figure 7.7). He will revisit those goals in the spring as he writes a letter to his next year's teacher for his Learner Profile.

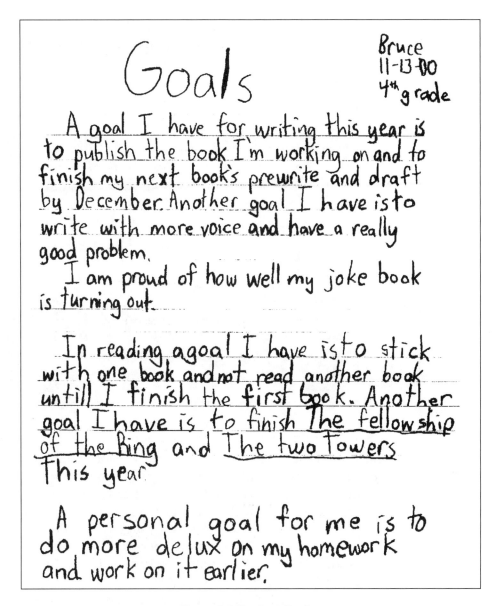

Figure 7.7 Student Goals

Unlike abstract goals, concrete objectives (like finishing the next two books by Tolkien) are easy to measure and to reach. Other goals are more challenging, such as Bruce's hope to write with more voice. The continuums, your focus lessons, the self-evaluations checklists, and rubrics all provide students with the language to set goals they can accomplish.

Connecting to the Continuums

In order for the continuums to become a living part of the classroom, it's important for students and teachers to refer to them on a regular basis. When the continuums are displayed in your classroom, you are more likely to use the language from the descriptors as you teach. You might want to enlarge and display all the continuum charts under your whiteboard or on a wall. Some teachers prefer to enlarge and laminate only the three or four stages that are appropriate to their group of students (Figure 7.8). However, if the charts are merely posted and neither students nor teachers refer to them, it's probably not a good use of wall space.

Figure 7.8 Continuum Charts

You may want to display the "student version" charts, which are included at the end of this chapter and on the CD-ROM. Each time you present a focus lesson or a shared reading or writing lesson, you can point to the appropriate skill or strategy on the continuum chart. For instance, Jan Peacoe, a teacher on Bainbridge Island, Washington, talked to one of her first graders in September about how leaving spaces between words would help her read his work. A few days later, Chris proudly showed Jan his story with correct spacing, which they both could read. Together, they looked at the continuum chart and found the descriptor that matched his new step as a writer. Jan used her anecdotal notes to record the conversation and watched for further evidence that Chris used correct spacing consistently as a Beginning writer.

Some teachers laminate the charts, then use an erasable overhead pen and place a check by the strategies they have introduced, practiced, or reviewed. You can then visually track what strategies you have taught and spot any instructional gaps. In addition, your students will soon become familiar with the descriptors, which makes it much easier for them to fill out the student self-evaluation checklists or self-evaluation version of the continuums.

Connecting Instruction to Assessment and Evaluation

What do you do with the assessment information you've collected about each student? For instance, what do you do with the insights you gain from individual reading conferences or running records? Such time-consuming assessment strategies are only worthwhile if the assessment information helps you fine-tune your teaching to better meet each child's needs. Both Anne Klein and Janine King make these connections intentionally. In both classrooms, students first develop the criteria for quality work in reading and writing. The criteria inevitably match the descriptors on the continuums. The teachers then identify one aspect to use for a series of focus lessons, such as learning how to choose appropriate books. Teachers share their own strategies as readers, then provide time for discussions and practice. Anne and Janine are then able to assess how well each student has internalized the strategy through observations during silent reading time and individual reading conferences. For instance, as students evaluate their growth as readers, one of the strategies they can assess is their ability to choose and finish books independently. In Anne Klein's classroom, her focus lessons, class discussions, and the student-generated chart about "Good Readers" provide the language and criteria for self-evaluation.

In this chapter, I have tried to show the links between teaching, assessment, and student self-evaluation. By letting children know the specific steps along the path to independent reading and writing, we take the mystery out of evaluation. Students can measure their own growth toward clearly defined targets. Learning how to use the continuums takes a great deal of time and energy for both teachers and students. If our goal is to nurture readers and writers who take responsibility for their own learning, it's worth the effort. The continuums, charts, and checklists in student language and the surveys can help you involve your students as partners in the assessment process. Student self evaluation based on criteria can lead naturally into portfolio reflections, goal setting, and student-led conferences. In this chapter, I explored ways in which to involve students in self-evaluation. Next, we'll look at how we can also involve families in the assessment process.

Staff Development

In grade level teams, divide up the continuum stages. Hand each group a copy of the "adult version" of the writing continuums. Ask teachers to put the descriptors into "kid language," using first person. This activity is a great way to clarify confusing descriptors and build consensus about the terminology. Discussions inevitably arise about how to teach some of these strategies. At the end of the activity, hand out the student self-evaluation continuum from this book and talk about what they notice. At a second staff meeting, do the same activity with the reading continuum.

Ask each teacher or grade-level team to share specific examples of student self- evaluation in reading or writing. You may want to bring a portfolio reflection, a survey, an example from the student self-evaluation checklist, or a student's comments from your anecdotal notes. Discuss ways in which to encourage student participation in the assessment process.

Spelling Survey

Name: _____ **Date:** _____

Are you a good speller? Why do you think so? _____

_____

_____

_____

_____

What do you do when you don't know how to spell a word? _____

_____

_____

_____

_____

What are other ways to figure out how to spell a word? _____

_____

_____

_____

What kinds of words are hard for you to spell? _____

_____

_____

_____

How do people get to be good spellers? _____

_____

_____

_____

When is correct spelling important? _____

_____

_____

_____

Writing Survey (Primary)

Name: _____ **Date:**_____

In general, how do you feel about writing? _____

_____

_____

_____

_____

What is the hardest thing about writing? _____

_____

_____

What have you written that you really like? _____

_____

_____

_____

How do you decide what to write about? _____

_____

_____

Who are some of your favorite authors? _____

_____

_____

What makes a good author? _____

_____

_____

_____

What would you like to learn to help you become a better writer? _____

_____

_____

_____

_____

Writing Attitude Survey (Intermediate)

Name: _____ **Date:** _____

In general, how do you feel about writing? _____

_____

_____

_____

What has helped you the most as a writer? _____

_____

_____

_____

What kinds of things do you like to write? (letters, poems, notes, stories, nonfic-

tion, etc.) _____

_____

_____

_____

What types of writing do people in your family do? _____

_____

_____

_____

What are other ways in which people use writing? _____

_____

_____

_____

What do you like best about writing? _____

_____

_____

_____

_____

cont.

Writing Attitude Survey (Intermediate) (continued)

What is the hardest part of writing? _____

_____

_____

_____

What have you written that you really like? _____

_____

_____

_____

How do you decide what to write about? _____

_____

_____

_____

Who are some of your favorite authors? _____

_____

_____

_____

What makes a good author? _____

_____

_____

_____

Why is it important to write well? _____

_____

_____

_____

What would you like to learn to help you become a better writer? _____

_____

_____

Reading Survey (Primary)

Name: _____ **Date:** _____

What are some of your favorite books you've read by yourself? _____

_____

_____

_____

_____

What are some of your favorite books someone has read aloud to you? _____

_____

_____

_____

What kinds of books would you like to read this year? _____

_____

_____

_____

What do you do when you are reading and come to a word you don't know? __

_____

_____

_____

Do you think you are a good reader? Why or why not? _____

_____

_____

_____

What would you like to learn to help you become a better reader? _____

_____

_____

_____

_____

Reading Attitude Survey (Intermediate)

Name: _____ **Date:** _____

How do you feel about reading? _____

_____

_____

_____

When and how did you learn to read? _____

_____

_____

_____

What kinds of things do you like to read? (which magazines, newspapers, favor-

ite genres) _____

_____

_____

_____

Do you read to anyone in your family? Who? When? How often? How do you

feel about it? _____

_____

_____

_____

Does anyone in your family read to you? Who? When? How often? How do you

feel about it? _____

_____

_____

_____

What are your favorite books you've read at home? _____

_____

_____

cont.

Reading Attitude Survey (Intermediate) (continued)

What are your favorite books you've read in class? _____

_____

_____

_____

What are your favorite books your teachers have read aloud at school? _____

_____

_____

_____

Who are some of your favorite authors? _____

_____

_____

_____

How do you feel when you read aloud? _____

_____

_____

_____

Why is it important to be a good reader? _____

_____

_____

_____

How do you feel about yourself as a reader? _____

_____

_____

_____

Other comments about who you are as a reader: _____

_____

_____

Name: _____ Date: _____

Things I Can Do in Writing

Not Yet	Sometimes	Always	
❑	❑	❑	I draw pictures to tell my stories or ideas.
❑	❑	❑	I draw pictures and write a word or two about the pictures.
❑	❑	❑	I can write my name.
❑	❑	❑	I know that letters are used to make words and stories.
❑	❑	❑	My writing looks like letters.
❑	❑	❑	I write words using the letters I know.
❑	❑	❑	I can tell about my pictures and writing.

My Goal: _____

_____

_____

Comments: _____

_____

_____

Preconventional Writer

Name: _____ **Date:** _____

Not Yet	Sometimes	Always	**Things I Can Do in Writing**
❑	❑	❑	I use pictures and words to tell my stories and ideas.
❑	❑	❑	I write about my pictures.
❑	❑	❑	I copy names and some words.
❑	❑	❑	I know that each sound has a letter or letters.
❑	❑	❑	I print with mostly upper case letters.
❑	❑	❑	I match letters to their sounds.
❑	❑	❑	I use beginning sounds to write words.
❑	❑	❑	I use beginning and ending sounds to write words.
❑	❑	❑	I can almost read what I write.
❑	❑	❑	I see myself as a writer.
❑	❑	❑	I write new things and spell words on my own.

My Goal:_____

_____

_____

Comments:_____

_____

_____

Emerging Writer

Name: _____ **Date:** _____

Not Yet	Sometimes	Always	**Things I Can Do in Writing**
❑	❑	❑	I write 1–2 sentences about a topic.
❑	❑	❑	I write names and favorite words.
❑	❑	❑	I can think of ideas to write about.
❑	❑	❑	I write from top to bottom, left to right, and front to back.
❑	❑	❑	I use both upper and lower case letters.
❑	❑	❑	I use capitals correctly some of the time.
❑	❑	❑	I use periods correctly some of the time.
❑	❑	❑	I use spaces between my words.
❑	❑	❑	I use what I know about sounds and rhymes to write words.
❑	❑	❑	I sound out words when I spell.
❑	❑	❑	I use beginning, middle, and ending sounds to write words.
❑	❑	❑	I can read my own writing.

My Goal: _____

_____

_____

Comments: _____

_____

_____

Developing Writer

Name: _____ **Date:** _____

			Things I Can Do in Writing
Not Yet	Sometimes	Always	
❑	❑	❑	I can write several sentences about a topic.
❑	❑	❑	I write about what I see and true things about my life.
❑	❑	❑	I write true things about a topic (nonfiction) with help.
❑	❑	❑	I pick ideas to write about by myself.
❑	❑	❑	I read my own writing and can find mistakes with help.
❑	❑	❑	I add more to my writing with help.
❑	❑	❑	I use spaces between words.
❑	❑	❑	I make my letters neatly.
❑	❑	❑	I write pieces that I can read and others can read.
❑	❑	❑	I use my own spelling to write by myself.
❑	❑	❑	I spell easy words and some common words correctly.
❑	❑	❑	I sometimes use periods and capital letters correctly.
❑	❑	❑	I share my writing with others.

My Goal: _____

_____

_____

Comments: _____

_____

_____

Beginning Writer

Name: _____   **Date:** _____

Not Yet	Sometimes	Always	**Things I Can Do in Writing**
❏	❏	❏	I write short stories and poetry with help.
❏	❏	❏	I write short nonfiction (facts about a topic, letters, and lists) with help.
❏	❏	❏	I write with a main idea.
❏	❏	❏	I write with complete sentences.
❏	❏	❏	I organize my ideas to make sense in my writing with help.
❏	❏	❏	I find and use interesting language.
❏	❏	❏	I use prewriting strategies (web, brainstorm, picture) to get ideas with help.
❏	❏	❏	I listen to other people's ideas and give other people suggestions about their writing.
❏	❏	❏	I use other people's suggestions about my writing to make it better.
❏	❏	❏	I add description and details with help.
❏	❏	❏	I edit for capitals and punctuation with help.
❏	❏	❏	I publish some of my writing with help.
❏	❏	❏	I write so people can read my handwriting.
❏	❏	❏	I spell most common words and many other words correctly.
❏	❏	❏	I talk about what I do well as a writer and set goals with help.

My Goal: _____

_____

_____

Comments: _____

_____

_____

Expanding Writer

Name: _____ **Date:** _____

Not Yet	Sometimes	Always	**Things I Can Do in Writing**
❑	❑	❑	I write about my feelings and opinions.
❑	❑	❑	I write fiction with a clear beginning, middle, and end.
❑	❑	❑	I write poetry using carefully chosen language with help.
❑	❑	❑	I write organized nonfiction (reports, letters, and lists) with help.
❑	❑	❑	I use paragraphs to organize my ideas.
❑	❑	❑	I use strong verbs, interesting language, and dialogue with help.
❑	❑	❑	I ask for help and suggestions about my writing.
❑	❑	❑	I revise my writing to make sense with help.
❑	❑	❑	I make my writing more interesting by adding description and detail.
❑	❑	❑	I use a thesaurus or lists of words to make my writing better with help.
❑	❑	❑	I edit for punctuation, spelling, and grammar (correct English).
❑	❑	❑	I publish my writing in polished format with help.
❑	❑	❑	I spell more words correctly by using how a word looks, spelling rules, and word parts.
❑	❑	❑	I use commas and apostrophes correctly.
❑	❑	❑	I set my own writing goals with help.

My Goal:_____

_____

_____

Comments:_____

_____

_____

Bridging Writer

Name: _____ **Date:** _____

Not Yet	Sometimes	Always	**Things I Can Do in Writing**
❑	❑	❑	I write organized fiction and nonfiction (reports, letters, biographies, and autobiographies).
❑	❑	❑	I develop plots that have a problem and solution with help.
❑	❑	❑	I create characters in stories with help.
❑	❑	❑	I write poetry using carefully chosen language.
❑	❑	❑	I try writing different types of sentences.
❑	❑	❑	I try different types of leads and endings with help.
❑	❑	❑	I use description, details, and similes (comparing using "like" or "as") with help.
❑	❑	❑	I use dialogue in my stories with help.
❑	❑	❑	I use different prewriting strategies (web, outline, free write).
❑	❑	❑	I write for different purposes and audiences with help.
❑	❑	❑	I revise for writing traits (ideas, organization, word choice, sentence fluency, voice, and conventions) with help.
❑	❑	❑	I use people's suggestions about my writing with help.
❑	❑	❑	I edit accurately for punctuation, spelling, and grammar.
❑	❑	❑	I use tools (dictionary, word lists, and spell checker) to edit with help.
❑	❑	❑	I use what I know about good writing in different genres to make my writing better with help.

My Goal: _____

_____

_____

Comments: _____

_____

_____

Fluent Writer

Name: _____ **Date:** _____

Not Yet	Sometimes	Always	**Things I Can Do in Writing**
❑	❑	❑	I write persuasively about my ideas, feelings, and opinions.
❑	❑	❑	I create plots with problems and solutions.
❑	❑	❑	I develop main characters and describe detailed settings.
❑	❑	❑	I write organized and fluent nonfiction, including simple bibliographies.
❑	❑	❑	I write clear paragraphs that include reasons and examples with help.
❑	❑	❑	I use transitional sentences to connect paragraphs together.
❑	❑	❑	I use different types of sentences, leads, and endings.
❑	❑	❑	I use descriptive language, details, and similes.
❑	❑	❑	I use personal voice to get an emotional response from readers.
❑	❑	❑	I gather and use information on a topic from a variety of sources.
❑	❑	❑	I revise for writing traits (ideas, organization, word choice, sentence fluency, voice, and conventions).
❑	❑	❑	I use tools (dictionary, word lists, and spell checker) to edit independently.
❑	❑	❑	I publish some of my writing in polished format independently.
❑	❑	❑	I use complex punctuation (commas, colons, semicolons, and quotation marks) correctly.
❑	❑	❑	I set my own goals and identify ways to improve my writing in different genres.

My Goal: _____

_____

_____

Comments: _____

_____

_____

Proficient Writer

Name: _____ **Date**: _____

Not Yet	Sometimes	Always	

Things I Can Do in Writing

❑ ❑ ❑ I write in a variety of genres and forms for different audiences and purposes.

❑ ❑ ❑ I create plots with a climax.

❑ ❑ ❑ I create detailed, believable settings and characters in stories.

❑ ❑ ❑ I write organized, fluent, and detailed nonfiction independently, including bibliographies with correct format.

❑ ❑ ❑ I write cohesive paragraphs including reasons and examples.

❑ ❑ ❑ I use descriptive language, details, similes, and imagery to enhance my ideas.

❑ ❑ ❑ I use dialogue to enhance character development.

❑ ❑ ❑ I incorporate personal voice in my writing with increasing frequency.

❑ ❑ ❑ I integrate information on a topic from a variety of sources.

❑ ❑ ❑ I construct charts, graphs, and tables to convey information when appropriate.

❑ ❑ ❑ I use prewriting strategies effectively to organize and strengthen my writing.

❑ ❑ ❑ I revise for specific writing traits (ideas, organization, word choice, sentence fluency, voice, and conventions).

❑ ❑ ❑ I include deletion in my revision strategies.

❑ ❑ ❑ I incorporate suggestions from others about my own writing.

❑ ❑ ❑ I use complex punctuation (commas, colons, semicolons, and quotation marks) with increasing accuracy.

My Goal: _____

_____

_____

Comments: _____

_____

_____

Connecting Writer

Name: _____ **Date:** _____

Not Yet	Sometimes	Always	**Things I Can Do in Writing**
❑	❑	❑	I write organized, fluent, accurate, and in-depth nonfiction, including references with correct bibliographic format.
❑	❑	❑	I write cohesive, fluent, and effective poetry and fiction.
❑	❑	❑	I use a clear sequence of paragraphs with effective transitions.
❑	❑	❑	I use literary devices (imagery, metaphors, personification, and foreshadowing) in my writing.
❑	❑	❑	I weave dialogue effectively into stories.
❑	❑	❑	I develop plot, characters, setting, and mood (literary elements) effectively.
❑	❑	❑	I begin to develop a personal voice and style of writing.
❑	❑	❑	I revise through multiple drafts independently.
❑	❑	❑	I seek feedback from others and incorporate suggestions in order to strengthen my writing.
❑	❑	❑	I publish my writing for different audiences and purposes in polished format independently.
❑	❑	❑	I internalize the writing process.
❑	❑	❑	I use correct grammar (e.g., subject/verb agreement and verb tense) consistently.
❑	❑	❑	I write with confidence and competence on a range of topics.
❑	❑	❑	I persevere through complex or challenging writing projects.
❑	❑	❑	I set writing goals independently by analyzing and evaluating my writing.

My Goal: _____

_____

_____

Comments: _____

_____

_____

Independent Writer

Name: _____ **Date:** _____

Things I Can Do in Reading

Not Yet	Sometimes	Always	
❏	❏	❏	I choose things to read and have favorite books.
❏	❏	❏	I try to read signs, labels, and logos.
❏	❏	❏	I can read my own name.
❏	❏	❏	I hold a book and turn the pages correctly.
❏	❏	❏	I can show the beginning and end of a book.
❏	❏	❏	I know some letter names.
❏	❏	❏	I listen to books read aloud.
❏	❏	❏	I talk about the pictures in books.
❏	❏	❏	I read along when we share books, rhymes, poems, and songs.

My Goal: _____

_____

_____

Comments: _____

_____

_____

Name: _____ **Date:** _____

			Things I Can Do in Reading

Not Yet	Sometimes	Always	
❑	❑	❑	I have memorized some pattern books and poems.
❑	❑	❑	I read signs, labels, and logos.
❑	❑	❑	I like to read.
❑	❑	❑	I can almost read some books.
❑	❑	❑	I use the pictures to tell a story.
❑	❑	❑	I read from top to bottom, left to right, and front to back with help.
❑	❑	❑	I know most of my letter names and some letter sounds.
❑	❑	❑	I read some names and words.
❑	❑	❑	I make good guesses about what will happen next in a story.
❑	❑	❑	I can make rhymes and play with words.
❑	❑	❑	I read along when we read books I know.
❑	❑	❑	I connect the books we read to my own life with help.

My Goal: _____

_____

_____

Comments: _____

_____

_____

Emerging Reader

Name: _____ Date: _____

Not Yet	Sometimes	Always	**Things I Can Do in Reading**
❏	❏	❏	I read books with patterns.
❏	❏	❏	I can sometimes read my own writing.
❏	❏	❏	I can read to myself for a little while (5–10 minutes).
❏	❏	❏	I talk about what I'm reading with others.
❏	❏	❏	I use the words and pictures when I read.
❏	❏	❏	I can point to the words as I read.
❏	❏	❏	I know most letter sounds.
❏	❏	❏	I read some words.
❏	❏	❏	I make good guesses about what will happen next in a book.
❏	❏	❏	I can show the title and author's name in a book.
❏	❏	❏	I can tell the main idea of a book or story.
❏	❏	❏	I talk about a book or story during discussions.
❏	❏	❏	I think of myself as a reader.
❏	❏	❏	I explain why I like or don't like a story during discussions with help.

My Goal: _____

_____

_____

Comments: _____

_____

_____

Developing Reader

Name: _____ **Date:** _____

			Things I Can Do in Reading
Not Yet	Sometimes	Always	
❑	❑	❑	I read simple early-reader books.
❑	❑	❑	I read harder early-reader books.
❑	❑	❑	I read and follow simple written directions with help.
❑	❑	❑	I know about different types of writing (fiction, nonfiction, and poetry).
❑	❑	❑	I use punctuation marks when I read out loud.
❑	❑	❑	I can read by myself for 10–15 minutes.
❑	❑	❑	I choose what to read on my own.
❑	❑	❑	I learn information from reading and share what I learn with others.
❑	❑	❑	I use meaning (context) to make sense when I read.
❑	❑	❑	I use how English works (grammar) to make sense when I read.
❑	❑	❑	I use letter sounds and patterns (phonics) to make sense when I read.
❑	❑	❑	I read sight words easily.
❑	❑	❑	I sometimes correct myself when my reading doesn't make sense.
❑	❑	❑	I can retell the beginning, middle, and ending of a story with help.
❑	❑	❑	I can talk about the characters and events in a story with help.
❑	❑	❑	I can talk about what I do well as a reader with help.

My Goal: _____

_____

_____

Comments: _____

_____

Beginning Reader

Name: _____ Date: _____

Things I Can Do in Reading

Not Yet	Sometimes	Always	
☐	☐	☐	I read easy chapter books.
☐	☐	☐	I choose, read, and finish lots of different reading materials (books, poems, comics, and magazines) with help.
☐	☐	☐	I can sometimes read aloud smoothly.
☐	☐	☐	I can read by myself for 15–30 minutes.
☐	☐	☐	I read differently, depending on why and what I'm reading.
☐	☐	☐	I use what I know about word parts (prefix, contractions, and word families) to figure out hard words.
☐	☐	☐	I use meaning (context) when I'm reading to learn new words.
☐	☐	☐	I correct myself when my reading doesn't make sense.
☐	☐	☐	I follow written directions.
☐	☐	☐	I can find the chapter titles and table of contents in a book or magazine.
☐	☐	☐	I can retell the events from a story in order.
☐	☐	☐	I talk about how facts, characters, and events in books relate to my life.
☐	☐	☐	I can compare different characters and story events.
☐	☐	☐	I can "read between the lines" with help.
☐	☐	☐	I talk about what I do well as a reader and set goals with help.

My Goal: _____

_____

_____

Comments: _____

_____

_____

Expanding Reader

Name: _____ **Date:** _____

Not Yet	Sometimes	Always	**Things I Can Do in Reading**
❑	❑	❑	I read medium level chapter books.
❑	❑	❑	I choose things to read that are at my reading level.
❑	❑	❑	I understand the difference between genres (realistic fiction, historical fiction, and fantasy)
❑	❑	❑	I read aloud with expression.
❑	❑	❑	I can find information in the encyclopedia, on the computer, and in nonfiction with help.
❑	❑	❑	I can find information using the table of contents, captions, glossary, and index with help.
❑	❑	❑	I can gather information from graphs, charts, tables, and maps with help.
❑	❑	❑	I learn new words by reading and by using tools (dictionary and thesaurus) with help.
❑	❑	❑	I can talk about the difference between fact and opinion.
❑	❑	❑	I can follow complex written directions.
❑	❑	❑	I can discuss setting, plot, characters, and point of view with help.
❑	❑	❑	I can talk about the issues and ideas in literature as well as the facts or story events.
❑	❑	❑	I make connections to other authors, books, and points of view.
❑	❑	❑	I participate in small group literature discussions with help.
❑	❑	❑	I use reasons and examples to support my ideas and opinions with help.

My Goal: _____

_____

_____

Comments: _____

_____

_____

Name: _____ **Date:** _____

Not Yet	Sometimes	Always	**Things I Can Do in Reading**
❑	❑	❑	I read challenging children's books.
❑	❑	❑	I choose, read, and finish a wide variety of genres with help.
❑	❑	❑	I use strategies for picking good materials to read.
❑	❑	❑	I read aloud with fluency, expression, and confidence.
❑	❑	❑	I read silently for extended periods (30–40 minutes).
❑	❑	❑	I use different resources (encyclopedia, computer and nonfiction books) to find information.
❑	❑	❑	I can gather information using the table of contents, captions, glossary, and index on my own.
❑	❑	❑	I use tools (dictionary and thesaurus) to learn new words in different subject areas.
❑	❑	❑	I discuss literature by talking about setting, plot, characters, theme, and author's craft.
❑	❑	❑	I share thoughtful responses when I talk and write about literature with help.
❑	❑	❑	I use new vocabulary when I write and talk about what I read.
❑	❑	❑	I gain deeper meaning by "reading between the lines."
❑	❑	❑	I set goals and identify strategies to improve my reading.

My Goal: _____

_____

_____

Comments: _____

_____

_____

Fluent Reader

Name: _____ **Date**: _____

Not Yet	Sometimes	Always	**Things I Can Do in Reading**
❑	❑	❑	I read complex children's literature.
❑	❑	❑	I read and understand want ads, brochures, schedules, catalogs, and manuals with help.
❑	❑	❑	I can select reading materials on my own.
❑	❑	❑	I use resources (e.g., encyclopedias, articles, Internet, and nonfiction texts) to locate information independently.
❑	❑	❑	I gather and analyze information from graphs, charts, tables, and maps with help.
❑	❑	❑	I use information from many nonfiction sources to deepen my understanding of a topic with help.
❑	❑	❑	I use resources (e.g., dictionary and thesaurus) to increase my vocabulary independently.
❑	❑	❑	I can identify similes, metaphors, personification, and foreshadowing (literary devices).
❑	❑	❑	I discuss literature with reference to theme, author's purpose, style, and author's craft.
❑	❑	❑	I generate in-depth responses in small group literature discussions.
❑	❑	❑	I generate in-depth written responses to literature.
❑	❑	❑	I use more complex vocabulary when I talk and write about literature.
❑	❑	❑	I use reasons and examples to support my ideas and conclusions.
❑	❑	❑	I look for deeper meaning by "reading between the lines" in response to literature.

My Goal: _____

_____

_____

Comments: _____

_____

_____

Proficient Reader

Name: _____ **Date:** _____

Not Yet	Sometimes	Always	**Things I Can Do in Reading**
❑	❑	❑	I read complex children's literature and young adult literature.
❑	❑	❑	I select, read, and finish a wide variety of genres independently.
❑	❑	❑	I choose challenging reading materials and projects.
❑	❑	❑	I can integrate nonfiction information to develop a deeper understanding of a topic independently.
❑	❑	❑	I gather, analyze, and use information from graphs, charts, tables, and maps.
❑	❑	❑	I generate in-depth responses and sustain small group literature discussions.
❑	❑	❑	I generate in-depth written responses to literature.
❑	❑	❑	I can evaluate, interpret, and analyze reading content critically.
❑	❑	❑	I am beginning to develop criteria for evaluating literature.
❑	❑	❑	I seek recommendations and opinions about literature from others.
❑	❑	❑	I set my reading goals and challenges independently.

My Goal: _____

_____

_____

Comments: _____

_____

_____

Connecting Reader

Name: _____ **Date**: _____

Not Yet	Sometimes	Always	**Things I Can Do in Reading**
❑	❑	❑	I read young adult and adult literature.
❑	❑	❑	I choose and comprehend a wide variety of sophisticated materials with ease (e.g., newspapers, magazines, manuals, novels, and poetry).
❑	❑	❑	I read and understand informational texts (e.g., manuals, consumer reports, applications, and forms).
❑	❑	❑	I read challenging material for pleasure independently.
❑	❑	❑	I read challenging material for information and to solve problems independently.
❑	❑	❑	I persevere through complex reading tasks.
❑	❑	❑	I gather and analyze information from graphs, charts, tables, and maps independently.
❑	❑	❑	I analyze literary devices (e.g., metaphors, imagery, irony, and satire).
❑	❑	❑	I contribute unique insights and support my opinions in complex literature discussions.
❑	❑	❑	I add depth to responses to literature by making insightful connections to other authors, texts, and experiences.
❑	❑	❑	I evaluate, interpret, and analyze reading content critically.
❑	❑	❑	I develop and articulate criteria for evaluating literature.
❑	❑	❑	I pursue a widening community of readers independently.

My Goal: _____

_____

_____

Comments: _____

_____

_____

Independent Reader

Writing Continuum Key

▤ Types of Texts

🗁 Content and Traits

✂ Process

✍ Mechanics and Conventions

☺ Attitude and Self-Evaluation

Reading Continuum Key

📖 Types of Texts and Oral Reading

☺ Attitude

☑ Reading Strategies

👍 Comprehension and Response

↝ Self-Evaluation

Preconventional Writer

📄 I draw pictures to tell my stories or ideas.

📄 I draw pictures and write a word or two about the pictures.

📁 I know that letters are used to make words and stories.

✍ My writing looks like letters.

✍ I write words using the letters I know.

☺ I can tell about my pictures and writing.

Emerging Writer

📄 I use pictures and words to tell my stories and ideas.

📄 I write about my pictures.

📄 I copy names and some words.

📂 I know that each sound has a letter or letters.

✍ I print with mostly upper case letters.

✍ I match letters to their sounds.

✍ I use beginning sounds to write words.

✍ I use beginning and ending sounds to write words.

☺ I can almost read what I write.

☺ I see myself as a writer.

☺ I write new things and spell words on my own.

Developing Writer

📄 I write 1–2 sentences about a topic.

📄 I write names and favorite words.

📂 I can think of ideas to write about.

✍ I write from top to bottom, left to right, and front to back.

✍ I use both upper and lower case letters.

✍ I use capitals correctly some of the time.

✍ I use periods correctly some of the time.

✍ I sometimes use spaces between my words.

✍ I use what I know about sounds and rhymes to write words.

✍ I sound out words when I spell.

✍ I use beginning, middle, and ending sounds to write words.

☺ I can sometimes read my own writing.

Beginning Writer

📄   I can write several sentences about a topic.

📄   I write about what I see and true things about my life.

📄   I write true things about a topic (nonfiction) with help.

📁   I pick ideas to write about by myself.

✂   I read my own writing and can find mistakes with help.

✂   I add more to my writing with help.

✍   I always use spaces between words.

✍   I make my letters neatly.

✍   I write pieces that I can read and others can read.

✍   I use my own spelling to write by myself.

✍   I spell easy words and some common words correctly.

✍   I sometimes use periods and capital letters correctly.

☺   I share my writing with others.

Expanding Writer

▤   I write short stories and poetry with help.

▤   I write short nonfiction (facts about a topic, letters, lists) with help.

📁   I write with a main idea.

📁   I write with complete sentences.

📁   I organize my ideas to make sense in my writing with help.

📁   I sometimes find and use interesting language.

✂   I use prewriting strategies (web, brainstorm, picture) to get ideas with help.

✂   I listen to other people's ideas and give other people suggestions about their writing.

✂   I sometimes use other people's suggestions about my writing to make it better.

✂   I add description and details with help.

✂   I edit for capitals and punctuation with help.

✂   I publish some of my writing with help.

✎   I write so people can read my handwriting.

✎   I spell most common words and many other words correctly.

☺   I talk about what I do well as a writer and set goals with help.

Bridging Writer

▤ I write about my feelings and opinions.

▤ I write fiction with a clear beginning, middle, and end.

▤ I write poetry using carefully chosen language with help.

▤ I write organized nonfiction (reports, letters, and lists) with help.

📁 I sometimes use paragraphs to organize my ideas.

📁 I use strong verbs, interesting language, and dialogue with help.

✂ I ask for help and suggestions about my writing.

✂ I revise my writing to make sense with help.

✂ I make my writing more interesting by adding description and detail.

✂ I use a thesaurus or lists of words to make my writing better with help.

✂ I edit for punctuation, spelling, and grammar (correct English).

✂ I publish my writing in polished format with help.

✎ I spell more words correctly by using how a word looks, spelling rules, and word parts.

✎ I use commas and apostrophes correctly.

☺ I set my own writing goals with help.

Fluent Writer

📄 I sometimes write organized fiction and nonfiction (reports, letters, biographies, and autobiographies).

📄 I develop plots that have a problem and solution with help.

📄 I create characters in stories with help.

📄 I write poetry using carefully chosen language.

📂 I try writing different types of sentences.

📂 I try different types of leads and endings with help.

📂 I use description, details, and similes (comparing using "like" or "as") with help.

📂 I use dialogue in my stories with help.

✂ I use different prewriting strategies (web, outline, free write).

✂ I write for different purposes and audiences with help.

✂ I revise for writing traits (ideas, organization, word choice, sentence fluency, voice, and conventions) with help.

✂ I use people's suggestions about my writing with help.

✂ I edit accurately for punctuation, spelling, and grammar.

✂ I use tools (dictionaries, word lists, and spell checkers) to edit with help.

☺ I use what I know about good writing in different genres to make my writing better with help.

Proficient Writer

📄 I write persuasively about my ideas, feelings, and opinions

📄 I create plots with problems and solutions.

📄 I sometimes develop main characters and describe detailed settings.

📄 I sometimes write organized and fluent nonfiction, including simple bibliographies.

📁 I write clear paragraphs that include reasons and examples with help.

📁 I use transitional sentences to connect paragraphs together.

📁 I use different types of sentences, leads, and endings.

📁 I sometimes use descriptive language, details, and similes.

📁 I use personal voice to get an emotional response from readers.

📁 I sometimes gather and use information on a topic from a variety of sources.

✂ I sometimes revise for writing traits (ideas, organization, word choice, sentence fluency, voice, and conventions).

✂ I use tools (dictionaries, word lists, and spell checkers) to edit independently.

✂ I publish some of my writing in polished format independently.

✍ I sometimes use complex punctuation (commas, colons, semicolons, and quotation marks) correctly.

☺ I sometimes set my own goals and identify ways to improve my writing in different genres.

Connecting Writer

I write in a variety of genres and forms for different audiences and purposes.

I create plots with a climax.

I create detailed, believable settings and characters in stories.

I write organized, fluent, and detailed nonfiction independently, including bibliographies with correct format.

I write cohesive paragraphs including reasons and examples.

I use descriptive language, details, similes, and imagery to enhance my ideas.

I sometimes use dialogue to enhance character development.

I incorporate personal voice in my writing with increasing frequency.

I integrate information on a topic from a variety of sources.

I construct charts, graphs, and tables to convey information when appropriate.

I use prewriting strategies effectively to organize and strengthen my writing.

I revise for specific writing traits (ideas, organization, word choice, sentence fluency, voice, conventions).

I include deletion in my revision strategies.

I incorporate suggestions from others about my own writing.

I use complex punctuation (commas, colons, semicolons, and quotation marks) with increasing accuracy.

Independent Writer

🗎   I write organized, fluent, accurate, and in-depth nonfiction, including references with correct bibliographic format.

🗎   I write cohesive, fluent, and effective poetry and fiction.

📂   I use a clear sequence of paragraphs with effective transitions.

📂   I use literary devices (imagery, metaphors, personification, and foreshadowing) in my writing.

📂   I weave dialogue effectively into my stories.

📂   I develop plot, characters, setting, and mood (literary elements) effectively.

📂   I begin to develop a personal voice and style of writing.

✂   I revise through multiple drafts independently.

✂   I seek feedback from others and incorporate suggestions in order to strengthen my writing.

✂   I publish my writing for different audiences and purposes in polished format independently.

✂   I internalize the writing process.

✍   I use correct grammar (e.g., subject/verb agreement and verb tense) consistently.

☺   I write with confidence and competence on a range of topics.

☺   I persevere through complex or challenging writing projects.

☺   I set writing goals independently by analyzing and evaluating my writing.

Preconventional Reader

   📖   I choose things to read and have favorite books.

   📖   I try to read signs, labels, and logos.

   📖   I can read my own name.

   ☑   I hold a book and turn the pages correctly.

   ☑   I can show the beginning and end of a book.

   ☑   I know some letter names.

   👍   I listen to books read aloud.

   👍   I talk about the pictures in books.

   👍   I read along when we share books, rhymes, poems, and songs.

Emerging Reader

📖   I have memorized some pattern books and poems.

📖   I read signs, labels, and logos.

☺   I like to read.

☑   I can almost read some books.

☑   I use the pictures to tell a story.

☑   I read from top to bottom, left to right, and front to back with help.

☑   I know most of my letter names and some letter sounds.

☑   I read some names and words.

☑   I make good guesses about what will happen next in a story.

👍   I can make rhymes and play with words.

👍   I read along when we read books and poems I know.

👍   I connect the books we read to my own life with help.

Developing Reader

📖   I read books with patterns.

📖   I can sometimes read my own writing.

☺   I can read to myself for a little while (5–10 minutes).

☺   I talk about what I'm reading with others.

☑   I use both the pictures and the words when I read.

☑   I can point to the words as I read.

☑   I know most letter sounds.

☑   I read some words.

☑   I make good guesses about what will happen next in a book.

☑   I can show the title and author's name in a book.

👍   I can tell the main idea of a book or story.

👍   I talk about a book or story during discussions.

👓   I see myself as a reader.

👓   I explain why I like or don't like a story during discussions with help.

Beginning Reader

📖   I read simple early-reader books.

📖   I read harder early-reader books.

📖   I read and follow simple written directions with help.

📖   I know about different types of writing (fiction, nonfiction, and poetry).

📖   I use punctuation marks when I read out loud.

☺   I can read by myself for 10–15 minutes.

☺   I choose what to read on my own.

☺   I learn information from reading and share what I learn with others.

☑   I use meaning (context) to make sense when I read.

☑   I use how English works (grammar) to make sense when I read.

☑   I use letter sounds and patterns (phonics) to make sense when I read.

☑   I read sight words easily.

☑   I sometimes correct myself when my reading doesn't make sense.

👍   I can retell the beginning, middle, and ending of a story with help.

👍   I can talk about the characters and events in a story with help.

👍   I can talk about what I do well as a reader with help.

Expanding Reader

📖   I read easy chapter books.

📖   I choose, read, and finish lots of different reading materials (books, poems, comics, and magazines) with help.

📖   I can sometimes read aloud smoothly.

☺   I can read by myself for 15–30 minutes.

☑   I read differently, depending on why and what I'm reading.

☑   I use what I know about word parts (prefix, contractions, and word families) to figure out hard words.

☑   I use meaning (context) when I'm reading to learn new words.

☑   I correct myself when my reading doesn't make sense.

☑   I follow written directions.

☑   I can find the chapter titles and table of contents in a book or magazine.

👍   I can retell the events from a story in order.

👍   I talk about how facts, characters, and events in books relate to my life.

👍   I can compare different characters and story events.

👍   I can "read between the lines" with help.

〰   I talk about what I do well as a reader and set goals with help.

Bridging Reader

📖   I read medium level chapter books.

📖   I choose things to read that are at my reading level.

📖   I understand the difference between genres (realistic fiction, historical fiction, and fantasy)

📖   I read aloud with expression.

☑   I can find information in the encyclopedia, on the computer, and in nonfiction with help.

☑   I can find information using the table of contents, captions, glossary, and index with help.

☑   I can gather information from graphs, charts, tables, and maps with help.

☑   I learn new words by reading and by using tools (dictionary and thesaurus) with help.

☑   I can talk about the difference between fact and opinion.

☑   I can follow complex written directions.

👍   I can discuss setting, plot, characters, and point of view with help.

👍   I can talk about the issues and ideas in literature as well as the facts or story events.

👍   I make connections to other authors, books, and points of view.

👍   I participate in small group literature discussions with help.

👍   I use reasons and examples to support my ideas and opinions with help.

Fluent Reader

📖   I read challenging children's books.

📖   I choose, read, and finish a wide variety of genres with help.

📖   I sometimes use strategies for picking good materials to read.

📖   I read aloud with fluency, expression, and confidence.

☺   I read silently for extended periods (30–40 minutes).

☑   I sometimes use different resources (encyclopedias, articles, Internet, and nonfiction texts) to find information.

☑   I can gather information using the table of contents, captions, glossary, and index on my own.

☑   I use tools (dictionary and thesaurus) to learn new words in different subject areas.

👍   I discuss literature by talking about setting, plot, characters, theme, and author's craft.

👍   I share thoughtful responses when I talk and write about literature with help.

👍   I use new vocabulary when I write and talk about what I read.

👍   I sometimes gain deeper meaning by "reading between the lines."

〰   I sometimes set goals and identify strategies to improve my reading.

Proficient Reader

📖   I read complex children's literature.

📖   I read and understand informational texts (e.g., want ads, brochures, schedules, catalogs, and manuals) with help.

📖   I can select reading materials on my own.

☑   I use resources (e.g., encyclopedias, articles, Internet, and nonfiction texts) to locate information independently.

☑   I gather and analyze information from graphs, charts, tables, and maps with help.

☑   I use information from many nonfiction sources to deepen my understanding of a topic with help.

☑   I use resources (e.g., dictionary and thesaurus) to increase my vocabulary independently.

👍   I can identify similes, metaphors, personification, and foreshadowing (literary devices).

👍   I discuss literature with reference to theme, author's purpose, style, and author's craft.

👍   I sometimes generate in-depth responses in small group literature discussions.

👍   I sometimes generate in-depth written responses to literature.

👍   I use more complex vocabulary when I talk and write about literature.

👍   I use reasons and examples to support my ideas and conclusions.

👍   I look for deeper meaning by "reading between the lines" in response to literature.

Connecting Reader

📖 I read complex children's literature and young adult literature.

& I select, read, and finish a wide variety of genres independently.

☺ I sometimes choose challenging reading materials and projects.

☑ I can integrate nonfiction information to develop a deeper understanding of a topic independently.

☑ I sometimes gather, analyze, and use information from graphs, charts, tables, and maps.

👍 I generate in-depth responses and sustain small group literature discussions.

👍 I generate in-depth written responses to literature.

👍 I can sometimes evaluate, interpret, and analyze reading content critically.

👍 I am beginning to develop criteria for evaluating literature.

👍 I seek recommendations and opinions about literature from others.

〰 I set my reading goals and challenges independently.

Independent Reader

- 📖 I read young adult and adult literature.

- 📖 I choose and comprehend a wide variety of sophisticated materials with ease (e.g., newspapers, magazines, manuals, novels, and poetry).

- 📖 I read and understand informational texts (e.g., manuals, consumer reports, applications, and forms).

- ☺ I read challenging material for pleasure independently.

- ☺ I read challenging material for information and to solve problems independently.

- ☺ I persevere through complex reading tasks.

- ☑ I gather, analyze, and use information from graphs, charts, tables, and maps independently.

- 👍 I analyze literary devices (e.g., metaphors, imagery, irony, and satire).

- 👍 I contribute unique insights and support my opinions in complex literature discussions.

- 👍 I add depth in my responses to literature by making insightful connections to other authors, texts, and experiences.

- 👍 I evaluate, interpret, and analyze reading content critically.

- 👍 I develop and articulate criteria for evaluating literature.

- ➰ I pursue a widening community of readers independently.

Family Support

> The family, then, is where literacy begins and where the foundations of literacy are learned.
>
> —*Thomas, Fazio, and Stiefelmeyer, 1999a, p. 9*

In the last few chapters, we've examined what teachers and students can do to support learning, but what about the family's role in education? Many parents post the weekly spelling words on the refrigerator to practice with their children. Some family members might help with long-term projects or answer occasional questions about homework. Many parents read aloud to children when they are in the primary grades but stop reading aloud after second or third grade. What else can families do at home to support reading and writing? As a teacher, how can you build upon the early literacy activities that students experience at home? In this chapter, I'll suggest six important ways to connect learning at home and at school, then provide some ideas about how to share continuums with families.

Encourage and Celebrate Literacy at Home

Note that this chapter is called "*Family* Support." When possible, I consciously used the word "family" instead of "parents" since many students live with foster parents, aunts and uncles, grandparents, or even siblings. The more inclusive term of "family" indicates that any loving adult or older sibling can provide supportive literacy activities at home.

The Family Support document included at the end of this chapter and on the CD-ROM presents ideas for reading and writing at home, assuming that the students come to school with their basic needs met. Families whose children come to school without enough sleep, proper clothing, food, or adequate shelter should have those issues as their first priority. We should do everything in our power to help connect families with counselors, other teachers or families, and local or district services. Children are far more ready to learn to read and write when they arrive at school with warm clothes, an adequate breakfast, and a good night's sleep! Chris Crutcher, a family therapist and young adult author, states that if teachers knew a fraction of the challenges some children face at home, we would shake their hands each day when they enter our rooms. For some of our students, survival takes precedence over literacy. On the other hand, even in families where basic survival is a challenge, many adults do make an effort to get to the library, provide writing materials, and read with their children. We need to recognize and celebrate literacy activities wherever they occur.

Denny Taylor's (1983) ethnographic research in the 1970s and 1980s examined reading and writing in working class neighborhoods. She found that many homes were filled with print and literacy, even when parents were educationally or economically disadvantaged. Literacy was embedded in the daily activities of living, rather than a time set aside for "teaching reading." Literacy activities, however, may take other forms in different cultures and settings. For example, rather than reading picture books from libraries, literacy activities in some families may consist of reading from the Bible, clipping coupons, or writing letters to family members still living in another country.

For single parents, non-English speaking parents, or parents who work double shifts or late at night, reading with children may be a challenge. In some homes, television takes the place of reading and writing. For other families, the obstacles to reading may be after school schedules filled to the brim with soccer, gymnastics, Scouts, and piano lessons. Whatever the challenges families face, our first job as educators is to stress the vital importance of making reading and writing a fundamental part of children's lives. We should provide information and support the efforts families make. Margaret Mooney, a celebrated New Zealand educator, says that "everybody is someone's sweetie pie." We need to communicate to families that we know and value their child. The continuums and assessment strategies presented in this book can help you communicate more clearly with students and their families.

Get to Know Students and Families

As teachers, it's helpful to learn something about the languages, siblings, and interests of our students and their families, as well as the occupations of their parents. At the end of this chapter and on the CD-ROM, I have included a Primary Parent Survey (DC Form 8.1) and an Intermediate Parent Survey (DC Form 8.2) that you might want to send home during the first week of school or distribute at Back to School Night. You might tell students that this is their family's first homework assignment. Jan Colby, a kindergarten teacher on Bainbridge Island, Washington, created the welcoming introduction at the top of the Parent Surveys: "Dear Parents: Since you are your child's first and best teacher, we would like your perception of your child as a learner." In Sedro Wooley, Washington, Mim Abrose mails each family a note as the surveys are returned, commenting on what she learned and thanking parents for taking the time to fill it out. In addition to providing information about families' goals for their children, comments from surveys can help you match children to books and writing topics. Some teachers highlight specific responses on the survey that they find interesting or informative. These highlighted comments often serve as a springboard for conversations at conferences and show families that you value their input.

Great information about how to involve families in their children's education can be found in Shelley Harwayne's books, *Going Public: Priorities and Practice at The Manhattan New School* (1999, Chapter 5) and *Lifetime Guarantees: Toward Ambitious Literacy Teaching* (2000, Chapter 8). Throughout these books are glimpses of how families are invited to participate in this New York public school. The ways in which the school reaches out to families and the community are truly inspiring. For instance, rather than using a survey, Shelley Harwayne sends home an open-ended letter to each new student, asking the family to write about their child by including stories, as well as descriptions of the child's strengths, weaknesses, fears, and passions. She also asks families to tell the story behind their child's name.

What happens when you don't get all the family surveys or letters back? First of all, send a second copy. Sometimes the survey or letter might be buried under the deluge of paperwork that comes home from school. Secondly, it helps if you let families know at Back to School Night how you use the information. You can explain that you value their response on the surveys as a way to find out more about students' interests, attitudes, and hobbies, as well as a way to tap into the resources and areas of expertise in the community. Finally, learning more about the family's goals for their student will help you plan your instruction in order to meet each child's specific needs. For instance, knowing a child's interests and hobbies can be useful when your students have trouble finding a writing topic or a book to read. Once they understand how much you value the information from the surveys, families often make more of an effort to respond thoughtfully.

If you still have a few surveys that haven't been returned, you might offer to transcribe the responses or have parents or caretakers fill one out at the end of the conference. You have to be sensitive to your particular group of parents and discover if missing surveys might be due to limited reading and writing skills of parents or a language barrier. Adult volunteers or siblings can sometimes help translate the questions and answers for non-English speaking families. At the Manhattan New School, teachers display information about who speaks each language to help families make connections, translate letters or forms, and become resources for each other. Spanish versions of the Primary Parent Survey and the Intermediate Parent Survey are included in the EAL section on the CD-ROM. (Of course, you may also need a translation of the responses!) A Spanish translation of the reading and writing continuums are also included on the CD-ROM. If you translate the continuums, surveys, or Family Support documents into other languages, please send me a copy to share with other teachers.

Inform and Educate Families

In *Going Public* (1999), Shelley Harwayne states, "If we want parents to understand and support our ways of working with children, we must take parent education very seriously" (p. 164). The more you deviate from what family members remember about their own schooling, the more clearly you must articulate what you are doing and why. Since continuums will be new to virtually all of the families at your school, our third job should be to explain developmental continuums at Back to School Nights, parent conferences, and Curriculum Nights.

You can also inform families through classroom and school newsletters. For instance, the monthly bulletin at Brighton School contains a calendar, as well as information about changing report cards, book reviews, new curriculum, and educational research in parent-friendly language (Figure 8.1). You can slip bits of research on literacy acquisition or suggestions for family activities or books into your classroom newsletter as well. Some schools have developed a "Family Room" with cozy couches and pillows for reading with younger siblings, as well as a professional library for adults. Other schools have developed Family Literacy projects (Thomas, Fazio, and Stiefelmeyer, 1999a), parent workshops, or parent book clubs. Cliff Nelson, the principal at Brighton School, finds that school tours also give perspective families a chance to see teaching and learning in action.

Value Family Support

My mother had a special gift of marveling at my children and making me feel like a wonderful parent. How can we show families that we value what they do at home? We need to thank families for the great job they are doing. Much of the joy and the heartbreak of our work as teachers relate directly to the kinds of interactions that have happened at home for years before a child has started school. "We believe that all parents have their children's future largely in their hands. So much development has already taken place before children enter school that the teacher's role can be viewed as only supplementary to what has gone before at home" (Butler and Clay, 1979, p. 7). In her book, *Home Is Where Reading and Writing Begin*, Mary Hill (1989) comments that none of us went to school to learn how to be parents. We learned as we went, maybe read a few books along the way, talked to our own families and friends, and relied a great deal on our intuition. Many of the activities in the Family Support document are ones which many parents do naturally and may reflect their own upbringing. Parents may be surprised to realize how many of these simple activities they have been doing for years. For others, these very specific suggestions may be new ideas.

Suggest without Overwhelming

WARNING!! Many of us lead busy lives, always carrying some guilt along with us, whether it's about a house that could be cleaner, a lovely meal we didn't have time to make, the workout we missed, the time we didn't take to listen to our children, or a million things we should have done. This document is called "Family *Support*." You may want to nudge some parents or caretakers a bit, but you certainly don't want parents to feel inadequate, overwhelmed, or guilty. As you share this list with families, assure them that in all your years of teaching, you have never met a parent who did *everything* on these lists! These are merely suggestions gathered from many families and resources. Our fifth job should be to encourage families to pat themselves on the back for all they're already doing, then choose one or two new ideas to weave into the rhythm of their daily lives.

◆ Brighton Bulletin ◆

Week 10 - Monday, November 9, 1998   *A Nobel Learning Community*

BRIGHT◆N

SCHOOL

PRINCIPAL
CLIFF NELSON

ASS'T PRINCIPAL
JOANNE NELSON

NORTH CAMPUS
(GRADES 1 - 7)
6717-212TH ST SW
LYNNWOOD, WA
98036
(425) 672-4430
NORTH CAMPUS
OFFICE MANAGER:
KRIS McNELEY

SOUTH CAMPUS
(EARLY CHILDHOOD
EDUCATION AND
KINDERGARTEN)
21316-66TH AVE W
LYNNWOOD, WA
98036
(425) 776-5446
SOUTH CAMPUS
OFFICE
MANAGER:
LINDA SLEISTER

Continuums Used to Accurately Show Student Progress

For the past few years, Brighton teachers, along with teachers in several other Washington school districts, have been an integral part of developing reading and writing continuums which accurately show student progress in these areas. We have used these continuums as a part of our reporting system for three years. This year we will also add a math continuum to our reporting system in some grade levels, thanks to countless hours of work from our teachers, especially coordinator Linda Horn.

What is a continuum of learning? Simply speaking, it is a list of descriptors describing student academic behaviors that increase in difficulty through several different levels. As a student is able to do the things described in the list, those specific skills mastered are highlighted.

The learning continuums have 10 different levels of proficiency, ranging from *pre-conventional* (turns book correctly, recognizes own name in print, scribble-writes, etc.) to *independent* level, which includes skills that most adults have yet to master. Most students fall mainly in one level of the continuum for a subject, although there may be some skills at a higher level which they are able to do, or some at a lower level which they are still working on. A continuum allows parents to see which specific skills have been accomplished, and which still need mastery.

When you see these continuums in the conferences coming up this month, do not hesitate to ask questions. The continuums provide a wealth of information to both parents and teachers, and help us together set a course of growth for each child.

Students Make Excellent Showing on Levels Tests

Recently our students in grades 3 - 7 took "levels" tests in reading and math. These tests show how our students are faring compared to other students nationally.

We are pleased to announce that a large percentage of our students scored within the top quartile (highly above average) of students taking these tests. In all grade levels, more than half of our students scored in the upper 25% in both reading and math, and in many grade levels, the percentages were much higher. For example, 87% of our 6th grades scored in the top quartile in reading, 84% of our 5th graders scored in that range in math. Congratulations, students!

Full results are available in the office. Parents of students who took the test received an explanation booklet explaining the tests and the scores for their child.

INSIDE	
Tech News, Student Election	2
Bulletin Board/PTO News	3
Upcoming Dates/Calendar	3
Brighton "Reading Picks"	4

Figure 8.1 Brighton Bulletin

Providing Specific Suggestions

If we want to build a bridge between school and home, it helps to provide families with suggestions of ways to support their child's learning. You can highlight general recommendations, such as attending parent conferences and Curriculum Nights, reading school newsletters, checking homework, and helping with long-term projects (but not doing the work for children). Richard Gentry (1997), in his book *My Kid Can't Spell*, provides five specific recommendations:

- Turn off the television.
- Vote for smaller schools.
- Vote for fewer kids per classroom.
- Make a big deal about good teachers.
- Pay attention. Listen to your child and talk together.

Suggestions like these might be slipped into school or classroom letters and bulletins, repeated at Back to School Night, and celebrated when observed.

Our greatest emphasis should be on encouraging families to read together. Conflicting information exists about everything in education except for the well-researched fact that reading aloud to children pays off. The common factors that Dolores Durkin (1966) found in her famous study of children who read before they started school was that they all had access to books and they were all read to by siblings or parents. This research has been confirmed repeatedly in the past forty years since Durkin's landmark study.

Reading together is a great gift. Reading (and re-reading) books together should be fun and should begin at birth and continue for as long as possible. Urge parents not to stop reading aloud when their children learn to read on their own. Adults or older siblings can model fluency and a love of reading. They can read books aloud that are slightly above a child's reach. In addition, it's the conversations and interactions that occur around and about books that nurture readers.

Sharing Family Support Documents with Families

In addition to general recommendations, it's important to also share more specific suggestions for reading and writing for each stage of reading and writing. At the end of this chapter and on the CD-ROM, you'll find a list of activities that families could do at home with students at each stage on the reading and writing continuums. Notice that these aren't suggestions that require specific educational materials, kits, or training. Those of you who are parents probably enjoyed many of these literacy activities with your own children. Many of the recommendations can be woven into daily routines, such as reading before bedtime or playing word games in the car. Others require more time and energy. For instance, Deb Vanderhye, a parent at Brighton School, read aloud Bruce Coville's (1996) picture book, *William Shakespeare's a Midsummer Night's Dream* before she took her children to see the ballet. They also watched the movie and compared the three versions. You may want to modify the list on the CD-ROM to meet the needs of your particular group of students and families. You might also want to send a survey home at the end of the year to determine which activities were the most successful.

At some schools, the Family Support documents are shared during conferences. Rather than giving families the whole document, teachers at Brighton School give each family two pages (one for reading and one for writing) for the specific stage where most of their child's descriptors fall. Families are asked to highlight one activity for reading and one for writing to try at home. Teachers make a note of the choices for their own records and thank the family for their support. Most parents are grateful for these specific suggestions.

The Family Support document can also be shared at a Curriculum Night. You may want to begin with the continuum activity described in the Staff Development section in Chapter 1. When I present a family workshop on reading and writing development, I often begin by asking ten volunteers to come up to the front of the room. I choose a topic, such as "gardening" or "singing" and we arrange ourselves in a continuum from left to right. I choose several other topics and we re-arrange ourselves accordingly. This activity provides an easy and engaging way to introduce the concept of continuums to families.

After handing out the Narrative Portraits of Readers and Writers (Chapter 2), I ask parents to identify the stage where most of their own children's behaviors fall. I next pass out the Family Support document from the end of this chapter. It helps at this point to describe one student as a reader and writer at each stage on the continuum (it usually takes about 30 minutes). I show pictures and student work from each of the students described in the Case Studies in Chapter 2. You may prefer to describe students from your own school (with student and parent permission). These specific examples make it easy for parents to see where their child fits on the continuums. I highlight one or two suggestions of activities that families can do to support readers and writers at each stage.

At the back of the room, I usually have plastic tubs of representative books for each continuum stage, along with the list of Book List by Continuum Stages from Chapter 4. After the workshop, adults are invited to ask questions and to browse through the book tubs. Families take home a copy of the Reading and Writing Continuums, the Narrative Portraits (Chapter 2), the list of Books by Continuum Stages (Chapter 4), and the Family Support document (Chapter 8). At Dhahran Academy in Saudi Arabia, these documents are included in a Parent Handbook that is given to each new family. Families appreciate these materials and come away with a better understanding of developmental continuums and their child's reading and writing development. You may want to keep a copy of the Family Support documents in clear acetate slip-sheets in your Continuum Notebook.

Sharing the Continuums with Families

In education, we rarely show parents the targets. We may explain that their child is not performing at an acceptable level, but we seldom show examples of what we expect. Grant Wiggins (1994) states, "Few parents understand what constitutes an exemplary performance, however, because few schools disseminate samples of excellent work as a frame of reference" (p. 36). Charts of the student version for each stage on the reading and writing continuums are included in Chapter 7 and on the CD-ROM. You may want to these charts in your classroom and refer to them at Back to School Night. The continuum charts and samples of student work make reading and writing growth understandable to students and their families. You may also want to display the reading and writing continuum charts in a central location in your school to visually portray the developmental nature of reading and writing. You could post either the teacher version (CD-ROM) or the student version of the charts (Chapter 7 and CD-ROM). Some schools post the charts outside the library or in the front hallway as another form of communication with families.

At one school, the principal found that the displayed charts and samples of student work were helpful when talking to families. For instance, when parents were concerned about their child's report card, he set up a time to meet with the family. Before the meeting, he collected samples of the child's work. When the parents came to his office, he asked them to look through their child's folder, then refer to the student samples below the charts on the Continuum Wall. To his delight, this seemed to assuage many of the parents' concerns by providing a context and perspective on their child's work.

The Jefferson County School District in Colorado, has created an outstanding ten-minute videotape called *Learning to Read* in which they describe what families can do at each of the first six stages of the reading continuum. The order form for the videotape can be downloaded off the Jefferson County School District web site (http://204.98.1.2/isu/langarts/litmain). You may want to show this videotape at a Curriculum Night about reading development in the primary grades. I hope that Jefferson County School District or another district will create similar videotapes for reading in the intermediate grades and for writing.

You may want to share the continuums and Family Support materials with the families in your school. In addition, you may want to invite families to communicate with you informally through phone calls, email, and notes whenever they have questions, compliments, or concerns. The more you open the door to communication, the more you will feel like a partner with families in the important job of teaching children.

Staff Development

Before using the Family Support document, you might want to meet in grade-level groups to brainstorm ways in which families can support reading and writing at home. Next, hand out copies of the Family Support document and see which ideas match the lists you created. Using the CD-ROM, you can then add to or modify the suggestions. You might want to pick four or five ESSENTIAL ways in which parents across grade levels can help at home (such as reading to children) and emphasize these in school and classroom newsletters, on hallway bulletin boards, and at PTO/PTA meetings. The emphasis should not be on "one-more-thing-to-do" as a chore, but an invitation to celebrate reading and writing at home.

As a staff, plan a Family Night about continuums and reading/writing development. Make copies of the Reading/Writing Continuums, the Narrative Portraits (Chapter 2), the Books by Continuum Stages (Chapter 4), and the Family Support document (Chapter 8). Collect tubs of representative Books by Stages (see Chapter 4). Ask each grade-level team to choose a stage on the continuum and select one child as a "case study." Be sure to get written permission from the children and their parents. Have the team help the child's teacher prepare a five-minute presentation about one student as a reader and writer at that stage. Make overhead transparencies of a few pieces of that student's reading and writing to share at the Family Night. You may want to end the evening with the *Learning to Read* videotape from the Jefferson County School District. After the Family Night, discuss the parts of the presentation that were effective and what you would do differently next time.

What are other ways to share reading and writing development with families? One of the many great ideas in *Going Public* (Harwayne, 1999) is a bulletin board at the Manhattan New School. Shelley, the principal of the school, sent out a request for families to send in pictures of literacy activities at home. Students brought in photographs, along with a short written description of reading with grandparents, reading the Bible with an uncle, bedtime reading with siblings, and many more. Since their school has over 500 students, Shelley rotated the pictures as they were turned in at school, then put them in a Family Literacy Scrapbook that is kept in the front hall of the school for families to enjoy. What a visual way to celebrate all of the ways families read and write together! You may want to read Shelley's book for more ideas about the many ways that this remarkable staff connects with families and their wonderfully diverse community.

Family Support: Preconventional Writer (Ages 3–5)

◆ Read aloud to your child on a regular basis. By listening to books, young children begin to understand that print carries meaning.

◆ Provide writing materials (such as paper, pens, chalkboard, markers) and a corner or area for writing. You might want to have a writing box with paper, markers, and crayons in one convenient place.

◆ Provide magnetic letters on the refrigerator and plastic letters in the bathtub so your child can play with letters and words.

◆ Model everyday writing (such as lists, letters, notes). Ask your child to add a word or picture.

◆ Keep a grocery list on the refrigerator. Have your child add to the list.

◆ Share letters and birthday and holiday cards.

◆ Take pictures and make a book about your child as he or she grows up.

◆ Invite your child to write along with you when you're writing lists or letters.

◆ Have your child dictate a story to you and make it into a simple book.

◆ Respond to your child's awareness of the writing around them ("Wow, how did you know that said K-Mart? That's great reading!").

◆ Play with language by singing, pointing out signs, rhyming words, and talking about words and letters.

◆ When your child draws, scribbles, or writes random letters, ask him or her to tell you about the writing or drawing.

◆ Encourage risk-taking as your child learns to write and experiments with letters and words.

◆ Encourage your child to label drawings with a word or letter and sign his/her name.

◆ Respond enthusiastically to early attempts at writing.

Family Support: Emerging Writer (Ages 4–6)

◆ Read aloud to your child on a regular basis. Reading provides the foundation for writing and builds vocabulary.

◆ Provide writing materials where your child can get them easily.

◆ Provide Post-it notes for lists and notes.

◆ Invite your child to write alongside you as you use daily writing ("Could you write that for me on the grocery list?" "Why don't you put a sign on the door?" "Stick a Post-it note on the refrigerator so we don't forget.").

◆ Demonstrate the many ways you use writing as you make lists, address envelopes, pay bills, and write notes and letters.

◆ Keep a family calendar where you and your child can write down upcoming events and things to remember.

◆ Encourage invented spelling rather than spelling the words for your child, so he or she can become an independent writer (Ask, "What sounds do you hear?").

◆ Encourage your child to label things in his/her room or around the house.

◆ Encourage your child to write the names of family and friends.

◆ Encourage your child to add pictures and a few words to thank you notes or cards.

◆ Create a message center with a bulletin board or slots for mail. Encourage your child to write notes to members of the family.

◆ Play letter/word recognition games while driving ("Let's look for things that start with 'p' or look for license plates from different states.").

◆ Cut up words and letters from magazines and glue them together to make words and sentences.

◆ Write a story together.

◆ Encourage your child to make up plays and puppet shows.

Family Support: Developing Writer (Ages 5–7)

◆ Read aloud to your child on a regular basis. Reading helps children develop an ear for language and a love of reading.

◆ Make a writing center with Post-it notes, paper, stickers, staplers, pencils, and a pencil sharpener. Try to include inviting paper and bright pens or colorful markers.

◆ Make or buy an alphabet strip with upper and lower case letters to put in a writing area or on a desk.

◆ Display your child's artwork and writing.

◆ Leave simple notes in your child's lunchbox, under the pillow, on the mirror, or on the refrigerator.

◆ Make lists of jobs, friends, birthdays, favorite restaurants, good jokes, etc.

◆ Encourage your child to write notes and reminders ("Why don't you add that to the message board, refrigerator, or calendar?").

◆ Involve your child in writing party invitations, name tags, thank you notes, valentines, holiday cards, etc. Be sure to plan ahead enough so your child will have lots of time.

◆ Have your children send friends postcards when you're on a trip. Be sure to take stamps and their addresses with you.

◆ Tell "add-on" stories as you hike or on a car trip.

◆ Make simple books together after a trip, about your family, or about a subject your child finds interesting.

◆ Show your child how you use writing in your job and in daily life.

◆ Ask your child to tell you about the work that comes home from school. Have your child read to you what he or she has written. Focus on content.

◆ Encourage risk-taking and the use of invented spelling as your child first writes. This helps your child express ideas and feelings independently without becoming discouraged by the mechanics of writing.

◆ Save your child's work and compare with earlier writing to point out and celebrate growth.

Family Support: Beginning Writer (Ages 6–8)

◆ Read chapter books aloud to your child. Anticipating the next installment each night is motivating!

◆ Keep materials for writing available (old checks, music paper, telephone message pads, paper, chalk and chalkboard, markers, pens, and pencils).

◆ Encourage letter writing (pick a friend or relative who will answer!).

◆ If you have a computer, encourage your child to email friends and relatives.

◆ Keep a family journal of trips, favorite restaurants, funny stories, visitors, movies, etc. Ask your child to add comments and reactions.

◆ Make a family joke book. Check out joke books from the library and add your favorites.

◆ Have your child read you what he/she has written. Respond first to the content and ideas. At this stage, a child's confidence and attitude about writing are very important.

◆ Praise the "good ideas" evident in your child's writing and use of invented spelling ("That was a great guess. You got the first and the last letters.").

◆ Share your thinking as you write.

◆ Encourage the use of your child's own spelling (invented spelling) so he or she can become an independent writer. When asked, "How do you spell that?", encourage your child to write the sound he or she hears.

◆ Correct your child's spelling or punctuation only if asked. Focus on only one skill so your child doesn't become overwhelmed.

◆ Save your child's quality school work and art and keep it in a book or folder. Be sure to date the work and call attention to changes and growth.

Family Support: Expanding Writer (Ages 7–9)

◆ Read chapter books aloud to your child. Reading provides a model of story structure.

◆ Talk about lovely language, descriptions, and details in the books you read together.

◆ Point out the beginning, middle, and end of stories. Discuss the exciting parts or parts that made you want to read more.

◆ Provide empty notebooks or blank books to use as journals or diaries.

◆ Keep Post-it notes in the car and around the house for notes and messages.

◆ If you have a computer, provide writing programs (such as Creative Writer, Writer Rabbit).

◆ Give your child a children's dictionary.

◆ Discuss the types of writing you do at home and at work (such as checks, lists, and memos).

◆ Suggest writing topics (things you've done as a family, family stories, trips).

◆ Make books together about trips, events, holidays, and your family.

◆ Encourage your child to make books about their interests (such as soccer, horses).

◆ Encourage your child to write to friends and relatives who will answer promptly.

◆ Respond to the ideas and content first when your child shares his or her writing.

◆ Point out patterns in English as your child tries to spell challenging words.

◆ When asked, help your child by focusing on one skill at a time (for instance, only discuss how "y" is changed to "ies" when making a plural word like "babies").

◆ Be encouraging as your child tackles longer writing pieces and begins to revise and edit.

◆ Be a supportive audience for your child's writing.

Family Support: Bridging Writer (Ages 8–10)

◆ Read chapter books aloud to your child. Don't stop reading aloud when your child can read independently! Introduce your child to new authors and genres.

◆ As you read aloud, talk about the author's style and what makes powerful writing.

◆ Provide blank books for a personal journal (the ones with a key are particularly appealing at this age) as well as stamps, stationery, and writing materials.

◆ Purchase a dictionary and thesaurus and show your child how to use them.

◆ Point out words that are related (such as "sign" and "signal").

◆ Talk about root words, prefixes, and suffixes that help children see the patterns of English spelling.

◆ If you have a computer, show your child how to use email, the spell checker, and the Internet.

◆ Read a poem once a week at dinner. Let family members take turns picking poems.

◆ Encourage your child to write and/or perform plays at home.

◆ Help your child learn how to research a topic using the computer, nonfiction books, and magazine articles, as well as the encyclopedia. Encourage your child to take notes in his or her own words.

◆ Play word games, such as *Jr. Scrabble*, *Yahtzee*, or informal word games with similes and alliteration.

◆ On final drafts, help your child revise for meaning first. Revision involves communicating and presenting the ideas logically. Editing for spelling and punctuation come after revision. (A secretary can edit, but rarely revises.) Leave the pencil in your child's hands!

◆ Help with a few skills at a time so revision doesn't become overwhelming. Revising and editing are challenging for young writers.

Family Support: Fluent Writer (Ages 9–11)

◆ Read chapter books aloud to your child. Reading provides a model for good writing.

◆ Help your child locate information on the Internet, in encyclopedias, and in nonfiction materials.

◆ Involve your child in doing research before you make a major purchase or go on a trip.

◆ Encourage your child to send postcards to friends when you're on a trip. (Gather addresses and stamps before you leave.)

◆ Have your child keep the family journal on a trip.

◆ Take your child to hear a children's author speak about writing.

◆ Talk about how you revise and edit your own writing.

◆ Help your child revise for only one thing. Edit when asked for help.

◆ Ask your child to circle misspelled words and look them up, then check the words.

◆ Help your child become comfortable with writing tools, such as spell checkers, dictionaries, and a thesaurus.

◆ Encourage your child to share finished writing and to talk about his or her writing process.

◆ Find different audiences for your child's writing (friends, relatives, or contests).

◆ Subscribe to magazines, such as *Highlights*, *Cricket*, or *Stone Soup* that publish student writing. Encourage your child to submit a story, book review, or poem.

◆ Help your child identify his or her strengths as a writer and set realistic goals.

Family Support: Proficient Writer (Ages 10–13)

◆ Read chapter books aloud to your child. Read young adult novels that spark great discussions. Talk about point of view and the author's style.

◆ Help your child learn to locate information in encyclopedias, on the Internet, and in nonfiction materials.

◆ Do crossword puzzles together.

◆ Encourage your child to send editorials or letters to the editor with opinions, reactions, or concerns. Receiving a response can be very motivating.

◆ Encourage your child to submit his or her writing to contests.

◆ Encourage your child to write letters, plays, newspapers, movie reviews, etc.

◆ Have your child collect family stories and make them into a book as a gift.

◆ Encourage your child to write to favorite authors. (You can write to authors in care of the publisher. The publisher's address is near the copyright date at the front of the book.) Be sure to include a return envelope and postage.

◆ Discuss movies and TV shows together. Talk about the writer's or director's decisions and choices. Compare the book and the movie versions if available.

Family Support: Connecting Writer (Ages 11–14) and Independent Writer

◆ Read young adult and adult books aloud. You can begin to analyze and evaluate books together.

◆ Encourage your child to take writing classes in school or to form a writers club.

◆ Encourage your child to correspond via email.

◆ Encourage your child to take writing or journalism classes or to work on the school newspaper or literary magazine.

◆ Ask your child to share his or her writing with you.

◆ Analyze effective writing in literature and talk about the author's styles in the books you read.

◆ Provide support as your child tackles challenging writing projects.

Family Support: Preconventional Reader (Ages 3–5)

◆ Read books with appealing pictures that match your child's age and interests. Children at this age like books with rhythm, rhyme, and repetition.

◆ Have a cozy reading corner that invites reading.

◆ Read aloud daily, even if it's only for 10 minutes. Snuggle up on the couch or hold your child in your lap.

◆ Reading at bedtime is a wonderful way to end the day.

◆ Talk about the story and pictures in the books you read together. This time together should be natural and fun.

◆ Encourage risk-taking as children learn to read and memorize their first books. Have your child chime in on repeated lines or a chorus.

◆ Respond enthusiastically to early attempts at reading. Never say, "She's not reading. She has just memorized the book." Memorizing is one of the first steps in learning to read.

◆ Play with magnetic letters on the refrigerator or plastic letters in the tub.

◆ Encourage children to notice words in their world, such as signs, logos, and labels.

◆ Help your child learn to recognize his or her name in print.

◆ Share your love of books and reading.

◆ Sing together to develop an ear for the sounds of language and rhyme.

◆ Tell stories together.

◆ Visit bookstores and libraries with your child.

◆ Take your child to hear authors or storytellers at bookstores or the library.

◆ Make singing and talking together part of your daily routine.

◆ Watch TV shows together, such as *Sesame Street*, that incorporate reading and books.

◆ Buy or make tapes of favorite songs and books to listen to at home or in the car.

Family Support: Emerging Reader (Ages 4–6)

◆   Read aloud daily to your child.

◆   Make a cozy place to read at home.

◆   Talk about the books and materials you read with your child. Model reading.

◆   Go to the library regularly and visit bookstores. The people who work there can often help you find just the right books for your child.

◆   Check out books on tape from the library. Listen to them at bedtime or in the car.

◆   Take books everywhere you go. Keep books in the car and in every room.

◆   Write notes to your child (in his or her lunchbox, on the bed, on the mirror, or under the pillow) using simple words.

◆   Read picture books with predictable patterns and rhymes and familiar stories.

◆   Re-read favorite stories and poems.

◆   Encourage your child to chime in as you read stories, sing songs, or recite poems.

◆   Ask questions about what you read to help your child connect books with their life and experiences.

◆   Ask your child to guess what will happen next as you read aloud.

◆   Reinforce early reading attempts *without correcting mistakes*.

◆   Celebrate early memorizing as reading (it's the first step!).

◆   Point out words around you (such as signs, logos, commercials, and billboards).

◆   Tell stories and ask family members and friends to tell stories.

◆   Encourage your child to tell stories from pictures in magazines and newspapers.

◆   Tape record your child telling stories. Send the tape to relatives or friends.

Family Support: Developing Reader (Ages 5–7)

◆ Read different things aloud in addition to stories (such as recipes, letters, and directions).

◆ Subscribe to a magazine (such as *Sesame Street*, or *Ranger Rick*) and read it together.

◆ Visit bookstores and libraries regularly.

◆ Find books with patterns, rhythm, and rhyme that help children as they first begin to read on their own.

◆ Make "word cards" of the words your child can read. Make sentences with the words. The focus is on "playing with the words" rather than drilling!

◆ Encourage your child to read to friends, children in your family, or other relatives.

◆ As you read together, ask your child to predict what might happen next or talk about how the book relates to your child's life.

◆ Once in awhile, make a mistake while you're reading and problem-solve with your child about how to figure out what would make more sense.

◆ Talk about authors, illustrators, or interesting words.

◆ Talk about the characters in the books you read. Ask questions, such as, "Does that character remind you of anyone you know or a character in another book?"

◆ After reading a story aloud, retell it in your own words with your child's help.

◆ Keep a list of "Favorite Books We've Read" or a wish list of "Books to Buy."

◆ Ask friends and relatives to give books as gifts.

◆ Read the Sunday comics with your child.

◆ Watch educational TV shows together, like *Reading Rainbow*.

◆ Expose your child to computer games related to reading (such as *Reader Rabbit* and *Magic Schoolbus*).

Family Support: Beginning Reader (Ages 6–8)

◆ Read aloud daily. Your child might be ready for you to read a chapter book aloud, a chapter or two each night. Children also enjoy picture books, nonfiction, and joke books.

◆ Begin to read series books. If you read a few, children will often read the rest of the series on their own.

◆ Read poems, magazines, cartoons, recipes, maps, and nonfiction, as well as fiction.

◆ Provide time each night for your child to read on his or her own (10–15 minutes).

◆ Help your child find books at the right reading level, since at this stage children need lots of practice to become fluent readers. Ask your child's teacher for suggestions.

◆ Visit bookstores and libraries regularly.

◆ Talk about books you enjoyed when you were little.

◆ Give books as gifts.

◆ Watch television shows together (such as *Reading Rainbow*) or movies based on children's books.

◆ Be supportive as your child reads his or her first *I Can Read* books. Help with difficult words so your child can keep the flow of the story.

◆ Ask your child to make predictions as you read a story. ("What do you think this story will be about?" "What do you think will happen next?")

◆ Encourage your child to re-read a sentence when it doesn't make sense.

◆ Ask your child to retell a story you have read together.

◆ Point out ways to figure out words in addition to "sounding it out" (such as looking at the picture, breaking the word into smaller words, reading on, or thinking what would make sense).

◆ Point out punctuation as you read aloud. ("Oops, an exclamation mark! I'd better read that a little louder.")

◆ Talk about the strategies you use as a reader when you're looking for a book, when you come across a word you don't know, or want to learn more about something.

Family Support: Expanding Reader (Ages 7–9)

◆ Keep reading to your child, even when he or she can read independently.

◆ Provide time for your child to read at night (15–30 minutes).

◆ Encourage your child to practice reading aloud to siblings, relatives, or senior citizens.

◆ Use the public library for storyteller sessions, books on tape, book lists, and recommendations.

◆ Look for books that match your child's interests. (Bookstore staff, librarians, and your child's teacher can help you.)

◆ Talk about how you select books and the types of things you like to read.

◆ Have your child keep a list of books he or she finishes or would like as gifts.

◆ Help your child learn how to find information in books.

◆ Model how you look up words you don't know in a dictionary.

◆ Subscribe to children's magazines, such as *Kid City*, *Ranger Rick*, or *Contact Kids*.

◆ Talk about the characters from books, movies, and television programs.

◆ Read and compare several versions of a story (such as a fairy tale or folktale).

◆ When your child reads aloud and makes a mistake, don't correct your child right way. Provide enough time for your child to self-correct.

◆ Talk with your child about his/her reading strategies. Give positive encouragement.

◆ Play word games, such as *Boggle*, *Hangman*, or *Junior Scrabble*.

◆ Cook together. Ask your child to read and explain the directions.

◆ Ask relatives to send your child postcards when they go on trips.

Family Support: Bridging Reader (Ages 8–10)

◆ Continue reading aloud to your child. You can model fluent reading.

◆ Provide a reading routine when everyone in the family reads (30 minutes).

◆ Children at this age often delve into series books, such as *Goosebumps*, *Nancy Drew*, *The Baby-Sitter's Club* or *Animorphs*. This comfort zone helps build fluency. Go to the library so your child can get the next book in the series!

◆ Invite your child to read more challenging books, as well as books at his/her level.

◆ Encourage your child to try new genres of reading (poetry, fantasy, and nonfiction).

◆ Have your child keep a list of "Books I've Read" or "Favorite Books."

◆ Talk together about why you like or dislike certain books or authors.

◆ Talk about interesting words and language.

◆ Look up new words together in a dictionary.

◆ Talk about the characters, theme, and exciting or favorite parts in movies or books.

◆ Go to a local children's theatre. If the play is based on a book, read it together before you go, then compare the book and the play.

◆ Encourage your child to read aloud a favorite book, poem, or story to friends, relatives, or to younger children.

◆ Subscribe to children's magazines that match your child's interests, such as *Sports Illustrated for Kids*, *American Girl*, or *Zillions: Consumer Reports for Kids*.

◆ Discuss facts and opinions about community events or world news.

◆ When your child asks questions, seek answers together in books, encyclopedias, the newspaper, or on the Internet.

Family Support: Fluent Reader (Ages 9–11)

◆ Continue reading aloud to your child. Reading together opens the door for conversation about reading and life.

◆ Provide time for your child to read (30–40 minutes per day) on a regular basis. Research shows a direct correlation between how much a student reads during the day and reading achievement and success in school.

◆ Provide a quiet place for homework, writing, and reading.

◆ Listen to books on tape in the car, especially on long trips.

◆ Visit the public library regularly to check out books and tapes and to find information.

◆ Help your child find books. Keep up with new children's books by talking to teachers, friends, librarians, and bookstore staff. Encourage your child to try new genres and types of books.

◆ Read book reviews in newspapers and magazines, then look for those books in the library.

◆ Talk about the books and materials you read and how you find new books.

◆ Help your child find information in books, in articles, and on Internet.

◆ Look up the meaning of an interesting word together. Talk about the interesting words you find as you read.

◆ Ask your child to read aloud a favorite book, poem or story into a tape recorder and send the tape to a younger child far away as a gift.

◆ Encourage your child to participate in community programs that include reading and writing, such as writing contests, summer reading programs, or reading to younger children at the library.

◆ Point out what your child does well as a reader and celebrate successes.

Family Support: Proficient Reader (Ages 10–13)

- Continue reading aloud to your child. Read young adult novels together. It's an important way to stay connected as your child grows into adolescence.

- Read the newspaper and magazines and discuss articles together.

- Provide a quiet place for homework, writing, and reading.

- Help your child make time for reading and set goals as a reader.

- Visit the public library regularly to check out books and do research.

- Help your child find books. Keep up with new young adult and children's books by talking to teachers, friends, librarians, and bookstore staff. Read some of the books yourself so you can talk about them with your child.

- Join a parent/child book club.

- Collect books by a favorite author. Have your child write to the author. Send the letter to the publisher listed near the copyright information in the front of the book.

- Encourage wide reading of different genres and types of texts.

- Provide support as your child begins to read informational texts in different subject areas.

- Do crossword puzzles together.

- Discuss the concepts, symbols, well-written passages, and the author's craft as you read. Reading a book together also provides an opportunity to talk about issues.

- Talk about deeper levels of meaning in song lyrics.

- Talk about multiple perspectives and the complexity of issues in the news.

Family Support: Connecting Reader (Ages 11–14) and Independent Reader

◆ Continue reading aloud to your child. Read young adult or adult novels together. This may be the only time you can have genuine conversations with your teenager!

◆ Read the same books your child is reading so you can talk about the books together.

◆ Continue to visit the public library.

◆ Talk about the books and materials you are reading. Acknowledge your teen's mature interests and recommend appropriate adult books.

◆ Discuss the concepts, symbols, well-written passages, and the author's craft as you read.

◆ Help your child make time for reading and set goals as a reader.

◆ Help your child find books. Keep up with new books by talking to teachers, friends, librarians, and bookstore staff. Share book reviews.

◆ Encourage wide reading of many genres and types of texts.

◆ Ask your child to discuss his or her favorite genres, titles, and authors.

◆ Ask your child to explain why he or she likes or dislikes a book or author.

◆ Discuss articles and editorials from the newspaper. Share the sports page or entertainment section.

◆ Have your child read the map when you're going somewhere new.

◆ Provide support as your child reads informational texts in many subject areas.

◆ Provide encouragement as your child tackles challenging reading projects.

◆ Give your child a subscription to a teen or adult magazine based on his or her interests. Even if you might prefer a different subject matter, it will keep your child reading at an age when reading tends to decline.

◆ Start a mother-daughter book club with friends (or father-daughter, mother-son, etc.).

Parent Survey (Primary)

Name: _____ **Date:** _____

Child's Name: _____

Dear Parents: Since you are your child's first and best teacher, we would like your perception of your child as a learner. Thank you for your help!

How does your child feel about going to school? _____

_____

_____

_____

What are your goals for your child this year? _____

_____

_____

_____

What are your child's interests/hobbies/talents/activities? _____

_____

_____

_____

What types of activities do you like to do together as a family? _____

_____

_____

_____

Do you read together regularly? If so, when and how often? _____

_____

_____

_____

Do you usually read to your child or does your child read to you? _____

_____

_____

cont.

What types of books does your child enjoy? _____

_____

_____

_____

What are some of your child's favorite books and/or authors? _____

_____

_____

_____

Does your child discuss, retell, or "pretend read" stories/poems you read aloud? _____

_____

_____

_____

Does your child know how to read any books? If so, which ones? _____

_____

_____

_____

Does your child do any drawing or writing at home? If so, how often and what types? _____

_____

_____

_____

What are your observations about how your child plays? _____

_____

_____

_____

What are some other things you would like me to know about your child? _____

_____

_____

_____

Parent Survey (Intermediate)

Name: _____ Date: _____

Child's Name: _____

Dear Parents: Since you are your child's first and best teacher, we would like your perception of your child as a learner. Thank you for your help!

How does your child seem to feel about going to school? _____

_____

_____

_____

What are your goals for your child this year? _____

_____

_____

_____

What are your child's interests/hobbies/talents/activities? _____

_____

_____

_____

What types of activities do you like to do together as a family? _____

_____

_____

_____

Do you read together regularly? If so, when and how often?_____

_____

_____

_____

Do you usually read to your child or does your child read to you? _____

_____

_____

cont.

What types of books does your child enjoy? _____

_____

_____

_____

What are some of your child's favorite books and/or authors? _____

_____

_____

_____

Does your child do any drawing or writing at home? If so, how often and what types?

_____

_____

_____

What are your observations about how your child learns? _____

_____

_____

_____

What are some other things you would like me to know about your child? _____

_____

_____

_____

_____

_____

_____

_____

English as an Additional Language (EAL) Continuum

Learning to read and write is a challenging task in our native language. Imagine learning to read and write in two or even three languages! It is truly impressive to visit a classroom in Saudi Arabia and see six-year-olds learning to read and write in English (going from left to right) as well as in Arabic (moving from right to left). What a gift to be able to speak, read, and write in more than one language.

This chapter explores the use of continuums for students learning an additional language. In the United States, this broad topic is often referred to as ESL (English as a Second Language), ESOL (English to Speakers of Other Languages), ELL (English Language Learners), or EFL (English as a Foreign Language). In some cases, however, English could be a student's second, third, or even fourth language. For this reason, some schools in Britain and around the world use the term EAL (English as an Additional Language). I decided to use the term EAL since it seems to reflect a respectful view that speaking an additional language is an asset, rather than a disadvantage. I use the terms "home language," "first language," "mother tongue," and "native language" interchangeably.

All students move through the same stages of learning to read and write; the

415

pace is just slower when a child's learning includes a second language. With young students learning two languages simultaneously, the languages seem to develop in tandem. One may not be able to advance until the other does.

For this reason, EAL/ESL teachers found they could also use the reading and writing continuums with their second language students. The ages do not apply, but all students move through the same developmental progression in learning to read and write, whether in their native language or in another tongue. Of course, a great deal will depend on whether or not the child has learned to read and write in his or her native language (Goodman and Goodman, 1978; Hudelson, 1981). As many educators have observed, you only learn to read once. If a child has already learned to read in his or her native language, it's much easier to transfer that knowledge to reading in a related second language. Cynthia Ruptic, a teacher at the Osaka International School in Japan, notes that this is not true with Japanese, Chinese, and Korean students whose first language is so different from English. For these students, the entire encoding system ("pictorial" characters), grammar (tense, case, plurals), and even the order of the words is so markedly different that it is difficult to transfer language learning between the two languages. For students whose native language more closely matches English, learning the new language is significantly easier. For all students, however, we need a way to monitor and support their growing skills as English language learners. The reading and writing continuums provide a way to assess students' abilities to read and write in English, but how can you document students' growing ability to understand and speak English?

Developing the EAL Continuum

At Dhahran Ahliyya School in Saudi Arabia, the teachers in the girls' school have developed a non-graded form for reporting student progress to families. Anna Marie Amudi, the Supervisor for the English Department, and the other English teachers wanted to develop some form of assessment that demonstrated what students *could do*, rather than using letter grades that often took on a negative and competitive flavor. In 1996, the staff created a progress report using developmental stages for reading, writing, listening, and speaking. Their continuums were piloted and revised over the next two years.

When I visited Dhahran Ahliyya in February of 1999, I shared my reading and writing continuums, which were very similar to the ones they had developed. After lengthy discussions and comparisons, the staff at Dhahran Ahliyya decided to adopt my continuums for reading and writing. They felt these continuums provided a clearer picture of student growth and were easier for parents to understand than the ones they had developed. The teachers then put the listening and speaking continuums they had developed into a similar format.

While this was happening in the Arab school, a few kilometers away, two other teachers were discussing the possibility of developing their own listening and speaking continuum. Kathryn Blatch was the EAL teacher in the British section of Dhahran Academy, one of nine schools that form part of the International Schools Group in Saudi Arabia. Cecilia Vanderhye, the ESL teacher in the American school on the same campus, was also interested in oral language development, particularly for second language learners. Kathryn and Cecilia had been meeting on a regular basis to discuss issues related to language acquisition.

Both Kathryn and Cecilia were frustrated by traditional means of assessing and reporting student growth for students whose first language was not English. Kathryn felt that all too often, non English-speaking students were required to sit through several hours of standardized tests to determine if they qualified for ESL services. Cecilia wanted a way to document and report student progress that highlighted children's development toward becoming competent English speakers. Was there a way to assess students' language development in a more authentic way? How could teachers quickly assess and document growth in a student's ability to use English across the curriculum? Kathryn and Cecilia felt that a listening/speaking continuum, together with the reading and writing continuums, would successfully capture their students' growth as English language learners.

In the fall of 1999, Anna Marie gave a copy of her school's listening/speaking continuum to Kathryn and Cecilia. The three teachers began to meet on a regular basis in order to fine-tune the EAL continuum. They looked at several American, British, and Australian resources, which are listed in the References at the end of the book. Once the EAL Listening/Speaking Continuum was finished they created Narrative Portraits, a Glossary, Assessment Checklists, Anecdotal Notes Focus Questions, a Student Self-Evaluation Continuum, and Family Support documents. These documents parallel the reading and writing pieces in Chapters 2, 3, 5, 6, 7, and 8. As I had discovered with revisions of the reading and writing continuums, constructing a glossary and defining terms helped to clarify their thinking and led to further modifications. As the three teachers piloted the continuum and support documents in their classrooms, we made further changes.

We shared drafts of the EAL continuum and support materials with several ESL teachers, Monica Dilts from Denver Public Schools, Sally Nathenson-Mejía (a university professor at the University of Colorado, Denver), Cynthia Ruptic (classroom teacher and consultant in Osaka, Japan), and with Theresa Zanatta, (an educational consultant). We would like to thank these people and all the EAL professionals whose feedback helped us refine and clarify the continuums and support pieces. We have all found that the process itself was as valuable as, if not more valuable than the final product. In many ways, we wish you had the time and energy to create your own EAL continuum from scratch as we have done. The process has been a tremendous learning experience for all of us, particularly for me. The broad experiences of the teachers in these schools, who work with students from many countries around the world, is amazing. Each of the teachers brought her own experienced perspective to the table.

For instance, Cecilia worked for many years as a Spanish/English court interpreter in Phoenix. She is fluent in Spanish, Swedish, and English. Cecilia is now teaching at the International School of Brussels in Belgium. Kathryn taught English as a Foreign Language in Greece, EAL in England and Saudi Arabia, and is currently teaching in Thailand. Anna Marie has had a unique perspective as the Supervisor for the English Department in an Arab school for the past 13 years. She is married to a Saudi man and has two grown children who went to school at Dhahran Ahliyya and who are bilingual in Arabic and English. All three teachers often drew on their own experiences of learning another language. My role was that of editor and I provided feedback from a perspective outside the ESL community.

As I looked at draft after draft, I kept asking for simpler language and examples in order to understand the stages as clearly as possible. We decided to include the EAL continuum and support pieces in this book, but not without some misgivings. We wish we had another year to pilot and polish these pieces. However, as I have learned from my ten-year process with the reading and writing continuums, there will never be a time when the continuums are done. As we continue to share ideas and learn from research, the continuums will inevitably change and grow as well. Before we look at the general characteristics of English language learners, let's look at two very different students in Cecilia's program.

Case Studies

Case Study: Mali

Mali is a ten-year-old girl from Thailand who moved to Saudi Arabia. She was placed in third grade where she received ESL/EAL support in a pullout program. She began the year not knowing any English. She was extremely shy and her voice was rarely heard in school for the first eight months. Cecilia soon discovered that Mali was preliterate (not yet literate) in her home language. Her mother was Thai and could not read or write herself. Mali had had very little interaction with her Thai father. A year earlier, her father died and her mother subsequently married an American, whose job brought the family to Saudi Arabia. Learning to read and write in English presented a daunting challenge for this young girl.

After the first year of working on beginning reading and writing, Mali began to take risks. She used invented spelling to write very simple stories and personal narratives but often could not read her own writing. Her reading progressed more slowly. At the end of her first year at the school, Mali had a sight vocabulary of 30 words and could decode only the beginning sound of words with initial consonants. At first, her classroom teacher was discouraged about Mali's progress. Cecilia and the teacher filled out Mali's continuums together. They realized that, despite her slow start and her limited skills in English, the continuums reflected that she had actually made some progress in her reading and writing. At the end of her first year at the school, Mali was still at the Preconventional stage in reading and writing. By the end of the second year, she was at the Emerging stage in reading and at the Developing stage in writing. Mali's progress was extremely slow and her teachers were concerned about this child. Mali identified with Trisha, the struggling reader in Patricia Polacco's picture book, *Thank You, Mr. Falker* (1998). Despite her difficulties, Mali enjoyed school and liked to play with other girls.

Mali's listening and speaking skills progressed more quickly than her reading and writing. She began third grade at the New to English stage on the EAL continuum and after two years, she was at the Becoming Familiar stage. For students like Mali who have not learned to read in their home language, literacy acquisition often moves slowly until students are at the Becoming Fluent stage as speakers and listeners (Peregoy and Boyle, 1997b). It is almost as if they have to sink their roots into the language before they are ready to blossom as readers and writers. They need to develop a solid core of English words in order to "break the code." Mali's cognitive level of understanding was significantly less than that of her peers. There were several basic concepts she did not understand, even in her own language. For example, she did not understand the concept of "middle" in either English or Thai. Many experts believe that for a subject area concept to truly "take root," it must be taught in both languages. We sometimes underestimate the obstacles and challenges that confront some second language learners.

The classroom teachers were initially frustrated that Mali's skills were so far below those of her peers. Once she was assessed using the continuum, however, they were able to identify what this young girl could do and to plan instruction around her needs. She needed many opportunities to listen to stories read aloud. She was beginning to use phonics cues but needed support to learn how to use meaning and picture cues to piece together a story. As a writer, she was between the Emerging and Developing stages and had just begun to take risks, writing about her observations and experiences using invented spelling. She needed guidance on how to brainstorm and find topics about which she could write, as well as ample time to put her ideas on paper using invented spelling. Mali also needed encouragement and praise to develop her confidence as a reader and writer. The continuums allowed her classroom teacher to see her abilities more clearly and to identify and celebrate progress.

Case Study: Jonas

Jonas was also a third-grade student in Cecilia's program. Originally from Norway, Jonas started third grade speaking virtually no English except simple greetings. However, Jonas had excellent decoding skills in Norwegian when he arrived at the school. Because he was literate in his home language (which was close to English phonetically and grammatically), Jonas didn't have to learn basic reading concepts and skills. The leap he had to make in order to become a reader in English was a relatively small one. Once he learned the English letter sounds and acquired a basic oral vocabulary, he began to read some repetitive pattern books and beginning early readers.

Lynne Teter, his classroom teacher, and Cecilia were able to mark a few descriptors at the Developing and Beginning stages on the Reading continuum in November. By January, they were able to check off most of the descriptors in both stages. Jonas learned English quickly and by the end of the year, he was at the Expanding stage as a reader. His progress was similar in writing. In November, Jonas could demonstrate approximately two-thirds of the descriptors at the Beginning stage in writing. By January, his teachers marked the remaining descriptors in the Beginning stage and a few at the Expanding level. Jonas was performing at grade level by the end of the year as a strong Expanding writer. Cecilia believes that the success Jonas experienced was partly due to the fact that he was already literate in Norwegian and partly due to the fact that he received ESL/EAL support in the classroom.

Both of his parents are Norwegian and they speak only Norwegian at home. In addition, they both speak English well and encouraged Jonas to learn English. When Jonas first came to the school, he refused to speak English at all and would only play with one other Norwegian child so that he wouldn't have to speak English. His father was concerned and at first and tried to force him to speak English. Lynne and Cecilia reassured his father that a silent period was normal at first (Krashen, 1981) and that he would soon begin experimenting with his new language. This indeed proved to be true. His parents invited English-speaking friends to their house and provided opportunities for Jonas to be exposed to English without neglecting his home language. His parents also demonstrated support by attending Jonas' school activities and plays. He began the school year at the New to English stage, but by January, he was already at the Becoming Competent level. By the end of the year, Jonas was at the beginning of the Becoming Fluent stage, spoke English with confidence at school, and had many English-speaking friends. Jonas also had a great deal of support at home where he was praised for his success and encouraged to improve his English.

Unlike Mali, Jonas received ESL/EAL support in his classroom. Cecilia and the classroom teacher, Lynne, planned the morning language arts lesson together, incorporating activities that were helpful to all students but would particularly benefit the ESL students like Jonas. For example, Cecilia and Lynne would read the students' journals and identify phonemes that the EAL students found difficult. When the class played a weekly *Bingo* game with new vocabulary, the teachers incorporated words with those challenging phonemes and pointed out the sounds to the whole class, knowing that this would particularly benefit the EAL students in the room. When teaching students how to brainstorm ideas for writing, one of the strategies the teachers shared was to sketch their ideas, which again was particularly beneficial for students just learning English. For literature circles, Cecilia and Lynne would include some easier books in the choices and guide the EAL students toward those books. The EAL students were then paired with more capable readers so that part of the story could be read to them.

The teachers used modeling and role playing to demonstrate how to include quiet students in literature discussions. As the students responded to the text in their response journals, Cecilia provided individual support for Jonas and the other EAL students in the room. Cecilia notes, "I strongly believe that all of this contributed to how Jonas felt a part of the class from the beginning and to his willingness to participate in class even with his limited English. After only a few months, his oral language had progressed tremendously, he was able to understand more and more of what he read, and he began to participate in literature discussions." His oral language had to reach a level of proficiency before his reading and writing skills could develop (Peregoy and Boyle, 1997b). Both teachers believe their integrated program and team teaching contributed strongly to the speed at which Jonas and others in his class learned English. When students receive EAL support in the classroom, they feel part of the community of learners and have more opportunities to interact with peers and to benefit from curricular activities.

Factors that Influence Language Acquisition

As you can see from these two very different examples, there are many factors that influence how quickly a student absorbs a new language. Some learners internalize a new language quickly, while others take more time to become fluent. What do we know from research about learning a new language? Here are some of the factors that influence how quickly a student learns a new language:

Degree of Immersion and Interaction

Parental attitude toward the new culture may affect the amount of social interaction families provide for their children. For example, some cultures may not allow teenage children much freedom to mix with their peers, while imposing little or no restrictions on younger children. Most likely, younger children who are exposed to more playing time with their friends will have more authentic practice using their new language and will pick it up more quickly. For instance, Jonas played with English-speaking children outside of school, because his parents recognized how much this social interaction helped him learn a new language. On the other hand, Mali had very little time for playing with other children, since much of her time after school was spent helping her mother do chores and clean the house.

Studies have also shown that language acquisition occurs over time and that true bilingual immersion has the greatest long-term effect. Students who learn academic content in both languages through elementary school have the greatest gains by the end of high school (Thomas and Collier, 1995). The least effective programs are the pullout ESL programs most often found in schools in the United States (Collier and Thomas, 1997). Yet in states like California, legislation has removed bilingual education from many schools where the primary language for the majority of students is Spanish. Decisions like this fly in the face of both research and our experience as educators. What can you do? In *Literacy at the Crossroads* (1996), Regie Routman urges us to wield our votes carefully and to speak out against unfair and unsound practices. We also need to educate our families and communities about second language acquisition.

Age

Age is also a factor in language acquisition at school. In the primary grades, students come into language-rich classrooms where all children are learning language and concepts together in a non-threatening environment. Learning alongside their native English-speaking peers provides many natural opportunities to try speaking English – opportunities that are lost when students are pulled out of their classrooms. On the other hand, older learners, especially in middle school and high school, have to bridge a larger gap before they can function successfully in school (Peregoy and Boyle, 1997b) and inclusion models become more challenging.

Age also affects learners' ability to pronounce and use their new language competently. In most cases, children who begin to learn a new language before puberty are far more likely to achieve a true native-like accent. Children who begin learning a second language when they are 15 or younger are also more apt to be as competent in grammar as their native counterparts (Ellis, 1996).

Family Literacy Level and Expectations

In cases where home literacy level is low, some parents can fail to see the need for children to become proficient in reading and writing. Sometimes the situation may be the reverse, where parents do not want their children to experience the barriers they have experienced and encourage their children to study and do well in school. Literate parents are more capable of helping their children with schoolwork. For example, his parents often helped Jonas with homework and made time to read to him in both English and Norwegian. They recognized that this support would accelerate his English language learning and allow Jonas to be more successful in school. Mali's mother tried to help, but her lack of native language literacy skills and her inability to speak English meant that her help with schoolwork was minimal. She felt that keeping a clean house was important, so Mali's time after school was primarily spent doing chores.

Personality and Motivation

People with out-going personalities will most likely develop their oral language skills in English faster than a shy person will. They are often more willing to take risks and to try to use their limited language skills. In Mali's case, she was very shy and her silent period lasted at least a year and a half, especially in her regular classroom. Jonas was more eager to become part of the class and began speaking English very quickly, even when his vocabulary was still quite limited.

It's also worth noting that ESL/EAL students often make a dramatic "leap" at some point, especially those who are reluctant to use their new language until it is "perfect." For instance, at Osaka International School in Japan, Meelad (Iranian) entered school in first grade but never said a word in English for eight months, although he had the skills. He understood and could read (one-on-one, very quietly, or preferably, in private). When he did begin to speak in April, his oral and written language came in full sentences that were grammatically correct. His teacher, Cynthia Ruptic, said the same thing occurred with a third grader, Solene from France. She came to OIS in September with no English and cried continuously for a month. Suddenly, in October, she began writing in English and spoken English soon followed. By December, she was quite fluent. She did not even lose her newly acquired English during the three week winter break spent in France.

Cultural Background

Jonas came from a Norwegian culture where children in school are encouraged to speak up and are not reprimanded for giving the "wrong answer." Mali came from the Thai school system where she had to stand up and read in front of the class. She was hit with a ruler every time she made a mistake, which in Mali's case was quite often. In her school culture, children were not asked to give their opinions about what was read or presented. They were not encouraged to speak as freely as children in Scandinavian schools. Although this is a general statement about different school cultures and much will depend on the individual school and teacher, it is an important factor for teachers who work with students from other countries to consider. There is a cultural adjustment children go through in moving from one country's school system to another. As teachers, we must take this period of adjustment into account and help students learn the new expectations in a way that will minimize trauma and feelings of inadequacy.

Language Similarities and Differences

Norwegian and English are much more similar than English and Thai. For Jonas, understanding the different parts of speech and syntax helped him make the connection between his native language and English. Mali, however, had to learn many new rules and grammatical structures that do not exist in the Thai language, such as the use of articles. In addition, Thai and English have significant phonological differences. In English, a different tone or pitch indicates differences in emotion or a question versus a statement. In Thai, a difference in tone can signal a whole new word and change the meaning completely. The similarity of the grammatical structures, encoding system, and word order between students' native language and the new language will have a significant impact on how quickly they learn English.

Learning Disabilities

Students with learning disabilities will no doubt have more challenges learning a new language, particularly as they begin to read and write. According to a special education teacher at Mali's school, she probably had some learning disabilities and significant problems with short and long term memory. It's very difficult to assess ESL/EAL students for learning disabilities, since they should be tested in their native language, which is often impossible in school settings. Jonas, on the other hand, did not have any learning disabilities. Once he overcame the language barrier, he was able to fully benefit from the curriculum.

Teacher Expectations

From the very beginning, Jonas was expected to participate in class. Cecilia and Lynne took into consideration his language limitations and adapted activities as much as possible, but never used his limited English as an excuse not to participate. His teachers were always able to find a level at which he could take part in class, which did take time and planning. The benefit was that Jonas and the other EAL/ESL students felt a part of the group and understood that they were expected to do their best, just like their English-speaking peers. Mali's teachers found it difficult to adapt classroom activities because the gap between her language and skills and those of her peers was several years. Despite parent and high school volunteers and a modified curriculum, it was difficult to meet Mali's needs in the classroom. Classroom teachers must devote a significant amount of time to adapt activities and the curriculum to meet the needs of students like Mali. Teachers who have additional planning time and who can use the support and expertise of EAL/ESL teachers like Cecilia are more able to meet the needs of all the students in their classrooms. Even within the same school, classroom teachers utilized the expertise and time of the EAL/ESL support staff in different ways. Some teachers preferred to have Cecilia pull the EAL students out of the classroom for small group instruction. Others, like Lynne, viewed Cecilia as a team teacher and intentionally set aside time to plan together.

Using the Continuum

It is important to keep in mind that the continuum stages pertain to language acquisition skills and are not age specific. The EAL continuum should apply to anyone learning English at any age. Therefore, when you look at the descriptors for each stage, the behaviors must be viewed through a developmental lens. For instance, the skills of a six-year-old student who "communicates competently in social and academic settings" will be quite different from the behaviors of a high school student. A good way to determine expectations would be to compare the learner to his or her native English-speaking peers. It's also important to realize that no child's behaviors fall neatly into one stage. Most students demonstrate behaviors in two or even three adjacent continuum stages.

We also discussed the concept of correct pronunciation at great length as we created and revised the EAL continuum. In the end, we decided to use the term "clearly" to indicate pronunciation that can be understood. We did this purposely in order to avoid an emphasis on only one form of pronunciation (e.g., American, British, or Australian) or dialect.

The EAL continuum was created originally for schools where English is the language of instruction, with additional instruction provided for students whose native language is not English. We wonder if the same continuum could be used in other language classes, such as Spanish, French, or Arabic. Of course, minor changes might have to be made, based on the characteristics and grammar of a specific language, but the same developmental progression should still apply. We would be very interested to know if the Listening/Speaking continuum would be useful for assessing students learning any new language. In that case, we would want to re-name it as the Additional Language Listening/Speaking continuum.

EAL Continuum, Student Self-Evaluation Continuum, Narrative Portraits, and Glossary

At the end of this chapter and on the CD-ROM, you will find the EAL Listening/Speaking Continuum. We also created the student self-evaluation version of the EAL continuum. Of course, students will probably not be able to read the descriptors until they are at the Becoming Competent or Becoming Fluent stage. You could, however, use the student version with children in the last three stages of the EAL continuum, with older students, or even with families. If you do plan to use the EAL continuum with students, you might consider translating it into the child's native language and explaining the descriptors in a one-to-one setting. For instance, the French teachers at the International School of Brussels in Belgium are currently translating the EAL continuum into French. As I discovered with the Spanish translation of the reading/writing continuums, anyone who provides a translation must not only be fluent in both languages, but be able to translate terminology specific to education. Please send any translations to me through Christopher-Gordon Publishers so that I can share them with other teachers whose students and families do not speak English.

We also developed Narrative Portraits in which students at each stage of the EAL continuum are described in general terms. You may want to include the Narrative Portraits in an EAL Parent Handbook, on a web site, or pass them out at parent conferences. We also developed a Glossary of the terms used in the EAL continuum. Classroom teachers and EAL support staff may want to keep copies of the EAL continuums and support documents in a Continuum Notebook or Assessment Tools Notebook.

Assessment Tools

As you use the EAL continuum, you should collect evidence using a variety of assessment tools. Although you probably have several assessment tools that you already find useful, you may also want to use or adapt some of the forms and techniques described in Chapter 5. Samples of the Anecdotal Notes Focus Questions and Assessment Checklists (DC Form 9.1–9.6) are included in this chapter and on the CD-ROM. In the next section, you will find a list of some of the assessment tools Anna Marie, Kathryn, and Cecilia use in their EAL/ESL classrooms to collect information about their students. These teachers stress that no one has time to use all of these assessment ideas. You may already use one or two of these and may want to try using one or two new ideas. The following chart shows how often the assessment information is collected.

Assessment Tool	2–3 Times Year	3–4 Times Year	Weekly or Ongoing
Taped Journals			X
Taped Retelling	X		
Language Samples			X
Videotape		X	
Informal Student Interview	X		
SOLOM	X		
Listening Comprehension	X		
Oral Language Observation Chart		X	
Barrier Game		X	
Anecdotal Notes/Observation			X
Performance Checklists	X		

Assessment Tool Directions

1. Taped journals: Each child receives a cassette on which the teacher has recorded a welcoming message. The child then responds to the message, starting an ongoing dialogue between the child and teacher. The message can be taped at home or at school.
2. Taped retelling of a story: The student reads a story, then retells it into a tape recorder. This can be done individually or as a group activity. It can be a simple retelling or an invented story based on a familiar tale.
3. Language samples: While children are talking, the teacher focuses on one child, writing down the actual words the child says. The language sample can also be tape recorded, then transcribed. This sample can help the teacher analyze the child's oral language using the EAL continuum.
4. Videotapes: Each child has his or her own videotape. The children can be videotaped during group discussions and oral presentations through-

out the year in order to show growth. The videotape can be helpful in filling out the EAL continuum.

5. Informal student interviews: The teacher records observations about the student's language abilities during a one-to-one conversation. Teachers can focus on one or two language skills or continuum strands (e.g., Oral Expression).

6. SOLOM (Student Oral Language Observation Matrix): Observation matrix published by the California State Department of Education (see Krashen, 1981). This tool also appears in *Reading, Writing, and Learning in ESL* (Peregoy and Boyle, 1997b).

7. Listening comprehension assessment: A listening comprehension exercise in which students listen to the teacher or a tape, then are given a task in order to show their listening/comprehension skills.

8. Oral language observation chart: A form to record a running record of an entire interaction with one student, focusing on language forms and functions (Peregoy and Boyle, 1997b).

9. Barrier game: Two students who are separated by a barrier communicate with each other to perform a task (e.g., spot the difference between two pictures or give instructions about what to draw). This activity can be used to assess whether or not students can ask questions properly, follow instructions, or use subject area language (Gibbons, 1998).

10. Classroom observations and anecdotal notes: The EAL Anecdotal Notes Focus Questions can provide a framework for recording observations about students during class. The focus questions are based on the EAL Listening/Speaking continuum.

11. Performance checklists: Checklists based on the Listening/Speaking EAL continuum to use during classroom observations of students.

Sharing the EAL Continuum with Families

As the teachers at these three schools developed the EAL continuum, they felt it was essential to share this information with families at the beginning of the school year. They wanted parents to understand the developmental progression of second language acquisition, as well as the purpose for using the continuums. Sandi Detwiler, an ESL teacher at the International School in Dhaka, Bangladesh, wrote about the power of using the reading, writing, and EAL continuums with families:

> For parent conferences in October, I highlighted various descriptors that described each child's consistent performance. Then I went back with a different color highlighter in December in preparation for report cards. Wow! What a useful tool to clearly and explicitly show my students' proficiencies and where they need to improve. I shared my markings on the three continuums with the classroom teachers when we conferred about students. They, too, commented on the depth of information the continuums offer. As a bonus, the descriptors are written in language that can be easily understood by parents. Looking at the continuums made my ESL students' progress evident to all.

Teachers at Dhahran Academy in Saudi Arabia use the continuums in a similar way. In addition, the reading and writing continuums, Narrative Portraits, Glossary, and Family Support documents are all included in a Parent Handbook, as described in Chapter 8. In the future, they plan to include the EAL Listening/Speaking continuum as well. The EAL Family Support document can be found at the end of this chapter and on the CD-ROM.

At Open House and during conferences, teachers refer to each of these pieces in the Parent Handbook. Cecilia found that families with students who were learning English appreciated the very concrete suggestions in the Family Support document about what they could do at home to support their child's next steps as learners. For instance, Elsa, a mother from Belgium, described how the EAL continuum had provided helpful information for their family:

> I have two daughters in the ESL program, one in fourth grade and one in second grade. As parents, we felt our oldest daughter was progressing well in English. She is an avid reader and will talk more about what she is doing and learning. But we were concerned about our youngest daughter. When we saw the continuums, we were surprised to discover that both girls were at approximately the same stage. We then realized how well our youngest daughter was doing. The continuum clearly showed growth which we would not have seen otherwise. Only then did we realize how well she was doing as an English language learner.

We are sharing the EAL continuum and support pieces with you with the hope that you will try them in your classroom and send us your feedback. What questions do you have? What changes would you make? What else is needed? You may want to provide translations of the EAL continuum and Family Support documents for parents who do not speak English. Our hope is that you will adapt these documents to match your particular setting and group of students. Keep in mind that the Family Support section may include suggestions that are inappropriate for some cultures or which present challenges for low-income or non-literate families. Feel free to adapt the Family Support ideas to best meet the needs of your particular population. Many of the suggestions assume that parents will communicate with their children in their home language and not in English. Parents with limited English can still provide opportunities for their children to hear English through tapes, music, television, computer games, and by providing opportunities for their children to play with English-speaking friends. These support pieces are intended to be a starting point for professional conversations and communication between teachers and families.

Staff Development

Ask each ESL/EAL teacher to choose two students at different levels of English proficiency. Collect samples of student writing, reading, and oral language from both their ESL/EAL class and from the child's regular classroom. Videotape the child speaking in several contexts (on the playground, reading, sharing information in class, and telling a story). Use the samples and videotapes to complete the EAL continuum together for each student (with parent permission). Ask the regular classroom teacher to fill out the EAL continuum, then discuss your perceptions. How are they the same or different? What might account for the differences?

Plan an inservice for classroom teachers to develop their awareness and improve their skills in working with EAL/ESL learners in their classrooms. In small grade-level groups, talk about each of the descriptors. When questions arise, you may want to use the EAL Anecdotal Notes Focus Questions and checklists for further observations. Share your findings about the students and their families with their classroom teachers. Discuss your general insights with the rest of the staff. Many of the Family Support suggestions may be adaptable to the classroom setting.

Create a videotape of one child at each of the six stages of the EAL/ESL continuum. This video could be used for staff development and parent education. Conversations about the continuum will lead naturally into discussions about appropriate and effective teaching techniques at each stage.

Design a series of one-hour Family Nights for EAL parents. You might want to begin with a continuum activity. Ask teachers and parents to line up (from left to right) according to their fluency in French, Spanish, English, and a few other languages. You can also make a continuum with other categories, such as cooking, mechanical abilities, singing, or reading maps. This activity provides a helpful introduction to the concept of continuums. Ask parents who speak other languages to translate the word "continuum" into their native language and write the translations on a chart. If there are several EAL/ESL teachers, you could each be responsible for describing a few stages, along with examples of how families can support learners at different stages of second language acquisition.

Create an EAL Parent Handbook. The EAL continuums, the Narrative Portraits, and the Family Support documents could be included in this EAL Parent Handbook and distributed when new students enter the program or at a parent workshop.

English as an Additional Language (EAL) Listening & Speaking Continuum

New to English

- 👂 Listens attentively to an English speaker with guidance.
- 👂 Follows one-step directions.
- 👂 Uses context cues to respond appropriately to classroom routines.
- 🍎 Responds to greetings with nods and gestures.
- 🍎 Responds to simple questions with guidance.
- 🍎 Expresses needs in English with single words and gestures.
- 🍎 Responds during classroom discussions with nods and gestures.
- 🍎 Participates non-verbally in the classroom.
- 📖 Names simple objects with guidance.
- ◆ Repeats English words and phrases with guidance.
- ◆ Echoes single words and/or short phrases.
- ☑ Produces single words and/or stock phrases with guidance.
- ☺ Demonstrates enthusiasm about learning English.

Early Acquisition

- 👂 Begins to follow illustrated stories and classroom instruction
- 👂 Follows two-step directions.
- 🍎 Responds to greetings with single words and/or phrases.
- 🍎 Begins to respond to simple questions with one-word answers.
- 🍎 Begins to express needs and give basic information (e.g., "I'm fine" and "this car").
- 🍎 Participates orally in classroom discussions with guidance.
- 📖 Uses some basic classroom vocabulary.
- 📖 Understands everyday classroom and subject area language with guidance.
- ◆ Begins to repeat new English words and phrases clearly.
- ☑ Begins to communicate using short phrases and simple language patterns, producing telegraphic sentences (e.g., "I want to go shop buy toy.").
- ☺ Practices English and tries new words and phrases.

Becoming Familiar

- 👂 Begins to listen attentively to an English speaker.
- 👂 Follows multi-step directions.
- 🍎 Begins to use English in social situations.
- 🍎 Responds to greetings with phrases.
- 🍎 Responds to simple questions with more than one-word answers.
- 🍎 Uses different language functions in discussions (e.g., predicting and describing) with guidance.
- 🍎 Participates in classroom discussions and offers opinions and feedback with guidance.
- 📖 Begins to understand classroom and subject area language.
- 📖 Begins to use expanding vocabulary that is less context-bound.
- ◆ Begins to speak English clearly.
- ☑ Communicates using short phrases and simple language patterns.
- ☑ Begins to use connected discourse (e.g., "Yesterday I go pool and I swam.").

Becoming Competent

- 👂 Begins to contribute to group discussions and offer opinions and/or feedback during discussions.
- 🍎 Paraphrases oral information with guidance.
- 🍎 Uses English in social situations.
- 🍎 Begins to respond to more complex questions.
- 🍎 Expresses needs and gives information independently.
- 🍎 Begins to ask questions to clarify content and meaning.
- 🍎 Begins to use more complex language functions (e.g., hypothesizing and reasoning) within an academic context.
- 📖 Begins to use an extensive vocabulary, using some abstract and specialized subject area words.
- 📖 Understands classroom and subject area language with repetition, rephrasing, or clarification.
- ◆ Speaks English clearly.
- ☑ Produces longer, more complex utterances using phrases, clauses, and sequence words (e.g., "next" and "then").
- ☑ Begins to use correct form when asking questions.
- ☑ Begins to use correct verb tense to express present, past, and future.
- ☺ Shows interest in improving language skills and accuracy.

Becoming Fluent

- 👂 Listens attentively to an English speaker.
- 👂 Listens to others and offers opinions and/or feedback.
- 🍎 Begins to paraphrase oral information.
- 🍎 Uses language appropriately across the curriculum for different purposes and audiences.
- 🍎 Responds to complex questions independently.
- 🍎 Asks questions to clarify content and meaning.
- 🍎 Develops awareness that there are appropriate forms and styles of language for different purposes and audiences.
- 🍎 Begins to speak with confidence in front of a group.
- 📖 Uses more extensive vocabulary, using abstract and specialized subject area words independently.
- 📖 Understands classroom and subject area language at nearly normal speed.
- ◆ Speaks English with near-native fluency; any hesitation does not interfere with communication.
- ◆ Begins to vary speech appropriately using intonation/ stress.
- ☑ Uses correct form when asking questions.
- ☺ Speaks confidently and uses new vocabulary flexibly.

Fluent

- 👂 Contributes to group discussion with ideas and appropriate suggestions.
- 👂 Paraphrases oral information independently.
- 🍎 Communicates competently in social and academic settings.
- 🍎 Participates and performs competently in all subject areas.
- 🍎 Employs a full range of language functions independently, using abstract and complex language to express ideas and opinions appropriate to age.
- 🍎 Speaks with confidence in front of a group.
- 📖 Understands a wide range of classroom and subject area language with native competence.
- 📖 Uses vocabulary approximating that of a native speaker.
- ◆ Speaks as fluently as a native speaker.
- ◆ Varies speech appropriately using intonation and stress independently.
- ☑ Uses a wide range of language patterns and complex compound tenses to create properly connected discourse (e.g., "Tomorrow I will be going on a long trip and I will see my good friend.").

👂 Listening and Comprehension   🍎 Oral Expression   📖 Vocabulary   ◆ Pronunciation and Fluency   ☑ Grammar   ☺ Attitude

English as an Additional Language (EAL) Listening & Speaking Continuum for Student Self-evaluation

New to English

- I can listen to someone speaking English when my teacher reminds me.
- I can do what my teacher tells me, one step at a time.
- I watch others to know what I'm supposed to do.
- I answer "hello" and "goodbye" by nodding and using my body.
- I can answer simple questions (like "How are you?").
- I ask for things I need with one word or I use my hands to show what I mean.
- I understand some of what people say but I use my body to answer.
- I understand what is happening in the classroom, but I can't use English words yet.
- I know the names of things we learned in class.
- I can repeat English words and short sentences with help from my teacher and friends.
- I can repeat English words when I hear them.
- I can speak some English with help.
- I like learning English.

Early Acquisition

- I enjoy stories in English if there are pictures that tell me what the words mean.
- I can do as my teacher tells me, two steps at a time.
- I can answer "hello" and "goodbye" with one or two words in English.
- I can use one word to answer questions.
- I can say more English words and can answer when someone talks to me (like "I'm fine" and "this car").
- When my teacher helps me, I can answer some questions in class.
- I can use some words I learned in class.
- When my teacher helps me, I can understand what goes on in class.
- Sometimes people can understand what I say in English.
- I can use simple sentences that people understand (like "Girl go shop buy toy.").
- I practice English and try new words and sentences.

Becoming Familiar

- I can pay attention when I listen to someone speaking English.
- I follow directions without help.
- I like to speak to others in English and ask questions.
- When people ask me questions, I can answer in English.
- I can answer questions with more than one word.
- I know what to say if my teacher asks me different types of questions (like, "What will happen if...?" or "What does it look like?").
- I usually understand what we are learning in class.
- I can talk about things that are not in the classroom.
- People usually understand me when I speak English.
- I use short and easy sentences when I talk.
- I can speak in sentences (e.g., "Yesterday I go pool and I swam.").

Becoming Competent

- I sometimes participate in discussions and say what I think.
- I can retell what someone says with my teacher's help.
- I like to speak in English and ask people questions.
- I can sometimes answer harder questions (like "Why do you think some parents don't let their kids have pets?").
- I can easily ask for things and give information.
- I sometimes ask questions when I don't understand.
- I can talk about what we are studying in class, sometimes saying what might happen and why.
- I can talk about feelings and use new words about what we are studying in class.
- I usually understand what we are learning, but sometimes need some help or explanations.
- I speak English clearly and others understand me.
- I use longer sentences and connecting words (like "next" and "then").
- I usually ask questions in the right way.
- I can speak using the present, past, and future verb tenses.
- I want to speak better English so people can understand me more easily.

Becoming Fluent

- I can pay attention to someone speaking English.
- I listen to others and share my ideas and opinions.
- I can usually retell what someone else has said.
- I use English in different subject areas for different reasons (such as to predict or explain).
- I can answer difficult questions (such as, "Why will the rock sink if I throw it in a bucket of water?").
- I ask questions when I don't understand something.
- I know how to speak in different ways to different people (such as to other kids vs. a report or to adults).
- I sometimes speak in front of a group without getting nervous.
- I can talk about feelings and use new words about what we are studying in class.
- I understand what we are learning in class in English.
- I speak English almost as easily as my home language.
- I usually change my voice when I ask questions or to show excitement.
- I ask questions the right way.
- I speak with confidence and try new words and phrases.

Fluent

- During discussions, I listen to others, share my ideas, and make good suggestions.
- I can retell what someone has said, including the most important information and some details.
- I speak English fluently in school and outside of school.
- I can participate and do my work in English in all my classes.
- I use English for many reasons (to tell, predict, explain) in all subjects and I can talk about feelings and ideas.
- I feel confident when I speak in front of a group in English.
- I understand what is said in all my classes as well as my English-speaking classmates.
- I use big words just like my English-speaking friends.
- I speak English as easily as I speak my home language.
- I speak with expression.
- I use correct grammar and tenses (e.g., "Tomorrow I will be going on a long trip and I will see my good friend.").

Legend: Listening and Comprehension · Oral Expression · Vocabulary · Pronunciation and Fluency · Grammar · Attitude

Narrative Portraits of EAL Speakers and Listeners

Learners New to English

- Listens attentively to an English speaker with guidance.
- Follows one-step directions.
- Uses context cues to respond appropriately to classroom routines.
- Responds to greetings with nods and gestures.
- Responds to simple questions with guidance.
- Expresses needs in English with single words and gestures.
- Responds during classroom discussions with nods and gestures.
- Participates non-verbally in the classroom.
- Names simple objects with guidance.
- Repeats English words and phrases with guidance.
- Echoes single words and/or short phrases.
- Produces single words and/or stock phrases with guidance.
- Demonstrates enthusiasm about learning English.

It is important for students' cognitive and emotional growth that they continue to communicate freely in their native language as they learn English. Learners usually experience a silent period while they build up competence in the second language. Although they may not be speaking in English, they are building up a core vocabulary and internally constructing rules about how English works. Students at this stage are able to follow one-step directions that have been clearly demonstrated. Learners often watch carefully what others are doing. They are often quite proud and excited to say one-word utterances on their own.

These learners may use single words or simple phrases to communicate, such as "Finished" to show they have completed a task, or "Me go?" to ask permission to leave. They most likely use some non-verbal gestures to indicate meaning, particularly for likes and dislikes, fulfillment of personal needs, and in response to social questions. For example, children who want paper or a crayon may point to themselves and then to the item they want. Students begin to label objects and describe simple actions. These learners may echo single words or short phrases as they learn to pronounce new words. Some children play with sounds in English that may sound "fun" or strange. This is a period of absorbing and exploring a new language. Learners are often enthusiastic about the prospect of learning a new language.

Early Acquisition

- Begins to follow illustrated stories and classroom instruction.
- Follows two-step directions.
- Responds to greetings with single words and/or phrases.
- Begins to respond to simple questions with one-word answers.
- Begins to express needs and give basic information (e.g., "I'm fine" and "this car").
- Participates orally in classroom discussions with guidance.

cont.

- Uses some basic classroom vocabulary.
- Understands everyday classroom and subject area language with guidance.
- Begins to repeat new English words and phrases clearly.
- Begins to communicate using short phrases and simple language patterns, producing telegraphic sentences (e.g., "I want to go shop buy toy.").
- Practices English and tries new words and phrases.

At this stage, learners are gaining more understanding of the English language. Although they may still be silent most of the time, they can concentrate on discussions for longer periods and can listen attentively to stories with supportive illustrations. They are able to follow two-step oral directions, classroom instructions, and simple conversations and stories. Students may be more apt to speak English in one-to-one and small group situations.

These students are able to demonstrate an understanding of classroom and simple subject-area vocabulary. They respond with English words and phrases to express needs, participate orally in class, and respond to social questions. As they speak, students may leave out non-essential words, such as articles and prepositions, and produce telegraphic sentences, such as, "Me go bike park." They begin to pronounce English words clearly and their use of vocabulary is expanding; however, their conversations are context bound and stated in present tense. Students begin to include simple adjectives and adverbs, such as "big," "red," "slow," and "fast." They respond to questions with one-word answers. Learners at this stage are absorbing a great deal of information about how English works. They need to be exposed to the new language as much as possible. Learners need time to experiment and take risks as they try new words and phrases in a stress-free environment. At this stage, students need encouragement and opportunities to communicate successfully in their new language.

Becoming Familiar

- Begins to listen attentively to an English speaker.
- Follows multi-step directions.
- Begins to use English in social situations.
- Responds to greetings with phrases.
- Responds to simple questions with more than one-word answers.
- Uses different language functions in discussions (e.g., predicting and describing) with guidance.
- Participates in classroom discussions and offers opinions and feedback with guidance.
- Begins to understand classroom and subject area language.
- Begins to use expanding vocabulary that is less context-bound.
- Begins to speak English clearly.
- Communicates using short phrases and simple language patterns.
- Begins to use connected discourse (e.g., "Yesterday I go pool and I swam.").

Learners at this stage are becoming more confident with the English language. They can listen attentively to an English speaker for a longer period. They can answer questions and respond with some teacher support. These students begin to anticipate their turn to speak in a group. They are able to concentrate for longer periods because they understand more of the discussion. At this stage, learners are more interested in communicating meaning than in "correctness."

At the Becoming Familiar stage, students begin to participate in classroom discussions, using a wider range of language functions for different purposes. They begin to ask questions. Students still use short phrases and simple language patterns, but they are beginning to use more connected speech as they expand their vocabulary. They begin to use different verb tenses and modifiers, such as adjectives and adverbs. Students begin to speak English clearly and use their restricted vocabulary creatively to communicate meaning. They take more risks as they begin to communicate in English with others.

If learners have experienced success and feel secure in their attempts to communicate, they will continue to develop their new skills. However, if their success has been limited or if they experience ridicule or teasing, they may show signs of resistance, frustration, or a lack of interest. These students sometimes adopt an "I don't care" attitude. Learners at this stage are vulnerable, and it is important to create a climate for risk-taking and experimentation. It is also important at this stage to praise early attempts at communication and to celebrate growth.

Becoming Competent

- Begins to contribute to group discussions and to offer opinions and/or feedback during discussions.
- Paraphrases oral information with guidance.
- Uses English in social situations.
- Begins to respond to more complex questions.
- Expresses needs and gives information independently.
- Begins to ask questions to clarify content and meaning.
- Begins to use more complex language functions (e.g., hypothesizing and reasoning) within an academic context.
- Begins to use an extensive vocabulary, using some abstract and specialized subject area words.
- Understands classroom and subject area language with repetition, rephrasing, or clarification.
- Speaks English clearly.
- Produces longer, more complex utterances using phrases, clauses, and sequence words (e.g., "next" and "then").
- Begins to use correct form when asking questions.
- Begins to use correct verb tense to express present, past, and future.
- Shows interest in improving language skills and accuracy.

At this stage, learners show greater confidence in using English in most social situations. They speak English clearly. Their increasing fluency, however, may mask the need for support in developing the academic vocabulary used for science investigations, mathematics, or historical research. Although their oral reading sounds fluent, they may still have a significant lag in comprehension. Students understand classroom and subject area language when it is simplified, repeated, paraphrased, or clarified. They begin to paraphrase and offer opinions or feedback during conversations.

Learners at this stage produce more complex sentences, using phrases, clauses, and sequence words, such as "then" and "after." They also begin to use present, past, and future tenses correctly. At this stage, learners use the English language in social situations, give information freely, and respond to more complex questions. Students begin to use a wider range of language for different purposes, such as predicting, describing, and hypothesizing. Students at this stage begin to use correct grammar as they express themselves.

Successful learners will continue to show an interest in improving their language skills and accuracy. Learners who are not as successful may demonstrate a lack of motivation and frustration in their attempts to move beyond this stage. Now that they have the basic skills, what learners need most at this stage is practice and support in developing academic vocabulary and an understanding of concepts. Students also need help in setting realistic goals, as they become increasingly competent in speaking English.

Becoming Fluent

- Listens attentively to an English speaker.
- Listens to others and offers opinions and/or feedback.
- Begins to paraphrase oral information.
- Uses language appropriately across the curriculum for different purposes and audiences.
- Responds to complex questions independently.
- Asks questions to clarify content and meaning.
- Develops awareness that there are appropriate forms and styles of language for different purposes and audiences.
- Begins to speak with confidence in front of a group.
- Uses more extensive vocabulary, using abstract and specialized subject area words independently.
- Understands classroom and subject area language at nearly normal speed.
- Speaks English with near-native fluency; any hesitation does not interfere with communication.
- Begins to vary speech appropriately using intonation/ stress.
- Uses correct form when asking questions.
- Speaks confidently and uses new vocabulary flexibly.

These learners are becoming much more confident with their new language. They can listen attentively to an English speaker for long periods. Their pronunciation can be very "native-like," especially if they are young children. At this stage, students begin to vary their speech with appropriate stress and intonation. Although their speech may be hesitant, they are easily understood. These learners can understand classroom discussions and instruction in different subject areas, even when spoken at nearly normal speed. They use specialized vocabulary, such as mathematical terms, as well as abstract concepts like "greed" or "empathy." Students can paraphrase and offer opinions with more confidence. At this stage, some children may be willing to interpret for their parents or to teach them English.

These students may begin to speak with confidence in front of a group. They use language appropriately across the curriculum. Learners are aware of appropriate forms and styles of language for different purposes, such as varying an oral presentation for a particular audience. They continue to use a wide range of language for different purposes, such as hypothesizing in science. Students begin to use compound verb tenses, simple modifiers, and conjunctions, (such as, *"Tomorrow I will make a big trip and see my friend."*). They use the correct form when asking questions and use new vocabulary flexibly (e.g., *"Can you pass me the water holder?"* when they can't think of the word *"pitcher"*). As these students become more fluent, they are able to express themselves clearly and accurately in most social and academic situations. They may experiment with new vocabulary and communicate with confidence in English.

Fluent

- Contributes to group discussion with ideas and appropriate suggestions.
- Paraphrases oral information independently.
- Communicates competently in social and academic settings.
- Participates and performs competently in all subject areas.
- Employs a full range of language functions independently, using abstract and complex language to express ideas and opinions appropriate to age.
- Speaks with confidence in front of a group.
- Understands a wide range of classroom and subject area language with native competence.
- Uses vocabulary approximating that of a native speaker.
- Speaks as fluently as a native speaker.
- Varies speech appropriately using intonation and stress independently.
- Uses a wide range of language patterns and complex compound tenses to create properly connected discourse (e.g., "Tomorrow I will be going on a long trip and I will see my good friend.").

Students at this stage are almost as fluent as native speakers. They understand a wide range of classroom and subject area language. Their vocabulary approximates that of a native speaker. Variations in pronunciation do not interfere with communication. However, these learners may continue to struggle with idiomatic expressions and figurative language, such as *"It's raining cats and dogs"* and they continue to benefit from vocabulary development activities. Fluent speakers contribute to group discussions with relevant ideas and suggestions, and can paraphrase oral information accurately. Students speak confidently in front of a group, in conversations, and in collaboration with English-speaking peers.

These learners use a full range of language patterns, including grammatically correct compound verb tenses, modifiers, and conjunctions (e.g., *"Tomorrow I'm going on a long trip and I'll get to see my good friend."*). They ask questions to clarify content and meaning in classroom and social settings. These learners are able to enrich their vocabulary by using sources such as a thesaurus, dictionary, newspaper, or magazine. They may switch between languages with ease. Although reading and writing in English may be more limited than their oral skills, their spoken English approximates that of native English speakers.

EAL Listening and Speaking Continuum Glossary

abstract words: words describing a quality or intangible concept (e.g., vocabulary dealing with hope, love, or evil).

academic setting: classroom environment where learning takes place.

begins to: indicates the first steps students take as they perform an activity or task on their own. Students still need help from an adult or peer. They may demonstrate a strategy some of the time, but not yet consistently.

classroom language: vocabulary related to school routines (e.g., where things are located, how to put materials away, when to line up for lunch).

clause: a group of related words that has both a subject and a predicate. A clause may or may not indicate a complete thought (e.g., *"While the sun is shining,"* is an incomplete thought. On the other hand, *"The sun is shining."* is a complete thought.).

clearly: pronunciation that is easy to understand but not necessarily like that of a native speaker.

competently: adequately or correctly.

complex questions: open-ended questions that require the listener to draw upon prior knowledge.

compound verb tenses: verb tenses that are made up of more than one word. For example, *"I **have found** a pencil."*

conjunctions: words used to connect words, phrases, or sentences (e.g., "and," "or," and "but").

connected discourse: coherent and fluent speech that includes different verb tenses, modifiers, and conjunctions (e.g., *"Yesterday I went to the mall and I bought red shoes."* as opposed to *"Yesterday I go mall. I shoes buy."*).

context-bound: vocabulary that deals with concrete objects or the present situation (e.g., words used to describe a photograph that is in front of a student).

context cues: information available to the listener by hearing key words, looking at pictures or signs, observing the surrounding environment, or watching people (their actions, body language, or gestures) that helps the listener make meaning.

EAL: English as an Additional Language.

EFL: English as a Foreign Language.

ELL: English Language Learner.

ESL: English as a Second Language.

ESOL: English to Speakers of Other Languages.

echo: to repeat or imitate what someone else says.

feedback: to make a comment or give a suggestion or opinion about what someone has said. Also to accept or receive suggestions from others.

fluency: ability to communicate easily in a smooth and accurate manner.

gestures: body language used to help communicate (e.g., a nod of the head or shrug of the shoulders).

home language: the language or languages a learner speaks with his or her family at home (e.g., the learner may speak Arabic with her parents and grandparents). Also referred to as "native language," "first language," or the "mother tongue."

hypothesize: making an informed guess about what will happen next and providing a rationale.

intonation: the manner of pronouncing words or speaking, especially with regard to the rise and fall of the pitch of the voice.

language functions: purposes for using language, such as describing, predicting, reasoning, questioning, narrating, and comparing (e.g., *"This apple is bigger than the pear."* [comparing] or *"We added sodium carbonate to the vinegar."* [reporting]).

language pattern: expressions or formulaic speech that language learners acquire in "chunks" or phrases rather than as separate words. These expressions are learned as phrases with an open slot. For example, after learning the phrase, "Can I have a ___?" as a whole, learners can "fill in the blank" with the appropriate missing word.

modifier: a word, phrase, or clause that limits the meaning of another word or group of words (e.g., *"A red umbrella"* or *"The man who walked down the hill slowly is my uncle."*).

native language: see "home language."

paraphrase: to re-state what someone has said using different words.

phrase: a group of related words which lacks either a subject, a verb, or both (e.g., *"this girl's book," "running full speed,"* or *"through the house"*).

predict: in relation to language function, to use an appropriate grammatical structure when stating a possible outcome (e.g., *"The water will turn cloudy."*).

prior knowledge: information, ideas, and concepts based on previous life experiences that learners bring with them to the classroom.

pronunciation: the way in which a person utters or articulates the sounds of letters and words in a language.

reason: to draw conclusions or inferences from facts or premises.

scaffolding: in education, the gradual withdrawing of adult assistance and support as students are able to accomplish a task more independently.

sequence words: words that help connect speech in a logical manner (e.g., *"next," "then,"* and *"finally,"* or *"first, second, third"*).

simple questions: questions that require the student to recall and process a piece of information and which require a *"yes"* or *"no"* answer or short response (e.g., *"Is the girl going to fall?"* or *"What color is her dress?"*).

stock phrases: commonly used phrases that are learned as a complete chunk (e.g., *"Good morning,"* *"Thank you,"* and *"I've finished."*).

stress: the relative loudness in the pronunciation of syllables or words in a sentence.

subject area language: vocabulary related to a specific topic (dinosaurs) or subject (science or math).

telegraphic sentences: sentences that omit non-essential words, as in a telegraph message (e.g., *"I go mall yesterday."*).

utterance: a spoken word or words.

verb tense: all verb tenses, such as present, past, and future.

with guidance: the student performs an activity or task with direction or support from a teacher, another adult, or peer. Scaffolding (support) is gradually withdrawn, as the student becomes more independent. Students at this level still need adult help most of the time.

EAL Anecdotal Notes Focus Questions

🜂 Listening and Understanding
1. Is the student able to follow directions? (one-step, two-step, multi-step?)
2. Does the student listen attentively to an English speaker?
3. Does the student listen to others in class?
4. Is the student able to follow classroom routines?
5. Is the student able to follow illustrated stories?
6. Is the student able to follow classroom instruction?
7. Is the student able to paraphrase oral information?
8. Is the student able to ask questions or clarify content or meaning?

🜂 Oral Expression
1. How does the student respond to greetings? (nods/gestures? one word? phrase?)
2. How does the student respond to simple questions? (gestures? one word? phrases?)
3. How does the student respond to complex questions?
4. Is the student able to express needs?
5. Does the student use English in social situations?
6. Is the student able to give basic information?
7. Does the student participate in classroom discussions?
8. Is the student able to offer opinions and feedback? state ideas? make relevant suggestions?
9. Is the student able to use a variety of language functions in the classroom?
10. Does the student show confidence when speaking in front of the class?

📖 Vocabulary

1. Is the student able to name simple objects?
2. Does the student use basic classroom vocabulary?
3. Can the student understand subject area language?
4. Is the student's vocabulary expanding and becoming less context-bound?
5. Is the student able to use abstract and subject area words?
6. Does the student's vocabulary approximate that of a native speaker?

👄 Pronunciation and Fluency

1. Does the student echo words and phrases?
2. Does the student repeat words and phrases?
3. Can the student pronounce words clearly enough so others can understand?
4. Does the student speak English fluently enough so it does not interfere with communication?
5. Does the student speak English as fluently as a native speaker?
6. Does the student begin to vary intonation and stress when appropriate?

☑ Grammar

1. Does the student use simple words and stock phrases?
2. Does the student use short sentences and simple language patterns?
3. Does the student use phrases, clauses, and sequence words?
4. Does the student ask questions using the correct form?
5. Does the student use correct verb tenses (present, past, and future)?
6. Does the student use complex compound tenses?

☺ Attitude

1. Does the student show enthusiasm about learning English?
2. Does the student practice English and try new words and phrases?
3. Does the student show interest in improving his or her language skills and accuracy?
4. Does the student take risks and try new vocabulary?
5. Is the student confident when speaking in front of a group?
6. Does the student speak with confidence and use new vocabulary flexibly?

⟨ **Listening and Comprehension Checklist**

The student is able to ...	with guidance	begins to	independently
follow one-step directions			
follow two-step directions			
follow multi-step directions			
listen attentively to a speaker			
follow classroom routines			
follow classroom instruction			
follow illustrated stories			
paraphrase information			
ask questions to clarify meaning			
participate in group discussions			

Comments:

☑ **Grammar Checklist**

The student is able to . . .	with guidance	begins to	independently
respond to simple questions			
respond to complex questions			
ask simple questions			
ask complex questions			
ask questions to clarify meaning			
	nods and gestures	**yes/no or single words**	**phrases or sentences**
answers questions with			

Comments:

● Oral Expression Checklist

The student is able to . . .	gestures and single words	phrases	short sentences
express needs			
give information			
contribute to group discussions			
	with guidance	begins to	independently
listen to others			
offer feedback or opinions			
contribute ideas and relevant suggestions			
ask questions to clarify meaning			
show confidence speaking in front of a group			
respond to social greetings			
respond to questions			
initiate conversation			

Comments:

❦ Oral Expression (Language Functions) Checklist

The student is able to . . .	with guidance	begins to	independently
predict			
retell			
reason			
describe			
compare			
contrast			
persuade			
hypothesize			
summarize			
explain			
report			
narrate			
draw conclusions			

Comments:

📖 **Vocabulary Checklist**

The student is able to . . .	with guidance	begins to	independently
name simple objects			
understand classroom vocabulary			
use subject area language			
use abstract and subject area language			
use less context-bound vocabulary			
use new vocabulary flexibly			

Comments:

❧ Pronounciation/Fluency Checklist

The student is able to . . .	with guidance	begins to	independently
repeat words and phrases clearly			
speak English clearly enough for others to understand			
vary intonation and stress appropriately			
speak English as fluently as a native speaker			

Comments:

EAL Family Support

General Introduction to Parents

If your native language is not English, we hope you continue to speak and read to your child in your home language. Speaking in your native language will *not* make it more difficult for your child to learn English. In fact, an important part of language development is learning a first language well. Research shows that learners may be able to interact with peers and adults in a second language within six months to two years after arriving in a new country. However, it will take learners five or more years to meet the academic demands of school, both orally and in writing, at a level comparable to that of their peers. Furthermore, learners who have had no prior schooling and no primary language support can take as long as seven to ten years to demonstrate academic competence in a new language.

Speaking English might not be natural during your daily routine. If this is the case, you might want to set time aside to play games in English, such as *Bingo* with colors, numbers, or school vocabulary words. You can also designate a certain time each week for speaking English at home, such as Monday nights during dinner. It's important to also continue talking with your child about school in your native language to show that you value their efforts and what they are learning.

If you speak English, you can help by explaining concepts in your native language. For instance, Kim recorded what she was learning in her science log in Korean and took it home each night. Her father would help translate key concepts into English, then they would discuss them in Korean to be sure Kim understood the concepts. Her father did the same thing when the EAL/ESL teacher was trying to teach Kim about parts of speech. You can provide a language bridge for challenging concepts by supporting your child's understanding in both languages.

Here are ten general suggestions that will help your child's acquisition of the English language, whether they are just beginning to speak English or are approaching fluency:

Helping Your EAL Learner at Home

- ☑ Find some time every day to listen and talk with your child about his or her school day in your home language.
- ☑ Attend school presentations whenever possible.
- ☑ Read to your child in your native language.
- ☑ Explain challenging concepts to your child in your native language.
- ☑ Provide your child with videos, tapes, and CDs of stories in English. If possible, have versions of these in both English and your child's home language.
- ☑ Provide your child with a dual language dictionary or picture dictionary for use at school as well as at home.
- ☑ Encourage your child to watch some television programs in English that are of educational value.

---

cont.

☑ Provide an authentic purpose for learning English, such as asking where to find something at a grocery store or ordering at a restaurant.
☑ Allow your child to teach you English.
☑ Do not force your child to speak in English.

Let's take a look at specific activities you can do at home, based on your child's specific needs at each stage on the EAL Listening/Speaking continuum.

Family Support: New to English

- Read books to your child, either in English or your home language. The books should have pictures that closely match the meaning of the words on the page.
- Talk about English language stories in your home language.
- Provide your child with tapes of English books and songs.
- Read English signs to your child (such as store signs and road signs).
- Provide your child with interactive computer games in English.
- Encourage your child to play with English-speaking children.
- Praise your child's attempts to speak in English and do not worry if the child makes mistakes. The focus should be on building confidence and communicating meaning.

Family Support: Early Acquisition

- Share English books with your child. Talk about the illustrations and the story in your home language.
- Talk about English language books in your home language.
- Help your child read English signs (such as store signs and road signs).
- Encourage your child to share new words, rhymes, and/or songs learned at school.
- Encourage your child to read books from school to you, then tell you the story in your home language.
- Review vocabulary words and books used at school.
- Provide your child with a tape recorder to record songs and stories learned at school.
- Provide your child with interactive computer games in English.
- Encourage your child to invite English-speaking children over to play.
- Praise your child's attempts to speak in English and do not worry if the child makes mistakes. The focus should be on building confidence and communicating meaning.

Family Support: Becoming Familiar

- Talk about English language books in your home language.
- Encourage your child to read books from school to you, then tell you the story in your home language.
- Encourage your child to make up stories from pictures.

- Encourage your child to tell you in your home language what he or she is learning at school.
- Review English vocabulary and school work with your child.
- Encourage your child to share new words, rhymes, and songs learned at school.
- Help your child read English informational texts (such as store signs, road signs, labels, menus, and instructions).
- Encourage your child to watch some television programs in English that are of educational value.
- Provide your child with tapes, videos, and CDs of stories in English. If possible, have versions in both English and your home language.
- Provide your child with interactive computer games in English.
- Provide your child with a tape recorder to record songs and stories learned at school.
- Encourage your child to invite English-speaking children over to play.
- Praise your child's attempts to speak in English and do not worry if the child makes mistakes. The focus should be on building confidence and communicating meaning.

Family Support: Becoming Competent and Becoming Fluent
- Encourage your child to read books from school to you, then tell you the story in your home language.
- Encourage your child to make up stories from pictures.
- Encourage your child to tell you in your home language what she or he is learning at school.
- Review English vocabulary and school work with your child.
- Encourage your child's use of a thesaurus to add more interesting words to oral presentations.
- Encourage your child to express his or her opinion in your home language about news reports, movies, or television programs you watch together.
- Provide your child with tapes, videos, and CDs of stories in English. If possible, have versions in both English and your home language.
- Provide your child with interactive computer games in English.
- Encourage your child to invite English-speaking children over to play.

Family Support: Fluent
- Encourage your child's use of a thesaurus to add precise or interesting words to oral presentations.
- Encourage your child to tell you in your home language what she or he is learning at school.
- Encourage your child to express his or her opinion in your home language about English news reports, movies, or television programs you watch together.
- Encourage your child to invite English-speaking children over to play.

Middle School Challenges

Chapter 10

> You never stop learning, even when you are old.
>
> —*Kendal, First-Grade Student*

The focus in the previous chapters was on using continuums at the elementary level. However, as Kendal points out, the process of learning — and of accurately assessing learning — continues throughout life. The continuums present a different set of challenges in junior high or middle school.

Challenges

In most elementary schools, teachers may use the continuums for 20–30 students. In a typical junior high schedule with 50-minute periods, teachers might work with 120–150 students. Getting to know students and meeting their instructional needs is overwhelming enough; filling out that many continuums would seem almost impossible. Given the sheer numbers of students that teachers interact with each day, I would first suggest that continuums only make sense when a staff fully supports a developmental middle school philosophy. Continuums are far more feasible in middle schools where block schedules and teaming allow teachers to interact with fewer numbers of students. This method of assessment and reporting would be most effective, for example, when the middle school language arts teachers are responsible for filling out the continuums for three or four classes. The continuum would also seem appropriate in middle schools with a Language Arts/Social Studies block. Using the continuums with large numbers of students also becomes more manageable when teachers have the same students for more than one year. As teachers see students over time, it's easier to get to know them as readers and writers. Another alternative would be to fill out the continuum only for those students about whom you are concerned.

The second challenge is that the descriptors look very similar in the last four stages of the continuums. You teach many of the same skills to sixth, seventh, and eighth graders. The two main differences between these grade levels are the sophistication of the materials and your expectations. As students move through middle school, you withdraw the scaffolding as you help students internalize strategies and move toward independence.

Benefits

Reading and writing growth is very clear in the elementary years. Since change is less dramatic in middle school, sixth through eighth grade teachers at Brighton School considered the possibility of filling out the continuums only once a year. They decided, however, that it's important to have baseline data in the fall in order to document growth. In addition, filling out the continuums also holds teachers accountable for assessing and documenting student learning. The information helps them get to know their students. As teachers fill out the continuums, the descriptors guide their observations as well as their teaching. Finally, the continuums can become a vehicle for student self-evaluation as students become more adept at evaluating their own literacy growth. Self-evaluation is perhaps the most powerful reason for using continuums in middle school.

Self-Evaluation

The elementary teachers at Brighton School have used the continuums successfully for several years. The middle school teachers at the school also valued the continuums and philosophically supported a developmental method of assessment and reporting. Since each middle school teacher works with several classes, they were daunted by the sheer number of continuums they would be expected to fill out. They decided that since their goal is to develop students who can evaluate their own work, it would make sense for the students to become increasingly responsible for filling out their own continuums. The goal of student growth in self-evaluation also meets one of the four Washington State reading and writing standards.

Middle school teachers at Brighton School see students every other day for 100-minute blocks of time. Janine King teaches language arts, and she is the teacher primarily responsible for filling out the reading and writing continuums for three classes of sixth, seventh, and eighth graders. She assesses students using anecdotal notes, rubrics, surveys, student self-evaluation forms, as well as by looking at their work. An equal share of responsibility for completing the continuums, however, lies in the hands of her students.

Janine asks her sixth, seventh, and eighth graders to fill out the student versions of the reading and writing continuums twice a year (January and May). Since Brighton students have been using continuums for several years and Janine ties her focus lessons to the continuums, the task is fairly straightforward for most students. If questions arise, Janine and her students in sixth grade can refer to their continuums from the elementary school, since they are included with a copy of each year's report card in the students' Learner Profiles. She provides more support for the sixth graders and students who are new to the school. After students have filled out the continuums, Janine confers with each student to talk about reading and writing growth and to set goals. In order to hold them accountable, Janine makes her students responsible for providing documentation. They are expected to show evidence of reading/writing achievement from their reading logs, journal entries, writing folders, published pieces, and portfolios. Let's take a look at how Janine provided support in January as her students learned how to self-evaluate using the reading/writing continuums.

Assessing Reading

Assessing Types of Texts

On Monday, Janine began the process by introducing one continuum strand at a time. She started by focusing on the Types of Texts that students read independently, designated by an icon of an open book (📖). In the back of the room, Janine placed five tubs, each containing 10–20 books representing each of the last five stages on the reading continuum. She chose books from the Books by Continuum Stages list in Chapter 4.

Janine handed out the student version of the reading continuum and the list of Characteristics of Books and the List of Books by Continuum Stages from Chapter 4. Janine discussed the general characteristics of books at each stage, providing a few examples of benchmark titles. She pointed out the symbol for the Types of Texts and Oral Reading strand on the continuum (📖). The students used the book tubs and lists to identify the continuum level for books (when possible) on their Reading Logs (DC Form 10.1 and 10.2). Of course, not every book students had read was on the list, but they could at least match some titles to their reading logs (Figure 10.1).

Most middle school teachers require reading outside of class. Reading logs provide an easy way to see if students transfer the reading strategies practiced in class to their independent reading. You can also note when book talks by peers, class author studies, and your read aloud choices spark students' reading outside of school. Finally, you can note the difficulty level of the books students are choosing. For instance, Laura had just finished reading *Getting Near to Baby* (Audrey Couloumbis, 1999) and *Our Only May Amelia* (Jennifer Holm, 1999) from the Connecting stage. She had also read *A Long Way from Chicago* (Richard Peck, 1998) from the Proficient stage and *Waiting for Odysseus* (Clemence McLaren, 2000) from the Independent stage. In general, most of Laura's reading was at the Connecting stage, so she used a pencil to place a check by the Connecting stage on the continuum to indicate the types of texts she reads independently.

Figure 10.1 Reading Self-Evaluation

As Janine collected the logs and continuums from each class, she noted how students had evaluated their reading range. Most students were both honest and accurate in their self-assessment. Janine realized that although most students were reading books at the right level, a few were struggling through books that were far too difficult. Others needed to be nudged to try new genres or authors. These quick checks helped Janine hold students accountable and showed her which students needed support in choosing books. She finds that when students are picking books that are too hard, they become more interested in reading when she can help them find an easier book at their reading level. Goal setting occurs informally as she helps connect students with good books and monitors their comprehension through book talks, literature circles, and class discussions.

Several descriptors in this strand are particularly challenging to assess since students are to demonstrate the skill *independently*. As teachers, we may not observe those skills being used in class and may have to rely on student self-assessment and ask students to collect evidence. For instance, at the Proficient stage, how do you know when a student "Develops strategies and criteria for selecting reading materials independently"? Janine simply asks students how they pick books in informal interviews and on surveys, then observes them choosing books in class. Some students simply read familiar authors or pick a book at random off the shelf, while others ask peers for recommendations and develop preferences for specific authors and genres. She can also determine students' criteria for evaluating books by examining their literature journal responses.

Another challenging descriptor to assess is whether or not middle school students read a wide range of sophisticated material independently. Janine asks students to include any reading material on their logs, including manuals, the sports page from the newspaper, poetry, and magazines, as well as novels. She also records her observations about what students read during silent reading time on Fridays and asks about the range of their reading on student surveys.

Assessing Attitude and Self-Evaluation

The middle school students had completed a reading survey (DC Form 7.2 and 7.5) at the beginning of the year. On Tuesday, students looked over their surveys, rubrics, and Janine's comments on their papers, response journal entries, and projects. The students then used a pencil to place check marks by the appropriate descriptors on the Reading Attitude (☺) and Self-Evaluation (↶) strands on the reading continuum. Janine used her anecdotal notes that she took during silent reading, literature circle discussions, and weekly Friday Book Talks, to note any discrepancies between her assessment and the students' self-evaluation.

Assessing Reading Comprehension

Janine focused on Reading Comprehension and Response (🜂) on Wednesday. She explained the descriptors in that particular strand, using student samples from other years as examples of strong comprehension and quality responses. Janine reminded students of assignments and projects they had done in class that would be helpful to refer to as they looked at the continuum descriptors. She provided as many examples as possible. For instance, Janine referred to students' literature circle response journals and shared specific examples of "in-depth written responses to literature," which is one of the descriptors at the Proficient and Connecting stages. For instance, Andy's response to *When Zachary Beaver Came to Town* (Kimberly Willis Holt, 1999) shows his understanding of the metaphors and deeper levels of meaning of the book:

> January 5
>
> This book is like an onion in the sense it has many layers of plot (not that it makes you cry). On the top layer, you have the conflict of Zachary Beaver and the rest of the town trying to figure out what his story is. Next, there is the problem of Toby's mom not being home and Cal's brother off in Viet Nam. Peeling the onion back one more layer reveals Toby's inner turmoil caused by all the changes in his life and how he reacts to it.

> January 19
>
> This book had several climaxes. One was the releasing of the ladybugs. It is also known as the Ladybug Waltz, a tradition started by Wayne, Cal's older brother who died in the Viet Nam War. It summed up his life and was not only a way of releasing the ladybugs to protect the fields, but was a way of renewing the community and healing the pain and loss from Wayne's absence. This book was filled with loss and redemption. It made me realize that no matter how bad life can get, it will always get better.

> When Zachary Beaver is made fun of, that is demeaning and counter to his rights as a human being. I wonder if we are all trapped in the "trailers" of our own subconscious by our doubts and fears. All any of us need is someone to make us take some steps and the courage to step outside of our comfort zone.

Students looked through their response journal entries, rubrics, and response projects as they assessed Reading Comprehension and Response (Figure 10.2). Again, Janine used her anecdotal notes and observations to compare her information with the students' self-evaluation.

Figure 10.2 Writing Self-Evaluation

At the Fluent and Proficient stages, students also begin to refer to literary elements such as characters and theme, as Laura did in her response to *Good Night Mr. Tom* (Michelle Magorian, 1981):

> I think the theme of the book is strength and friendship. It is about Willie's strength and courage as he begins a new life with a strange old man, and his strength as he develops his own opinions, and breaks away from his mother's controlling views on life. It is as if he has been locked up in his mother's apartment all his life and, with the help of good friends, he is able to escape from his mother.
>
> The book is also about friendship because without the help of all of his new friends, none of the changes would have happened. Mr. Tom was the one who helped the most and I think that their unlikely friendship helped both of them recover from the past.

You can also assess when students at the Bridging stage make connections to other books or authors. For instance, Laura mentioned how the format in *Monster* by Walter Dean Myers (2000) reminded her of the style in *Letters from the Inside* (John Marsden,1991), since they were both written from inside prison. She also commented about the flashbacks in *Monster*, stating that "except for one or two pages in *Absolutely Normal Chaos* (Sharon Creech, 1990), I haven't seen this format before. It gives you an inside view of the character's thoughts."

What does it mean at the Fluent, Proficient, and Connecting stage when s students "generate in-depth responses in small group literature discussions"? Students' comments in their literature circles response journals provide a way to assess the depth of their discussions. For example, Cora wrote, "Our discussion today ranged all over the place. It seemed like it was more of a conversation than a discussion. We tied the book to other things we've read, seen, and heard. We talked about why Martin Luther King, Jr. was written about more than Malcolm X, but how both of them made the same difference in our world."

The discussion rubric the class created expands on the continuum descriptor and makes it more assessable. For instance, at the end of a literature circle set on *Roll of Thunder, Hear My Cry* (Mildred Taylor, 1976), the students used the Literature Discussion Rubric (CBA Form 9.13). Kelsey used a pink highlighter to note the strategies she used independently. She used a yellow highlighter to indicate her goals for the next round of literature circle discussions. Kelsey's written reflection (Figure 10.3) shows that she understands what it means to contribute effectively to a literature discussion and that she's able to set goals independently. The class discussions, the continuum, and the rubric provide the specificity students need to self-evaluate and plan their next steps as readers and writers.

> Today I helped clear up misunderstandings about certain passages, asked questions and answered questions to keep the discussion going. I listened to everyone's thoughts, ideas, and questions. I added my oppinions and answered questions to clear things up. I also contributed to our discussion of the author's clarity.
>
> Next time I would compare the book to other books I've read more!

Figure 10.3 Student Reflection

Assessing Reading Strategies

On Thursday, Judy Cromwell, the social studies teacher at Brighton School walked students through Reading Strategies (☑), the final strand on the reading continuum. She focused specifically on descriptors relating to students' research and presentation skills. As she explained these descriptors, Judy shared examples of student work and referred to projects they had done in social studies class. Students then used a pencil to check the Reading Strategies descriptors on the continuum.

Assessing Writing

The next week, Janine completed similar activities with the writing continuums. Students looked through their working portfolios, which contain all their writing assignments from the year. As Janine explained each descriptor, she again referred to assignments where students might find evidence of particular skills. She also provided specific examples: "If, in your short story, you could create a plot with a climax independently, you would be at the Connecting level. If you can create a story with a problem and a solution, but still need help building a climax, you would mark the descriptor at the Proficient stage." Janine observed that referring to writing assignments and using examples were essential in helping students use the continuums for self-assessment.

Types of Texts and Content

On Monday, students looked through their Working Portfolio to determine the Types of Texts (📄) and Contents and Traits (🗁). To a large extent, the range of writing in middle school reflected Janine's assignments in class. As she planned her curriculum, she used the continuum descriptors to ensure that she provides practice in writing a wide variety of genres throughout the year for each grade level.

Writing Process

The next day, students referred to Janine's comments on their drafts of several recent writing projects to assess their ability to revise and edit on the Writing Process (✂) strand. They also used the rubrics the class constructed for specific assignments and genres. For instance, in sixth grade, Laura evaluated her myth using a rubric based on criteria the class developed (Figure 10.4). Janine added these comments: "Your name choices and play on words makes your myth very entertaining to read! Your writing has strong voice and is almost perfect in the conventions department. Organization is good, too." She drew an arrow to the criteria for developing a strong plot, and commented, "this would be a good next step to focus on when writing stories." Rubrics tied to writing traits help students see their areas of strength, as well as areas in which they can improve.

MYTH RUBRIC

Name: Laura   Date: 11-2-99

Check the boxes that apply to this piece of writing, then mark an "X" in the top bar to indicate approximate placement on a continuum. Use the back for comments: what you noticed as strengths and weaknesses, and what you found interesting and unique.

NOVICE	APPRENTICE	PRACTITIONER	EXPERT
☐ has a title	☐ interesting title	☒ interesting title that indicates myth theme	☐ interesting and original title that reflects myth theme
☐ cover has illustrations	☒ cover has neat and colorful illustrations	☒ cover has neat and colorful illustrations that complement the story	☐ cover has neat and colorful illustrations with direct correlation to the story
☐ includes very few details or descriptive words	☐ includes some details and descriptive words	☐ includes many details and descriptive words	☒ has voice in addition to many interesting details and descriptive words
☐ plot may lack clarity or may not be fully developed; problem and/or solution not clear	☐ plot is developed with clear beginning, middle, and end; includes a problem and solution	☒ plot is well-developed with clear beginning, middle, and satisfying ending; at least one problem builds tension; clear climax and resolution	☐ plot is well-developed with clear beginning, middle, and satisfying ending; more than one problem builds tension; clear climax and resolution
☐ common words spelled incorrectly	☐ most common words spelled correctly, but may contain a few spelling errors	☐ most words spelled correctly	☒ contains few or no spelling errors
☐ contains errors in writing conventions such as: paragraphing, use of capital letters and punctuation	☐ contains a few errors in writing conventions such as: paragraphing, use of capital letters and punctuation	☐ correct use of most writing conventions such as: paragraphing, use of capital letters and punctuation	☒ correct use of most writing conventions such as: paragraphing, use of capital letters and punctuation, including dialogue

Comments:

Figure 10.4 Myth Rubric

Mechanics and Conventions

One of the most concrete skills to assess in writing is the student's use of proper Mechanics and Conventions (✍). On Wednesday, students looked at their drafts and published pieces to determine how much editing they were able to do independently. The section in the rubric on conventions also reflected students' ability to edit their own writing. This skill was also easy to see in their daily grammar exercises. Janine uses *Caught 'Ya: Grammar with a Giggle* (Kiester, 1990) which presents grammar in an appealing form for middle school students. As students looked back at their corrections on the daily exercises, it was easy to determine their ability to edit for punctuation, spelling, and grammar.

Attitude and Self-Evaluation

On Thursday, students referred to the Writing Survey (DC Form 7.2) they had completed in the fall as they assessed the Attitude and Self-Evaluation (☺) strand. They commented how difficult it was to fill out the continuums themselves. For instance, Ben noted, "It was easy for reading, but it was hard for writing. This is true because I don't think a lot about my writing." Self-evaluation is a new skill for many students. As with all skills, reflection improves with modeling and practice.

Comparing and Communicating Results

After Janine King and Judy Cromwell helped the middle school students complete their reading and writing continuums, they met during their planning time to share the students' continuums. Judy looked specifically at descriptors about students' use of research and presentation skills. Since her students do a great deal of reading and writing in social studies, she was often able to corroborate or supplement Janine's observations.

For example, in social studies, students in each grade do an extensive research report. Judy focused on reading and writing strategies as she watched students during the research process and examined their notes, drafts, and final products. In Figure 10.5 and 10.6 below, the gray shading shows the descriptors on the continuums that Judy could assess in her social studies class (approximately one-third of the reading and writing descriptors). These two continuums are also included on the CD-ROM. In reading, the two strands that Judy found particularly easy to assess were her students' Reading Strategies (☑) and Types of Texts (▤). The writing skills she observed were scattered more widely across all five strands on the writing continuum. The information Judy collected helped support Janine's assessments in her language arts classes. As you and your colleagues look over students' continuums, you can sometimes catch specific skills that students demonstrate but do not mark or strategies which students marked but do not yet demonstrate consistently.

WRITING CONTINUUM (Social Studies)

Preconventional Ages 3–5
- Relies primarily on pictures to convey meaning.
- Begins to label and add "words" to pictures.
- Writes first name.
- Demonstrates awareness that print conveys meaning.
- Makes marks other than drawing on paper (scribbles).
- Makes random recognizable letters to represent words.
- Tells about own pictures and writing.
- Sees self as writer.
- Takes risks with writing.

Emerging Ages 4–6
- Uses pictures and print to convey meaning.
- Writes words to describe or support pictures.
- Copies signs, labels, names, and words (environmental print).
- Demonstrates understanding of letter/sound relationship.
- Prints with upper case letters.
- Matches letters to sounds.
- Uses beginning consonants to make words.
- Uses beginning and ending consonants to make words.
- Pretends to read own writing.
- Sees self as writer.
- Takes risks with writing.

Developing Ages 5–7
- Writes 1–2 sentences about a topic.
- Writes names and familiar words.
- Generates own ideas for writing.
- Writes from top to bottom, left to right, and front to back.
- Intermixes upper and lower case letters.
- Experiments with capitals.
- Experiments with punctuation.
- Begins to use spacing between words.
- Uses growing awareness of sound segments (e.g., phonemes, syllables, rhymes) to write words.
- Spells words on the basis of sounds without regard for conventional spelling patterns.
- Uses beginning, middle, and ending sounds to make words.
- Begins to read own writing.

Beginning Ages 6–8
- Writes several sentences about a topic.
- Writes about observations and experiences.
- Writes short nonfiction pieces (simple facts about a topic) with guidance.
- Chooses own writing topics.
- Reads own writing and notices mistakes with guidance.
- Revises by adding details with guidance.
- Uses spacing between words consistently.
- Forms most letters legibly.
- Writes pieces that self and others can read.
- Uses phonetic spelling to write independently.
- Spells simple words and some high frequency words correctly.
- Begins to use periods and capital letters correctly.
- Shares own writing with others.

Expanding Ages 7–9
- Writes short fiction and poetry with guidance.
- Writes a variety of short nonfiction pieces (e.g., facts about a topic, letters, lists) with guidance.
- Writes with a central idea.
- Writes using complete sentences.
- Organizes ideas in a logical sequence in fiction and nonfiction writing with guidance.
- Begins to recognize and use interesting language.
- Uses several prewriting strategies (e.g., web, brainstorm) with guidance.
- Listens to others' writing and offers feedback.
- Begins to consider suggestions from others about own writing.
- Adds description and detail with guidance.
- Edits for capitals and punctuation with guidance.
- Publishes own writing with guidance.
- Writes legibly.
- Spells most high frequency words correctly and moves toward conventional spelling.
- Identifies own writing strategies and sets goals with guidance.

Bridging Ages 8–10
- Writes about feelings and opinions.
- Writes fiction with clear beginning, middle, and end.
- Writes poetry using carefully chosen language with guidance.
- Writes organized nonfiction pieces (e.g., reports, letters, and lists) with guidance.
- Begins to use paragraphs to organize ideas.
- Uses strong verbs, interesting language, and dialogue with guidance.
- Seeks feedback on writing.
- Revises for clarity with guidance.
- Revises to enhance ideas by adding description and detail.
- Uses resources (e.g., thesaurus and word lists) to make writing more effective with guidance.
- Edits for punctuation, spelling, and grammar.
- Publishes writing in polished format with guidance.
- Increases use of visual strategies, spelling rules, and knowledge of word parts to spell correctly.
- Uses commas and apostrophes correctly with guidance.
- Develops criteria for effective writing to set own writing goals with guidance.

Fluent Ages 9–11
- Begins to write organized fiction and nonfiction (e.g., reports, letters, biographies, and autobiographies).
- Develops stories with plots that include problems and solutions with guidance.
- Writes poetry using carefully chosen language.
- Creates characters in stories with guidance.
- Begins to experiment with sentence length and complex sentence structure.
- Varies leads and endings with guidance.
- Uses description, details, and similes with guidance.
- Uses dialogue with guidance.
- Uses a range of strategies for planning writing.
- Adapts writing for purpose and audience with guidance.
- Revises for specific writing traits (e.g., ideas, organization, word choice, sentence fluency, voice, and conventions) with guidance.
- Incorporates suggestions from others about own writing with guidance.
- Edits for punctuation, spelling, and grammar with greater precision.
- Uses tools (e.g., dictionaries, word lists, and spell checkers) to edit with guidance.
- Develops criteria for effective writing in different genres with guidance.

Proficient Ages 10–13
- Writes persuasively about ideas, feelings, and opinions.
- Creates plots with problems and solutions.
- Begins to develop the main characters and describe detailed settings.
- Begins to write organized and fluent nonfiction, including simple bibliographies.
- Writes cohesive paragraphs including reasons and examples with guidance.
- Uses transitional sentences to connect paragraphs.
- Varies sentence structure, leads, and endings.
- Begins to use descriptive language, details, and similes.
- Uses voice to evoke emotional response from readers.
- Begins to integrate information on a topic from a variety of sources.
- Begins to revise for specific writing traits (e.g., ideas, organization, word choice, sentence fluency, voice, and conventions).
- Uses tools (e.g., dictionaries, word lists, spell checkers) to edit independently.
- Selects and publishes writing in polished format independently.
- Begins to use complex punctuation (e.g., commas, colons, semicolons, quotation marks) appropriately.
- Begins to set goals and identify strategies to improve writing in different genres.

Connecting Ages 11–14
- Writes in a variety of genres and forms for different audiences and purposes independently.
- Creates plots with a climax.
- Creates detailed, believable settings and characters in stories.
- Begins to write organized, fluent, and detailed nonfiction independently, including bibliographies with correct format.
- Writes cohesive paragraphs including supportive reasons and examples.
- Uses descriptive language, details, similes, and imagery to enhance ideas independently.
- Begins to use dialogue to enhance character development.
- Incorporates personal voice in writing with increasing frequency.
- Integrates information on a topic from a variety of sources to convey information when appropriate.
- Constructs charts, graphs, and tables to convey information when appropriate.
- Uses prewriting strategies effectively to organize and strengthen writing.
- Revises for specific writing traits (e.g., ideas, organization, word choice, sentence fluency, voice, and conventions) independently.
- Includes deletion in revision strategies.
- Incorporates suggestions from others on own writing independently.
- Uses complex punctuation (e.g., commas, colons, semicolons, quotation marks) with increasing accuracy.

Independent
- Writes organized, fluent, accurate, and in-depth nonfiction, including references with correct bibliographic format.
- Writes cohesive, fluent, and effective poetry and fiction.
- Uses a clear sequence of paragraphs with effective transitions.
- Begins to incorporate literary devices (e.g., imagery, metaphors, personification, and foreshadowing).
- Weaves dialogue effectively into stories.
- Develops plots, characters, setting, and mood (literary elements) effectively.
- Begins to develop personal voice and style of writing.
- Revises through multiple drafts independently.
- Seeks feedback from others and incorporates suggestions in order to strengthen own writing.
- Publishes writing for different audiences and purposes in polished format independently.
- Internalizes writing process.
- Uses correct grammar (e.g., subject/verb agreement and verb tense) consistently.
- Writes with confidence and competence on a range of topics independently.
- Perseveres through complex or challenging writing projects independently.
- Sets writing goals independently by analyzing and evaluating own writing.

Legend: Types of Texts   Content and Traits   Process   Mechanics and Conventions   Attitude and Self-Evaluation

Figure 10.5 Writing Continuum with Highlighted Descriptors

READING CONTINUUM (Social Studies)

Preconventional — Ages 3–5
- Begins to choose reading materials (e.g., books, magazines, and charts) and has favorites.
- Shows interest in reading signs, labels, and logos (environmental print).
- Recognizes own name in print.
- Holds book and turns pages correctly.
- Shows beginning/end of book or story.
- Knows some letter names.
- Listens and responds to literature.
- Comments on illustrations in books.
- Participates in reading of familiar books, rhymes, poems, and songs.

Emerging — Ages 4–6
- Memorizes pattern books, poems, and familiar books.
- Begins to read signs, labels, and logos (environmental print).
- Demonstrates eagerness to read.
- Pretends to read.
- Uses illustrations to tell stories.
- Reads top to bottom, left to right, and front to back with guidance.
- Knows most letter names and some letter sounds.
- Recognizes some names and words in context.
- Makes meaningful predictions with guidance.
- Rhymes and plays with words.
- Participates in reading of familiar books and poems.
- Connects books read aloud to own experiences with guidance.

Developing — Ages 5–7
- Reads books with simple patterns.
- Begins to read own writing.
- Begins to read independently for short periods (5–10 minutes).
- Discusses favorite reading material with others.
- Relies on illustrations and print.
- Uses finger-print-voice matching.
- Knows most letter sounds and letter clusters.
- Recognizes simple words.
- Uses growing awareness of sound segments (e.g., phonemes, syllables, rhymes) to read words.
- Begins to make meaningful predictions.
- Identifies titles and authors in literature (text features).
- Retells main event or idea in literature.
- Participates in guided literature discussions.
- Sees self as reader.
- Explains why literature is liked/disliked during class discussions with guidance.

Beginning — Ages 6–8
- Reads simple early-reader books.
- Reads harder early-reader books.
- Reads and follows simple written directions with guidance.
- Identifies basic genres (e.g., fiction, nonfiction, and poetry).
- Uses basic punctuation when reading orally.
- Reads independently (10–15 minutes).
- Chooses reading materials independently.
- Learns and shares information from reading.
- Uses meaning cues (context).
- Uses sentence cues (grammar).
- Uses letter/sound cues and patterns (phonics).
- Recognizes word endings, common contractions, and many high frequency words.
- Begins to self-correct.
- Retells beginning, middle, and end with guidance.
- Discusses characters and story events with guidance.
- Identifies own reading behaviors with guidance.

Expanding — Ages 7–9
- Reads easy chapter books.
- Chooses, reads, and finishes a variety of materials at appropriate level with guidance.
- Begins to read aloud with fluency.
- Reads silently for increasingly longer periods (15–30 minutes).
- Uses reading strategies appropriately, depending on the text and purpose.
- Uses word structure cues (e.g., root words, prefixes, suffixes, word chunks) when encountering unknown words.
- Increases vocabulary by using meaning cues (context).
- Self-corrects for meaning.
- Follows written directions.
- Identifies chapter titles and table of contents (text organizers).
- Summarizes and retells story events in sequential order.
- Responds to and makes personal connections with facts, characters, and situations in literature.
- Compares and contrasts characters and story events.
- "Reads between the lines" with guidance.
- Identifies own reading strategies and sets goals with guidance.

Bridging — Ages 8–10
- Reads medium level chapter books.
- Chooses reading materials at appropriate level.
- Expands knowledge of different genres (e.g., realistic fiction, historical fiction, and fantasy).
- Reads aloud with expression.
- Uses resources (e.g., encyclopedias, CD-ROMs, and nonfiction texts) to locate and sort information with guidance.
- Gathers information by using the table of contents, captions, glossary, and index (text organizers) with guidance.
- Gathers and uses information from graphs, charts, tables, and maps with guidance.
- Increases vocabulary by using context cues, other reading strategies, and resources (e.g., dictionary and thesaurus) with guidance.
- Demonstrates understanding of the difference between fact and opinion.
- Follows multi-step written directions independently.
- Discusses setting, plot, characters, and point of view (literary elements) with guidance.
- Responds to issues and ideas in literature as well as facts or story events.
- Makes connections to other authors, books, and perspectives.
- Participates in small group literature discussions with guidance.
- Uses reasons and examples to support ideas and opinions with guidance.

Fluent — Ages 9–11
- Reads challenging children's literature.
- Selects, reads, and finishes a wide variety of genres with guidance.
- Begins to develop strategies and criteria for selecting reading materials.
- Reads aloud with fluency, expression, and confidence.
- Reads silently for extended periods (30–40 min.).
- Begins to use resources (e.g., encyclopedias, articles, Internet, and nonfiction texts) to locate information.
- Gathers information using the table of contents, captions, glossary, and index (text organizers) independently.
- Begins to use resources (e.g., dictionary and thesaurus) to increase vocabulary independently.
- Begins to discuss literature with reference to setting, plot, characters, and theme (literary elements), and author's craft.
- Generates thoughtful oral and written responses in small group literature discussions with guidance.
- Begins to use new vocabulary in different subjects and in oral and written response to literature.
- Begins to gain deeper meaning by "reading between the lines."
- Begins to set goals and identifies strategies to improve reading.

Proficient — Ages 10–13
- Reads complex children's literature.
- Reads and understands informational texts (e.g., want ads, brochures, schedules, catalogs, manuals) with guidance.
- Develops strategies and criteria for selecting reading materials independently.
- Uses resources (e.g., encyclopedias, articles, Internet, and nonfiction texts) to locate information independently.
- Gathers and analyzes information from graphs, charts, tables, and maps with guidance.
- Integrates information from multiple nonfiction sources to deepen understanding of a topic with guidance.
- Uses resources (e.g., dictionary and thesaurus) to increase vocabulary independently.
- Identifies literary devices (e.g., similes, metaphors, personalization, and foreshadowing).
- Discusses literature with reference to theme, author's purpose, and style (literary elements), and author's craft.
- Begins to generate in-depth responses in small group literature discussions.
- Begins to generate in-depth written responses to literature.
- Uses increasingly complex vocabulary in different subjects and in oral and written response to literature.
- Uses reasons and examples to support ideas and conclusions.
- Probes for deeper meaning by "reading between the lines" in response to literature.

Connecting — Ages 11–14
- Reads complex children's literature and young adult literature.
- Selects, reads, and finishes a wide variety of genres independently.
- Integrates nonfiction information to develop deeper understanding of a topic independently.
- Begins to gather, analyze, and use information from graphs, charts, tables, and maps.
- Generates in-depth responses and sustains small group literature discussions.
- Generates in-depth written responses to literature.
- Begins to evaluate, interpret, and analyze reading content critically.
- Begins to develop criteria for evaluating literature.
- Seeks recommendations and opinions about literature from others.
- Sets reading challenges and goals independently.

Independent
- Reads young adult and adult literature.
- Chooses and comprehends a wide variety of sophisticated materials with ease (e.g., newspapers, magazines, manuals, novels, and poetry).
- Reads and understands informational texts (e.g., manuals, consumer reports, applications, and forms).
- Reads challenging material for pleasure independently.
- Reads challenging material for information and to solve problems independently.
- Perseveres through complex reading tasks.
- Gathers, analyzes, and uses information from graphs, charts, tables, and maps independently.
- Analyzes literary devices (e.g., metaphors, imagery, irony, and satire).
- Contributes unique insights and supports opinions in complex literature discussions.
- Adds depth to responses to literature by making insightful connections to other reading and experiences.
- Evaluates, interprets, and analyzes reading content critically.
- Develops and articulates criteria for evaluating literature.
- Pursues a widening community of readers independently.

Legend: Types of Texts and Oral Reading · Attitude · Reading Strategies · Comprehension and Response · Self-Evaluation

Figure 10.6 Reading Continuum with Highlighted Descriptors

The continuums provide a vehicle for conversations among teachers, as well as between teachers and students. A middle school student, Lauren, wrote, "I like the continuums because it gives you a chance to put down what you think your level is. Then you can look at what the teacher wrote. From there, you can think, 'Hmm . . . maybe I'm not doing this.' It can help you know that maybe you are/aren't doing stuff that you thought you were."

If there was disagreement between different observations or between the students' self-evaluation and their teacher's assessment, Janine asked the students to provide evidence of particular skills. For example, when Randy first began to fill out the reading continuum, he marked all the descriptors under the Independent stage. He reads adult novels, so he felt he was an independent reader in all aspects. Types of Texts, however, is only one strand on the continuum. By going over each descriptor and looking at his work with Janine, Randy was able to look at the continuum more closely and to create a more accurate assessment of his skills as a reader.

Janine found that if she disagreed with a student's evaluation, it was usually because the student misunderstood what the descriptor meant. Once Janine explained the skill and provided a few examples, most discrepancies were cleared up. As students fill out the continuums over time, these discrepancies will probably occur less often and Janine will have better examples to share with students. In fact, I hope Janine will write a book with examples of student work that illustrate specific skills and strategies that are used at each stage.

Marking the Continuums

In January, students first used a pencil to check the descriptors that matched their skills. After the team meetings and individual conferences, Janine then marked the descriptors on the reading and writing continuums with a yellow highlighter and the continuums were sent home as part of the middle school report card. Using the same process in June, students first filled out the continuums using a pencil. Janine then used a pink highlighter in the spring to show students' new skills and strategies. In this way, reading and writing growth can be captured visually for students and their families. At Brighton School, teachers send the continuums home as part of the report card in January and in June, then copies are placed in the Learner Profile that travels with students from year to year.

Allocating Time

You may be questioning the amount of time spent on evaluation and individual conferences. However, if your goal is honest and thoughtful self-evaluation, you must provide the modeling, time, and support for the process. The continuums provide a powerful assessment tool that can help you meet individual student's needs and help each student set goals.

Most of us scarcely have time to chat with colleagues about our weekend when we meet in the parking lot or pass in the hallways, much less to talk about individual students. By consciously allocating time to talk specifically about students' growth as readers and writers, you can make sure that no one "slips between the cracks." In addition, some students who struggle in one class may shine in another.

For example, Tracey had difficulty expressing her ideas in social studies, but wrote fluent prose in language arts class. Creative writing was one of Tracey's strengths, but research reports and technical writing were challenging tasks. Sharing information among teachers can help paint a more three-dimensional picture of each learner. By discussing learning across content areas, you can also ensure a consistent message to families about each student's needs and strengths.

Informal self-evaluation occurs throughout the year as Janine provides feedback on students' reading and writing. She also posts the continuum charts on the front wall of the classroom and refers to descriptors when appropriate. The more formal self-evaluation process took about two weeks in the fall, plus another week for individual conferences. Janine spent 30–45 minutes for four class periods focusing on the reading descriptors and the same amount of time the second week when students assessed themselves as writers. In the spring, the same process took only two weeks, since students were more familiar with the continuums, and usually only marked a handful of new descriptors. In addition, the teachers knew the students better by spring and had collected a great deal more assessment information. The process also becomes easier over time if teachers have the same students for more than one year.

Insights

The Brighton teachers and I learned several things as the middle school students filled out the continuums. First, it was interesting to see that the strong readers and writers were very accurate in their self-assessment. On the other hand, more struggling students often marked themselves far higher on the continuums than their work and teacher assessment indicated. In addition, students in middle school are often trying to "save face" and may hope that if they don't admit their weaknesses you might not notice! Many of these students did not seem to realize that their reading and writing were areas of concern. Goal setting becomes challenging when some students "don't know what they don't know." Struggling students often don't know what good readers or writers do or think or say. Only when Janine showed examples and asked them to provide evidence to support the skills they marked did they say, "Oh. That's what you mean. I guess I don't do that yet."

For instance, when Margaret marked "Generates in-depth responses to literature and sustains small group literature discussions" at the Connecting stage, Janine referred to her anecdotal notes. She had recorded that Margaret was often somewhat passive during discussions, sometimes building off others' comments, but rarely contributing her own original thoughts. When Janine provided examples of how students sustain a good discussion, Margaret realized what this descriptor meant and set a goal to become more of a leader in future discussions.

Second, we discovered that many of these young adults are reading adult novels, but without the level of understanding these books demand. The types of texts students read must be linked to comprehension. One of the challenges in middle school is helping students choose books at their reading level and then assessing their level of comprehension. Janine assesses comprehension during individual conferences, book talks, and literature circle discussions. She also measures comprehension through students' written response journals and extension projects.

To our surprise, in several reflections, students mentioned how helpful it had been when Janine went over each descriptor. Eric wrote, "I thought it was fairly easy because all the choices were clearly shown and easily read and with the teachers helping, it made it super easy." Janine had worried that she was spending too much time going over the continuums, but most students felt that the time was well spent.

By using the checklists described in Chapter 7, Janine also found that the behaviors and strategies of middle school students spread across three or even four stages. Students' strengths and weaknesses become more noticeable as the expectations increase in middle school. For instance, although most primary students willingly experiment with poetry, not all students in middle school write poetry "with carefully chosen language" easily or independently. Similarly, some students may be better than others at writing expository texts or reading nonfiction. Using the continuums and checklists enabled Janine to highlight students' strengths and helped them set goals.

The continuums have been part of the report card at Brighton School for seven years, but many students mentioned that marking the continuums *themselves* was quite a different experience from simply looking over the report card that a teacher filled out. The students also said that marking it themselves was hard work. When asked how she felt about using the continuums, Crissa wrote, "If Mrs. King had done it for us, then I still would have learned my strengths and weaknesses, but by filling it out myself, I really had to think and I learned more about myself." Melissa wrote, "I thought it was hard because I needed to think hard about what I was able to do and not what I *wished* I could do!" She added, "I learned how important the continuum is. I used to just glance over it. Now I take my time and read every one." Finally, students said that the continuums helped them see what they *can do* and showed them their next steps as readers and writers. Garret said, "I like how you can know exactly where you are and what you need to improve on."

Finally, it has become increasingly clear that in order for students to understand the continuum descriptors, we need to show them actual examples of what we expect. By starting your Anchor Papers Notebook and by focusing on a few strands or genres at a time, you can clarify the targets and help your middle school students learn to evaluate their own work.

Parent Communication

How do families know what their middle school students are learning? Occasional newsletters and quick glimpses of curriculum at Open House only present a broad overview. How much can a letter grade tell parents about these adolescent readers and writers? Reading and writing growth in middle school is quite different from growth in the primary years. Parents are used to seeing students move through one or even two stages a year in the elementary grades. By middle school, however, change occurs in terms of depth rather than in monumental leaps. For instance, students learn how to edit with adult guidance in second and third grade. They begin to use those skills on their own with some teacher support in the intermediate grades. It may not be until the end of middle school or even high school that students can truly edit their work independently. Part of the challenge for middle school teachers is developing a plan to educate families about growth in the middle years.

At Brighton School, middle school students are responsible for sharing the continuums with their families. In January, students arranged a time to explain the continuums to their parents. They described the process they went through, explained the descriptors that were marked, and shared their reading/writing goals for the remainder of the year. This exercise was valuable for three reasons. First, families made the time to talk with their child about school. At this age, young adolescents are leading busy lives and it becomes harder to find time to talk about school. Second, the students had to articulate what they had learned as reflected in the continuums. In addition, parents gained information about their student's strengths and areas for growth as readers and writers. Families appreciate the specificity of the continuums. One parent wrote, "Having specific behaviors to discuss is much more enlightening than a number or letter grade. I particularly like seeing where my son feels *he* belongs on the continuum."

Another challenge in middle school is the issue of scheduling parent conferences. If students have 4–6 teachers and each teacher works with over 100 students, conferences become logistically impossible. Faced with such challenges, most junior highs and middle schools have simply eliminated individual parent conferences. Yet, as parents and teachers, we know that students still need adult support at this age. Our children rarely come bursting in the door eager to talk about what they did at school. It becomes harder for parents to know what their children are learning in middle school. Student-led conferences provide a logical answer to many of these concerns.

Student-Led Conferences

In some middle schools, students share the continuums and their work samples, along with reflections about progress toward their goals, at student-led conferences in the fall and spring. Typically, three to five students and their families meet in each classroom for 30–45 minute conferences. The teachers circulate around the room as students explain the continuums and share their portfolios. If parents still feel that an individual teacher conference is necessary, a private conference is scheduled for another time. More specific information about student-led conferences will be included in the next two books in this assessment series, *Book Three: Student Portfolios and Reflection* and *Book Four: Reporting Student Growth*.

As parents, my husband and I found that it was a very powerful experience in the spring to listen to our daughter, Laura, explain what she had learned in sixth grade. She showed us her continuums, provided examples of her work, and explained how she had improved since September. Other parents were equally impressed. For instance, Emily's mother wrote, "It was interesting and informative to have Emily walk me through her thinking and evaluation. She seems to be pretty realistic about her progress. I'm a firm believer in self-evaluation, especially with follow-up with a teacher or parent."

Benefits of Continuums in Middle School

Most parents want to know what their child is learning and how they can provide support at home. Chapter 8 provides specific literacy activities for each stage on the continuum. The continuum itself is also beneficial as a starting point for conversations about reading and writing. One parent at Brighton School wrote, "This is an accurate evaluation of John's growth socially and academically. The time required to read and understand this continuum is worth it as we parents are given a detailed, multi-layered view of our student's growth and progress."

As a teacher, Janine feels that the continuums are valuable tools for helping middle school students begin to take some responsibility for their own learning. They are willing and able to do this, but only if you show them how and provide plenty of opportunities for self-evaluation. You also need to provide student samples that reflect quality work.

From a student's perspective, Kayleigh commented, "I find the continuums helpful because I can visually see where I am, and I can share that information with my parents. That way, they know how I'm doing in those subjects. I could see why it might be hard for teachers, but it wasn't that hard for me because I could look in my papers, see what level they were, and mark it down on my continuum."

The reading and writing continuums are being used successfully in elementary schools and districts around the world for both assessment and reporting. Many questions still remain about manageable and effective ways to use continuums in middle schools. Are continuums more useful for guiding instruction at this level, or can they be used for assessment and reporting as well? How can teachers find time to assess students and share that information with colleagues? What are effective ways in which to involve students in collecting evidence and reflecting on their learning? Five essential criteria necessary for using the continuums in middle school are listed in the following chart.

Key Factors for Using Continuums Successfully in Middle School

1. Filling out the continuums is more reasonable with block scheduling. Teachers with fewer students can more realistically assess and report growth.
2. Teachers need common planning time to share assessment information about students and to support each other in filling out the continuums.
3. Teachers must demonstrate and teach the process of self-evaluation.
4. Students need practice and support in collecting evidence and filling out the continuum themselves.
5. Teachers need to educate families about the nature of reading and writing development in middle school.

Middle school teachers at Brighton School can see both philosophical and practical connections among their beliefs, their curriculum, daily instruction, assessment, and reporting. It is a huge amount of work to align all these pieces. The teachers continue to explore ways to involve students and families in the evaluation process, using the continuums as a springboard for conversations about learning. In the next chapter, I'll suggest some ways in which the continuums can also be used to spark conversations about learning within a school or district.

Staff Development

At a middle school staff meeting, hand each teacher a copy of the reading continuum. Ask each teacher to highlight the descriptors that they teach or might see evidenced in their classes. For instance, math or science teachers might see evidence of students gathering information from charts and graphs. Social studies teachers could assess students' use of research skills.

At a second staff meeting, repeat the same activity with the writing continuum. These discussions provide a way for teachers in different content areas to see connections and possibilities for coordinating units or themes. You can also plan which teachers will focus on particular skills or strategies. Although the language arts teachers will be the ones primarily responsible for filling out the reading and writing continuums, other teachers can agree to teach certain skills and help collect evidence through student work.

At another staff meeting, ask each teacher to choose two or three descriptors to investigate by collecting student examples. For instance, the social studies teacher may want to collect examples to show the increasing level of expectations for writing bibliographies at the last four stages of the writing continuum. Language arts teachers could show how students improve in their use of dialogue or written response to literature. Teachers can then share these exemplars with their colleagues.

With permission, videotape a student-led conference in which a student shares his or her reading and writing continuums, work samples, and self-evaluations. At the end of the conference, ask the student and family to reflect upon the process. At a staff meeting, show clips from the videotape and discuss your concerns, questions, and insights.

READING LOG

Name:

Date	Title	Author	Rating 1–10	Stage BFPCI	Genre	Comments

READING LOG

Name:

Date	Title	Author	Stage	Genre	Comments

Stage: B = Bridging   F = Fluent   P = Proficient   C = Connecting   I = Independent

Data Collection
and Staff
Development

The continuums allow teachers to see students in terms of possibility and progress, rather than through a deficit lens. Every child is somewhere on the literacy journey, and every child has potential to move forward.

—*Carol Wilcox, Staff Developer, Denver, Colorado*

The last 10 chapters have focused on using continuums at the classroom level. As your colleagues become interested, however, you may decide to implement continuums at a grade level, school, or district level. As continuums are used on a larger scale, it becomes possible to collect data about particular stages, ages, and descriptors. Continuum data can then be aligned more closely to your district curriculum, as well as to your state tests and standards. This chapter is divided into two sections. In the first half, I examine ways in which data can be collected at the classroom, school, and district levels.

In the second part of this chapter, I explore the stages of continuum development and present some ideas for staff development. Interest in continuums often begins with a few teachers in a school and then starts to grow. This grass-roots implementation on the part of teachers has been far more effective than a top-down mandate from the district office. In order for the continuums to be successful on a larger scale, however, it is vital to have enough teacher interest, administrative leadership, time, and resources. Over the past 10 years as I have helped schools and districts implement continuums, common questions and concerns often arise.

The continuums help you know where your students are as readers and writers, but how can you step back to see the growth of your whole class? How can you be sure that your assessments align with those of other teachers at your grade level? When your colleagues place students on the continuums, how well do your results match those of teachers at the grade below or the grade above? Are the age ranges in Seattle the same as in Winnipeg and Saudi Arabia? Collecting large-scale data can help answer some of these questions.

Developmental Range

In most classrooms, students' behaviors fall into a range of two or three stages on the reading/writing continuums. This can be considered the typical developmental range for any particular grade level. Of course, you may also have a couple of students who demonstrate some skills in an earlier or later stage. You may have a range of chronological ages within your classroom as well. For example, most first graders at the beginning of the year are six or seven years old. You may have a few who turn six and some who turn eight during the school year. In the primary grades, it is also interesting to graph the ages of your students, then note if some of the students at the earlier stages on the continuum are your younger students.

Despite this range, curriculum and teaching materials are frequently designed as if all the children in the class were the same age with the same developmental needs. Too often, children are forced to fit the curriculum, rather than the curriculum being designed around the needs of students. The continuum has been one way to encourage developmentally appropriate instruction based on a student's age, proficiencies, and needs. On the other hand, with 20–30 students, it would be overwhelming to create totally individualized learning plans. You can probably target some of your instruction to whole class demonstrations or focus lessons. Other skills are best taught through small-group or individual focus lessons or conferences. Some teachers use the continuum in order to group students for guided or shared reading. Unlike a test, continuum placement is backed by classroom-based assessment and samples of student work.

Collecting Data within Your Classroom

At Brighton School, Diana Kastner starts a Writing Development Class Profile (DC Form 11.1) and a Reading Development Class Profile (DC Form 11.2) in the fall by listing her students' names in the left column of both charts. As she prepares for parent conferences in October, she places a dot (.) on the Class Profile by the appropriate stage for each student. She does the same thing at the end of the year, using an (X) to mark each student's developmental stage on the Class Profile. Diana uses this information to group students for reading and writing instruction at the beginning of the year.

Sharing Data with Families

Diana often deals with a few overly concerned parents every year. Particularly if it's their first child in school, parents sometimes panic if their child isn't reading in first grade. Each year during conferences, Diana shares the child's portfolio, their writing and reading samples, and information from her classroom based assessment. Inevitably, at least one parent asks at the end of their conference, "But how is my child doing?"

There are several issues lurking beneath the surface of this simple question. The first is our American obsession with numbers and the desire to quantify everything. Some parents feel that a test score is more objective and reliable than the range of the classroom-based evidence you have collected about their child. In addition, continuums and portfolios are still fairly new for many families and are quite different from the letter grades and tests they remember as students. There is also a competitive edge to the question. Parents want to know how their child compares to the rest of the class and to other students the same age. They want know how their child is doing in relation to other students at the same grade level. Finally, parents are inundated with negative messages about education. They are genuinely worried that their children may not be getting the education they need for the future. How can Diana possibly assuage all these concerns in the last five minutes of a parent conference?

You may want to introduce the continuum at Back to School Night and at a Parent Evening, as discussed in Chapter 8. The more parents understand the developmental nature of literacy acquisition, the more able they are to move away from the old paradigm of ranking students. Diana finds that the Class Profile form also helps provide some perspective to answer parents' concerns. At conferences, Diana covers up the other students' names and shows parents where their child fits in the Class Profile. For most parents, this visual proof that their child is in the normal developmental range is tremendously reassuring. At this point, you should already have had several conferences with families of any students who fall outside the normal developmental range. Both highly capable children and students who are struggling require individual plans to provide the extra support or challenge they need at home and at school.

When she taught on Bainbridge Island, Washington, Cynthia Ruptic also used the continuums and Class Profile during parent conferences. She writes,

> Over and over again, parents asked in conference, "Yes, but how does my child compare with the rest of the class?" As a teacher, I had been trained to steer parents away from such questions; however, as a parent, I understood their need to know if their child was "in the ballpark." Don't we all wonder how our child fits in his or her group and want assurance that our child is "where he or she should be?" Isn't this part of the purpose of parent-teacher conferences?

Cynthia found that most of her students fell within the expected age ranges on the continuums. If a child was at the lower or upper end, Cynthia and the parents were able to openly discuss the reasons and create a plan to meet that child's needs. All of the parents appreciated receiving clear and honest communication about their child. Families came away with a clear understanding of their child's individual growth, as well as knowledge about how their child was doing in terms of broad developmental expectations. By guiding meaningful conversation between teacher and parent, the continuums foster a home/school connection beyond what any other evaluation tool can provide.

Figure 11.1 shows a Class Profile from Christy Clausen's first-grade classroom. Christy had an IEP (Individual Educational Plan) in the fall for the four students who were at the Emergent stage and the two children who were at the Expanding stage as readers. She used the assessment tools described in Chapters 5 and 6 to fill out the continuum and then designate the general stage for each student in reading and writing. The data from this form helped Christy group students for instruction and share information with families at conference time. Two blank Class Profiles (DC Form 11.1 and 11.2) and an explanatory letter (DC Form 11.3) are included at the end of this chapter and on the CD-ROM.

EMERGENT READING DEVELOPMENT: CLASS PROFILE

Student	Emergent	Developing	Beginning	Expanding	Bridging
TM	•		X		
PT				•X	
TR			•	X	
MS		•	X		
AR			•	X	
TW			•	X	
CO	•		X		
JJ			•	X	
TP		•	X		
AZ	•	X			
AW			•	X	
LM			•	X	
KR		•	X		
SC	•		X		
RM		•	X		
KB			•	X	
TR			•	X	
BW			•	X	
CL			•	X	
PC		•	X		
MM			•	X	
BG		•	X		
PS				•	X
PA		•	X		

• = fall   X = spring

Figure 11.1 Class Profile

One of the advantages the continuums offer is that they provide families with a new way to talk about their child's learning. Ingrid Stipes, a fourth-grade teacher on Mercer Island, Washington, notes, "Instead of focusing on the numbers or grades on the report card, parents are using the language and concepts from the continuum to talk about their child's progress." The continuums provide a way to celebrate what the child does well and to discover specific ways in which parents can support reading and writing at home.

Sharing Data Within a School

You can also convert the information from your Class Profile into numerical data to capture yearly growth. After you have completed the Class Profile, divide the number of students in each stage by the total number of students in your class (e.g., 8 ÷ 27 students = 30%). By collecting this information in the fall and again at the end of the year, you can see how much your class has progressed. Teachers can use the information from the Continuum Data Collection forms (DC Forms 11.5 and 11.6) to set their own professional goals for the next year. Figure 11.2 shows an example of the reading and writing data Lisa Norwick collected for her second graders a few years ago. The chart shows how Lisa's students made significant growth as readers in one year. Instructions for filling out the Continuum Data Collection (DC Form 11.4) and the blank forms for Writing and Reading Data Collection forms (DC Form 11.5 and 11.6) are included at the end of this chapter and on the CD-ROM.

CONTINUUM DATA COLLECTION: READING
Teacher: Lisa Norwick   Grade: 2   Year: 1998-99

Continuum Stage	Fall # Students	Fall %	Spring # Students	Spring %
Preconventional				
Emerging	1	5%		
Developing	4	20%		
Beginning	10	50%	4	20%
Expanding	5	25%	11	55%
Bridging			4	20%
Fluent			1	5%
Proficient				
Connecting				
Independent				
Total	20	100%	20	100%

Figure 11.2 Continuum Data Collection

When you fill out your Class Profile and Continuum Data Collection forms, you will need to identify one continuum stage for each student. In reality, no child falls exactly into one stage or another. Most children exhibit skills and strategies in two or even three stages. When in doubt, place a child at an earlier, rather than later stage. It's also important to remember that reading and writing growth are much more dramatic in the first few years of school. Students may move through two or even three stages per year in kindergarten and first grade. The pace of growth slows in the intermediate and middle school years as students solidify and fine-tune their skills as readers and writers. In addition, the percentages on Christy Clausen's Class Profile and Lisa Norwick's Continuum Data Collection form reflect their local population and particular demographics and may not be representative of all first and second grades. The data could be collected at the school and district level and compared to the results from state tests. Whatever your percentages, the results can be a catalyst for professional conversations with your colleagues and administrators.

Staff development takes on a new tone when conversations begin with what students can do. As Roger Vanderhye at Dhahran Academy in Saudi Arabia states, "Our job as educators changed radically after the introduction of the continuums, as we began to record what children *could do* instead of what they *couldn't do*. The focus of assessment and evaluation shifted from comparing students to assessing children and measuring growth against developmental benchmarks."

Allocating Resources

As you complete the Class Profile and Data Collection forms at the beginning of the year, you may want to meet with other staff members to discuss the implications for allocating resources. Should teachers with a higher percentage of students below the normal developmental range be provided with additional resources? How can the school provide support for teachers who have the most students with significant needs? Should the literacy specialists, paraprofessionals, or ESL teachers spend extra time in classrooms with the greatest needs?

At the end of the year, you can meet in grade-level teams to analyze the results of the data collection and allocation of resources. Next, meet as a staff to share your insights and questions. Do the age ranges on the continuums reflect expectations in your school or district? What percentage of students fall outside those developmental age ranges? Are all those students in special programs or on Individual Learning Plans? What trends do you notice? Are there issues or areas of concern? The Class Profiles and Continuum Data Collection charts can be used to decide how best to meet the needs of all students.

Ensuring Consistency

At one school, a mother fumed because her second grader was marked at the Bridging stage on the reading continuum, while his third-grade sibling was assessed at the Expanding level. The teacher realized too late that her assessments were out of line with those of her colleague. I hope this won't happen at your school. If you have participated in the staff development activities suggested in this book, created an Anchor Papers Notebook, and collected a plethora of assessment information, you should feel confident about how you have marked the continuums. Another way to ensure consistency is to share the data collection with your colleagues each fall and spring. Are classrooms balanced in terms of students' skills as readers and writers? Do all third-grade classrooms show similar gains at the end of the year? It is also important to discuss the continuums using student work in order to ensure a common understanding about how the continuums are marked and what the descriptors mean. The data collection should be helpful for school administrators and can spark conversations within a school to ensure consistency.

Celebrating Growth over Time

The reading and writing continuums, classroom-based assessment tools, and portfolios show students' growth over the period of one year. Is there also a way to step back and record growth over a longer period of time? In some schools, teachers have attempted to pass their students' portfolios on to the next year's teachers. With all the best intentions, they hoped that the new teachers would recognize and celebrate the gains their students had made in order to build upon each child's strengths. In reality, the new teachers simply didn't have time to look at 30 bulging portfolios the first month of school. They were too busy getting to know the students and their families. In many classrooms, teachers' energy was focused on starting new student portfolios for the current year. As they got to know their students over time, they focused more on what they could do and were less interested in the path students took to get to that point.

The same problem arose with classroom-based assessment. Many teachers passed along their anecdotal notes, running records, and other assessment tools. They often felt discouraged when the students' teachers the next year didn't look at the information. In terms of both portfolios and assessment data, the problem is not that the information is not useful, but simply that it's *too much* information.

As a classroom teacher, would you prefer to look through each child's stack of running records from the previous year, or would you rather look at each child's placement on the reading continuum? Would you rather look through a stack of reading logs or see a one-minute video clip of the student reading? Would you prefer to look through 30 portfolios or read their "Letter to Next Year's Teacher" in which students describe their favorite subjects, what they've learned, their interests, and what they would like to learn during the upcoming year? Rather than passing along all your assessment information, it makes more sense to use all your data to fill out the continuums that get passed on. Teachers say that looking at the reading and writing continuums from the previous year is both manageable and informative.

Learner Profiles

Several years ago, in response to the questions above, teachers at Bainbridge Island, Washington, and Brighton School began a Learner Profile that is passed along from year to year. Initially, the teachers collected one item each month. In September, all the teachers in the school gathered students' self-portraits. The next month, they collected a writing sample from each student. The samples were kept in a three-ring binder with section dividers for each type of entry (self-portrait, writing sample, reading sample, math work, drawing, etc.). For instance, all the student's K–8 self-portraits will be in one section in chronological order, stored in clear acetate slip-sheets for protection. This "mini-portfolio" grew as teachers built the monthly Learner Profile entry into their schedule and realized the value of looking at growth over time. At this point, the Learner Profile list at Brighton School is quite a bit more extensive. Teachers collect fall and winter samples, then ask students to reflect on their own growth. The Learner Profile Checklist (DC Form 11.7) includes the list of the items teachers at Brighton School collect each month, which is kept in the front of the Learner Profile. The list begins with each student's goals and ends with a letter to next year's teacher about the progress made toward those goals, as well as their hopes for the upcoming year. The Learner Profile Checklist is also included on the CD-ROM as part of the Continuum Support materials for both reading and writing.

Students at Brighton School also keep a classroom portfolio with many more samples and reflections. These classroom portfolios go home at the end of the year. After all, parents are the ones most interested in poring through their child's work. In Figure 11.3, the top of the triangle includes all the work the student produces during the year. From that work, the students select representative pieces to be included in their portfolios. The bottom of the figure shows how work for the Learner Profile can be chosen from the student's portfolio as a smaller representative slice of their learning.

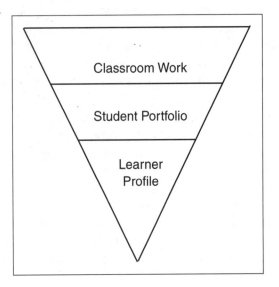

Figure 11.3 Learner Profile Data Collection

Students look through their Learner Profiles after their parent conferences. Both the student and their families enjoy looking through the binder together. In Figure 11.4, you can see my daughter, Laura, as a fifth grader, looking through her self-portraits from preschool through fifth grade. As an eighth grader next year, she will bring her Learner Profile home when she graduates from Brighton School. In one binder, we can trace her growth as a student from preschool through eighth grade through her self-portraits, goals, letters to the next year's teachers, reading logs, and work samples.

Figure 11.4 Laura's Learner Profile

Videotapes

The most popular item in the Learner Profile is the videotape that follows each child from year to year. The principal at Brighton School, Cliff Nelson, videotapes each of the 300 students in the school reading aloud in the fall and spring every year. Teachers sign up for a slot during the two or three weeks of videotaping. In preparation, teachers help each student select a page of a book he or she can read independently. You may want to monitor the books students choose to be sure that they have picked books that reflect their reading abilities. One at a time, the students bring their videotape to the office, Cliff tapes them reading for 30 seconds to one minute, then students return to class with their videotape. Depending on the number of students, it takes an hour to two hours to tape an entire class. Cliff has considered delegating the videotaping to a parent, but is unwilling to give up this enjoyable task. Unlike the classroom teachers, Cliff is able to see students' growth year after year. In addition, he enjoys this opportunity to match faces and names, as he gets to know new students. When Laura graduates next year from Brighton School, I will have a videotape of her reading aloud in the fall and spring from kindergarten through eighth grade.

Learner Profile Continuum Arrow

Some years, my children seemed to be growing out of their coats and jeans every three months. Other years, they were wearing the same clothes in June that they had worn the first week of school. Like their physical growth, academic learning also occurs in spurts. Remember the student you worried about all year and how relieved you were to hear from his next teacher that he finally blossomed as a reader? Is there a way we can step back and look at growth over several years in order to see patterns and changes? A copy of the reading and writing continuum stages without the descriptors is kept as the second page of the Learner Profile (DC Form 11.8). The Learner Profile chart is also included on the CD-ROM as part of the Continuum Support materials. As they fill out report cards in June, teachers mark the general stage where each student's behaviors fall at the end of the year. The Learner Profile is then handed to the child's new teacher in September. If students move, the contents of the binder and videotape are simply removed and given to the child's parents. If you have a highly mobile population, the Learner Profile may not be a reasonable option at your school.

The power of using Learner Profiles lies in looking at growth over time. At many schools, Learner Profiles have provided the solution to teachers' frustration about passing student portfolios on to the next teacher. In the next book in this assessment series, *Student Portfolios and Self-Evaluation*, I will further explore the possibilities of Learner Profiles and provide examples from various schools.

Sharing Data within a District

Jefferson County School District near Denver, Colorado, has been using the reading and writing continuums in a variety of ways since 1997. Interest in the continuums began with Carrie Ekey and a small group of Literacy Resource Teachers (LRTs) in this very large school district with over 100 elementary schools. In the next section, I'll describe how Carrie and this dedicated group of teachers have created links between the reading/writing continuums and other assessment tools over the past four years.

1. Connecting the Reading Continuum with Assessment Strategies

The major focus for Jefferson County in 1997 was to help teachers see the connection between the continuums and the newly mandated Colorado Basic Literacy Act (CBLA). Carrie Ekey, the Lead Literacy Resource Teacher, and her colleagues created a list of assessment tools and strategies for each stage on the reading continuum. For many classroom teachers, this was the first time they had ever heard of tools like running records, miscue analysis, literacy checklists, retelling, and continuums. Staff development was concentrated on helping teachers become familiar with and comfortable using these assessment strategies.

2. Connecting the Continuum with Guided Reading and Book Leveling

The team created a document directly linking the continuum stages with guided reading. They developed a Guided Reading Continuum with folders that contained suggestions for strategies and types of questions to ask before, during, and after reading. At the same time, they created a pamphlet of guided reading book characteristics to support teachers in the selection of books for guided reading groups. Stein Elementary, a low socioeconomic school in Jefferson County with a high proportion of ESL learners, was particularly interested in meeting the needs of their diverse population. They decided to group students for instruction by continuum levels. They also leveled hundreds of books in their school in order to match appropriate books to students and their individual needs. Now that these documents have been in place for several years, teachers are enthusiastic about the difference the continuums, leveled books, and intentional teaching and assessment have made in their school.

In the book room at Hutchinson Elementary in Jefferson County, Colorado, teachers put up the enlarged versions of the continuum descriptors at each continuum stage, along with the accompanying list of book characteristics and titles from Chapter 4. They organized books for guided reading by continuum stages. Now, when they work with a group of students at a particular stage, they use the book characteristics and book lists to choose appropriate titles for guided reading from the book room.

3. Connecting the Continuum with K–1 Literacy Screening

The following year, Carrie and the Literacy Resource Teachers created a K–1 Assessment screening instrument linked to the continuums. Each of the measures (letter/sound recognition, phonemic awareness, beginning reading skills, writing proficiency, and beginning reading process) included a rubric aligned with the Preconventional, Emerging, and Beginning stages on the reading and writing continuums. The Jefferson County K–1 Assessment was originally used to place students in Title I reading programs. It was revised to help guide instruction and evaluate the reading proficiency of kindergarten students, as required by the CBLA. First grade students who were not proficient in kindergarten were also monitored. Hundreds of K–1 teachers were trained in the use of this assessment. Carrie writes:

> In the first year, teachers were quite vocal about their frustration over being required to administer an individual assessment. One teacher complained about how the district's expectation of kindergartners was too high. The next year, this teacher, as well as many others were raving about the value of the assessment. She said that she knew her students as individual learners far better than she had in previous years. In addition, she acknowledged that the quality of her students' reading and writing had improved greatly over other years because her expectations were higher.

4. Connecting the Reading and Writing Continuums with Standards

Over the last few years, Jefferson County attempted several ways to align the continuums with district standards. Teachers had struggled to articulate what the standards would look like at their grade level. Since at the same time, the CBLA was requiring documentation of classroom assessment for reading proficiency for all K–3 students, Carrie and the Literacy Resource Teachers formatted the sequence of individual behaviors on the reading continuum to align with the district standards and required a "body of evidence." A similar type of reformatting was used to align the writing continuum with the writing process and Six-Trait Writing (Northwest Regional Educational Laboratory). Other districts in Colorado are now developing similar ways to help teachers see the connections between standards, district expectations, assessment, and continuums. By connecting testing and standards with continuums and classroom-based assessment, it's possible to maintain a balance between the political reality of our times and our professional knowledge about what is best for children. Laura Benson, an educational consultant in the Denver area, writes, "The issue of honoring a child's strengths – not just his/her needs – is a powerful and incredibly necessary practice in these times of high-stakes testing."

5. Connecting the Reading Continuum with Comprehension through Retelling

Teachers in the Jefferson County district were using the Developmental Reading Assessment (DRA, Beaver, 1997) to assess the reading proficiency of each K–3 student. The district supplemented the retelling portion of the test with a K–3 Retelling Rubric that they developed specifically linked to the reading continuum. This tool presented a challenge for many teachers who were still overwhelmed by the thought of individual assessment and data collection. By the end of the year, one teacher told Carrie, "I started using the retelling rubric in my guided reading, and I can see the difference in my students' comprehension. I know they will be proficient on the DRA, but more importantly, they are comprehending at a much higher level."

6. Connecting the Reading Continuum with Instructional Strategies

Last year, Jefferson County developed a list of very specific reading skills and strategies for each stage on the reading continuum. They created an Instructional Strategies pamphlet, a Reading Skills and Strategies guide, and pacing sheets. These support materials helped teachers see the connection between the continuum and their teaching. The district also aligned the writing continuum with district standards in the same way reading had been aligned the year before.

7. Connecting the Writing Continuum with Anchor Papers

In response to teachers' requests to "show me what writing should look like at my grade level," Carrie and the Literacy Resource Teachers collected sample papers from several schools and created a packet of Anchor Papers for K–3. They linked these samples to the continuum in a Six-Trait Writing Benchmarks K–3 Pacing Sheet which accompanies the Anchor Papers (called Writing Exemplars K–3). The positive response to this particular curricular piece has been overwhelming. One teacher stated, "This makes the writing continuum come alive! Now I can see what these descriptors mean in terms of real student work. Now I can show these Exemplars to students and parents so they have a picture of what we expect." Carrie commented, "Across our district, staff developers are having very rich, exciting conversations with teachers as they begin evaluating student writing in a much more knowledgeable manner. Teachers are evaluating writing and collaborating about writing instruction across grade levels and discussing instruction in a way that has never happened before."

8. Connecting the Reading Continuum with Parent Education

The final piece which the Jefferson County School District added last year was the *Learning to Read* video described in Chapter 8. This ten-minute video presents ways for parents of children in the first six stages of the reading continuum to support reading at home. A copy of the video was given to each of the 100 elementary schools and to each of the 30 preschools in the district.

9. Defining Continuum Terminology and Building Consistency

In the writing continuum, students at the Beginning stage are expected to write "some high frequency words correctly" and "most high frequency words correctly" by the Expanding stage. How do you know how many is "some" or "most"? This year, Jefferson County developed a recommended list of high frequency words that can help teachers assess their students' writing at each of the first five stages on the writing continuum. For instance, students would be expected to be able to write eight words by the end of kindergarten (including the child's first name). They should be able to write 26 words by the end of the Developing stage (mid-year first grade), 50 words by the end of first grade, 100 words at the end of the Beginning stage (mid-year second grade), and 150 words by the beginning of the Expanding stage (end of second grade). By the end of the Expanding stage, students should have moved toward conventional spelling of these high frequency words.

This does not mean that teachers should drill students on these words. Rather, the list is intended as a guideline and an assessment tool for monitoring correct spelling of high frequency words. Instruction of correct spelling of other words through patterns is also expected and assessed using other spelling assessment tools. Some of you may not want to operationalize the continuum at this level of specificity. If, however, you are collecting large-scale data and using the continuum in a large district, the work Jefferson County has done may be helpful. For copies of their list of high frequency words or the other seven continuum support pieces described in this chapter, you may want to contact Carrie Ekey (cekey@jeffco.k12. co.us) or the Jefferson County School District at (www.jeffconet. jeffco.k12.co.us/ isu/langarts/).

Correlating with Standards-Based Tests

Like many other states, Washington has implemented new state standards and testing at fourth, seventh, and tenth grades. Approximately 80% of the Washington State standards are incorporated into the reading and writing continuums. You may want to determine what percentages of your state standards are woven into the continuums. In some cases, you may want to use the CD-ROM version to adapt the continuums so that they align with your standards.

The good news in Washington is that the tests are rigorous, yet realistic, and reflect good teaching. The bad news is that the results are splashed across the front page of local newspapers and far too much importance is attached to the test scores. As teachers, we all know the limitations of such tests. They are small snapshots of learning, often culturally biased, and in the end, directly correlated to social economic status (SES). In addition, the results are often misinterpreted. However, tests are a reality in the world of education. Test results can be balanced with information from the continuums and classroom-based assessment.

In states like Colorado, test results are often used to evaluate schools and programs and to allocate funds and resources. Scores are scrutinized to determine changes from year to year. Parents, administrators, and politicians sometimes don't realize that results will be influenced by the composition of each group. For example, the results of the fourth-grade test are compared from year to year, yet the tests are given to different groups of students. In Figure 11.5 and 11.6, for instance, you can see the percentages for two different groups of fourth graders. Notice how in 1998, 87% of Nick Thompson's students were at the Bridging or Fluent stages in reading at the beginning of the year, with only four of his students starting the year as Expanding readers. The next year, only 27% of his students were Bridging readers and none of his students were Fluent readers. Most of his students were at the Beginning or Expanding stages. When the reading test scores for his class went down in 1999, Nick could compare test results with where he had placed students on the reading continuum at the beginning of the year. Although Nick knew intuitively that his group of students was quite different the second year, comparing test data and continuum information provided more specific information and facilitated conversations between grade levels. You may want to use the Data Collection forms (DC Form 11.5 and 11.6) for your own class, then share the results with your colleagues.

CONTINUUM DATA COLLECTION: READING

Teacher: *Nick Thompson*   Grade: *4* Year: *98 – 99*

Continuum Stage	Fall		Spring	
	# Students	%	# Students	%
Preconventional				
Emerging				
Developing				
Beginning				
Expanding	4	13%		
Bridging	24	80%	14	47%
Fluent	2	7%	15	50%
Proficient			1	3%
Connecting				
Independent				
Total	30	100%	30	100%

Figure 11.5 First Year Continuum Data

In the future, I hope that a large district that is using the continuums will decide to correlate continuum information with state test results. In Washington, for instance, a district could compare continuum placement with the results from the fourth-grade state test (WASL). If the continuums incorporate most of the state standards and the tests are based on standards, then the test results should match where teachers place students on the continuums. If not, we may want to re-examine either the continuums or the tests. However, until we have actual data to analyze, no claims can be made about statistical validity at this point. Such a study would make a fascinating doctoral dissertation! Although high standards are an admirable goal, the reality in education is that some students have far more obstacles and challenges to overcome before they can achieve these lofty goals. Our job is to discover and build upon the skills students *do* have and celebrate growth in their journey toward high standards. I hope that those of you reading this book who are using the continuum as a whole school or district will consider these ideas and contact me through Christopher-Gordon Publishers to share your results.

CONTINUUM DATA COLLECTION: READING

Teacher: *Nick Thompson*   Grade: *4* Year: *99-00*

Continuum Stage	Fall		Spring	
	# Students	%	# Students	%
Preconventional				
Emerging				
Developing				
Beginning	4	13%		
Expanding	18	60%	6	20%
Bridging	8	27%	22	73%
Fluent			2	7%
Proficient				
Connecting				
Independent				
Total	30	100%	30	100%

Figure 11.6 Second Year Continuum Data

Staff Development

Now let's take a look at how teachers' questions and practices change over time as they implement developmental continuums. Figure 11.7 shows the typical stages of continuum implementation over a period of five years.

Year One: Exposure

In most cases, the process begins when a teacher who learns about continuums shares the information with a few colleagues. Several teachers then express an interest in looking at the continuums more closely because they see the match between the continuums and their beliefs about teaching and learning. During the initial discussions about whether or not to use a continuum, the following rather broad questions usually emerge:

- What is a developmental continuum?
- How do continuums fit with my philosophy, curriculum, and teaching practices?

- How do continuums align with our current assessment practices?
- How do continuums match our state and district standards?

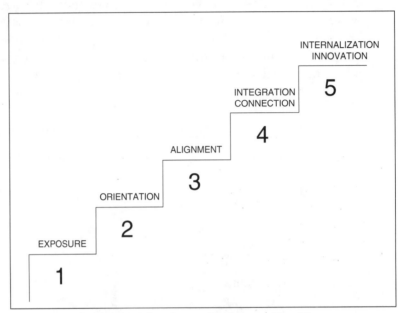

Figure 11.7 Continuum Implementation Stages

Once teachers are able to answer these questions satisfactorily, they usually develop a plan for a small group of teachers to pilot the continuum. The pilot group may want to meet regularly to share questions and to provide support for each other. At the end of the year, the pilot group can discuss the advantages of using continuums, as well as the teachers' concerns. Teachers can then decide if they want to use the continuum the next year on an individual voluntary basis, by grade levels, as a school, or as a district.

Year Two: Orientation

The second year often involves an official pilot on a wider scale. At West Mercer Elementary in Washington State, for instance, a small group of teachers informally piloted the continuums in 1997 and shared the information with some of their colleagues. The next year, they formed another unofficial pilot group with about ten other teachers in the school. As they talked about the advantages and wondered about the whole school implementing the continuum, they first had to address the following questions:

- How do the continuums fit with our state standards?
- How do the continuums fit with our district curriculum?
- Where do I store continuums?
- How do I mark continuums?
- What do some of the descriptors mean?
- How do I match assessment tools to the continuum?
- How do continuums fit with other priorities, projects, and practices?

This is a very concrete level of questioning. Teachers want to know how to fit the continuums in their Teacher Notebooks and how to mark them. Part of the process at this stage is deciding who will participate in the pilot. Will it be volunteers, a whole grade level, or an entire school? No matter how enthusiastic teachers are, it's important at this point to step back and decide how continuums fit with all the other projects and commitments at your school. Are you adopting a new math series and implementing performance tasks this year? How much time or energy will teachers have to put into learning how to use continuums and classroom-based assessment? In most schools, the problem is not resistance to new ideas, but simply overload. Before going any further, it's vital to decide if developmental continuums will be a priority at your school. For instance, when I worked with the teachers at the Saudi Arabian International School (SAIS) in Jeddah, Saudi Arabia, they were enthusiastic about every idea I shared. The principal, Tracey Carey, helped teachers prioritize the list and create a five-year plan and a time line for the rest of the school year (Figure 11.8).

Primary English Department 5- Year Plan December 1999

	This year	Next year	3-5 years
Pilot continuums		◆	
Implement continuum assessment by teacher only		◆	
Implement student self-evaluation w/ continuum		◆	
Learn more about literature circles for use w/ continuums	◆		
Pilot six traits writing		◆	
Complete identification of benchmarks	◆		
Incorporate benchmarks into unit plans		◆	
Develop consistent spelling approach	◆		
Incorporate continuum into reporting system			◆
Align six traits with Arabic program		◆	
Align continuum use with Arabic program		◆	
Continue with portfolios/writing samples	◆		
Writers workshop inservice	◆		
Six traits inservice	◆	◆	
Literature circles inservice		◆	
Review and reevaluate reporting system	◆	◆	
Develop science philosophy/essential agreements	◆		
Form book club/study group	◆		

Plans for the Remainder of this School Year

	This year
Learn more about literature circles for use w/ continuums	• Terry and Christine will pilot
Literature circles inservice	• May discuss in reading group
Complete identification of benchmarks	• Department meetings in February and March
Develop consistent spelling approach	• January – Department meetings
Continue with portfolios/writing samples	• Clarify expectations – December • Ongoing
Writers workshop inservice	• Jan – April course offered for credit
Six traits inservice	• Topic for book group • Show and tell in department meetings • Possible weekend workshops
Review and reevaluate reporting system	• Dot will initiate. Probably a lengthy process..
Develop science philosophy/essential agreements	• Bridget/Terry will bring model to revise /approve in department meeting
Form book club/study group	• Make selections in December • Begin meetings in January

Figure 11.8 Long-Term Staff Development Plan

The staff decided which ideas they would focus on for the remainder of the year and which new ideas would become the focus during the following year. For instance, teachers decided to begin the official continuum pilot in the fall of the 2000–2001 school year and hoped to have the continuums in place as part of the report card by 2001–2002.

Once you determine who will participate in the continuum pilot, the next step is to decide whether to begin with the reading continuum, the writing continuum, or both. Will you fill out the continuums two or three times a year? Will teachers in the pilot group fill out the continuum on a few students or all students? You may want to write a grant to fund the project so that the pilot teachers can be compensated for the additional work and time involved. Teachers also appreciate earning clock hours or credit.

At West Mercer Elementary in Mercer Island, Washington, teachers agreed to fill out the reading continuum on two or three students in the fall and all of their students by the end of the year. In other schools, teachers may plunge in and complete the continuums for all their students two or three times a year. By collecting baseline data in the fall, it's easier to see growth. In addition, once the continuum is filled out the first time, there are usually only a handful of new descriptors the next trimester or semester to check off. In the pilot stage, students are assessed with the continuums in order for teachers to become familiar with the descriptors and confident about the data they have collected. The data that is collected may or may not be shared with families at this point.

Staff Development

The most important staff development activity for participants in the pilot is providing time to talk about the continuums. The highlighter activity described in Chapter 3 is particularly helpful. This exercise usually assuages teachers' anxiety about filling out the continuum as they realize that most of the descriptors are ones that they already assess. If you are piloting the reading continuum, you may also want to take an hour or two for the book sorting activity described in Chapter 4. When Dan and Colleen Kryszak piloted the reading continuum in Tacoma, Washington, they said that the most important staff development activity they did was the book sort. Dan writes, "Doing the book leveling was hands-on and provided a way to see the continuum in a tangible way. The activity pointed out the range of readers in a classroom and, at times, the lack of books for kids at certain levels." Dan and Colleen served as facilitators as teachers discussed the continuum descriptors for each stage and asked questions. Teachers discussed what behaviors to look for and how to assess the skills of young readers. This simple staff development activity often helps teachers begin talking about books and readers in a new way.

The second year is a perfect time to introduce Teacher Notebooks (Chapter 5). At West Mercer Elementary, teachers identified three or four assessment tools at each grade level that they all agreed to use and recorded those on their Organizational Grid (DC Form 5.3). They shared student work and questions when they met informally throughout the year. At the end of the year, pilot participants will want to share their successes and concerns with the rest of the school or district administration in order to determine whether the pilot will continue another year, or if the continuums will be required the following year. If you decide to continue using the continuum, the pilot group may want to submit a list of recommendations based on their own experiences.

Year Three: Alignment

Year Three is the implementation year. Once again, you have to decide whether to use the reading or writing continuum or both, and how often the continuum will be filled out. Will the continuums be shared with parents at the "ballpark" level, in which teachers indicate the general stage where students fall, or will teachers use highlighters to fill out the continuum at the descriptor level? You may want to use the following chart to clarify expectations for using the continuums. This is the chart that each teacher at West Mercer used to indicate his or her preference for the implementation year. The results were tallied and discussed.

West Mercer Elementary: Continuum Consensus

Name: Grade Level:

Filled Out for:	Reading Continuum		Writing Continuum	
None of my students				
Some of my students	Ballpark	Descriptor	Ballpark	Descriptor
All of my students	Ballpark	Descriptor	Ballpark	Descriptor

At West Mercer Elementary, most of the K–4 teachers had already used the reading continuums, so the staff agreed that all K–4 teachers would complete the reading continuum in the fall and spring at the descriptor level for all students. The conversations soon shifted to a higher level as teachers looked at the match between their instruction and their assessment practices. Teachers also fine-tuned their understanding of the continuum as they became more familiar with the descriptors at their grade level.

The next challenge that often arises is how to share the continuum with other teachers, such as the resource teacher and Title I teachers. Ideally, the resource staff and the classroom teachers should both fill out the continuums and plan time to share the results in order to support students with specific needs. Classroom teachers and the ESL teachers in your building may also want to fill out the EAL Speaking and Listening continuum from Chapter 9 for students who are learning to speak English.

Finally, how will the continuum be shared with families? Will you provide an overview of the continuum at a Curriculum Night as described in Chapter 8? At West Mercer Elementary, I conducted a night for parents on reading and writing development. Teachers distributed the Narrative Portraits (Chapter 2), a list of Books by Stages (Chapter 4), and the Family Support documents (Chapter 8). I showed samples and video clips from the Case Studies described in Chapter 2. Teachers also explained the continuums at Back to School Night. Some teachers gave families a copy of the reading continuum at parent conferences. You should decide how to share the continuums with families at the beginning of the implementation year. Here are some of the other questions that typically arise, as continuums are used school wide:

- What do some of the descriptors mean?
- How do I provide enough documentation to mark the continuums? How much is enough?
- How can I weave assessment practices into my classroom in a manageable and organized way?
- Where are our instructional gaps as a school?
- How do we share continuum/assessment information with other teachers (reading teachers, ESL, special education)?
- How do we share the continuums with parents and administration?

Staff Development

You may want to repeat the highlighting and book sorting exercise as other teachers use the continuums for the first time. Teachers from the pilot group can share their Teacher Notebooks, Organizational Grids, and Anchor Papers Notebook and explain how they fill out the continuums. You may want to provide a half-day of release time for a support team to help the new teachers create their notebooks and grids. A continuum committee may also want to create some support documents that show how the continuums align with your curriculum and state standards.

During the 1999–2000 school year, all of the K–4 teachers at West Mercer Elementary used the reading continuum. In order to build consistency within the district, the Literacy Team decided to create a writing continuum pilot project for the following year. Kay Grady, the literacy coordinator, wrote a grant for a writing continuum pilot project for the 2000–2001 school year. Her original grant was for six teachers per school to participate from the three elementary schools in the district. To her amazement, almost 50 teachers requested to be part of the pilot! Kay scrambled to write an additional grant, which eventually was funded. This year the writing continuum pilot consists of 48 teachers from the three elementary schools in the district. The participating teachers received copies of the continuums and support materials, as well as a Teacher Notebook with dividers. They also attended a full-day workshop on continuums and another half-day workshop on writing assessment. Grade-level support meetings were offered several times during the year after school, as well as optional book study groups on writing. As part of the grant, teachers were also released for an hour in the fall and in the spring to meet in grade-level teams to share their successes and concerns about writing assessment and the continuum.

The principals, the literacy leads in each building, and the literacy coordinator for the district were all extremely supportive of the teachers. They provided time, materials, professional books, and responded to teachers' needs and concerns. Of course, not every district has the administrative backing or resources to provide this type of support, but you may be able to incorporate some of these suggestions based on your own situation. Administration support is invaluable if change is to occur at the district level. This is also a good time to form a report card committee if you are considering incorporating the continuum into your report card in the future.

Year Four: Integration and Connections

In Year Four, the continuum is used for both assessment and reporting. Although teachers may have been using the continuum for assessment, this is usually the first year that the continuums are included as an official supplement to the report card. In many schools, teachers are allowed to cross out the reading and/or writing boxes on the report card and write "See Continuum." This is a more manageable step than trying to figure out how to put the continuums on the report card itself. It makes more sense to begin with the educational challenge of using a continuum, rather than becoming bogged down by trying to change the whole report card or facing the technological challenge of creating a computer program for the continuum and report card. Learning to use the continuum is enough of an undertaking in itself!

By this time, you probably have a good understanding of most of the continuum descriptors. Now the questions shift from "What is a literary element?" to "When my fifth graders write in their literature response journals, what does a thoughtful written response look like?" At this point, it's important to build some consistency within and between grade levels. The best way to do this is to provide time to bring actual samples of student work to discuss in staff meetings or at a workshop. As you look at student samples, conversations inevitably turn to instruction. These discussions can become an exciting venue for professional growth as you address some of the following questions:

- What do some of the descriptors really mean (fine-tuning)?
- How do we build consistency between and within grade levels?
- What are the staff needs for further professional development?
- How can we involve students in the assessment process?
- How can we put the continuum on the computer?
- How do we introduce the continuums to parents and educate the community?

Staff Development

At West Mercer Elementary in Washington State, teachers held monthly grade-level team meetings focusing on assessment. During the meetings, teachers looked at their Organizational Grids and reviewed the assessment tools they planned to collect that month. These team meetings were a powerful forum for professional conversations and sharing. For instance, Kay Grady, the district literacy coordinator, arranged for "floating substitutes" to free each grade-level team to meet with me for an hour in the fall and again in the spring at each of the three schools. We discussed the continuums and they shared their Organizational Grids and Teacher Notebooks. Because I was coming, some teachers scrambled to put together their notebooks the night before. Just like students, teachers are also on a continuum in terms of their knowledge of assessment and continuums. By October, some teachers already had filed their parent and student surveys in their Teacher Notebook, had started reading conferences, and had taken several anecdotal notes for each student. As these teachers shared their enthusiasm about how well they knew their students, many of their colleagues left the meetings ready to begin collecting and organizing their own Teacher Notebook. Whenever I facilitate this type of meeting, I am struck by how hard teachers work and by how grateful they are for this type of professional dialogue.

You may also want to create a Continuum Wall at your school and begin an Anchor Papers Notebook with exemplary work from students at each stage on the continuum for different genres (e.g., nonfiction writing, written response to literature, poetry). Each grade level may also want to identify one child at each stage on the continuum and create your own version of the Case Studies that fit your particular community. The process of identifying these 10 students and collecting their work can help clarify the continuum descriptors and create a common framework and understanding of literacy acquisition.

Principals may want to provide time before the school year begins for teachers to put together their Teacher Notebooks and create a new Organizational Grid for the next year. Teachers can share which tools were most effective and fine-tune their assessment plans. Principals may also want to pair the new teachers in the building with those who have used Teacher Notebooks and continuums successfully.

The schools where teachers are most confident and enthusiastic about assessment and continuums are most often the ones in which principals have provided strong leadership. For instance, Nancy Emerson, the principal at West Mercer Elementary has linked the teachers' Organizational Grids to their professional goals and her classroom observations. Teachers are required to turn in their grids to her at the beginning of the year. As much as possible, she also tries to attend the monthly team meetings in which teachers share their Teacher Notebooks and assessment tools. Ingrid Stipes writes, "The continuums have provided a common language that we now share among grade levels throughout the building, among parents, with other schools in the district, and with our students. Teachers now meet in grade levels to share materials, ideas, and observations using 'continuum-ese!' Teaching doesn't seem as lonely as it once did. The continuums have truly opened up our channels of communication."

Kay Grady, the literacy team, and principals like Nancy Emerson have done a great deal to maintain a supportive tone in the district as teachers have piloted the continuums. They provide release time for staff development, substitutes for monthly meetings and classroom observations in other schools, as well as professional study groups on literacy instruction and assessment. Change is certainly easier in such a supportive district.

It's also important to have the support of the district administration. In the Tacoma School District in Washington State, the reading and writing continuums have been used for several years on the K–3 report card. When the new report card with the reading and writing continuums was first adopted, Gail Miller, Director of Elementary Education/Early Childhood, presented a two-hour workshop at each of the district's 37 elementary schools. Her enthusiasm and the fact that the presentation was given by a high-level administrator helped teachers see that the continuum report card was supported by the district. Cheryl Perkins was a teacher in Tacoma. She writes, "I was involved in the adoption of continuums in the Tacoma School District. Now, five years later, I am working on a similar adoption with the American Community School in Abu Dhabi in the United Arab Emirates." As Cheryl notes, "best practices" are the same anywhere in the world.

Once teachers have become more comfortable filling out the continuums and sharing them with parents, the next logical step is to involve students in the assessment process, as described in Chapter 7. You may want to display the continuum charts in your room and refer to them as you teach. With modeling and practice, your students can also learn to fill out the student self-evaluation version of the continuums or the student self-evaluation checklists. The continuums also provide a perfect segue into portfolio reflections and goal setting. During student-led conferences, students can share the continuum with their parents and use their portfolios to provide evidence for what they've learned. You may want to offer another Curriculum Night about reading and writing development for parents during which you hand out copies of the continuums and the support pieces (Narrative Portraits, Family Support, and Books by Stages) in a Parent Handbook.

As a staff, you may want to collect feedback about the continuums with a survey. What did parents like about the continuums? What did they find difficult? For instance, one parent wrote the following response about the continuums, "It informed me about how and if the child was performing at the expected rate in relation to their age group, showing what has been done and what's to come." This type of information is invaluable as you decide whether or not to include the continuum as part of the report card for the following year. The concept of a continuum is so radically different from what most parents experienced growing up that you will face a great deal of resistance unless parent education is woven into the report card revision process. The biggest obstacle to using a continuum is the almost universal familiarity with number and letter grades. Before the continuums can be implemented as part of the report card, this issue has to be confronted directly.

If you have been including the continuums as a supplement to your report card, you may next want to consider putting the continuum on the computer as part of your report card; however, creating such a program is extremely time consuming. Becky Walsh, a primary teacher in Marysville, Washington, launched a report card pilot for the Marysville School District. She created a computer program that can also be used as a classroom database for managing student information. Using Becky's program, you can also print mailing labels and send mail-merged parent letters. Teachers who have used Becky's report card with the continuum and the accompanying database have been extremely pleased. If you're interesting in putting the continuum on a computer, you may want to start by contacting Becky Walsh (rwalsh@sos.net) for advice and information. Bill and Karen Bliven in Issaquah, Washington, have also created a computer program with continuums that can be used for assessment and reporting. With their program, you can click on continuum descriptors, scan in student portfolio samples, and record oral reflections. You may want to look at their website (www.halcyon.com/bliven/kids.htm) for more information.

When I first started teaching, report cards were revised only every five years because they were so expensive to run on NCR paper. With changes in technology, we currently have many more creative options. Now, teachers can look creatively at report cards and reporting practices. With the advent of computers, changes can be made each year, based on feedback from the pilot and parent surveys. These types of technological connections are very exciting and will be explored further in the fourth book in this assessment series, *Reporting Student Growth*. In that book, I will also address the challenges of evolving report cards and describe ways in which many districts have successfully incorporated developmental continuums as part of the reporting process.

Year Five: Internalization and Innovation

By Year Five, the continuums have been integrated as part of the report card and are being used for both assessment and reporting. The focus now becomes strengthening the connections between instruction, assessment, and reporting. Teachers at this stage make conscious links between the continuums, student portfolios, and student-led conferences as they consider the following questions:

- How can we better involve students in self-evaluation?
- How can continuums connect to portfolios and student-led conferences?
- How can we document student growth within and between grade levels?
- What changes do we want to make on the report card or continuums?

At the Saudi Arabian International School (SAIS) in Jeddah, Jill and Jack Raven and the other first-grade teachers literally cut apart the reading and writing continuums and paste them into their students' evaluative portfolios. The continuum descriptors are surrounded by samples of student work and photographs as support. For instance, a student at the Developing stage in writing might have a story, a list, and a poem next to the descriptors for that stage. How would you show reading growth? In Figure 11.9, you can see how Jill documented a student's reading skills with a sample page from a book he could read independently and with photographs of the student sharing books and response projects with the class. The student samples and photographs bring the continuums to life!

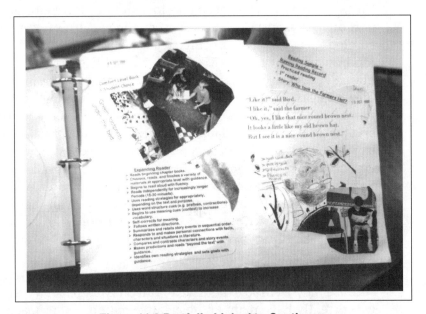

Figure 11.9 Portfolio Linked to Continuum

Kevin Baxter from the Aramco school in Abqaiq, Saudi Arabia writes, "In our first-grade classroom, continuums are a huge part of our daily life. Our student portfolios are updated regularly, using the continuums as a way to monitor and report progress. The students are becoming familiar with the vocabulary, which helps them see where they are as readers and writers. The continuums and portfolios become informative pieces of evidence to share with parents during conferences."

What are other ways to communicate with parents about their children's growth? Brighton School has used the school web site (www.brightonschool.com) to display the continuums, Narrative Portraits, and Family Support documents. You may also want to create a team of "Continuum Parents" who would be willing to explain the continuums to new families. Once continuums are in place, data can be collected at the school and district level. You may want to correlate test results with teacher assessment on the continuums. You can use the CD-ROM to make modifications to the continuum based on your findings. As continuums become an integral part of your curriculum, assessment, and reporting plan, you may want to use the Class Profile and Data Collection forms described in the first half of this chapter.

Cliff Nelson, the principal, described the central role of the continuums at Brighton School:

> At Brighton School, the reading and writing continuums have been part of our teaching, assessment, and reporting system for five years. It is the cornerstone of our academic program. The continuums set standards for what we want our students to know and be able to do at age appropriate levels. As the principal, I share the continuums on every tour of prospective enrollees. What I am able to say to parents is that we have standards, but we also teach developmentally. We teach students where they are. If they have mastered a particular skill, we move on to the next set of learnings. If students need more of a foundation to meet standards, we teach them what they need. The continuums also help us design professional growth opportunities for teachers as we plan more effective teaching and assessment strategies.
>
> The continuums are invaluable to teachers, students, and families. The continuums are not just a tangible guide for literacy growth. They are also the center of our philosophy and a way of defining our targets, teaching students at their own level, assessing progress, and reporting accurately to students and parents.

Many schools in Winnipeg, Manitoba have been using continuums for several years. Gayle Robertson, an Early Years Consultant for the Winnipeg School Division Number 1 feels that the continuums also provide a way to encourage professional dialogue. She writes:

> Continuums are one of the most useful tools I have found for sparking the interest of teachers in working together with colleagues as a team. Often, when a teacher first discovers continuums, the reaction is "Hey, this is great. It's just what I needed to track the progress of my students." In the next stage, teachers begin to look more closely at the indicators, adjusting the language to fit their personal understandings. As teachers begin to think about using the continuums as a tool for sharing information with colleagues and parents, the best part begins and teacher-to-teacher conversations blossom.
>
> Conversations about educational issues are the heart of professional staff development. There is nothing more exciting than to see a group of teachers bring their insights, understanding, and experi-

ence together to forge a shared framework for observing, recording, and communicating information about students' learning. I have seen teachers bring research, examples of student work, anecdotal notes, and personal stories to share with their colleagues. I have teachers work together as a staff to develop school-wide continuums which are used to record progress and communicate with families. I believe that continuums are a useful tool for assessment, evaluation, and reporting. In addition, continuums also provide a valuable tool for staff development.

Continuum Implementation

It's helpful to think of continuum implementation as a five-year plan. It is better to start slowly and provide enough time, support, and resources so that the process can be successful. At West Mercer Elementary, the process began with a handful of teachers who informally used the reading continuum in 1997. The reading continuum was piloted by teachers in 1999 and the writing continuum in 2000.

CONTINUUM IMPLEMENTATION
West Mercer Elementary, Mercer Island, Washington

Year	Reading	Stage
1997–1998	1	Exposure
1998–1999	2	Orientation
1999–2000	3	Alignment
2000–2001	4	Integration

Year	Writing	Stage
1997–1998		
1998–1999	1	Exposure
1999–2000	2	Orientation
2000–2001	3	Alignment

Brighton School in Lynnwood, Washington has been using the reading and writing continuums since 1995. They began using a math continuum in 1997, including it on the report card in 1999. The math continuum is still being revised. You'll want to look at the priorities in your own building and district to determine a long-range plan for using developmental continuums and classroom-based assessment.

CONTINUUM IMPLEMENTATION
Brighton School, Lynnwood, Washington

Year	Reading/Writing	Stage
1995–1996	1	Exposure
1996–1997	2	Orientation
1997–1998	3	Alignment
1998–1999	4	Integration
1999–2000	5	Innovation
2000–2001		

Year	Math	Stage
1995–1996		
1996–1997		
1997–1998	1	Exposure
1998–1999	2	Orientation
1999–2000	3	Alignment
2000–2001	4	Integration

Using the Continuums at the University Level

Katherine L. Schlick Noe is a professor in the School of Education at Seattle University. She has used the reading and writing continuums for several years with her preservice students in the Master in Teaching program. One of the biggest challenges for beginning teachers is getting a sense for what their students know and can do as readers and writers. Instinct or panic prompts many inexperienced teachers to start with their curriculum and work through a published program. But then they encounter readers who don't fit a fixed curriculum—the first grader reading a *Harry Potter* book, the fourth grader struggling to figure out the most basic words who forgets what she's reading long before she finishes a passage, the third grader spending his library time poring over books on aircraft, soaking up technical specifications just as others crave fantasy. Readers don't always fit the curriculum. And that's where the continuum comes into play.

The continuums help Katherine's students focus first on the learner. What do children do as they develop as readers and writers? How do they move toward more sophisticated literacy behaviors? Her class tackles these questions before they delve into instruction. Using the continuums as a framework sets the stage for everything her students learn about literacy instruction. Assessment helps the preservice teachers develop a stance of "kid watchers." They learn that everything their students do can provide them with information about the learner as a reader and writer. The continuums describe concrete behaviors to watch for.

In Katherine's course, students use the continuums in several specific ways. Their first task is to conduct a literacy profile on a student in their student teaching classroom. They select someone they and their cooperating teacher have questions about — perhaps a child who is new to the classroom, or someone whose challenge with English may mask what they know as a learner, or simply someone they can't figure out. The beginning teachers use the continuums to make preliminary conjectures about their students' strengths and needs. ("Preliminary" because this is only one assessment at one moment in time. Throughout the course, they talk about how assessments need to be made over time and in a variety of areas to get a full picture of a student's strengths and needs).

Students also plan a reading strategy lesson in which they blend the continuum descriptors with the Washington State Essential Academic Learning Requirements (EALR's). Using the continuums helps them see how the state standards apply to what we know about readers and writers. It also helps these beginning teachers figure out how to plan specific literacy lessons that are based on what their students need at any given time.

The continuums give preservice teachers the language to explain how students behave as literacy learners. As beginning teachers, they will be better able to walk into a classroom and focus on learners, rather than on the curriculum. That, in turn, enables them to make effective use of their school or district curriculum. They develop an eye for assessment and feel that they are better able to teach to each student's individual needs. Katherine notes that this also helps them deal proactively with the testing mania many of them face once they begin teaching. As beginning teachers, they come armed with an understanding of literacy development, some skills in assessing literacy strengths and needs, and experience in designing and teaching lessons to meet those needs. They begin to see how an emphasis on good teaching focused on individual students' specific needs can result in higher student achievement. For more information about how Katherine Schlick Noe uses the continuums in her assessment and literacy courses, you can contact her at kschlnoe@seattleu.edu or visit her web sites: Literacy Resources K–12 (http://fac-staff.seattleu.edu/kschlnoe/Literacy.html) and the Literature Circles Resource Center (http://fac-staff.seattleu.edu/kschlnoe/LitCircles).

WRITING DEVELOPMENT: CLASS PROFILE

Teacher Name: _____   Grade Level: _____

School: District:

Initials					

• = Fall   X = Spring

READING DEVELOPMENT: CLASS PROFILE

Teacher Name: _____   Grade Level: _____
School: District:

Initials					

• = Fall   X = Spring

Class Profile Directions

Dear Teachers,

We would like to collect some data about the reading and writing continuums. The continuums are being used in many schools and communities around the world. In order to determine the validity of the age ranges, we would like to collect information from your classroom. Please ask any colleagues who are also using the continuums to participate in this study.

We recognize that in real life, no child's behaviors fall neatly into one continuum stage or the other. However, for our purposes, we need you to place each student in one stage. In the fall, simply mark a DOT (•) where each child is in your class before the first parent conferences as you fill out the reading and writing continuums. If you are already using the continuum, this probably won't be very hard. Don't put them 1/2 in one stage and 1/2 in another. Just pick the stage where MOST of their behaviors fall. When in doubt, place them in the earlier stage.

Do the same thing again at the end of the year and mark an X for the stage where most of their behaviors fall. By covering up the names, you can share this information with parents during spring conferences. You will also have a picture of reading and writing growth of your students this year.

Please put your name, school, grade level(s) and district on the form. You can either put your students' names by initials or numbers, but that information will not be shared in any way since we'll simply be tallying •'s and x's.

Notice there are no stages on the top of the data collection form, so it could adapted for any grade level. Simply write the five appropriate stages into which most of your students fall in the boxes at the top of the form. I have included a sample page so that you can see the portrait of a first-grade class.

Please collect the data this fall and again in the spring, then send the results to me at the end of the year. It will be interesting to see if the ages on the continuum are consistent across communities and countries. Please share this form with as many teachers as you can find who are willing to help with this project!

Thank you for your help! If you have any further questions about this continuum data collection, please contact me through Christopher-Gordon Publishers.

Sincerely,

Bonnie Campbell Hill

Continuum Data Collection Directions

1. We are collecting ROUGH ESTIMATES of where your students are in the fall and spring on the reading/writing continuums. In reality, no child falls exactly into one stage or another. Record the numbers of students in each stage. Divide that number by the total number of students in your class to calculate the PERCENTAGE of students (rounded off to nearest %) at each stage in the fall and again in the spring for both Reading and Writing.

2. What percentage of your class falls outside of the normal developmental range indicated by the ages on the continuums?

Outside Typical Developmental Stages

	Fall	Spring
Reading		
Writing		

How many of those students are in Title I, Special Education/Resource Room, ESL, a Gifted/Enrichment, or another special program?

3. Do you feel the age spans truly reflect the "ballpark" for the developmental range you see in your classroom? If not, what would be your recommendations?

4. Comments:

Continuum Data Collection: Writing

Teacher:_____ Grade: _____Year: _____

Continuum Stage	Fall		Spring	
	# Students	%	# Students	%
Preconventional				
Emerging				
Developing				
Beginning				
Expanding				
Bridging				
Fluent				
Proficient				
Connecting				
Independent				
Total		100%		100%

Continuum Data Collection: Reading

Teacher:_____ Grade: _____ Year: _____

Continuum Stage	Fall		Spring	
	# Students	%	# Students	%
Preconventional				
Emerging				
Developing				
Beginning				
Expanding				
Bridging				
Fluent				
Proficient				
Connecting				
Independent				
Total	100%		100%	

LEARNER PROFILE: CHECKLIST

Student:

Year

Teacher

Starting Date: Exit Date:

Month		Pre K	K	1	2	3	4	5	6	7	8
September	Goals										
	Self-Portrait										
	Drawing Sample										
October	Writing Sample										
November	Reading Log										
	Reading Video										
December	Math Sample										
January	School Photograph										
February	Content Area Sample										
March	Math Sample + Reflection										
April	Reading Log + Reflection										
	Reading Video										
May	Writing Sample + Reflection										
	Self-Portrait										
June	Content Area Sample + Reflection										
	Date Continuum Arrow										
	Letter to Next Teacher										

LEARNER PROFILE: DEVELOPMENTAL CONTINUUMS

Reading Continuum

Preconventional   Emerging   Developing   Beginning   Expanding   Bridging   Fluent   Proficient   Connecting   Independent

Writing Continuum

Preconventional   Emerging   Developing   Beginning   Expanding   Bridging   Fluent   Proficient   Connecting   Independent

EAL Continuum

New to English   Early Acquisition   Becoming Familiar   Becoming Competent   Becoming Fluent   Fluent

* Date continuum in January (yellow) and June (pink)

Chapter 12

Conclusion

When we actually tell students what the target is and we hold it still for them and we allow them to see it, most students can hit the target.

—Richard Stiggins

Developmental continuums can provide a powerful framework for teaching and learning. The reading and writing continuums outline the targets for literacy acquisition and capture a picture of each student's growth and progress. Continuums also provide a common language for teachers, students, and their families.

At the Dhahran Ahliyya School in Saudi Arabia, Anna Marie Amudi lists four ways in which the continuums have made a difference in the English department in their school. The first shift (which is a monumental one) is that students, teachers, and parents have moved from looking at what students *cannot do* to what they *can do* in order to help learners grow. As a result, discussions between parents and teachers focus first on children's strengths, rather than on test scores or grades. Second, teachers are more aware of the need to document student learning in a variety of ways. Teachers collect data using anecdotal notes, running records, checklists, and other classroom-based assessment tools. The third change is reflected in the professional dialogue at their school. Discussions have moved from analyzing test results to discussions about expectations at various ages. Anna Marie states, "It has changed the way we look at our students." Teachers are also sharing instructional ideas as they examine student work. Finally, teachers are becoming classroom researchers as they collect samples and develop indicators that signify growth. The continuums have provided a spark for professional conversations.

Guiding Instruction and Assessing Students

The continuum descriptors can guide your teaching and provide the framework for assessing students. The four notebooks described in Chapter 1 can help you feel organized and confident. Your Continuum Notebook contains copies of the continuums and support documents described in this book. All of the assessment forms you plan to use are kept in your Assessment Tools Notebook. Your Organizational Grid (Form 5.3) with your assessment plan for the year and all the information about each of your students are kept in your Teacher Notebook. Your Anchor Papers Notebook contains examples of quality student reading and writing for each continuum stage.

Involving Students in Self-Evaluation

Students participate in the assessment process by using class-generated rubrics, assessment forms, and the student self-evaluation continuums or checklists. Their portfolio selections and reflections are directly linked to the continuums. The continuums make it easy for students to understand your expectations and to set goals for their next steps as readers and writers.

Communicating with Families

You can provide general information about literacy acquisition with families through newsletters and curriculum nights. More specific information about literacy can be included in a Parent Handbook, which may include the Narrative Portraits (Chapter 2), the Glossary (Chapter 3), the lists of Books by Stages (Chapter 4), and the Family Support documents (Chapter 8). Very specific information about each child's strengths, areas for growth, and goals can be communicated through student-led conferences and continuum-based report cards. The Learner Profile that travels with each student from year to year also captures growth over time.

Putting the Pieces Together

Several years ago, I was extremely fortunate to have Julie Ledford as my daughter's fifth-grade teacher at Brighton School. In Figure 12.1, you can see the array of assessment information that Julie collected throughout the year. Her anecdotal clipboard is in front of her, along with her Teacher Notebook, open to Laura's section. By her right hand are the reading and writing continuums, which include our state standards. Julie used her anecdotal notes and the information in her Teacher Notebook to fill out the continuums. On the left side of the table is Laura's portfolio, in which she had collected samples of her best work and evidence of growth.

Laura referred to her portfolio as she filled out the student version of the continuums. Propped up in the middle of the table is Laura's Learner Profile, which contains representative work from each year that Laura has been at Brighton School, as well as the videotape of her oral reading each year. As a parent, I feel confident that Julie knows my daughter well. Julie has created a solid framework upon which to build her instruction and assessment in a manageable and organized way.

Figure 12.1 Julie Ledford's Assessment Tools

Missing Pieces

This book has been the result of over 10 years of work with hundreds of brilliant and dedicated teachers around the world. I am deeply grateful for their continued willingness to exchange ideas. It has been a source of deep pleasure to show the continuums to teachers around the world who then extend the work by developing additional materials, such as the EAL continuums in Chapter 9.

There are three areas I still see as gaps in the work on continuums. The first is the challenge of creating a math continuum. I hope the teachers at Brighton School and other teachers around the world will continue to refine the math continuum and to develop parallel support materials. Next, as some of you translate assessment forms and continuum support pieces into other languages, please send me copies, so that the continuums can become accessible to families from a wider range of countries and cultural and linguistic backgrounds. Finally, the database of books by stages is a never-ending project. As you use books with students, you will inevitably find discrepancies between my list of books and stages and your own experience. I would appreciate hearing your suggestions for levels and for new titles, which can then be added to future editions of this book and the database.

The focus of this book was to show the connections between classroom-based assessment and the continuums. The next two books in the series, *Student Portfolios* and *Reporting Student Growth* will explore additional ways in which to involve students and families in the assessment and reporting process by connecting continuums to report cards, portfolios, and student-led conferences.

References

Allington, R. L. (2001). *What really matters for struggling readers: Designing research-based programs*. Reading, MA: Addison-Wesley.

Beaver, J. (1997). *Developmental reading assessment*. Parsippany, NJ: Celebration Press.

Bird, L., Goodman, K., & Goodman, Y. (1994). *The whole language catalog: Forms for authentic assessment*. Columbus, OH: SRA.

Booth, D. (1992). *Censorship goes to school*. Markham, Ontario: Pembroke.

Braunger, J. & Lewis, J. P. (1998). *Building a knowledge base in reading*, 2nd Ed. Porland, OR: Northwest Regional Educational Laboratory.

Butler, D., & Clay, M. (1979). *Reading begins at home: Preparing children for reading before they go to school*. Portsmouth, NH: Heinemann.

Clay, M. (1993a). *An observation survey of early literacy achievement*. Portsmouth, NH: Heinemann.

Clay, M. (1993b). *Reading recovery: A guidebook for teachers in training*. Portsmouth, NH: Heinemann.

Clay, M. (2000a). *Concepts about print: What have children learned about the way we print language?* Portsmouth, NH: Heinemann.

Clay, M. (2000b). *Follow me, moon*. Portsmouth, NH: Heinemann.

Clay, M. (2000c). *No shoes*. Portsmouth, NH: Heinemann.

Clay, M. (2000d). *Running records for classroom teachers*. Portsmouth, NH: Heinemann.

Collier, V., & Thomas, W. (1997). *School effectiveness for language minority students*. (http://www.ncbe.gwu.edu and http://www.crede.ucsc.edu)

Culham, R. (1998). *Picture books: An annotated bibliography with activities for teaching writing*, 5th Ed. Portland, OR: Northwest Regional Educational Laboratory.

Curriculum Corporation. (1990). *Literacy profiles handbook: Assessing and reporting literacy development*. Victoria, Australia: Curriculum Corporation.

Curriculum Corporation. (1994). *English: A curriculum profile for Australia schools*. Victoria, Australia: Curriculum Corporation.

Durkin, D. (1966). *Children who read early*. NY: Teacher College Press.

Ellis, R. (1996). *The study of second language acquisition*. Oxford: Oxford University Press.

Fletcher, R. (1993). *What a writer needs*. Portsmouth, NH: Heinemann.

Fletcher, R., & Portalupi, J. (1998). *Craft lessons: Teaching writing K–8*. York, ME: Stenhouse.

Fletcher, R., & Portalupi, J. (2001). *Nonfiction craft lessons: Teaching writing K–8*. York, ME: Stenhouse.

Fountas, I., & Pinnell, G. S. (2001). *Guiding readers and writers grades 3–6: Teaching comprehension, genre, and content literacy*. Portsmouth, NH: Heinemann.

Fountas, I., & Pinnell, G. S. (1999). *Matching books to readers: Using leveled books in guided reading, K–3*. Portsmouth, NH: Heinemann.

Fox, M. (1993). *Radical reflections: Passionate opinions on teaching, learning, and living*. San Diego, CA: Harcourt Brace.

Gentry, J. R., & Gillet, J. (1993). *Teaching kids to spell*. Portsmouth, NH: Heinemann.

Gentry, J. R. (1997). *My kid can't spell! Understanding and assisting your child's literacy development*. Portsmouth, NH: Heinemann.

Gibbons, P. (1998). *Learning to learn in a second language*, (Barrier Games on pages 35–41). Australia: Primary English Teaching Association.

Graves, B. (1988). First novels. In *Book Links*, 7 (5), p. 51–55.

Griffin, P., Smith, P., & Burrill, L. (1995). *The American literacy profile scales: A framework for authentic assessment*. Portsmouth, NH: Heinemann.

Goodman, K. & Goodman, Y. (1978). *Reading of American children whose language is a stable rural dialect of English or a language other than English*. (Final Report No. C-003-0087). Washington, DC: National Institute of Education.

Harp, B. (2000). *The handbook of literacy assessment and evaluation*, 2nd Ed. Norwood, MA: Christopher-Gordon.

Harris, T. B., & Hodges, R. (Eds.). (1995). *The literacy dictionary: The vocabulary of reading and writing*. Newark, DE: The International Reading Association.

Harwayne, S. (1999). *Going public: Priorities and practice at The Manhattan New School*. Portsmouth, NH: Heinemann.

Harwayne, S. (2000). *Lifetime guarantees: Toward ambitious literacy teaching*. Portsmouth, NH: Heinemann.

Heard, G. (1989). *For the good of the earth and sun: Teaching poetry*. Portsmouth, NH: Heinemann.

Heard, G. (1999). *Awakening the heart: Exploring poetry in elementary and middle school*. Portsmouth, NH: Heinemann.

Heinemann. (1996). *First steps program*. Portsmouth, NH: Heinemann.

Heinemann. (1997). *First steps oral language resource book.* (1997). (Barrier Games on pages 109–119). Portsmouth, NH: Heinemann.

Hill, M. (1989). *Home is where reading and writing begin.* Portsmouth, NH: Heinemann.

Hill, B. C., Johnson, N. J., & Schlick Noe, K. L. (1995). *Literature circles and response.* Norwood, MA: Christopher-Gordon.

Hill, B. C., & Ruptic, C. (1994). *Practical aspects of authentic assessment: Putting the pieces together.* Norwood, MA: Christopher-Gordon.

Hill, B. C., Ruptic, C., & Norwick, L. (1998). *Classroom based assessment.* Norwood, MA: Christopher-Gordon.

Hill, B. C., Schlick Noe, K. L., & Johnson, N. J. (2001). *The literature circles resource guide.* Norwood, MA: Christopher-Gordon.

Hudelson, S. (Ed.). (1981). *Learning to read in different languages.* Washington, DC: Center for Applied Linguistics.

Jefferson County School District. (2000). *Learning to Read Video.* Denver, CO: Jefferson County School District (Download the order form from http://204.98.1.2/Isu/langarts/litmain). (For continuum support materials, contact Carrie Ekey at cekey@jeffco.k12.co.us).

Juneau School District. (1993). *Language arts portfolio handbook for the primary grades.* Juneau, AL: Juneau School District. (1-907-463-1967)

Kiester, J. B. (1990). *Caught'ya: Grammar with a giggle.* Gainsville, FL: Maupin House.

Krashen, S. (1981). Bilingual education and second language acquisition theory. In California State Department of Education (Ed.), *Schooling and language minority students: A theoretical framework.* Los Angles, CA: Evaluation, Dissemination and Assessment Center, California State University.

Lane, B. (1993). *After the end: Teaching and learning creative revision.* Portsmouth, NH: Heinemann.

Lehr, S. (Ed.). (1995). *Battling dragons: Issues and controversy in children's literature.* Portsmouth, NH: Heinemann.

Leslie, L., & Caldwell, J. (1995). *Qualitative reading inventory (QRI-II).* NY: HarperCollins.

Masters, G. & Forster, M. (1996a). *Developmental assessment: Assessment resource kit.* Camberwell, Victoria, Australia: Australian Council for Educational Research, 19 Prospect Hill Road, Camberwell, Victoria, Australia, 3124 (Email: sales@acer.edu.au).

Masters, G. & Forster, M. (1996b). *Progress Maps: Assessment resource kit.* Camberwell, Victoria, Australia: Australian Council for Educational Research, 19 Prospect Hill Road, Camberwell, Victoria, Australia, 3124 (Email: sales@acer.edu.au).

Ministry of Education, British Columbia. (1992). *Supporting learning: Understanding and assessing the progress of children in the primary program.* Victoria, British Columbia, Canada: Ministry of Education.

Ministry of Education, British Columbia. (1994). *Evaluating reading across the curriculum: Using the reading reference set to support learning and enhance communications.* Victoria, British Columbia, Canada: Ministry of Education.

Northwest Regional Educational Laboratory. 101 SW Main Street, Suite 500, Portland, OR 97204 (www.nwrel.org or 1-800-547-6339/1-503-275-9519).

Peregoy, S. & Boyle, O. (1997a). SOLOM: Student oral language observation matrix. In *Reading, writing, and learning in ESL.* White Plains, NY: Longman.

Peregoy, S. & Boyle, O. (1997b). *Reading, writing, and learning in ESL,* 2nd Ed. NY: Longman.

Power, B. M. (1996). *Taking note: Improving your observational notetaking.* York, ME: Stenhouse.

Rhodes, L. K. & Shanklin, N. (1993). *Windows into literacy: Assessing leaners K–8.* Portsmouth, NH: Heinemann.

Rhodes, L. K. (Ed.). (1993). *Literacy assessment: A handbook of instruments.* Portsmouth, NH: Heinemann.

Rickards, D., & Cheek, E., Jr. (1999). *Designing rubrics for K–6 classroom assessment.* Norwood, MA: Christopher-Gordon.

Routman, R. (2000). *Conversations: Strategies for teaching, learning, and evaluating.* Portsmouth, NH: Heinemann.

Routman, R. (1996). *Literacy at the crossroads: Crucial talk about reading, writing, and other teaching dilemmas.* Portsmouth, NH: Heinemann.

Spandel, V. (1997). *Seeing with new eyes: A guidebook on teaching and assessing beginning writers,* 4th Ed. Portland, OR: Northwest Regional Educational Laboratory.

Spandel, V. & Stiggins, R. (1997). *Creating writers: Lining writing assessment and instruction.* NY: Longman.

Strickland, K. & Strickland, J. (2000). *Making assessment elementary.* Portsmouth, NH: Heinemann.

Taylor, D. (1983). *Family literacy: Young children learning to read and write.* Portsmouth, NH: Heinemann.

Thomas, W., & Collier, V. (1995). Language minority student achievement and program effectiveness. *California Association for Bilingual Education Newsletter,* 17 (5), 19–21.

Thomas, A., Fazio, L., & Stiefelmeyer, B. (1999a). *Families at school: A guide for educators.* Newark, DE: International Reading Association.

Thomas, A., Fazio, L., & Stiefelmeyer, B. (1999b). *Families at school: A handbook for parents.* Newark, DE: International Reading Association.

Wiggins, G. (1994). Toward better report cards. *Educational Leadership,* 52 (2), 28–37.

Woodward, H. (1994). *Negotiated Evaluation: Involving children and parents in the process.* Portsmouth, NH: Heinemann.

Subject Index

Author Index

About The Author

Bonnie Campbell Hill taught elementary school for 7 years in Boulder, Colorado. She received both her undergraduate and masters degree from the University of Colorado. In 1985, she moved to Seattle, Washington where she taught elementary school for 2 more years before returning to graduate school. She received her doctorate in Reading/Language Arts in 1991 from the University of Washington.

She has taught courses in writing, children's literature, reading, and assessment at Seattle Pacific University and Seattle University. Bonnie is currently a consultant with many school districts in the United States and in many countries around the world. She often presents at local, state, national, and international conferences. Bonnie is the mother of 3 children, ages 10, 12, and 17.

She has written a book on assessment and portfolios with Cynthia Ruptic, called *Practical Aspects of Authentic Assessment: Putting the Pieces Together* (1994). Her second book, *Literature Circles and Response* (Hill, Johnson, and Schlick Noe), was published by Christopher-Gordon in 1995. A supplementary book, *The Literature Circles Resource Guide* was published with her co-authors, Katherine Schlick Noe and Nancy Johnson in 2001. In 1998, she published *Classroom Based Assessment* (Hill, Ruptic, and Norwick, 1998), the first book in the four-part *Corner Pieces* assessment series. *Developmental Continuums* is the second book in the series. The last two books will be *Student Portfolios*, and *Reporting Student Growth*.

How To Use The CD

There are two major components on this CD-ROM: the CD-ROM Resources (MENU.PDF) and the Database of Children's Books (DATABASE.EXE).

The CD-ROM Resources include continuums and other forms from the book, *Developmental Continuums*, as well as forms from the book, *Classroom Based Assessment*. To use the CD-ROM Resources menu, you must have Adobe Acrobat Reader installed on your computer. This is a free program that you can install by running the program, **Reader 4.05 Installer**, included on this CD-ROM, or you can download the latest version from the Adobe web site at www.adobe.com. All of the CD-ROM Resources documents were created with Microsoft Word, and may be edited with that program. If you do not have Microsoft Word, you can still view and print the documents with Acrobat, although you will not be able to edit them. More information is available by reading the "Introduction" section on the CD-ROM Resources menu. The CD-ROM Resources require approximately 25 MB of disk space if you install it on your hard drive, but it can also be run directly from the CD-ROM.

The Database of Children's Books was created with Filemaker and is distributed in a royalty-free runtime version. No additional software is required. The Database of Children's Books requires approximately 8 MB of disk space and must be installed on your hard drive to use.

Windows 95/98/NT Installation and System Requirements

The install process runs automatically when the CD-ROM is inserted in the drive; follow the directions on the screen. To install both programs on your hard disk, select "Typical" installation. If you choose "Compact" installation, only the Database of Children's Books will be installed on your hard disk; you must have the CD-ROM inserted in your computer to use the CD-ROM Resources.

To run the program, double-click the appropriate icon on the desktop ("Database of Children's Books" or "Developmental Continuums") or start the program from the Windows Start Menu (Start > Programs > Developmental Continuums > "Database of Children's Books" or "CD-ROM Resources").

To directly access the CD-ROM, double-click "My Computer", Right-click the CD-ROM icon for "Developmental Continuums," then select "Open". Double-click "MENU.PDF" for the Resources. Double-click "Using the Database.PDF" for a printable version of database instructions.

Minimum PC System Requirements:

- Intel Compatible 486/33MHz PC (recommended 133MHz Pentium)
- At least 16 MB of RAM (recommended 32 MB)
- Hard disk with at least 20 MB of free space (50 MB if the CD-ROM Resources are installed)
- CD-ROM drive
- 600 x 800 pixel minimum video screen area
- Windows 95 or later, with Internet Explorer 4.0 or later, or Windows NT 4.0 (with Service Pack 3 or later)

To remove the programs from your computer, open Windows Control Panel and then select Add/Remove Programs. Highlight "Developmental Continuums" and select "Add/Remove".

For MacIntosh Users

Mac OS Installation and System Requirements

To install both the Database of Children's Books and CD-ROM Resources on your hard drive, create a new folder on your computer and name it "Developmental Continuums". Open the CD-ROM and drag each folder from it along with the file "MENU.PDF" to the new folder you created. To install only the Database of Children's Books, drag only the folder DATABASE from the CD-ROM to the new folder your hard drive.

To start the CD-ROM Resources, double-click the MENU.PDF file icon (either in the folder you created on your hard drive, or on the CD-ROM). To open the Database of Children's Books, open the DATABASE folder on your hard disk and double-click the DATABASE file icon.

Minimum Mac System Requirements:

- Power Macintosh or Mac OS computer with a PPC 601 processor or higher
- At least 16 MB of RAM (recommended 32 MB)
- Hard disk with at least 24 MB of free space (54 MB if the CD-ROM Resources are installed)
- CD-ROM drive
- 600 x 800 pixel minimum video screen area
- System 8.1 or later